STUDIES IN CHRISTIAN HISTORY AND THOUGHT

Puritan Spirituality

The Fear of God
in the Affective Theology of George Swinnock

D1602537

STUDIES IN CHRISTIAN HISTORY AND THOUGHT

Puritan Spirituality

The Fear of God
in the Affective Theology of George Swinnock

J. Stephen Yuille

Foreword by J. I. Packer

WIPF & STOCK · Eugene, Oregon

Wipf and Stock Publishers
199 W 8th Ave, Suite 3
Eugene, OR 97401

Puritan Spirituality
The Fear of God in the Affective Theology of George Swinnock
By Yuille, J. Stephen
Copyright©2007 Paternoster
ISBN 13: 978-1-55635-867-8
Publication date 2/20/2008

This Edition Published by Wipf and Stock Publishers by arrangement with Paternoster

Series Preface

This series complements the specialist series of *Studies in Evangelical History and Thought* and *Studies in Baptist History and Thought* for which Paternoster is becoming increasingly well known by offering works that cover the wider field of Christian history and thought. It encompasses accounts of Christian witness at various periods, studies of individual Christians and movements, and works which concern the relations of church and society through history, and the history of Christian thought.

The series includes monographs, revised dissertations and theses, and collections of papers by individuals and groups. As well as 'free standing' volumes, works on particular running themes are being commissioned; authors will be engaged for these from around the world and from a variety of Christian traditions.

A high academic standard combined with lively writing will commend the volumes in this series both to scholars and to a wider readership.

Series Editors

Alan P.F. Sell, Visiting Professor at Acadia University Divinity College, Nova Scotia, Canada

David Bebbington, Professor of History, University of Stirling, Stirling, Scotland, UK

Clyde Binfield, Professor Associate in History, University of Sheffield, UK

Gerald Bray, Anglican Professor of Divinity, Beeson Divinity School, Samford University, Birmingham, Alabama, USA

Grayson Carter, Associate Professor of Church History, Fuller Theological Seminary SW, Phoenix, Arizona, USA

For Alison

Contents

Foreword

In every movement that moves a jargon develops as ordinary words acquire special in-group nuances and overtones. In the seventeenth-century Puritan movement the words *sweet* and *solid* became instances of this. *Sweet* characterized communication, oral or written, as bringing peace, joy and assurance, or re-assurance, to the Christian heart. *Solid* was used to rate the communication as well grounded in Scripture, well set out and argued, and wisely applied to life. Pastor George Swinnock, so totally a mainstream Puritan as to contribute nothing at all of his own to the history of ideas, was gifted and perceived as sweet and solid in the highest degree, which makes him well worth studying today. It is our good fortune that Dr. Yuille's guide to Swinnock captures his spirit so well.

What will the reader gain from this weighty monograph? It seems to me that three benefits wait to be received.

First, we have here a full and exact anatomizing of the life of experiential communion with God as Swinnock understood it, appropriately organized as an exposition of the fear of God as the Christian's true principle of practice. Swinnock's concept of filial fear, built up in the way Dr. Yuille describes, does in fact go to the sometimes elusive heart of the insight into Christian existence that the Puritan school of thought maintained, fed as it was by Augustine, Calvin, and the Bible read as both had read it. The parallels to Swinnock that Dr. Yuille deploys at point after point show this abundantly. No more thorough analysis of essential Puritan piety exists anywhere, so far as I know.

Second, we have here, in text and footnotes, a full and exact mapping of the questions, disputes and tangles that the academic study of Puritanism during the past two generations has thrown up. As in other explorations of the history of ideas, so it is here: accounts of Puritan teaching are sometimes skewed by the prejudices and blind spots of its expositors, and the sorting out of the cross-currents of opinion is itself a sizeable scholarly task. Dr. Yuille, it seems to me, keeps his footing throughout, and proves himself a very safe guide in all of this.

Third, we have here a plain, straightforward pathway into what the Puritans, Swinnock and his peers, took to be the inner reality of biblical devotion as the psalms, the prophets, the gospels and the epistles present and exemplify it. All who see Puritan piety as an integral element in the church's evangelical heritage will find Swinnock's teaching, both in his own writings and as set forth here, a rich and reliable resource for practice as they beat their way through the undergrowth of competing spiritualities that our times have produced so prodigally in both East and West.

For successfully distilling the essence of George Swinnock, and fruitfully deploying what he has found, Dr. Yuille must be profoundly thanked. It gives me great pleasure to commend his work, and wish it the circulation and readership that it deserves.

J. I. Packer

Preface

This book is about George Swinnock, a seventeenth century English Puritan. It begins by defining his Puritanism as a spiritual movement to which political, ecclesiastical, and theological concerns were related in terms of cause and consequence. This is followed by an assessment of those influences that contributed in some way to the development of his spirituality.

Chapters three and four explore the foundation of Swinnock's spirituality. At its root is a teleological understanding of the image of God in humanity that is based upon faculty-humour psychology. This means Swinnock views sanctification as the proper ordering of the soul's faculties after the image of God. In other words, the head and heart perceive God to be the greatest good, resulting in renewed affections.

Chapters five to eight consider the expression of Swinnock's spirituality. As a result of the proper ordering of the soul's faculties, the individual delights in God's law. Furthermore, the rational appetite exercises control over the sensitive appetite. According to Swinnock, this self-control (or moderation) is evident in every area of life – all actions, vocations, relations, and conditions. To facilitate this mastery of the rational over the sensitive, he devotes himself to spiritual duties such as reading and praying. He views these as conduit-pipes whereby the Holy Spirit imparts grace to the soul. Among spiritual duties, meditation occupies the place of distinction for Swinnock by virtue of the fact that the mind is the leading faculty of the soul. It is, therefore, the principal means by which the Holy Spirit excites the affections.

This entire paradigm is included in Swinnock's concept of the fear of God; hence, the title for this book: *Puritan Spirituality: The Fear of God in the Affective Theology of George Swinnock*. Throughout, Swinnock's convictions are placed in a historical context, stretching back through Calvin to Augustine. In addition, they are expounded in the context of his contemporaries in order to confirm his place within the Puritan tradition.

Acknowledgements

The present work is my PhD thesis, completed at London School of Theology. I wish to express my sincere thanks to those who made this research possible. Seven years ago, Dr Victor Shepherd introduced me to the Puritans in a course at Tyndale Seminary, Toronto. They have been an integral part of my life ever since. Dr James Packer unknowingly stirred my desire to study Puritan spirituality through his book, *A Quest for Godliness: The Puritan Vision of the Christian Life*. Special thanks are due to my research supervisor, Dr Anthony Lane, who offered many helpful suggestions and corrections (only one or two) along the way. There are many college students and church members (too many to mention), who will recognize portions of this work from lectures and sermons. I appreciate the opportunity to have shared these insights with you. Thank you for your encouragement. I also owe a great debt to my parents, William and Naomi Yuille, and my parents-in-law, Claire and Irene Richardson, for their support. Finally, I am extremely grateful to Alison, my wife, who has loved me these many years. 'The grace of our Lord Jesus Christ be with you all!'

J. Stephen Yuille

Sermons preached, or men's words, pass away with many like wind – how soon are they buried in the grave of the oblivion! but sermons printed are men's works, live when they are dead, and become an image of eternity: 'This shall be written for the generation to come.'

George Swinnock, *The Christian Man's Calling* in *The Works of George Swinnock*, ed. James Nichol (London, 1868; rpt., Edinburgh: Banner of Truth, 1992) I:57.

Introduction

George Swinnock was born in 1627 at Maidstone, Kent. He graduated B.A. from Cambridge University (1647) and M.A. from Oxford University (1650). Upon receiving the latter, he resigned his fellowship to become vicar at St. Mary's chapel, Rickmansworth, Hertfordshire. After eleven years, he moved to St. Nicholas' chapel, Great Kimble, Buckinghamshire.[1] Upon his ejection for nonconformity, he entered the household of Richard Hampden to minister as family chaplain.[2] With the easing of restrictions in 1672, he returned to his home of Maidstone to become pastor. He occupied this position for less than a year, dying at the age of forty-six.[3]

According to Edmund Calamy, Swinnock 'was a man of good abilities, and a serious, warm, and practical useful preacher.'[4] Thomas Manton refers to Swinnock as 'a name well known to most serious Christians by his former savoury and useful works, published for the good of the church.'[5] Commenting on one of these works, Thomas Watson writes, 'For the Author... though I have

---

[1] This is where John Hampden voted in 1635 against the payment of ship money. He is famous for his support of the parliamentary forces. See *Dictionary of National Biography* (hereafter *DNB*), ed. S. Lee (London: Smith, Elder & Co., 1909).

[2] Richard Hampden (son of John Hampden) befriended several ejected ministers. Swinnock commends him for his support: 'The place to which I am presented hath not half a maintenance, nor so much as a house belonging to the minister; but the Lord hath given you such a compassion to souls, that you have given me both a convenient dwelling and a considerable maintenance, besides the tithes, above seventy pounds per annum out of your own inheritance, that I enjoy, through the good hand of my God upon me, a competent encouragement and comfortable employment.' *Christian Man's Calling; or, A treatise of making religion ones business: Parts I, II, III* in *The Works of George Swinnock*, ed. J. Nichol (London, 1868; rpt., Edinburgh: Banner of Truth, 1992) I:5-6. Nichol's edition contains all of Swinnock's works except *The Life and Death of Mr. Thomas Wilson, Minister of Maidstone, in the County of Kent, M.A.* (London, 1672). See bibliography for a complete list. Unless otherwise indicated, all quotations are taken from Nichol's edition. As for other authors, original sources are used as much as possible. When unavailable, reprints are used. In the case of originals, misspelling has been maintained whilst lettering has been standardized.

[3] See *DNB* and *Works of George Swinnock*, V:ix-xiv. Apart from these few details, very little is known of Swinnock. There is no available funeral sermon or collection of letters. There are scant references in the writings of his contemporaries.

[4] Edmund Calamy, *Nonconformist's Memorial* (London, 1802) I:303-304.

[5] Thomas Manton, 'To the Reader' in Swinnock, *Sinner's Last Sentence to eternal punishment, for sins of omission: wherein is discovered the nature, causes and cure of those sins*, V:267.

not had much knowledge of him, yet by that little converse had with him, I judge him to be a man of a serious and gracious spirit; it is excellent when the vessels of God's house retain in them a relish and savour of that good wine which they pour out to others.'[6]

Despite these favourable critiques, Swinnock is essentially a forgotten Puritan. Writing in the nineteenth century, James Hamilton notes, 'Except to a few collectors, the writings of Swinnock are almost unknown.'[7] The same is true today. Swinnock is conspicuously absent from academic research into English Puritanism, and he is seldom mentioned in the secondary literature related to the time period. Perhaps this absence is explained by his seemingly 'unspectacular' life. Apart from his ejection in 1662, there is no record of any involvement in noteworthy political or ecclesiastical struggles.[8] His teaching was uncontroversial in relation to the major tenets of English Reformed theology. He was rarely polemical in his writing. In short, he appears inconsequential to the great developments of the seventeenth century, thereby limiting his importance to both the historian and theologian. If this is indeed the cause of Swinnock's anonymity, then it serves to reveal a significant imbalance in the study of English Puritanism.

Without minimizing the validity of the political, ecclesiastical, and theological approaches to this field of study, this thesis argues that the essence of Puritanism is found in its spirituality. As Gordon Rupp states:

> In the last thirty years attention has centred on first one and then another aspect of Puritanism, on logic and theology, on ecclesiastical polity, on casuistry, on developing notions of freedom and toleration which presaged the future, and millenarian ideas which seem to peg down prophecy, together with the sociological context and the implications, conscious and unconscious, of their beliefs, for the development of political ideas and of science. Too little attention

---

[6]   Thomas Watson, 'To the Reader' in Swinnock, *Door of Salvation; or, A treatise containing the nature, necessity, marks and means of regeneration: as also the duty of the regenerate.* This letter is not found in Nichol's edition, but in the third edition published in 1671.

[7]   James Hamilton as quoted by Nichol in *Works of George Swinnock*, V:xii.

[8]   Swinnock was Presbyterian, yet he never writes polemically on the subject. See *Gods Are Men; or, Magistrates are mortal*; and *Men Are Gods; or, The dignity of magistracy, and the duty of the magistrate.* Thomas Hall, who published *The Beauty of Magistracy* in conjunction with the aforementioned works, remarks, 'The Presbyterian government is that government which by covenant we are bound to promote, it being that government which all the reformed churches of Christ do practice; and the only platform of government which carries a *Jus divinum* in the forehead of it.' *Works of George Swinnock*, IV:153.

has been paid to their spirituality, to what they have to say of Christian experience, of their devotion to Christ, and about the joy of Christian religion.[9]

There is some discussion of Puritan spirituality in the earlier secondary literature, as seen in Perry Miller's 'Augustinian piety,'[10] William Haller's 'spiritual brotherhood,'[11] and Geoffrey Nuttall's 'mystical union.'[12] There remains, however, a need for more comprehensive analyses. As an exemplar of seventeenth-century practical theology, Swinnock provides an excellent case study.

The primary objective of this thesis is to demonstrate that Swinnock's Puritanism is his spirituality as shaped by his understanding of sanctification. The second objective is to identify the foundation to Swinnock's doctrine of sanctification. It is his concept of the fear of God as the proper ordering of the soul's faculties after the image of God. Central to this is his teleological understanding of the image of God in humanity's threefold state: innocence, apostasy, and renewal. Swinnock shares this paradigm with his contemporaries, yet there has been no significant research as to its contribution to the development of their spirituality. This study confirms the prevalence of this paradigm within Puritanism and, therefore, Swinnock's place within the movement. The third objective is to locate Swinnock's spirituality in a historical tradition extending back to Augustine through Calvin. Whilst not becoming immersed in the 'Calvin versus the Calvinists' debate,[13] this thesis challenges the notion of discontinuity. Swinnock is not an innovator. He works within a received tradition that is neither an exact copy of Calvin nor a radical departure from him. Therefore, he develops the experimental implications of Calvin's theology whilst remaining committed to its foundations.

---

[9]   Gordon Rupp, 'A Devotion of Rapture in English Puritanism,' *Reformation, Conformity and Dissent: Essays in Honour of Geoffrey Nuttall*, ed. R. B. Knox (London: Epworth Press, 1977) 119.

[10] Perry Miller, *The New England Mind: The Seventeenth Century* (Harvard University Press, 1963) 3-34.

[11] William Haller, *The Rise of Puritanism* (New York: Harper Torchbooks, 1957) 49-82.

[12] Geoffrey Nuttall, *The Holy Spirit in Puritan Faith and Experience* (University of Chicago Press, 1992) 22-26.

[13] Swinnock's theology is firmly rooted in the *Westminster Confession of Faith* (hereafter *WCF*). The link between the *WCF* and Calvin has generated much discussion. Anthony Lane notes a tension in Calvin 'between the universal and the particular, between God's purposes for mankind as a whole and his purpose for the elect in particular.' 'The Quest for the Historical Calvin,' *Evangelical Quarterly* 55 (1983) 96. The Calvinists, according to Lane, tend to emphasize the 'particular' at the expense of the 'universal,' thereby resulting in modifications to Calvin's understanding of – among other things – faith and assurance. For this reason, Lane asks, 'Was Calvin a Calvinist?' *Ibid.*, 95.

In brief, Swinnock stakes his life's ambition upon Ecclesiastes 12:13 where the Preacher declares, 'Let us hear the conclusion of the whole matter: Fear God, and keep his commandments: for this is the whole duty of man.'[14] This 'conclusion' is at the core of Swinnock's spirituality. Outlined in the following pages is the manner in which he develops and expresses this in life. It is intended that this discussion should contribute to a greater appreciation for this 'serious, warm, and practical useful preacher' and, by consequence, to a better understanding of Puritan spirituality.

---

[14]   *Christian Man's Calling*, I:388. Unless otherwise indicated, Bible quotations are from the New American Standard Bible.

Chapter One

Puritanism

The term *Puritan* is used to describe Thomas Cartwright, John Preston, William Ames, John Goodwin, John Bunyan, John Milton, Oliver Cromwell, John Owen, Richard Baxter, John Cotton, and countless others. Yet, it is impossible to define *Puritanism* in a manner that encompasses all these men.[1] Richard Greaves attributes this confusion to the term's 'multiplicity of meanings' in the Elizabethan and Jacobean era.[2] A survey of the secondary literature confirms this.

Ecclesiastical Movement

In the words of Horton Davies, 'Puritanism is most accurately defined as the outlook that characterized the radical Protestant party in Queen Elizabeth's day, who regarded the Reformation as incomplete and wished to model English church worship and government according to the Word of God.'[3] This

---

[1]   For definitions of Puritanism, see Ian Breward, 'The Abolition of Puritanism,' *Journal of Religious History* 7 (1972) 20-34; Paul Christianson, 'Reformers and the Church of England under Elizabeth I and the Early Stuarts,' *Journal of Ecclesiastical History* 31 (1980) 463-482; Patrick Collinson, 'A Comment: Concerning the Name Puritan,' *Journal of Ecclesiastical History* 31 (1980) 483-488; Michael Finlayson, 'Puritanism and Puritans: Labels or Libels?' *Canadian Journal of History* 8 (1973) 203-223; Basil Hall, 'Puritanism: The Problem of Definition' in *Humanists and Protestants: 1500-1900* (Edinburgh: T & T Clark, 1990) 237-254; Christopher Hill, *Society and Puritanism in Pre-Revolutionary England* (London: Panther Books, 1969) 15-30; Martyn Lloyd-Jones, *The Puritans: Their Origins and Successors* (Edinburgh: Banner of Truth, 2002) 237-259; John Morgan, *Godly Learning: Puritan Attitudes Towards Reason, Learning, and Education, 1560-1640* (Cambridge University Press, 1986) 9-22; James Packer, *A Quest for Godliness: The Puritan Vision of the Christian Life* (Wheaton: Crossway Books, 1990) 21-48; and Leonard Trinterud, 'The Origins of Puritanism,' *Church History* 20 (1951) 37-57.

[2]   Richard Greaves, 'The Puritan-Nonconformist Tradition in England, 1560-1700: Historiographical Reflections,' *Albion* XVII (1985) 449. This article provides an excellent overview of Puritan studies.

[3]   Horton Davies, *The Worship of the English Puritans* (Morgan: Soli Deo Gloria, 1997) 1. For additional views of Puritanism as an opposition movement within the Church of England, see Christianson, 'Reformers and the Church of England,' 463-

dissatisfaction with the condition of the church was the result of events dating back to Henry VIII, whose personal confrontation with the pope over his marriage to Catherine was a symptom of the ongoing clash between political and ecclesiastical powers.[4] In a word, Henry 'wanted to be supreme with all the sources of power in his own hands.'[5] This power struggle came to a head when Parliament passed the Supremacy Act by which Henry was declared 'the only supreme head in earth of the Church of England.'[6] This Act focused upon the authority of the pope, not the doctrines of the Roman Church. At heart, Henry still accepted many of Roman Catholicism's practices, as is evident in the Six Articles passed by Parliament in 1539.[7] There were those, however, who disagreed with these Six Articles, viewing the Reformation as more than freedom from papal intrusion into domestic affairs. Therefore, from the outset, the English Reformation actually 'embraced two distinct tendencies.'[8] The first was semi-Roman whilst the other was anti-Roman.

When Elizabeth I ascended the throne in 1558, most of the English Protestants, who had fled to the Continent during the reign of Mary, returned to England. Some were discouraged with the state of the church, desiring to remove all remnants of the Roman Church such as using the surplice and kneeling at communion. Some of them also desired to reform the church's government on the basis of Presbyterianism.[9] Consequently, they were named *Puritans*. These Puritans encompassed a broad spectrum of opinion, yet all shared one common denominator – dissatisfaction with the extent of the Reformation in England. As Neil Keeble notes:

482; Trinterud, 'The Origins of Puritanism,' 37-57; Marshall Knappen, *Tudor Puritanism: A Chapter in the History of Idealism* (University of Chicago Press, 1970); and Paul Seaver, *Puritan Lectureships: The Politics of Religious Dissent 1560-1662* (Stanford University Press, 1977).

[4]   Henry VIII had additional motives. As Hugh Trevor-Roper notes, 'The temptation offered by the vast estates of the Church was not to be resisted.' *Archbishop Laud* (London: Phoenix Press, 2000) 8.

[5]   Helen White, *English Devotional Literature [Prose] 1600-1640* (New York: Haskell House, 1966) 23.

[6]   *Documents of the Christian Church*, ed. H. Bettenson (Oxford University Press, 1963) 227.

[7]   They condemn all who oppose transubstantiation, vows of chastity, private masses, and auricular confession, and all who support the giving of the cup to the laity and the marriage of the clergy. *Ibid.*, 233-234.

[8]   Philip Schaff, *The Creeds of Christendom* (Grand Rapids: Baker Books, 1998) I:704.

[9]   For an overview of the Admonition to Parliament in 1572, see Peter Lake, *Anglicans and Puritans? Presbyterianism and English Conformist Thought from Whitgift to Hooker* (London: Unwin Hyman, 1988). Of interest is his assertion that John Whitgift and Thomas Cartwright shared a 'formal doctrinal consensus' whilst differing as to its application. *Ibid.*, 25.

The term 'Puritan' became current during the 1560s as a nickname for Protestants who, dissatisfied with the Elizabethan Settlement of the church by the Act of Uniformity of 1559, would have subscribed to the contention of the Admonition to Parliament of 1572 that 'we in England are so far off, from having a church rightly reformed, according to the prescript of God's word, that as yet we are not come to the outward face of the same.'[10]

Their endeavour for 'a church rightly reformed' continued during the reign of James I,[11] and came to a head during the reign of Charles I, who advocated some aspects of Roman Catholicism with its head at Canterbury rather than Rome. Similarly, his archbishop, William Laud, claimed that the altar was 'the greatest place of God's residence upon earth – yea, greater than the pulpit.'[12] Parliament deposed both, and convened the Westminster Assembly in order to establish a new government and liturgy.[13] This victory was short-lived, however, as Oliver Cromwell's rise to power spelt the end of the aims of the Westminster Assembly; namely, one Presbyterian Church of England, Wales, Scotland, and Ireland. With the death of Cromwell, Charles II ascended the throne. The Independents hoped for 'toleration' whilst the Presbyterians aimed at 'comprehension' in the new religious establishment.[14] In 1662, Parliament passed an Act of Uniformity according to which all who had not received Episcopal ordination had to be re-ordained by bishops. Ministers had to declare their consent to the entire Book of Common Prayer and their rejection of the Solemn League and Covenant. As a result, approximately 2,000 ministers left the Church of England.

For many scholars, this ecclesiastical struggle is the essence of Puritanism. 'Before 1642,' writes Basil Hall, 'the "serious" people in the Church of England, those who followed "exact walking" and who desired some modifications in Church government and worship were called Puritans.'[15] He then argues that, after 1642, the term *Puritan* loses significance and should be replaced with *Presbyterian, Independent,* or *Baptist,* because 'each of these

---

[10] Neil Keeble, 'Puritan Spirituality' in *The Westminster Dictionary of Christian Spirituality,* ed. G. S. Wakefield (Philadelphia: Westminster Press, 1983) 323.
[11] For an overview of James' response to Puritan grievances, see Kenneth Fincham and Peter Lake, 'The Ecclesiastical Policy of King James I,' *Journal of British Studies* 24 (1985) 169-207.
[12] William Laud, *A Relation of the Conference Between William Laud and Mr. Fisher the Jesuit* in *The Works of William Laud,* ed. J. H. Parker (Oxford, 1857) VI:I:57. For an example of Laud's treatment of Puritans, see G. Gorman, 'A Laudian Attempt To "Tune the Pulpit:" Peter Heylyn and His Sermon Against the Feoffees for the Purchase of Impropriations,' *Journal of Religious History* 8 (1975) 333-349.
[13] For Marc Schwarz's thesis that Laud's intolerance alienated him from lay Anglicanism, thereby facilitating his downfall, see 'Lay Anglicanism and the Crisis of the English Church in the Early Seventeenth Century,' *Albion* 14 (1982) 1-19.
[14] Michael Watts, *The Dissenters* (Oxford: Clarendon Press, 1978) 217.
[15] Hall, 'Puritanism: The Problem of Definition,' 245.

names carries greater precision of meaning to the informed than the generalizing use of the word Puritan.'[16] He adds, 'Once a Puritan withdrew from the Church of England to set up a Church with a distinct ecclesiology of its own, he forthwith ceased to be clearly a Puritan.'[17] In making this assertion, Hall appears to lose sight of his own definition of *Puritan*. After 1642, this term is too broad for those who desire 'some modifications in Church government and worship.' However, it remains an appropriate designation for those who follow 'exact walking,' because their piety actually transcends the ecclesiastical convictions of Presbyterians, Independents, and Baptists.

Political Movement

As John Marlowe explains, 'The political aim of the Reformation in England had been not only to sever the temporal and spiritual allegiance which bound Englishmen to Rome, but to transfer that allegiance from the Roman Pontiff to the English Crown.'[18] In such a climate, church and state politics were inseparable.[19] For this reason, the desire for 'a church rightly reformed' brought many of the Puritans into direct conflict with the Stuart kings.[20] In addition, many Englishmen feared that Charles I intended to govern as an absolute monarch rather than in co-operation with Parliament, thereby alienating them from the country's political and economic affairs. According to Philip Schaff, Charles and Laud 'fairly represented in congenial alliance the principle and practice of political and ecclesiastical absolutism, and the sovereign contempt for the rights of the people, whose sole duty in their opinion was passive obedience.'[21] As a result, the English middle classes 'identified their cause and

---

[16] *Ibid.*, 251. This 'greater precision of meaning' is not so obvious. Finlayson demonstrates that the terms *Presbyterian* and *Independent* are themselves the source of some ambiguity. 'Puritanism and Puritans: Labels or Libels,' 215-220.

[17] Hall, 'Puritanism: The Problem of Definition,' 252. For a similar position, see Peter Toon, *Puritans and Calvinism* (Swengel: Reiner Publications, 1973) 49-50.

[18] John Marlowe, *The Puritan Tradition in English Life* (London: Cresset Press, 1956) 28.

[19] As Conrad Russell rightly explains, 'One of the major difficulties of seventeenth century England was that it was a society with several religions, while still remaining a society with a code of values and a political system which were only designed to be workable with one.' *The Causes of the English Civil War* (Oxford: Clarendon Press, 1990) 63.

[20] For a review of the relationship between royal absolutism and episcopacy, see J. P. Sommerville, 'The Royal Supremacy and Episcopacy "Jure Divino," 1603-1640,' *Journal of Ecclesiastical History* 34 (1983) 548-558. For Puritan political influence, see James Maclear, 'The Influence of the Puritan Clergy on the House of Commons: 1625-1629,' *Church History* 14 (1945) 272-289.

[21] Schaff, *Creeds of Christendom*, I:710.

ennobled their destiny in religious terms' – Puritanism.[22]

For eleven years, Charles fuelled discontent by refusing to convene Parliament, because it had requested the surrender of some measure of royal control over trade, religion, and taxes. However, in 1640, he was left with no other option. Three years earlier, he had attempted to impose the Book of Common Prayer upon Scotland. When the Scots signed the Solemn League and Covenant, Charles resorted to military force. Having suffered defeat, he needed to pay an indemnity to the Scots. This required an act of Parliament, which immediately seized the opportunity to exert itself. Eventually, the power struggle led to civil war.[23] In 1643, Parliament recognized that more decisive military action was required to defeat Charles; hence, it signed the Covenant with Scotland. Charles surrendered in 1646. However, the spread of independency within the Parliamentary army meant opposition to a national Presbyterian church. Perceiving this split, the king entered into an alliance with Scotland whereby he pledged to accept Presbyterianism in exchange for military support. However, he suffered defeat in August 1648. He was executed the following year.

Cromwell's own death precipitated another political crisis. The return of the Stuart monarchy appeared to provide the best solution; hence, Parliament restored Charles II to the throne. James II followed, again asserting royal absolutism and favouring Roman Catholicism. In the words of Gerald Cragg, 'The popish peril... persuaded the Protestants of England that beliefs on which they were agreed were vastly more important than the questions about which

---

[22] Charles George, 'A Social Interpretation of English Puritanism,' *The Journal of Modern History* XXV (1953) 336.

[23] Marlowe divides the 'Puritan Revolution' into three periods: (1) 'from the Millenary Petition in 1603 to the Three Resolutions in 1629, during which time a series of Parliaments summoned fairly regularly offered passive opposition to the exercise of the Royal Prerogative;' (2) 'from the dissolution of Parliament in 1629 to the calling of the Long Parliament in 1640, during which period the King attempted to govern without Parliament;' and (3) 'from the summoning of the Long Parliament in 1640 to the outbreak of the Civil War in 1642, during which period Parliament, under the leadership of Pym, openly and actively asserted the sovereignty of Parliament against the sovereignty of the King.' *The Puritan Tradition in English Life*, 20. For an overview of the events, leading to civil war, see Anthony Fletcher, *The Outbreak of the English Civil War* (New York University Press, 1981). He focuses upon 'the struggle against popery and the preservation of true religion.' *Ibid.*, 415. For another good treatment of this subject, see Russell, *The Causes of the English Civil War.* He identifies three 'long-term' causes: (1) 'multiple kingdoms;' (2) 'religious division;' and (3) 'breakdown of a financial and political system in the face of inflation and the rising cost of war.' *Ibid.*, 213. For events in Ireland that also contributed to civil war, see Crawford Gribben, *The Irish Puritans: James Ussher and the Reformation of the Church* (Auburn: Evangelical Press, 2003).

they were divided.'[24] A united Parliament offered the throne to James's daughter, Mary, who was married to William of Orange. In 1689, William and Mary were crowned king and queen upon their acceptance of a set of constitutional principles enacted by Parliament. This laid the foundation for constitutional monarchy in England.

Many view this political movement, spanning the reigns of the four Stuart kings, as the essence of Puritanism. Peter Lewis objects, stating, 'National, political and social elements which were closely allied with the idea of Puritanism at various stages of its progress have largely obscured the vital religious and spiritual meaning of the term.'[25] Brian Armstrong echoes this sentiment, stating, 'My misgivings arise... when the religious impulses which lie behind Puritan ideology are given short shrift and when we are left with the impression that political or social or economic considerations were the driving force of the movement.'[26] This is not to deny the relevance of 'political' and 'social' definitions, but to affirm that they are secondary.

Theological Movement

Dewey Wallace argues that Puritanism is a theological movement, shaped by the Reformed theology of grace.[27] He traces the influence of Swiss Reformers

---

[24] Gerald Cragg, *Puritanism in the Period of the Great Persecution, 1660-1688* (Cambridge University Press, 1957) 29. For more on the English perception of the 'popish peril,' see Carol Wiener, 'The Beleaguered Isle: A Study of Elizabethan and Early Jacobean Anti-Catholicism,' *Past and Present* 51 (1971) 27-62.

[25] Peter Lewis, *The Genius of Puritanism* (Morgan: Soli Deo Gloria, 1996) 11.

[26] Brian Armstrong, 'Puritan Spirituality: The Tension of Bible and Experience' in *The Roots of Modern Christian Tradition*, ed. E. R. Elder (Kalamazoo: Cistercian Publications, 1984) 232.

[27] There are divergent opinions concerning the issue of theological uniformity within the Church of England during the Elizabethan and Jacobean era. John New contends that Anglicans and Puritans differed on topics such as anthropology, ecclesiology, and eschatology. *Anglican and Puritan: The Basis of Their Opposition, 1588-1640* (Stanford, 1964). Michael McGiffert believes the Puritans were marked by a predilection for covenant theology. 'The Perkinsian Moment of Federal Theology,' *Calvin Theological Journal* 29 (1994) 117-148. John Coolidge sees a difference in their view on the sufficiency of Scripture. *The Pauline Renaissance in England: Puritanism and the Bible* (Oxford: Clarendon Press, 1970). J. Sears McGee believes there is a difference in their approach to the law. *The Godly Man in Stuart England: Anglicans, Puritans, and the Two Tables, 1620-1670* (Yale University Press, 1976). Other scholars stress a consensus in terms of predestinarian theology. See Nicholas Tyacke, *Anti-Calvinists: The Rise of English Puritanism, c. 1590-1640* (Oxford: Clarendon Press, 1987); Peter Toon, *Puritans and Calvinism*; and Dewey Wallace, *Puritans and Predestination: Grace in English Protestant Theology, 1525-1695* (Chapel Hill: University of North Carolina Press, 1982). Whilst acknowledging such a consensus, Robert Kendall distinguishes between 'experimental' and 'creedal'

upon English Protestants, concluding that 'with respect to the central matter of the theology of grace... the English Reformation was uncompromisingly Protestant.'[28] During the reign of Elizabeth I, this 'theology of grace' was further entrenched as many Marian exiles returned from Europe – where they had learned at the feet of the Swiss Reformers – to assume key leadership positions in the Church of England. Wallace notes, 'The theological standards of the Elizabethan settlement clearly were grounded in Reformed theology and reaffirmed the pattern of the theology of grace that had emerged in earlier English Protestantism.'[29] This dominance continued until the reign of James I, who, despite his condemnation of the Dutch Arminians, 'advanced to the English episcopate churchmen who sympathized with the heretics he denounced, largely because they were the staunchest upholders of his prerogatives.'[30] Nicholas Tyacke equates this advent of Arminianism with the Synod of Dort, writing:

> This international Calvinist gathering, which condemned the doctrines of the Dutch Arminians in 1619, acted as a catalyst on the English religious thought of the early seventeenth century... One result was that differences among English theologians, hitherto often implicit, were brought out into the open... Dissenters from Calvinism came increasingly to be identified as a group, and they in turn felt obliged to seek out allies in defence of a common cause. Indeed the Synod of Dort was, to an extent, responsible for the creation of an Arminian party in England.[31]

It was at this time that the Reformed theology of grace was increasingly –

---

predestinarianism. *Calvin and English Calvinism to 1649* (Oxford University Press, 1979) 1-13.

[28] Wallace, *Puritans and Predestination*, 28.

[29] *Ibid.*, 30.

[30] *Ibid.*, 83. For a brief summary of Arminius' theological position, see Carl Bangs, 'Arminius and the Reformation,' *Church History* 30 (1961) 155-170. For the relationship between Arminianism and 'royal rule by divine right,' see Bangs, '"All the Best Bishoprics and Deaneries:" The Enigma of Arminian Politics,' *Church History* 42 (1973) 5-16.

[31] Tyacke, *Anti-Calvinists*, 87. For a review of Tyacke's thesis, see Anthony Milton, 'Review of Nicholas Tyacke's "Anti-Calvinists: The Rise of English Arminianism,"' *Journal of Ecclesiastical History* 39 (1988) 613-616. There is some question concerning the 'Calvinism' of James I. Some argue that he rejected the appointment of Vorstius to Arminius' vacant chair at Leiden because of Vorstius' Socianism, not Arminianism. In addition, some claim that he adopted a 'Calvinistic' position regarding the Synod of Dort, because he desired uniformity. See Bangs, 'All the Best Bishoprics and Deaneries,' 12-16; Peter White, 'The Rise of Arminianism Reconsidered,' *Past and Present* 101 (1983) 34-54; Peter Lake, 'Calvinism and the English Church, 1570-1635,' *Past and Present* 114 (1987) 32-76; and Frederick Shriver, 'Orthodoxy and Diplomacy: James I and the Vorstius Affair,' *The English Historical Review* 336 (1970) 449-474.

though not exclusively – associated with Puritanism, thus marking its emergence as a theological movement.[32] From this time, many of the Puritans saw the crucial issue facing the Church of England not in terms of ecclesiology, but soteriology. Previously, as Wallace observes, 'the bishops and leaders of the Elizabethan church did not consider that their views of the theology of grace differed from those of more radical nonconforming Protestants who were eventually dubbed Puritans.'[33]

The theological divide within the Church of England widened when, under Charles I, 'William Laud... became the architect of an "Arminian" church renewal in theology, liturgy, and administration that was to attempt a drastic alteration in the character of the Protestant Church of England.'[34] According to Tyacke, 'Laud... so elevated the role of sacraments, and the grace which they

---

[32]   Jonathan Atkins makes an important distinction between those who were prepared to remain silent regarding the advent of Arminianism and those who were not. The former included many 'Calvinist bishops,' who 'accepted the doctrine of election,' but also 'accepted the English Protestant tradition based on the Thirty-nine Articles and the Book of Common Prayer... when confronted with the prospect of an Arminian church, the mindset of the Calvinist bishops inclined them to uphold the unity of the national church rather than risk the peace of the church over predestinarian Calvinism.' 'Calvinist Bishops, Church Unity, and the Rise of Arminianism,' *Albion* 18 (1986) 412-413.

[33]   Wallace, *Puritans and Predestination*, 36. Tyacke agrees. *Anti-Calvinists*, 8. Peter White challenges this view, stating, 'Within the Elizabethan church there was a spectrum of views on the doctrine of predestination.' He believes other issues (e.g., the Spanish war) 'threatened that delicate balance, especially on the point of predestination.' 'The Rise of Arminianism Reconsidered,' 54. For more on this, see William Lamont, 'The Rise of Arminianism Reconsidered,' *Past and Present* 107 (1985) 227-231. Julian Davies also challenges Tyacke's thesis, offering 'Carolinism' and 'Laudianism' as the causes of Puritan 'radicalisation,' adding, 'religion became the major cause of the British Civil War not because of the bugbear of Arminianism but because Charles I was in conscious rebellion against lay and popular Protestantism – the very Reformation itself.' *The Caroline Captivity of the Church: Charles I and the Remoulding of Anglicanism, 1625-1641* (Oxford: Clarendon Press, 1992) 2,17. David Hoyle upholds Tyacke's thesis whilst adding 'popery' as the 'other half of a familiar equation.' 'A Commons Investigation of Arminianism and Popery in Cambridge on the Eve of the Civil War,' *Historical Journal* 29 (1986) 419-425. Peter Lake acknowledges a 'Calvinist consensus,' but warns that this 'does not necessarily imply that all the English who regarded themselves as Protestant in the period before 1625 were explicitly Calvinist,' adding, 'hegemony is not monopoly.' 'Calvinism and the English Church,' 33-34. Lake adopts Kendall's distinction between 'creedal' and 'experimental' predestinarianism, the latter placing predestination at the centre of practical divinity, resulting in a certain 'style of piety.' *Ibid.*, 39.

[34]   Wallace, *Puritans and Predestination*, 83-84.

conferred, as effectively to supplant the grace of predestination.'[35] The Puritan position briefly gained the ascendancy with the publication of the *WCF*. After the Restoration, however, many associated the Reformed theology of grace with the anti-Episcopal government of Cromwell.[36] As a theological movement, therefore, Puritanism was indistinguishable until the reign of James I. From that time until 1662, it was an active force within the Church of England. After 1662, it was coupled increasingly with nonconformity.

In the opinion of some scholars, this Reformed theology of grace is at the heart of Puritanism. Whilst acknowledging this, it is important to remember Calvin's warning that theology 'is not apprehended by the understanding and memory alone, as other disciplines are, but it is received only when it possesses the whole soul, and finds a seat and resting place in the inmost affection of the heart.'[37] The Puritans would agree wholeheartedly. As Martyn Lloyd-Jones notes, 'There is nothing that they more deplored than a mere academic, intellectual, theoretical view of the Truth.'[38] David Sceats concurs, 'Puritans would hardly have acknowledged the notion of "pure theology" and would have been distinctly uncomfortable with the idea that theology might have been studied as an academic discipline without reference to its situational application.'[39] Their approach is entrenched in the words of William Ames, 'Theology is the doctrine or teaching of living to God.'[40]

Spiritual Movement

James Packer affirms that 'Puritanism was at heart a spiritual movement, passionately concerned with God and godliness.'[41] Jerald Brauer prefers the

---

[35] Tyacke, *Anti-Calvinists*, 7.

[36] Wallace, *Puritans and Predestination*, 159.

[37] John Calvin, *Institutes of Christian Religion* in *The Library of Christian Classics: Vol. XX-XXI*, ed. J. T. McNeill (Philadelphia: Westminster Press, 1960) III:VI:4.

[38] Lloyd-Jones, *The Puritans*, 55.

[39] David Sceats, 'The Experience of Grace: Aspects of the Faith and Spirituality of the Puritans,' *Grove Spirituality Series* 62 (1997) 12.

[40] William Ames, *Medulla Theologiae (The Marrow of Theology)* translated from the third Latin edition by J. D. Eusden (1629; Grand Rapids: Baker Books, 1997) I:I:1.

[41] Packer, *Quest for Godliness*, 28. According to Haller, 'English Puritanism, denied opportunity to reform the established church, wreaked its energy during a half century and more upon preaching and, under the impetus of the pulpit, upon unchecked experiment in religious expression and social behaviour.' *Rise of Puritanism*, 15. In other words, Puritanism changed its emphasis from reform to regeneration and its interest from political to spiritual. C. John Sommerville echoes Haller's viewpoint. 'Interpreting Seventeenth-Century English Religion as Movements,' *Church History* 69 (2000) 756-757. In sharp contrast to Haller and Sommerville, Richard Lovelace views Puritanism as 'the natural development of a further stage in the Reformation, which had begun by restructuring doctrine and the

term 'piety' rather than 'spirituality,' especially given the fact that the latter is rarely found in Puritan literature.[42] He is correct. Nevertheless, if *spirituality* is defined properly, then it is an acceptable designation for what the Puritans refer to as *godliness, holiness, piety,* or *religion.* For Lucien Richard, 'Spirituality means the forms that holiness takes in the concrete life of the believer.'[43] Dewey Wallace defines it as 'the communion of persons with the divine, with emphasis on the nature of the devotion by which the divine is approached.'[44] Alister McGrath defines it as 'the outworking in real life of a person's religious faith – what a person does with what they believe.'[45]

With these definitions in view, it is evident that Puritan spirituality is simply the 'outworking' of their 'religious faith,' which Ernest Kevan describes as 'Calvinistic.'[46] The term *Reformed* is preferable to *Calvinistic*;[47] nevertheless, Kevan's point is well made – the Puritans adhered to the Reformed theology of grace. This is evident by simply comparing William Perkins's *A Golden Chain* (1590)[48] with the *WCF* (1647).[49] In regards to the first step in the order of

---

exterior order of the church, and which was now turning to the development of its own inner life, heeding the clear biblical teaching that all was worthless without this last step.' 'The Anatomy of Puritan Piety: English Puritan Devotional Literature, 1600-1640' in *Christian Spirituality III*, eds. L. Dupré and D. E. Saliers (New York: Crossroad Publishing, 1989) 301.

[42]   Jerald Brauer, 'Types of Puritan Piety,' *Church History* 56 (1987) 39.

[43]   Lucien Richard, *The Spirituality of John Calvin* (Atlanta: John Knox Press, 1974) 1.

[44]   Dewey Wallace, *The Spirituality of the Later English Puritans* (Macon: Mercer University Press, 1987) xi.

[45]   Alister McGrath, *Christian Spirituality* (Oxford: Blackwell Publishers, 1999) 2.

[46]   Ernest Kevan, *The Grace of Law* (Ligoneir: Soli Deo Gloria, 1993) 40. For Brauer, there are four types of Puritan spirituality: Evangelicalism, Nomism, Rationalism, and Mysticism. 'Types of Puritan Piety,' 45-52. However, he includes Antinomians, Ranters, Seekers, and Quakers in his analysis. Elsewhere, he notes, 'The great central body of Puritans can be characterized in their piety as evangelicals.' 'The Nature of English Puritanism: Three Interpretations,' *Church History* 23 (1954) 106. There is, therefore, a mainstream of Puritan spirituality that possesses a particular theological foundation, thereby differentiating it from other movements dubbed 'Puritan.'

[47]   Lane warns against viewing Calvin as the only figure in Reformed theology – a misconception fostered by the use of the word 'Calvinist' for 'Reformed.' 'The Quest for the Historical Calvin,' 96.

[48]   Perkins's work is indicative of 'first generation' Puritan theology. For his importance, see Louis Wright, 'William Perkins: Elizabethan Apostle of "Practical Divinity,"' *Huntington Library Quarterly* III (1940) 171-196.

[49]   As Toon comments, 'Without doubt the *Westminster Confession* is the statement parexcellence of the (developed) Reformed Faith. It stands as an explanation of what seventeenth-century British, Calvinistic Protestants understood to be the doctrines of the Christian faith.' *Puritans and Calvinism*, 52. The Congregational *Savoy Declaration* (1658) and the Baptist *Confession of Faith* (1689) are also indicative of

salvation, Perkins comments, 'Gods decree, in as much as it concerneth man, is called Predestination: which is the decree of God, by which he hath ordained all men to a certaine and everlasting estate: that is, either to salvation or condemnation, for his owne glory.'[50] Similarly, the *WCF* states, 'By the decree of God, for the manifestation of his glory, some men and angels are predestined unto everlasting life, and others foreordained to everlasting death.'[51] It is significant that both equate predestination with God's decree, identify the purpose of predestination as God's glory, and emphasize double-predestination. Perkins proceeds to explain how God executes his decree of predestination. It involves four 'degrees:' effectual calling, justification, sanctification, and glorification.[52] The *WCF* identifies these same four 'degrees' as 'means.'[53] From Perkins to the *WCF*, the Puritans view this *ordo salutis* as the definitive statement of God's grace. Having been predestined, called, and justified, they advance in sanctification whilst awaiting their glorification. For John Owen:

> Sanctification is an immediate work of the Spirit of God on the souls of believers, purifying and cleansing of their natures from the pollution and uncleanness of sin, renewing in them the image of God, and thereby enabling them from a spiritual and habitual principle of grace, to yield obedience unto God, according unto the tenor and terms of the new covenant, by virtue of the life and death of Jesus Christ.[54]

In this statement, two aspects of sanctification are prevalent: the 'cleansing... from the pollution and uncleanness of sin;' and the 'renewing... of the image of God.' Thomas Watson identifies these as the 'privative part' (i.e., that which lies in the purging out of sin) and the 'positive part' (i.e., that which lies in the spiritual refining of the soul).[55] However, the more common Puritan terms are *vivification* and *mortification*.

In describing vivification, Owen states, 'In the sanctification of believers,

---

third generation Puritan theology. In terms of the Reformed theology of grace, they do not represent a serious modification of the *WCF*.

[50]   William Perkins, *Armilla Aurea (A Golden Chain; or, The description of theologie containing the order and the causes of salvation and damnation, according to Gods word)* in *The Works of William Perkins* (London: John Legate, 1608) I:16.

[51]   *WCF*, III:III.

[52]   Perkins, *Golden Chain, Works*, I:78-93.

[53]   *WCF*, X:II, XI:I, XIII:I, XXXII:I.

[54]   John Owen, *Discourse on the Holy Spirit* in *The Works of John Owen*, ed. W. H. Gould (London: Johnstone & Hunter, 1850; rpt., Edinburgh, Banner of Truth, 1977) III:386. For a detailed analysis of Owen's understanding of sanctification, see Randall Gleason, *John Calvin and John Owen on Mortification* (New York: Peter Lang, 1995). He argues convincingly for continuity between Calvin and Owen on this particular theme.

[55]   Thomas Watson, *A Body of Divinity Contained in Sermons Upon the Westminster Assembly's Catechism* (1692; 1890; rpt., London: Banner of Truth, 1958) 167.

the Holy Ghost doth work in them, in their whole souls, their minds, wills, and affections, a gracious, supernatural habit, principle, and disposition of living unto God; wherein the substance or essence, the life and being, of holiness doth consist.'[56] In brief, to vivify means to make alive. This is precisely the work that Owen here ascribes to the Holy Spirit, who produces in the individual 'a disposition of living unto God.' To explain this work, the Puritans appeal to Romans 8. At the beginning of this chapter, the apostle Paul affirms that, in the Christian, there is a new principle: 'the law of the Spirit of life in Christ Jesus.' This principle has set the Christian free from 'the law of sin and of death.'[57] Consequently, the governing principle (i.e., the flesh) has been replaced with another governing principle (i.e., the Spirit). This means that Christians walk after the Spirit, who empowers them to live in submission to God's will.[58]

Mortification, on the other hand, refers to the killing of sin. As already mentioned, this need exists because the corruption of nature remains in the regenerate. Owen explains:

> There are yet in them inclinations and dispositions to sin, proceeding from the remainders of a contrary habitual principle. This the Scripture calls the 'flesh,' 'lust,' the 'sin that dwelleth in us,' the 'body of death;' being what yet remaineth in believers of that vicious, corrupted depravation of our nature, which came upon us by the loss of the image of God, disposing the whole soul unto all that is evil.[59]

For Owen, the 'sin that dwelleth in us' has three characteristics.[60] First, there is the old man: the root and principle of sin, which possesses all the faculties of the soul. Second, there is the body of sin: the inclination and operations of the principle of sin. Third, there is actual sin: the effects, fruits, and products of the soul's inclination to sin. Mortification includes all of these. In describing the act of mortification itself, Owen again turns to Romans 8, where the apostle Paul states, 'For if you are living according to the flesh, you must die; but if by the Spirit you are putting to death the deeds of the body, you will live.'[61] From this verse, Owen derives several important principles. First, the object of mortification is the lusts.[62] Second, the duty of mortification belongs to the Christian.[63] Third, the cause of mortification is the Holy Spirit, who makes our hearts to abound in grace, helps us to destroy the root and habit of sin, and brings the cross of Christ to us by faith.[64]

---

[56] Owen, *Holy Spirit*, *Works*, III:386.
[57] Rom. 8:2.
[58] Rom. 8:7.
[59] Owen, *Holy Spirit*, *Works*, III:488.
[60] *Ibid.*
[61] Rom. 8:13.
[62] Owen, *The Mortification of Sin*, *Works*, VI:8.
[63] *Ibid.*, VI:9.
[64] *Ibid.*, VI:19.

For the Puritans, this is the Christian's present condition – a life long journey of sanctification. Haller appropriately describes it as the 'war,' 'epic,' or 'duel' of the two Adams.[65] In this conflict, there are two essential marks: growth in holiness and pursuit of holiness. This zeal for holiness stands at the centre of Puritan spirituality. According to Randall Gleason, 'The fundamental nature of spirituality within Puritanism is found in its insistence that the converted soul must go beyond conversion to actual holiness of life.'[66]

Conclusion

In the primary literature, the term *Puritan* is often used to describe such zeal. At the end of the sixteenth century, William Perkins remarks, 'For the *pure heart* is so little regarded, that the seeking after it is turned to a by-word, and a matter of reproach. Who are so much branded with vile termes of Puritans and Precisians, as those, that most endevour to get and keepe the puritie of heart in a good conscience?'[67] Writing in 1611, Robert Bolton comments, 'The world is come to that wretched pass, and height of profaneness, that even honesty and sanctification is many times odiously branded by the nick-name Puritanism.'[68] In 1641, Thomas Wilson notes that 'zeale' or 'fervency in religion' is branded with the terms 'indiscretion, rashnesse, puritanisme or headinesse.'[69] In 1658, Richard Baxter mentions that those who 'will not take a dead profession, joined with civility, for true sanctification' are branded 'with the name of puritans.'[70] Swinnock makes the same observation, quoting his opponents' slanderous remark, 'What! he give credit to the doctrine, and submit to the severe discipline of a few whimsical puritans, that must be wiser than all their neighbours!'[71] Whilst his ecclesiastical and political convictions may also earn him this label, Swinnock himself acknowledges that he is a Puritan by virtue of his 'serious piety.'[72]

---

[65] Haller, *Rise of Puritanism*, 152,158,160.

[66] Gleason, *John Calvin and John Owen on Mortification*, 83.

[67] William Perkins, *A Godly and Learned Exposition upon Christs Sermon in the Mount* in *The Works of William Perkins* (London, 1631) III:15.

[68] Robert Bolton, *A Discourse about the State of True Happinesse: Delivered in certaine sermons in Oxford, and at Pauls Crosse* (London, 1611) 132.

[69] Thomas Wilson, *David's Zeal for Zion, a sermon preached before the honourable House of Commons, April 4, 1641* (London, 1641) 14.

[70] Richard Baxter, *Directions and Persuasion to a Sound Conversion* in *The Practical Works of Richard Baxter: Select Treatises* (London: Blackie & Son, 1863; rpt., Grand Rapids: Baker Book House, 1981) 530.

[71] *Door of Salvation*, V:206.

[72] *Christian Man's Calling*, I:7,21.

Chapter Two

George Swinnock

Spirituality is never developed in a vacuum; thus, any appraisal of Swinnock's 'serious piety' necessitates an analysis of the context in which it evolved. In *Christian Man's Calling*, he encourages his readers to 'retire out of the world's company, to converse with the word of thy God.'[1] In typical fashion, he proceeds to meditate upon God's Word by unfolding its causes.[2] The efficient cause is God: the 'glorious and supreme Majesty of heaven and earth.' The moving cause is the Holy Spirit whereby 'the penman and scribes... were men extraordinarily inspired.' The instrumental cause is the provision of 'a perfect rule,' which 'informeth us fully in our carriage towards God, and towards men.' The formal cause is the stimulation of the individual's 'highest esteem and hottest affection' for the Bible because of its 'exact conformity to the will of God.' And the final cause is 'the glory of the great God, and the salvation of lost man.' For Swinnock, these five causes demonstrate that the Bible is 'the rule of all truth.' He concludes:

> It is not what sense saith, or reason saith, or what fathers say, or what general councils say, or what traditions say, or what customs say, but what Scripture saith, that is to be the rule of faith and life. Whatsoever is contrary to Scripture, or beside Scripture, or not rationally deducible from Scripture, is to be rejected as spurious and adulterate.[3]

---

[1] *Christian Man's Calling*, II:429.

[2] *Ibid.*, II:430-434.

[3] *Ibid.*, II:440. See *WCF*, I:VI:X. Swinnock is equally opposed to the opposite extreme, Quakerism, commenting, 'A man may follow the light within him to the chambers of utter darkness.' *Door of Salvation*, V:62. Also see *Men Are Gods*, IV:321,354,360. For the differences between Puritanism and Quakerism, see Nuttall, *Holy Spirit*, 155-157. Also see E. Glenn Hinson, 'Baptist and Quaker Spirituality' in *Christian Spirituality III*, eds. L. Dupré and D. E. Saliers (New York: Crossroad Publishing, 1989) 324-338. Jerald Brauer makes an interesting argument for the relationship between mysticism (Quakerism) and liberalism in 'Puritan Mysticism and the Development of Liberalism,' *Church History* 19 (1950) 151-170. The Puritans' rejection of the 'inner light' does not mean that they are rationalists. Packer explains, 'Sin within us... promises a universal unresponsiveness to spiritual truth and reality that the New Testament calls hardness and blindness of heart. More

Church history testifies to the fact that an assertion of the authority and sufficiency of Scripture is no guarantee that all will agree as to its interpretation as there are many influences at work when people read the Bible. Nevertheless, Swinnock seeks to be objective in his use of 'authorities,' bearing in mind that there is only one rule: 'what Scripture saith.' Given this conviction, it is no surprise to find that Swinnock's works are saturated with Scriptural references and allusions, forming the basis of his thinking. This observation is crucial, because it means that those individuals who influence Swinnock's understanding of the Bible make the greatest contribution to the development of his spirituality.

The School of Religion

There are insufficient details available to piece together all of Swinnock's childhood influences. It is known that he spent much of this time in the home of his uncle. When speaking of his cousin, Caleb Swinnock, he comments, 'I had the happiness some time to be brought up with him in his father's, Mr. Robert Swinnock's, family.'[4] Whatever the circumstances surrounding this stay, Swinnock describes it in a positive light as he recalls that his uncle's house 'had holiness to the Lord written upon it.' He explains:

> His manner was to pray twice a day by himself, once or twice a day with his wife, and twice a day with his family, besides singing psalms, reading, and expounding Scriptures, which morning and evening were minded. The Sabbath he dedicated wholly to God's service, and did not only himself, but took care that all within his gate should spend the day in secret and private duties, and in attendance on public ordinances; of their proficiency by the last, he would take an account upon their return from the assembly.[5]

It was in this 'school of religion'[6] that Swinnock lived until he departed for Cambridge in 1643, when he was sixteen. Given the fact that the first sixteen years of life are crucial in the formation of a person's character and convictions, it is certain that Swinnock was greatly influenced by his uncle's piety.

---

rational instruction thus proves ineffective; only the illumination of the Holy Spirit, opening our hearts to God's word and God's word to our hearts, can bring understanding of, conviction about, and consent to, the things that God declares.' *Quest for Godliness*, 83. His italics.

[4] *Fading of the Flesh and Flourishing of the Faith; or, One cast for eternity: with the only way to throw it well: as also the gracious persons incomparable portion*, III:409.

[5] *Ibid.*

[6] *Ibid.*

The Eminent Servant

This influence intensified with the arrival of Thomas Wilson (1601-1653). After a brief stint as a tutor, Wilson had several preaching posts before settling at Otham, Kent. The events surrounding his appointment are noteworthy. Swinnock mentions that 'many serious understanding Christians' at Maidstone, near Otham, were 'much troubled and dejected at the deadness and dulness of that Ministry under which they lived.'[7] Upon the death of the preacher at Otham, the responsibility for finding a replacement fell upon one of the aldermen from Maidstone, Robert Swinnock, who was determined to bring a 'godly' minister to a church so close to home.[8] Having heard Wilson preach elsewhere, he invited him to Otham. From that time, the 'serious' Christians journeyed from Maidstone to hear Wilson's sermons. Furthermore, it was Wilson's custom to have supper every Sunday at the home of his patron.[9] This means that, from infancy, Swinnock was raised under Wilson's preaching and catechising.

In April 1634, upon refusing to read the Book of Sports in the church, Wilson was called before the Court of High Commission and suspended.[10] He moved to Maidstone where he received support – undoubtedly from Robert Swinnock – until his suspension was lifted in 1639. However, the next year, upon refusing to read the prayer against the Scots,[11] a warrant – bearing the signature of Archbishop Laud – was issued for his arrest.[12] He hid in the country until the convening of Parliament in 1640 when he appealed to the house. Edward Dering, one of the members for Kent, spoke on his behalf: 'Mr. Wilson, for so is your Petitioner named, a Man Orthodox in his Doctrine, conformable in his Life, labourous in Preachings, as any we have, or I do know; He is now seperated from his People, to both their griefs, for 'tis not with him as with others, who are glad to set a Pursivant a work, that they may have an

---

[7]   *Life and Death of Mr. Wilson*, 8.

[8]   Robert Swinnock and his father had 'three or four times enjoyed the highest honour, and exercised the highest office' at Maidstone, Kent. *Fading of the Flesh*, III:409.

[9]   *Life and Death of Mr. Wilson*, 29. 'Wilson... wielded a considerable influence over puritan sentiment in his parish and in neighbouring Maidstone, the home of his patron, alderman Robert Swinnock. During the 1630s a number of the town's worthies, including Swinnock and his wife, had been prosecuted in the church courts for deserting the ministry of Robert Barrell at their parish church of All Saints in preference for Wilson's preaching at Otham.' Jacqueline Eales, 'Kent and the English Civil Wars, 1640-1660' in *Government and Politics in Kent, 1640-1914* (Kent: Boydell Press, 2001) 15.

[10] *Life and Death of Mr. Wilson*, 12.

[11] Wilson defended himself against this charge by arguing that 'in the Rubrick before the Common Prayer, it was enjoined that no prayer should be publicly read, except those that were in the Book of Common Prayer, but this Prayer against the Scots was not there.' *Ibid.*, 15-16.

[12] *Ibid.*, 18.

excuse to be out of the Pulpit; It is his delight to preach.'[13]

Having been reinstated by Parliament, Wilson had an opportunity to preach before the house in 1642. He took this opportunity to exhort his audience to stand firm in the struggle against 'Arch-B. *W. L.* and the rest of the Prelates,' whom he refers to as 'wicked men.'[14] In his sermon, he makes three observations, based upon Hebrews 11:30.[15] First, the walls of the church's enemies cannot protect them.[16] For Wilson, these include principality and prelacy, i.e., the Roman Church and its allies among the English bishops. Second, the walls of the church's enemies are destroyed by faith.[17] With this in mind, he encourages his audience to promote preaching, provoke prayer, and provide the seals of the covenant of God in order to cultivate faith among God's people. Third, the faith that brings down the enemy's walls is active.[18] Hence, Wilson admonishes his audience to demonstrate their faith by resisting the enemy. He declares, 'Receive that counsell, *put your selves in Aray against Babylon round about*; all ye that bend the bow *shoot at her*, spare no arrowes, for she hath sinned against the Lord.'[19] Later, he adds, 'A leprosie was discovered in Queen *Mary* her dayes, after that zealous Prince King *Edward* the sixt, but all was new plaistered in the Raigne of that *Englands Deborah*, Queen *Elizabeth*: but the plague is broken out againe, wherefore downe must the house, leave not one stone upon another unthrowne downe.'[20] In short, Wilson affirms that the Roman Church is an abomination – the whore of Babylon.[21] Like many of his contemporaries, he believes it is the source of those heresies that had corrupted the Church of England and polluted the nation.[22]

---

[13] *Ibid.*, 21-22. Lamont explains that 'Wilson was to emerge as one of the most extreme "root and branch" advocates.' *Godly Rule*, 85. When he did, Dering disassociated himself, contending that he was not aware of his colleague's radicalism. Fletcher maintains that Dering 'was impulsive by nature and thus susceptible to the persuasions of the radical cleric Thomas Wilson.' *Outbreak of the English Civil War*, 96.

[14] Thomas Wilson, *Jerichoes Down-Fall, As it was Presented in a Sermon preached in St. Margarets Westminster, before the Honourable House of Commons at the late Solemne Fast, September 28, 1642* (London, 1643) 16.

[15] 'By faith the walls of Jericho fell down after they had been encircled for seven days.'

[16] Wilson, *Jerichoes Down-Fall*, 4.

[17] *Ibid.*, 17.

[18] *Ibid.*, 29.

[19] *Ibid.*, 33. His italics.

[20] *Ibid.*, 36. His italics.

[21] 'And on her forehead a name was written, a mystery, "BABYLON THE GREAT, THE MOTHER OF HARLOTS AND OF THE ABOMINATIONS OF THE EARTH"' (Rev. 17:5).

[22] In this regard, John Wilson writes, 'The Puritans were English patriots who construed their nation's historical destiny in terms of the biblical drama. England had been the seat of the pure church and the great locus of resistance to Antichrist

In some respect, Wilson's fiery sermon marks the end of his seven-year ordeal in which he experienced constant harassment due to his religious convictions. His perseverance was further rewarded in 1643 when the divines gathered at Westminster Assembly. Swinnock proudly remarks that Wilson was 'a Member of the Reverend, Pious and Learned Assembly of Divines, which sat at *Westminster*' and that 'he was much esteemed in the Assembly, for his solid judicious Discourses as occasion was offered, and his meek humble behaviour.'[23] At this time, Swinnock was a student at Cambridge. Undoubtedly, he followed the proceedings at Westminster with great interest, particularly, the participation of his minister.[24] Regarding the *WCF* itself, Benjamin Warfield notes, 'The architectonic principle of the Westminster Confession is supplied by the schematisation of the Federal theology, which had obtained by this time in Britain, as on the Continent, a dominant position as the most commodious mode of presenting the *corpus* of Reformed doctrine.'[25] This federal theology is foundational to any understanding of Swinnock's spirituality.

Shortly after his appointment to the Assembly, Wilson finally became minister at Maidstone. In the words of Swinnock, 'At last by the good hand of God, Mr. *Wilson* and the people of *Maidstone* (who brought him first into *Kent*) who were long before joyned together in heart, were joyned together in Habitation, amongst whom he continued with much love and faithfulness, till God called him out of this World.'[26] At the time of Wilson's death in 1653, Swinnock was twenty-six. From his childhood, through his years at university, into his first pastorate at Rickmansworth, Swinnock was attached to this man whom he calls 'an eminent servant of the Lord Jesus.'[27] He remarks to the inhabitants of Maidstone: 'I must ingenuously acknowledge, that it was a great mercy to me that I was born amongst you, and brought up under as pious and powerful a ministry there, as most in England.'[28] The impact of Wilson's 'pious and powerful ministry' upon Swinnock is made abundantly clear in Swinnock's funeral sermon for Wilson, in which he reviews Wilson's life and ministry, focusing on those features that actually exemplify his own spirituality.

---

throughout Christian history. In turn they believed it would be the fountainhead of a purified Europe delivered from the Roman incarnation of Antichristian power.' *Pulpit in Parliament: Puritanism during the English Civil Wars 1640-1648* (Princeton University Press, 1969) 20.

[23] *Life and Death of Mr. Wilson*, 22.

[24] In a poem, written upon the death of Thomas Wilson, Swinnock praises the 'great Assembly.' *Ibid.*, 93.

[25] Benjamin Warfield, *The Westminster Assembly and Its Work* in *The Works of Benjamin Warfield* (Grand Rapids: Baker Books, 2003) VI:56.

[26] *Life and Death of Mr. Wilson*, 24.

[27] Ουρανος και ταρταρος; *or, Heaven and hell epitomized: the true Christian characterized, as also an exhortation with motives, means and directions to be speedy and serious about the work of conversion*, III:245.

[28] *Fading of the Flesh*, III:408.

The Universities

Swinnock arrived at Emmanuel College, Cambridge University, in 1643. The university had been at the centre of the English Reformation. From 1511 to 1514, Erasmus lectured in Greek whilst preparing his translation of the New Testament and his edition of Jerome's writings.[29] In so doing, he sent a clear message to his fellow scholars; namely, the importance of the original sources – the Scriptures and the Fathers. Within ten years, William Tyndale prepared his English translation from Erasmus' text. By the 1520s, Luther's works were circulating at Cambridge among the likes of Thomas Bilney and Hugh Latimer. In the next decade, the university aligned itself with Henry VIII in his struggle against the Roman Church by pronouncing that marriage with a brother's widow was contrary to the teaching of Scripture. In 1534, Cambridge accepted Parliament's Act of Supremacy, thus recognizing the king as the head of the Church of England. And, in 1549, the divinity chair was offered to Martin Bucer, thereby demonstrating the success of the Cambridge reformers.[30]

Cambridge was also at the centre of Puritanism. During the reign of Mary, many Cambridge reformers fled to Germany and Switzerland where they were exposed to the churches of Calvin and others.[31] Upon returning to Cambridge, some were dissatisfied with the condition of the church. They preached against perceived 'Roman' abuses. In the 1590s, these ecclesiastical struggles were overshadowed by more important theological questions regarding the nature of grace. Peter Baro argued that God's work of predestination is based upon his foreknowledge of an individual's faith and works. Baro's assertions paralleled developments on the Continent where the Lutheran Saxon Visitation Articles were published in 1592.[32] These went so far as to identify the 'false and erroneous doctrine of the Calvinists;' namely, that Christ died only for the elect, that God created most of humanity for destruction, that the elect cannot fall from grace, and that the reprobate are necessarily damned. At Cambridge, William Perkins responded with several literary works.[33] Others, such as William Whitaker, reacted by convening a synod in 1595, at which they

---

[29] Harry Porter, *Reformation and Reaction in Tudor Cambridge* (Cambridge University Press, 1958) 21-40.

[30] *Ibid.*, 51. For J. William Black's thesis that Bucer envisioned a 'pastor-led reformation' as opposed to a 'legislated reformation' in England, see 'Richard Baxter's Bucerian Reformation,' *Westminster Theological Journal* 63 (2001) 327-349.

[31] For a brief consideration of the impact of the Marian exiles upon Cambridge, see Richard Bauckham, 'Marian Exiles and Cambridge Puritanism: James Pilkington's "Halfe a Score,"' *Journal of Ecclesiastical History* 26 (1975) 137-148.

[32] Schaff, *Creeds of Christendom*, III:181-189.

[33] For more on this controversy, see Mark Shaw, 'William Perkins and the New Pelagians: Another Look at the Cambridge Predestination Controversy of the 1590s,' *Westminster Theological Journal* 58 (1996) 267-301.

produced the Lambeth Articles.[34] These clearly affirm the doctrines of predestination and reprobation, the irresistibility and certainty of saving grace, and the sovereignty of God in salvation.

By the 1620s, the Puritan party was in ascendancy at Cambridge.[35] However, Laud soon opposed their control. Unlike at Oxford University, he did not possess any official position at Cambridge. Therefore, his control could only be exerted through the king. In several colleges, he was able to secure royal appointments that facilitated his influence. However, the Puritan party still maintained a majority. Thus, in May 1635, Laud notified both Cambridge and Oxford of his intention to visit them.[36] Both universities resisted this advance by affirming that, as royal foundations, they were only subject to royal visitation. However, the king gave his approval to the plan. The next year, Laud drew up a paper of 'disorders' that required his intervention at Cambridge.[37] He never carried them out as trouble in Scotland soon diverted his attention.

By 1643, the Long Parliament was convened, the Westminster Assembly was gathered, Laud was imprisoned, the Court of High Commission was abolished, the civil war was underway, and the Solemn League and Covenant was signed. This was the state of the nation when Swinnock arrived at Cambridge. He could not have attended the university from 1643 to 1648 without witnessing events that would influence him for the rest of his life. There is no doubt that he was exposed to a multitude of conflicting opinions. There is also no doubt that he became acquainted with some great preachers.

As for Emmanuel College, it was founded 'for the education of young men in all piety and good letters and especially Holy Writ and Theology, that being thus instructed they may hereafter teach true and pure religion, refute all errors and heresies, and by the shining example of a blameless life excite all men to virtue.'[38] From the outset, it was known for its Puritan sympathies.[39] J. C. Ryle explains:

> Sir Walter Mildmay of Chelmsford, in Essex, was the founder of Emmanuel College, and even from its very foundation in 1585, it seems to have been notorious for its attachment to Puritan principles. Fuller, in his history of

[34] Schaff, *Creeds of Christendom*, III:523-525.
[35] For an example of the on-going struggle, see Stephen Bondos-Greene, 'The End of an Era: Cambridge Puritanism and the Christ's College Election of 1609,' *Historical Journal* 25 (1982) 197-208.
[36] Trevor-Roper, *Archbishop Laud*, 206.
[37] *Ibid.*, 209.
[38] 'Emmanuel Statutes' as quoted in C. Brooke and R. Highfield, eds., *Oxford and Cambridge* (Cambridge University Press, 1988) 162.
[39] It was also known for the number of leading divines who passed through its doors; e.g., Joseph Hall, Edward Reynolds, Stephen Marshall, Jeremiah Burroughs, Thomas Shepard, Thomas Hooker, John Preston, Stephen Charnock, Ralph Venning, and Thomas Watson.

Cambridge, relates that on 'Sir Walter Mildmay coming to court, soon after he had founded his college, Queen Elizabeth said to him, "Sir Walter, I hear you have erected a puritan foundation." "No, madam," saith he, "far be it from me to countenance anything contrary to your established laws; but I have set an acorn, which, when it becomes an oak, God alone knows what will be the fruit thereof."'[40]

Therefore, Swinnock was trained at a college where the entire atmosphere was decidedly Puritan. There is no doubt that his character and convictions were further influenced by this exposure.

Having completed his B.A., he departed for Oxford, where he entered Magdalen Hall as a commoner in 1648. He soon became a fellow at Balliol College. By the 1630s, Laud – as vice-chancellor of Oxford – had suppressed all dissenting voices. Hugh Trevor-Roper remarks, 'As for the Puritan opposition, he had smitten it hip and thigh, and it was discomfited. Wherever it had sought to organize itself, he had overthrown it. Wherever it was articulate, he had silenced it.'[41] During the Civil War, Oxford remained loyal to the archbishop and king. It was actually the centre of military operations for the Royalists until 1646. The following year, Parliamentary visitors arrived to re-order the university in a manner more favourable to their supporters. Thus, from April 1648 to January 1650, they made 400 appointments,[42] including Swinnock to his fellowship at Balliol.[43]

The Christian Heathen

At medieval Cambridge and Oxford, the regular arts course consisted of the trivium (i.e., grammar, rhetoric, logic), the quadrivium (i.e., music, arithmetic, geometry, astronomy), and the philosophies (i.e., natural, moral, metaphysical).[44] Once students completed the B.A. and M.A., they proceeded to the higher faculties such as theology, law, and medicine. Since the time of Augustine, it was believed that these arts and philosophies provided the

---

[40]   J. C. Ryle, 'A Biographical Account of the Author' in William Gurnall, *The Christian in Complete Armour: A Treatise of the Saints' War against the Devil* (London: Blackie & Sons, 1864; rpt., Edinburgh: Banner of Truth, 1995) xix.

[41]   Trevor-Roper, *Archbishop Laud*, 295.

[42]   Brooke and Highfield, eds., *Oxford and Cambridge*, 193.

[43]   For professors, masters, and fellow students, see *Historical Register of the University of Oxford to the End of the Trinity Term 1888* (Oxford: Clarendon Press, 1888) 26-50,175; and John Jones, ed., *Balliol College: A History 1263-1939* (Oxford University Press, 1942) 290.

[44]   Charles Mallett, *A History of the University of Oxford* (New York: Barnes & Noble, 1968) I:182-183. For a discussion of the nature of education at this time, see Jefferson Looney, 'Undergraduate Education at Early Stuart Cambridge,' *History of Education* 10 (1981) 9-19.

necessary foundation for theological study.[45] This emphasis was still in vogue when Swinnock appeared on the scene in the 1640s. Generally speaking, the Puritans were in favour of this program of study. Davies notes, 'It is erroneous to suppose that the Puritans despised the achievements of human reason because they subordinated them to the Divine Revelation.'[46] They insisted that original sin had ruined humanity's capacity to understand spiritual truth, however they also insisted that humanity retained the ability to penetrate into the mysteries of nature. Consequently, they had no inhibitions about learning from the ancients. They simply studied them with great care. Edward Reynolds articulates this mindset as follows: 'And here I might first alledge the honour which God himselfe hath beene pleased to give, unto Inferiour, and Naturall knowledge... And if we looke into the Ancient Christian Churches, or into these of later times, wee shall finde that very many Ecclesiasticall persons have not denied unto the world, their Philosophicall and Poeticall labors, either whole and alone, or mixed, and directed to Theologicall Ends.'[47] Likewise, Baxter affirms that 'we may... make use of all true human learning'[48] whilst remembering that 'the dark philosophers groping after the knowledge of God, did frequently stumble, and did introduce abundance of logical and physical vanities, uncertainties, and falsities, under the name of philosophy.'[49]

This is certainly Swinnock's approach. He depends heavily upon the ancients for stories and allegories to colour his own material.[50] He also draws on their thoughts to support his own arguments. However, he only does so as long as they are in agreement with Scripture. He remarks, 'Theology is the mistress, all other sciences and arts are but handmaids; and then they know their places, and serve for the right purpose, when they are, as the spoils which David took from the Gentiles, consecrated to the temple.'[51]

Swinnock's approach is evident in his handling of the moralists. He finds so

---

[45]   D. Leader, *A History of the University of Cambridge* (Cambridge University Press, 1994) I:171.

[46]   Davies, *Worship of English Puritans*, 6. For further discussion, see Morgan, *Godly Learning*, 41-78,172-244.

[47]   Edward Reynolds, 'A Preface to the Reader' in *A Treatise of the Passions and Faculties of the Soul* (London, 1640).

[48]   Baxter, *Christian Directory*, 722.

[49]   *Ibid.*, 721.

[50]   Swinnock's favourite historian is Plutarch, naturalist – Pliny, and orator – Cicero. C. John Sommerville notes that Aristotle, Plato, Plutarch, Cicero, Seneca, and the ancient naturalists and poets were a frequent source of illustrations among the Dissenters. *Popular Religion in Restoration England* (University of Florida, 1977) 67. At times, it is unclear whether or not Swinnock actually views his illustrations as reliable. By way of example, he remarks, 'What some observe of horse-hairs, that, though lifeless, yet lying nine days under water, they turn to snakes.' *Christian Man's Calling*, I:81.

[51]   *Ibid.*, I:369.

much in Seneca's thought, corresponding to his own, that he actually calls him a 'Christian heathen,'[52] yet he never appeals to him as an authority. Rather, he judges Seneca's writings in the light of Scripture. In a discussion of Psalm 73:26,[53] Swinnock writes, 'I confess the master of moral philosophy, whom I most admire of all heathen, seemeth to harp upon the same string as the psalmist. Those, saith he, whom God approveth and loveth, he exerciseth and afflicteth; those whom he seemeth to spare, he reserveth for future sufferings. But an ordinary capacity may perceive by the treatise, though there may be many excellent things in it, how far the moralist came short of Christianity.'[54] Swinnock's precaution is also evident in his handling of the philosophers.[55] He displays an understanding of various philosophical systems but leans heavily upon Aristotle – the 'prince.'[56] He employs aspects of Aristotle's thinking that serve his own purposes whilst avoiding any dependence upon this 'blind heathen.'[57]

The Historic Witness

In the century prior to Swinnock's attendance at Cambridge and Oxford, a significant change had occurred in the study of theology. In short, the empire of the Fathers and Reformers had replaced that of the Scholastics and Romanists.[58] Lovelace notes the impact of this revolution among the Puritans:

> In Puritan devotional literature, authorities lean heavily on patristic sources: Augustine is by far the most cited, followed by Chrysostom, Ambrose, the Cappadocians, and Gregory the Great. A large scattering of pagan authors is among those cited, chief among them Seneca; but among the schoolmen Bernard is the only one widely appealed to, except a few stray references to Aquinas. Of scholastic authors, there are a few citations. Of mystical writers (save for Bernard and Augustine), there is no mention. The Puritans quoted heavily from the Patristics and Reformers because it was with these that they felt the deepest spiritual sympathy.[59]

Lovelace's observations are confirmed in Swinnock. To begin with, Swinnock

---

[52] *Heaven and Hell*, III:227. Also see *Christian Man's Calling*, I:38,69,306, II:10,149.
[53] 'My flesh and my heart may fail, But God is the strength of my heart and my portion forever.'
[54] *Fading of the Flesh*, III:419-420.
[55] There are at least fifty citations from Aristotle in Swinnock's works. Plato is a distant second.
[56] *Christian Man's Calling*, I:425,450,478, II:86,203,294; and *Fading of the Flesh*, III:407,427, IV:8.
[57] *Christian Man's Calling*, I:308; and *Fading of the Flesh*, V:37.
[58] This is not to suggest that the Puritans were exempt from the shadow of Scholasticism. It still dominated a large part of the accepted curriculum.
[59] Lovelace, 'The Anatomy of Puritan Piety,' 296.

rarely quotes the medieval writers. The most frequently mentioned is indeed Bernard, whilst there are only sporadic references to Thomas Aquinas and Peter Lombard. Similarly, Swinnock's use of Roman Catholic authors is sparse. Robert Bellarmine, Stephen Gardiner, and Cornelius a Lapide are among the few mentioned. Swinnock finds some use for Lapide; as for the rest, his comments are usually negative. He quotes Gardiner – 'that Popish prelate' – as having said that justification by faith 'was a good supper doctrine, though not so good a breakfast one.'[60] He refers to Bellarmine 'with the rest of the papists' as 'wilfully blind.'[61] He is blunt in his criticism of the Roman Church, believing that superstition is a 'brat the devil hath long put out to nurse to the Romish church, which hath taken a great deal of pains to bring it up for him; and no wonder, when she is so well paid for its maintenance, it having brought her in so much worldly treasure and riches.'[62]

In terms of the Fathers, Lovelace notes that the four most popular among the Puritans are Augustine, Chrysostom, Ambrose, and the Cappadocians. For Swinnock, the only difference is the inclusion of Jerome after Augustine.[63] Unsurprisingly, there are more references to Augustine than all of the other fathers combined.[64] In terms of the Reformers, Sommerville observes that 'Continental reformers loomed larger than English ones' among the Puritans.[65] This is true of Swinnock who quotes – in order of popularity – Calvin, Luther, Beza, Zanchi, and Melanchthon. There are occasional references to Tremellius, Bucer, and Bullinger. Swinnock clearly stands in the tradition of Reformed theology as opposed to Lutheran theology. Apart from Luther and Melanchthon, he does not quote from anyone who would fall within the camp of Lutheranism.[66] Yet, he is not captive to just one Swiss Reformer. Without question, he has great respect for 'judicious Calvin.'[67] However, Calvin is only one figure in the tradition from which he draws.

The Pious Divines

Continuing with Swinnock's reading, it is clear that he was familiar with his

---

[60] *Christian Man's Calling*, I:6. Also see *Heaven and Hell*, III:310.

[61] *Sinner's Last Sentence*, V:308.

[62] *Christian Man's Calling*, I:80-81. For Swinnock's comments on the Genevan memorial, *Post tenebras, lux*, see I:165.

[63] Interestingly, Erasmus favoured Jerome. 'Shall the names of Scotua, Albertus, and writers still less polished be shouted in all the schools, and that singular champion, exponent and light of our religion who deserves to be the one persons celebrated, – shall he be the only one of whom nothing is said?' As quoted by Porter in *Reformation and Reaction*, 23.

[64] Sommerville confirms this trend among the Dissenters. *Popular Religion*, 67.

[65] *Ibid.*

[66] His use of Luther is always illustrative as opposed to theological or polemical.

[67] *Heaven and Hell*, III:203.

fellow Puritans.[68] In terms of those who contributed to his spirituality, William Perkins merits some attention. According to Ian Breward, what makes Perkins 'so important is that by the end of the sixteenth century his writings had begun to displace those of Calvin, Beza, and Bullinger.'[69] Edward Reynolds is also worth mentioning.[70] His book, *A Treatise of the Passions and Faculties of the Soul of Man*, sheds some light on Swinnock's understanding of the affections. Another noteworthy divine is Joseph Hall. His *Contemplations, Holy Observations, Heaven Upon Earth*, and *Meditations* are important, given Swinnock's emphasis upon meditation.

Swinnock also quotes a number of 'affectionate writers,' including Richard Baxter,[71] Thomas Shepard, William Gurnall, and Robert Bolton. He sees his own convictions mirrored in these authors. This is significant, in that they transcend the divide between Royalists and Parliamentarians, Episcopalians and

---

[68] In addition to those mentioned in this section, Swinnock refers to Richard Greenham, Thomas Cartwright, William Ames, Jeremiah Burroughs, Arthur Hildersham, Richard Rogers, Richard Sibbes, Joseph Caryl, and Thomas Manton.

[69] Ian Breward, 'The Significance of William Perkins,' *Journal of Religious History* 4 (1966) 116.

[70] *Life and Death of Mr. Wilson*, 34. Undoubtedly, Swinnock heard Reynolds preach on many occasions. He was certainly familiar with his printed sermons. *Christian Man's Calling*, I:370; *Heaven and Hell*, III:277,357,359; *Gods Are Men*, IV:104; and *Door of Salvation*, V:103,233. Reynolds graduated D.D. from Cambridge in 1648 – the same year Swinnock departed the university. A few months later, he was one of the Parliamentary visitors at Oxford, where he eventually became vice-chancellor. *Historical Register of the University of Oxford*, 26,195. Undoubtedly, he played a significant role in Swinnock's appointment as fellow at Balliol. In an introductory letter to one of Swinnock's treatises, Reynolds writes, 'there are two things which commend a book – the worthiness of the matter therein handled, and the skillfulness of the hand that contrived it.' *Door of Salvation*, V:9. In 1649, contention arose between Reynolds and the Parliamentary committee overseeing the university. The latter (mainly Independents) insisted that all members of the university subscribe to an Engagement to be faithful to the Commonwealth as established without king or House of Lords. Reynolds requested permission to submit to a promise to live peaceably under the government. It was refused. As a result, he was forced to resign his position. It is around this time that Swinnock resigned his fellowship at Balliol College.

[71] In an introductory letter, Baxter encourages the reader to study 'this savoury treatise,' though, as he admits, 'I know not the author.' *Door of Salvation*, V:13. They likely met in 1665, when Baxter was the guest of Richard Hampden. Baxter provides an interesting description of the minister's library, dividing it into three categories: the poorest, the poorer, and the poor. In terms of the first ('the smallest library that is tolerable'), he names Swinnock among 'affectionate practical English writers.' *Christian Directory*, 732.

Presbyterians, Conformists and Non-Conformists.[72] Furthermore, they are representative of the entire seventeenth century. Stephen Charnock should also be included in this group despite the fact that Swinnock never quotes him. Both studied at Emmanuel College, Cambridge. In 1649, Charnock obtained a fellowship at New College, Oxford, where Swinnock was chaplain. The similarity between their literary works is striking. Charnock's greatest treatises include *Discourses on the Existence and Attributes of God* and *Discourses on Regeneration*. After *Christian Man's Calling*, Swinnock's most notable works are *Incomparableness of God* and *Door of Salvation Opened by the Key of Regeneration*.

Some attention must also be given to Swinnock's use of spiritual biographies such as *The Life and Death of Mr. Robert Bolton*.[73] These biographies describe salvation according to the pattern of Romans 8:29-30.[74] In other words, they focus on the unfolding of the order of salvation in the individual's experience of conviction and forgiveness. In so doing, they portray conversion as an intense experience in the tradition of Augustine. As Miller notes, 'There survive hundreds of Puritan diaries and thousands of Puritans sermons, but we can read the inward meaning of them all in the Confessions.'[75]

Conclusion

The observations made in this chapter suggest that Swinnock stands within the tradition of English Reformed theology as developed upon the thought of Augustine within the framework of the Swiss Reformers (particularly Calvin) and as encapsulated in the *WCF*. This is the particular context that contributed to the development of his 'serious piety.' For this reason, there will be some interaction in subsequent chapters with Augustine, Calvin, and the Westminster divines.

Also evident from this chapter is the fact that Swinnock is not an anomaly.

---

[72] To further demonstrate the points of commonality among these groups, reference will be made in subsequent chapters to John Owen, John Flavel, John Bunyan, Thomas Watson, Ralph Venning, William Gouge, and others.

[73] According to E. Bagshawe, God humbled Bolton 'not by any soft and still voice, but in terrible tempests and thunder, the Lord running upon him as a giant, taking him by the neck and shaking him to pieces... by laying before him the ugly visage of his sins, which lay so heavy upon him.' *The Life and Death of Mr. Robert Bolton* in R. Bolton, *The Four Last Things: Death, Judgment, Hell, Heaven* (London, 1635) 15. This deep conviction of sin lasted for several months before he finally received 'an invincible courage and resolution for the cause of God.' *Ibid.*, 16.

[74] 'For those whom He foreknew, He also predestined to become conformed to the image of His Son, so that He would be the firstborn among many brethren; and these whom He predestined, He also called; and these whom He called, He also justified; and these whom He justified, He also glorified.'

[75] Miller, *New England Mind*, 5.

On the contrary, he stands as part of a movement. To ensure that he is rightly understood in that setting, there will also be some interaction with Baxter, Charnock, Reynolds, Gouge, and others. Further to this, Swinnock's position on various themes will be expounded together with that of his contemporaries in order to confirm his place within the Puritan tradition.

Chapter Three

The Whole Man

According to Genesis 1:27, 'God created man in His own image.' For Swinnock, this image is found in the faculties of the soul as characterized by knowledge, righteousness, and holiness. His entire theological framework rests upon his understanding of this image in the context of humanity's threefold state: 'innocency, apostasy, and recovery.'[1] And it is this framework that invariably gives rise to his spirituality.

The Faculties of the Soul

Perry Miller maintains that the Puritans discuss the faculties in 'passing references' that 'constitute an extended treatise upon psychology, the outlines of a doctrine upon which all Puritans agreed, of a premise for all their thinking, that can be said to have influenced them all the more extensively because it was unformulated and taken as axiomatic.'[2] This 'premise' is known as 'faculty-humour psychology.'[3] Miller describes it as follows:

> Plants have a 'vegetative soul,' which contains the powers of nourishing and propagating; animals have a 'sensible soul,' which contains the powers of nourishing and propagating, and, in addition, the senses and animal spirits, the 'interior senses' of common sense, imagination and memory, the passions and the sinews capable of motion; men have a 'rational soul,' which contains all the powers and faculties of the vegetative and sensible, and, in addition, the distinguishing faculties of the rational creature, reason and will.[4]

Miller's description is confirmed in Swinnock, who believes there are three types of 'souls' (also known as 'appetites' or 'faculties'): vegetative, sensitive,

---

[1]   *Christian Man's Calling*, II:433.

[2]   Miller, *New England Mind*, 242-243.

[3]   For a detailed description of faculty-humour psychology, see Charles Cohen, *God's Caress: The Psychology of Puritan Religious Experience* (Oxford University Press, 1986) 25-46. Of particular importance is Cohen's comment that the Puritans 'did not accept it uncritically, for like all knowledge, it had to pass muster with Scripture.' *Ibid.*, 26.

[4]   Miller, *New England Mind*, 240.

and rational.[5] The 'rational soul' is 'the greatest thing in man,' because it is the 'breath of Almighty God.'[6] Swinnock identifies three faculties in this rational soul: 'the understanding to conceive, the will to choose, the affections to love and desire.'[7] Steve Griffiths affirms that this threefold division was 'a standard medieval position' and 'accepted teaching within the Reformed tradition.'[8] In actual fact, this tripartite division is a minor alteration of the more common bipartite division within the 'Reformed tradition.' John Calvin states, 'The soul consists of two faculties, understanding and will.'[9] Similarly, Edward Reynolds identifies the understanding and will as the soul's 'principal parts.'[10] Neither of these men denies the function of the affections, but prefers to include them under the banner of the will. For them, the will has two components: inclination (or affections) and choice. By Swinnock's time, however, it was common practice among the Puritans to designate the affections as a faculty in its own right.[11] As Owen Watkins confirms, 'The Puritans... were concerned mainly with the relations between the faculties of the rational soul: the mind, the will,

---

5   *Christian Man's Calling*, I:3,11-13,16,271-272,286,389,399-400, II:165,233,253, III:196. For Baxter, see *Divine Life, Practical Works*, 129. For John Flavel, see *Pneumatologia: A Treatise on the Soul of Man* in *The Works of John Flavel* (London: W. Baynes and Son, 1820; rpt., London: Banner of Truth, 1968) II:493. For John Bunyan, see *The Greatness of the Soul, And unspeakableness of the loss thereof, &c.* in *The Miscellaneous Works of John Bunyan* (Oxford: Clarendon Press, 1981) IX:144.

6   Job 33:4. *Christian Man's Calling*, I:53. For more on Swinnock's view of the 'unconceivable value and excellency' of the soul, see II:174.

7   *Christian Man's Calling*, II:194. At times, Swinnock speaks in terms of a bi-partite division: mind and will (including inclination and choice). *Fading of the Flesh*, IV:36-37.

8   Steve Griffiths, *Redeem the Time: Sin in the Writings of John Owen* (Ross-shire: Christian Focus, 2001) 58-59. Griffiths identifies John Owen's concept of the image of God as foundational to his theological framework. His observations are noted throughout this chapter, thereby demonstrating the centrality of this concept among the Puritans.

9   Calvin, *Institutes*, I:XV:7.

10 Reynolds, *Passions and Faculties*, 403.

11 By way of example, see Thomas Shepard, *The Sincere Convert: Discovering the Small Number of True Believers and the Great Difficulty of Saving Conversion* in *The Sincere Convert and The Sound Believer* (Boston Doctrinal Tract and Book Society, 1853; rpt., Morgan: Soli Deo Gloria, 1999) 18-19; William Gurnall, *The Christian in Complete Armour: A Treatise of the Saints' War against the Devil* (1662-1665; London: Blackie & Sons, 1864; rpt., Edinburgh: Banner of Truth, 1995) I:292,294,297, II:3,8-10,30-32,279,370,468-469,568; and Stephen Charnock, *A Discourse of the Nature of Regeneration* in *The Works of Stephen Charnock*, ed. J. Nichol (London, 1865; rpt., Edinburgh: Banner of Truth, 1986) III:97,107.

and the affections.'[12] In the final analysis, the difference between a bipartite or tripartite division of the faculties is unimportant, given the fact that the function of the affections remains the same in both paradigms.[13] For the present discussion, the important point is that Swinnock identifies these faculties as the basis for the image (or likeness)[14] of God in humanity.

This emphasis dates back to Augustine, who asserts that, since the triune God made humanity in his image, there must be a trinity in humanity.[15] He identifies this trinity in the human mind: it exists, it knows it exists, and it delights in itself.[16] Elsewhere, he describes this trinity in terms of memory, understanding, and will.[17] Clearly, for Augustine, the image of God primarily exists in these faculties. Whilst rejecting Augustine's trinity of the mind,[18] Calvin agrees with his stress upon the faculties, writing, 'the primary seat of the divine image was in the mind and the heart, or in the soul and its powers, there.'[19] The Puritans adopt this same approach.[20]

The Nature of the Image

On the one hand, Swinnock believes the faculties of the rational soul constitute the image of God in humanity – they are the 'breath of Almighty God.' On the other hand, he believes the faculties are the means by which the image of God is communicated to the soul. Baxter elucidates this idea by distinguishing between the 'natural image of God' (i.e., the faculties) and the 'moral image of

---

[12] Owen Watkins, *The Puritan Experience* (London: Routledge & Kegan Paul, 1972) 6.

[13] In the next century, Jonathan Edwards argues for the inclusion of the affections under the faculty of the will, adding, 'It must be confessed, that language is here somewhat imperfect, the meaning of words in a considerable measure loose and unfixed, and not precisely limited by custom which governs the use of language.' *A Treatise Concerning Religious Affections* in *The Works of Jonathan Edwards* (1834; rpt., Peabody: Hendrickson Publishers, 1998) I:2.

[14] Swinnock makes no distinction between the 'image' and 'likeness' of God. He would agree with Calvin's assertion that some 'interpreters seek a nonexistent difference between these two words.' *Institutes*, I:XV:3.

[15] Augustine, *The City of God* in *A Select Library of the Nicene and Post-Nicene Fathers of the Christian Church: Vol. II*, ed. P. Schaff (New York: Random House, 1948) XI:26.

[16] Also see Augustine, *The Trinity, Select Library: Vol. III*, IX:4:4.

[17] *Ibid.*, X:11:17-X:12:19.

[18] Calvin, *Institutes*, I:XV:4.

[19] *Ibid.*, I:XV:3.

[20] For a discussion of the psychology taught at Cambridge University, see William Costello, *The Scholastic Curriculum at Early Seventeenth Century Cambridge* (Harvard University Press, 1958) 94-97.

God' (i.e., holiness).[21] According to this paradigm, the image of God in humanity is not merely the faculties of mind, affections, and will, but these faculties characterized by knowledge, righteousness, and holiness.[22] According to Perkins:

> The image of God, is nothing els but a conformitie of man unto God, whereby man is holy as God is holy: for Paul saith; *Put on the new man, which after God, that is, in Gods image, is created in righteousness and holiness.* Now I reason thus: wherein the renuing of the image of God in man doth stand, therein was it at the first: but the renuing of Gods image in man doth stand in righteousness and holiness: therefore Gods image wherein man was created at the beginning, was a conformitie to God in righteousness and holiness.[23]

The Westminster divines are in full agreement with Perkins: 'After God had made all other creatures, he created man, male and female, with reasonable and immortal souls, endued with knowledge, righteousness, and true holiness, after his own image.'[24] This concept is not derived from the Genesis creation account, but from the description of the renewal of God's image in humanity as described in Ephesians 4:24[25] and Colossians 3:10.[26] This is Augustine's position.[27] It is also found in Calvin, who writes:

> 'The new man is renewed... according to the image of his Creator' (Col. 3:10). With this agrees the saying, 'Put on the new man, who has been created according to God' (Eph. 4:24). Now we are to see what Paul chiefly comprehends under this renewal. In the first place he posits knowledge, then pure righteousness and

---

[21] Baxter, *Divine Life, Practical Works*, 146,227. Also see *A Call to the Unconverted to Turn and Live, Practical Works*, 438; and *The Mischiefs of Self-Ignorance and the Benefits of Self-Acquaintance, Practical Works*, 762. Charnock writes, 'The image of God consists not so much in the substance of the soul as in a likeness to God in a holy nature.' *Discourse of the Efficient of Regeneration, Works*, III:259,272,296. Also see *Nature of Regeneration, Works*, III:85,88,117; and *Discourses upon the Existence and Attributes of God* (London: Robert Carter & Brothers, 1853; rpt., Grand Rapids: Baker Books, 1990) I:191.

[22] *Heaven and Hell*, III:359. See Baxter, *Divine Life, Practical Works*, 149,226; and *A Treatise of Conversion Addressed to the Ignorant and Ungodly, Practical Works*, 322,336; Charnock, *Existence and Attributes of God*, I:191, II:112,127-128,173; and Gurnall, *Christian in Complete Armour*, I:408.

[23] Perkins, *An Exposition of the Symbole or Creede of the Apostles, according to the Tenour of the Scriptures, and the Consent of the Orthodoxe Fathers of the Church, Works*, I:153.

[24] *WCF*, IV:II.

[25] 'And put on the new self, which in the likeness of God has been created in righteousness and holiness of the truth.'

[26] 'And have put on the new self who is being renewed to a true knowledge according to the image of the One who created him.'

[27] Augustine, *Trinity, Select Library: Vol. III*, XIV:16:22-XIV:17:23.

holiness. From this we infer that, to begin with, God's image was visible in the light of the mind, in the uprightness of the heart, and in the soundness of all the parts.[28]

In explaining Calvin's view, Brian Gerrish remarks, 'The soul is not itself all that Calvin means by the divine "image." To have God's image includes an activity; it is a mode of personal existence rather than simply human nature as such, a relationship rather than simply a natural endowment. Often, though not always, Calvin has in mind a reflection in a mirror: the soul with its faculties is then the mirror, and the image is the reflection.'[29]

Thomas Shepard provides the following insights into how the moral image of God is reflected in the natural image of God. First, it appears in the understanding: 'As God saw himself, and beheld his own infinite, endless glory and excellency, so man was privy to God's excellency, and saw God most gloriously.'[30] Second, it appears in the affections: 'As God, seeing himself, loved himself, so Adam, seeing God, loved this God more than the world, more than himself... As God delighted in himself, so did Adam delight in God, took sweet repose in the bosom of God.'[31] Third, it appears in the will: 'As God only willed himself as his last end, so did Adam will God as his last end... As God willed nothing but good, so did Adam will nothing, though not immutably, but good; for God's will was his.'[32]

The Purpose of the Image

Swinnock concurs with Shepard's description of how the image of God is reflected in the faculties. The understanding sees 'God's infinite, endless glory' and the affections delight in him; consequently, the will chooses – 'though not immutably' – God as its 'last end.' Swinnock is convinced this explains the purpose of God's image in humanity. He states:

> Now the beauty of man consisteth in this, that he was made like unto God (Gen. 1:26); and his end and use is this, that he was made for God; first to serve him, and after to enjoy him, for the Lord hath set apart him that is godly for himself; therefore to recover the image of God, which consisteth in knowledge,

---

28   Calvin, *Institutes*, I:XV:4.

29   Brian Gerrish, *Grace and Gratitude: The Eucharist Theology of John Calvin* (Minneapolis: Fortress Press, 1993) 42-43. Thomas Torrance states, 'When Calvin says that the proper seat of the image is in the soul, he does not mean that the *imago dei* is the soul, or any natural property of the soul, but that the soul is the mirror which reflects in it or ought to reflect in it the image of God.' *Calvin's Doctrine of Man* (Grand Rapids: Eerdmans, 1957) 53.

30   Shepard, *Sincere Convert*, 18.

31   *Ibid.*, 19.

32   *Ibid.*, 19.

righteousness, and true holiness, to work to the service and glory of God, to aspire to the possession and fruition of God, must needs be man's greatest good.[33]

For Swinnock, God created humanity in his image so that people would serve him and enjoy him. This is humanity's 'last end' and 'greatest good.'[34] 'The great God,' writes Swinnock, 'according to his infinite wisdom, hath designed all his creatures to some particular ends, and hath imprinted in their natures an appetite and propensity towards that end, as the point and scope of their being.'[35] Swinnock's contemporaries share this teleological emphasis. Gurnall declares, 'Man's happiness stands in his likeness to God, and his fruition of God.'[36] Shepard comments, 'No unregenerate man hath fruition of God to content him, and there is no man's heart but it must have some good to content it; which good is to be found only in the fountain of all good, and that is God.'[37] Baxter states, 'Every soul that hath a title to this rest, doth place his chief happiness in God. This rest consisteth in the full and glorious enjoyment of God.'[38] Griffiths sees the same approach in Owen, who 'was firmly convinced that the image of God in man serves one primary purpose, namely, enjoyment of life with God, with all the benefits and duties that that entails.'[39] In brief, the Puritans believe that the image of God is the means by which humanity experiences 'happiness in God.'[40] This conviction finds its clearest expression in the first question of the *Westminster Shorter Catechism*: 'What is the chief

[33]   *Heaven and Hell*, III:359.
[34]   For a modern-day approach to this entire discussion, see John Piper, *Desiring God: Meditations of a Christian Hedonist* (Sisters: Multonomah Press, 1996).
[35]   *Christian Man's Calling*, I:47.
[36]   Gurnall, *Christian in Complete Armour*, I:415.
[37]   Shepard, *Sincere Convert*, 62.
[38]   Baxter, *The Saints' Everlasting Rest*, *Practical Works*, 54. Also see *Call to the Unconverted*, *Practical Works*, 444.
[39]   Griffiths, *Redeem the Time*, 30.
[40]   According to Norman Fiering, William Ames rejects the idea that happiness is the individual's ultimate aim. *Moral Philosophy at Seventeenth-Century Harvard: A Discipline in Tradition* (Chapel Hill: University of North Carolina, 1981) 76. Fiering is correct in his observation that Ames believes εὐζωία (living well) is 'more excellent' than εὐδαιμονία (living happily). Consequently, people should not strive for 'happiness which has to do with our own pleasure, but goodness which looks to God's glory.' *Marrow*, I:I:8. However, Fiering neglects the very next paragraph, in which Ames states, 'life is the spiritual work of the whole man, in which he is brought to enjoy God.' *Ibid.*, I:I:9. Later, Ames explains that 'rational creatures' are 'directed towards an eternal state of happiness or unhappiness in accordance with their own counsel and freedom.' *Ibid.*, I:X:2. Still later, he speaks of the new covenant, leading 'man to happiness.' *Ibid.*, I:XXIV:16. Ames believes happiness is the individual's ultimate aim, found in the enjoyment of God. What he condemns is happiness that is tied to 'our own pleasure' – sensual pleasure.

end of man? Man's chief end is to glorify God, and to enjoy him forever.'[41]

The framework for this teleological view of the image of God is found in Aristotle, who writes, 'there is some end (τέλος) of the things we do, which we desire for its own sake.' This 'end' is 'the chief good' (happiness), which is 'always desirable in itself and never for the sake of something else.'[42] For Aristotle, the conclusion is primarily ethical; that is, the happy man is the virtuous man – virtue being the mean between two extremes.[43] As Brian Gerrish observes, Calvin adopts the Aristotelian notion of the *summum bonum*, stating, 'When he adds that the highest human *good* is the very same thing – to know and glorify God – his point is simply that human happiness consists in fulfillment of the end for which humans were created.'[44] John Leith agrees, 'Calvin was certain that the highest human good was comprehended in communion with God.'[45]

Like Calvin, Swinnock employs Aristotle's teleological framework without accepting his view of the virtuous man. He agrees with Aristotle's assertion 'that those things only content the several creatures which are accommodated to their several natures.'[46] In relation to humanity, Swinnock believes this is God, for three reasons. First, God is perfect: 'That which makes man happy must have no want, no weakness in it. It must be able both to secure him against all evil, and to furnish him with all good.'[47] Second, God is suitable: 'It is an unquestionable truth, that nothing can give true comfort to man but that which hath a relation and beareth a proportion to his highest and noblest part, his immortal soul.'[48] Third, God is eternal: 'The soul can enjoy no perfection of happiness if it be not commensurate to its own duration.'[49] In a word, God alone can satisfy humanity because he alone meets the needs of the soul. Swinnock adds, 'According to the excellency of the object which we embrace in our hearts, such is the degree of our happiness; the saint's choice is right, God alone being the soul's centre and rest.'[50]

Swinnock also agrees with Aristotle's assertion that happiness consists 'in

---

[41] According to Warfield, 'The ultimate source of the declaration is almost as easily identified as its proximate source. This must undoubtedly be found in John Calvin, who, in his "Institutes" and in "Catechisms" alike, placed this identical idea in the forefront of his instruction.' *Westminster Assembly, Works*, VI:380. See *Geneva Catechism*, question 1.

[42] Aristotle, *Nicomachean Ethics, Works: Vol. IX*, I:2,4,7.

[43] *Ibid.*, I:13.

[44] Gerrish, *Grace and Gratitude*, 36. His italics. See Calvin, *Institutes*, II:I:4.

[45] John Leith, *John Calvin's Doctrine of the Christian Life* (Louisville: John Knox Press, 1989) 40.

[46] *Fading of the Flesh*, IV:8.

[47] *Ibid.*, IV:3.

[48] *Ibid.*, IV:8.

[49] *Ibid.*, IV:10.

[50] *Ibid.*, IV:2.

the knowledge of the chiefest good.'[51] Having identified God as humanity's chief good, he comments, 'Thy happiness dependeth wholly upon thy taking of the blessed God for thine utmost end and chiefest good.'[52] In this regard, Swinnock is firmly rooted in the Augustinian tradition. He quotes Augustine as saying, 'Thou hast made our heart for thee, and it will never rest till it come to thee; and when I shall wholly cleave to thee, then my life will be lively.'[53] God is the 'chiefest good,' therefore humanity's happiness is found in him. This means that individuals experience this happiness when they 'know' God who is 'the sweetest love, the richest mercy, the surest friend, the chiefest good, the greatest beauty, the highest honour, and fullest happiness.'[54]

Finally, Swinnock agrees with Aristotle's assertion that humanity has 'a propensity towards that in which they place their felicity.'[55] People move towards that which makes them happy and away from that which makes them unhappy. This is the purpose of the image of God, in that the faculties of the soul – marked by knowledge, righteousness, and holiness – are the means by which humanity finds happiness in God.[56] The understanding perceives God to be the soul's chief good. The affections desire God, and the will chooses God. This is the religious life – 'which consisteth in exalting God in our affections, as our chiefest good, and in our actions, as our utmost end.'[57] For Swinnock, this makes 'the holiest man... the happiest man.'[58]

The Corruption of the Image

When Adam sinned, this image of God was corrupted. This does not mean he lost his faculties; on the contrary, his soul still consisted of understanding, affections, and will. Rather, it means he lost knowledge, righteousness, and holiness. Charnock explains, 'We have the same faculties of understanding, will, and affection, as Adam had in innocence; but not with the same light.'[59] Lewis Bayly remarks, 'The felicity lost was, first, the fruition of the image of God, whereby the soul was like God in knowledge, enabling her perfectly to understand the revealed will of God; secondly, true holiness, by which she was free from all profane error; thirdly, righteousness, whereby she was able to

---

[51] *Ibid.*, IV:37.

[52] *Ibid.*, IV:22.

[53] *Ibid.*, IV:36. See Augustine, *Confessions, Select Library: Vol. I*, X:28:39.

[54] *Fading of the Flesh*, IV:28.

[55] *Ibid.*, IV:2.

[56] *Ibid.*, III:405,415, IV:2,12,28.

[57] *Christian Man's Calling*, I:4.

[58] *Pastor's Farewell and wish of welfare to his people; or, A valedictory sermon*, IV:62; and *Men Are Gods*, IV:367. According to Baxter, 'holiness is the way to happiness.' *Directions to Weak Christians for their Establishment, Growth, and Perseverance, Practical Works*, 674.

[59] Charnock, *Existence and Attributes of God*, I:350.

incline all her natural powers, and to frame uprightly all her actions, proceeding from those powers.'[60] Even earlier, Perkins writes:

> Wee must know, that there were in *Adam*, before his fall, three things not to be severed one from the other; the Substance of his body and soule; the Faculties and powers of his body and soule; and the Image of God, consisting in a straightnesse, and conformitie of all the affections and powers of man to Gods will. Now, when *Adam* fals, and sinnes against God, what is his sinne? Not the want of the two former, (for they both remained) but the very want and absence of the third thing, namely, of conformitie to Gods will.[61]

This view of the effect of Adam's fall is known as the Augustinian principle, which Calvin states as follows: 'the natural gifts in men were corrupted, but the supernatural taken away.'[62] The 'natural gifts' refer to the faculties of the soul whereas the 'supernatural gifts' refer to knowledge, righteousness, and holiness.[63] As John Leith notes, for Calvin, 'The image of God in which human beings were created involved two dimensions or relationships: the human and the divine. Natural human talents have been corrupted by sin, but the supernatural ones have been taken away.'[64]

There is some controversy surrounding the place of the Augustinian principle in Calvin's thought. A full analysis of the debate is beyond the scope of this chapter; however, a brief synopsis is important given the fact that Swinnock shares Calvin's view. Dewey Hoitenga maintains that Calvin's adherence to the Augustinian principle necessarily implies that when he 'comes to describe the components of the will and intellect in their fallen state, he will need to include the very components he attributes to them in their created state – even though neither power is any longer sound and whole, but weakened and

---

[60] Lewis Bayly, *The Practice of Piety: Directing a Christian How to Walk, that He May Please God* (1613; London: Hamilton, Adams, and Co., 1842; rpt., Morgan: Soli Deo Gloria, 2003) 32.

[61] Perkins, *The Whole Treatise of the Cases of Conscience, Distinguished into Three Bookes* (London, 1632) 6. Also see *Creede of the Apostles, Works*, I:165.

[62] Calvin, *Institutes*, II:II:4,12,14,18.

[63] Gerrit Berkouwer writes of the 'broader sense' and 'narrow sense' of the image of God, explaining, 'The broader sense of the image is used to stress the idea that man, despite his fall into sin and corruption, was not bestialized or demonized, but remained man. The narrow sense of the image is used to stress the idea that man lost his communion with God – his religious knowledge, his righteousness, his holiness, his conformity (*conformitas*) to God's will. This latter was a radical change in man's nature, which originally was wholly turned towards God, and now after the Fall is turned completely away.' *Studies in Dogmatics – Man: The Image of God* (Grand Rapids: Eerdmans, 1978) 38.

[64] Leith, *John Calvin's Doctrine of the Christian Life*, 44-45. See Calvin, *Institutes*, II:II:12.

corrupted".[65] In short, this means that the mind must retain its ability to discern between good and evil whereas the will must retain its ability to choose between good and evil because it possesses 'something of its created inclination to goodness besides its new inclination to evil.'[66] However, Hoitenga argues that Calvin fails to do precisely this, thereby revealing a glaring inconsistency in his thought: 'Calvin simply ignores a third alternative, required by the Augustinian principle, that something of the will's own created inclination to goodness might persist into the fallen state, without being wholly lost in the way that the supernatural gifts were lost.'[67]

Hoitenga's thesis is certainly overstated. Admittedly, as Torrance observes, 'the student of Calvin is faced with a difficult problem here, for in spite of taking this total view of man's corruption, Calvin can still admit that something remains in fallen man... Calvin says that there is still a portion of the image of God in fallen man.'[68] However, this problem does not imply an inconsistency. Calvin never denies the fallen will's ability to choose between good and evil;[69] rather, he denies that the fallen will's choice of good is good in God's sight (i.e., pleasing to him). Torrance explains, 'There is a sense... in which Calvin can speak of an external image of righteousness, or a lifeless image, or an outward semblance. There is no true righteousness or virtue here, and therefore nothing that really images the glory of God.'[70] Gerrish comments, 'The ambiguity in Calvin's statements about the effects of sin on the *imago dei* – was the image lost, or only damaged? – arise in part out of the two-sidedness of his conception of the image itself, which is both an endowment and its proper use.'[71] Calvin is adamant that only those choices and actions that mirror the image of God, thereby glorifying God, are good.[72] By virtue of the fall,

---

[65] Dewey Hoitenga, *John Calvin and the Will: A Critique and Corrective* (Grand Rapids: Baker Books, 1997) 73.

[66] *Ibid.*

[67] *Ibid.*, 84. As a remedy to Calvin's apparent discrepancy, Hoitenga makes two suggestions. First, we should affirm the free choice of the will. 'By free choice is meant the natural capacity for contrary choice between the morally good and evil alternatives with which the course of human life and action is now filled, together with the possibility of exercising this capacity for the development of moral virtues and vices'. Second, we should emphasize the inability of the will to convert itself back to God. 'The supernatural gifts required for this conversion have indeed been lost by the fall and depend for their restoration upon the special saving and regenerating grace of God'. *Ibid.*, 108-109. However, Hoitenga fails to demonstrate satisfactorily the inconsistency between his remedy and Calvin's position.

[68] Torrance, *Calvin's Doctrine of Man*, 88.

[69] Calvin, *Institutes*, I:V:6, II:I:11, II:II:13, II:III:3, III:XIV:2.

[70] Torrance, *Calvin's Doctrine of Man*, 94.

[71] Gerrish, *Grace and Gratitude*, 46 (f. 115).

[72] Perkins agrees, 'Thus the Heathen failed in doing good workes, in that the things which they did, for substance and matter were good and commandable, being done

humanity has lost this image. Therefore, when people exercise their natural powers (i.e., faculties) in choosing between good and evil, they fail to do so from a right principle. For this reason, these choices are not good in God's sight. In relation to Calvin's position, Anthony Lane remarks, 'It is true that outward virtue and respectability are to be found in the ungodly... As the inner motivation is wrong and there is no zeal for God's glory, such outward virtue has no merit before God.'[73] According to Berkouwer, 'Calvin denies all value to what appears praiseworthy in unholy man, but he means thereby that man in the very reception of these gifts contaminates them with his ambition, and that in all of life there can be found no passion to act to the glory of God... If this is not the aim, then true righteousness is lacking in all these "virtues," since our obligation is weighed not according to deeds, but according to intentions.'[74] Similarly, John Hesselink writes, 'The only obedience which deserves the name is that which honors God, the obedience of faith, and it is precisely this of which natural humanity is totally incapable.'[75]

Therefore, Calvin's adoption of the Augustinian principle is consistent with his assertion that the natural man is incapable of choosing what is good in God's sight. The issue is that the supernatural gifts are gone and, therefore, humanity is unable to make such a choice for the only motive that is acceptable to God, namely, his glory. Perkins echoes Calvin:

> A naturall man may doe good workes for the substance of the outward: but not in regard of the goodness of the manner: these are two diverse things. A man without supernaturall grace may give almes, doe justice, speake the truth, &c. which bee good things considered in themselves; as God hath commanded them; but he cannot doe them well... the good thing done by a naturall man is sinne in respect of the doer: because it failes both for his right beginning, faith unfained; as also for his end which is the glorie of God.[76]

Similarly, Swinnock never denies the individual's ability to choose between good and evil. However, like Calvin and Perkins, he affirms that the fallen will's choice of good is not good in God's sight because it fails to image his glory. When it comes to obedience, therefore, Swinnock distinguishes between

---

upon civill and honest respects, and referred to the common good: yet in truth their actions were no better than sins of omission, in as much as they issued from corrupted fountaines, hearts void of faith: and aimed not at the maine end, and scope of all humane actions, the honour and glory of God.' *Cases*, 14.

[73] Anthony Lane, 'Did Calvin Believe in Free Will?' *Vox Evangelica* 12 (1981) 72-90.

[74] Berkouwer, *Man: The Image of God*, 149-150.

[75] I. John Hesselink, *Calvin's Concept of the Law* (Allison Park: Pickwick Publications, 1992) 64-65.

[76] Perkins, *A Reformed Catholike; or, A declaration shewing how neere we may come to the present Church of Rome in sundry points of Religion: and wherein we must for ever depart from them*, *Works*, I:553.

'manner' and 'principle.'[77] Both the regenerate and unregenerate may 'be found traveling in the same path,' that is, they may share the same manner. However, 'according to the principle of man, such is his end.'[78] The regenerate's obedience proceeds from 'the fear of his God.'[79] This makes obedience acceptable, for 'nothing will be commendable in God's eye, which doth not flow from his awe.'[80]

The Nature of Sin

By virtue of the fall, humanity no longer possesses this 'principle.' Swinnock appeals to Ephesians 4:18[81] in order to show that humanity's alienation from 'the life of God' has resulted in the darkening of the mind, the hardening of the affections, and the enslaving of the will.[82] Here, Swinnock echoes Augustine's belief that 'what are called vices in the soul are nothing but privations of natural good.'[83] Believing that God is good, Augustine affirms that sin is the privation of God. In other words, when Adam was separated from God at the time of the fall, he was inclined to disobedience because this deprivation had a negative impact upon his faculties. His will was no longer directed by an understanding that knew God or affections that desired God. This means that sin has no formal existence. According to Perkins, sin 'is properly a want or absence of goodness.'[84] Swinnock is in complete agreement. For him, this is the essence of original sin. He elaborates:

> So hath original sin debauched the mind, and made it think crooked things straight, and straight things crooked; loathsome things lovely, and lovely things loathsome; perverted the will, and made it, as a diseased stomach, to call for and eat unwholesome meat against his own reason; enthralled his affections to sensuality and brutishness; chained the whole man, and delivered it up to the law of sin, and laid those strengths of reason and conscience in fetters, by which it might be hindered in its vicious inclinations and course of profaneness.[85]

Here, Swinnock says that original sin has 'debauched the mind,' 'perverted the will,' and 'enthralled his affections.' In essence, original sin has 'chained the

---

[77]   *Christian Man's Calling*, II:216.

[78]   *Ibid.*

[79]   *Ibid.*

[80]   *Ibid.*, II:217.

[81]   'Being darkened in their understanding, excluded from the life of God because of the ignorance that is in them, because of the hardness of their heart.'

[82]   Charnock makes the same appeal. *Existence and Attributes of God*, I:107,161, II:180. For Calvin on this text, see *Institutes*, II:III:1.

[83]   Augustine, *Enchiridion, Select Library: Vol. III*, III:XI.

[84]   Perkins, *Cases*, 7.

[85]   *Christian Man's Calling*, II:166.

whole man.' Baxter echoes this sentiment, stating, 'his mind is dark, his will perverse, and his affections carry him head-long.'[86] Charnock has the same view: 'Sin has made its sickly impressions in every faculty. The mind is dark (Eph. 4:18), he cannot know (1 Cor. 2:14); there is stoniness in the heart, he cannot bend (Zech. 7:12); there is enmity in the will, he cannot be subject (Rom. 8:7).'[87] Bolton comments, 'My mind is blind, vain, foolish, my will perverse and rebellious, all my affections out of order, there is nothing whole or sound within me.'[88] Bunyan affirms that the soul's faculties are in the 'service of Sin and Satan.'[89] In relation to John Owen, Griffiths provides an excellent summary: 'Thus whilst teaching sin as privation, Owen acknowledged its very real power and dominion when in harness with the categories of the soul... The enemy within, the active power that corrupts and depraves, that separates humanity from God, is not so much sin but the marred mind, will and affections after the fall.'[90]

This has been the predicament of Adam's posterity ever since the fall. Because of the corruption of his own nature, Adam could not transmit the perfect nature of his soul to his descendants. Instead, he transmitted the corrupt nature acquired by the fall. Swinnock explains, 'Adam begat a son after his own (not God's) image (Gen. 5:3).'[91] At this point, Swinnock clearly separates himself from Pelagianism, stating, 'The Pelagian error is, that no sin came in by propagation, but all by imitation.'[92] In marked contrast, Swinnock affirms that a sinful nature originates in all individuals at the commencement of their existence, writing, 'My infants are not innocents... They are estranged from the womb, and as full of wickedness as the ocean is of waters... I bring forth my children defiled with sin, like to Satan, and loathsome to God... have not I transmitted to my posterity the seeds both of sin and hell?'[93] He refers to children as 'all dead in sin' and 'polluted in the womb.'[94] In brief, for Swinnock, 'sin cometh in first by propagation.'[95] Similarly, Gurnall affirms that original sin 'is derived and propagated to us by natural generation. Thus Adam is said to beget a son in his own likeness, sinful as he was, as well as mortal and

---

[86] Baxter, *Call to the Unconverted, Practical Works*, 476.

[87] Charnock, *Efficient of Regeneration, Works*, III:171. Also see III:206.

[88] Robert Bolton, *The Carnal Professor, Discovering the Woeful Slavery of a Man Guided by the Flesh* (1634; London: Hamilton, Adams, and Co., 1838; rpt., Ligoneir: Soli Deo Gloria, 1992) 19.

[89] Bunyan, *Greatness of the Soul, Miscellaneous Works*, IX:148.

[90] Griffiths, *Redeem the Time*, 53.

[91] *Door of Salvation*, V:38.

[92] *Christian Man's Calling*, II:243. For a selection of documents on the Pelagian controversy, see *Documents of the Christian Church*, ed. H. Bettenson, 52-61.

[93] *Christian Man's Calling*, I:429-430.

[94] *Ibid.*, I:434.

[95] *Heaven and Hell*, III:222.

miserable.'[96] According to the *WCF*, 'Our first parents' are the 'root of all mankind,' therefore 'the same death in sin and corrupted nature conveyed to all their posterity descending from them by ordinary generation.'[97]

In his doctrine of original sin, Swinnock is firmly rooted in a tradition stretching back through the Reformers to Augustine.[98] Calvin makes it clear that Adam's fall had an impact not only upon Adam himself but also upon his descendants. In this regard, he comments, 'Adam, by sinning, not only took upon himself misfortune and ruin but also plunged our nature into like destruction. This was not due to the guilt of himself alone, which would not pertain to us at all, but was because he infected all his posterity with that corruption into which he had fallen.'[99] For his part, Augustine remarks, 'Thence, after his sin, he was driven into exile, and by his sin the whole race of which he was the root was corrupted in him, and thereby subjected to the penalty of death.'[100]

Sin in the Mind

For Swinnock, the mind is the 'supreme faculty of the soul.'[101] He writes, 'Though the motions of the understanding and will are in some respect circular, yet the understanding is the first mover and the leading faculty.'[102] He shares this view with his contemporaries. For example, Flavel remarks, 'This faculty is by *philosophers* rightly called το ηγεμονιχον [sic], *the leading faculty*; because the will follows its practical dictates. It sits at the helm, and guides the course of the soul; not impelling, or rigorously enforcing its dictates upon the will; for the will cannot be so imposed upon; but by giving it a directive light, or pointing, as it were, with its finger, what it ought to chuse, and what to refuse.'[103] Sinclair Ferguson observes that 'for Owen the mind (*nous*) is the leading and ruling faculty in man, the channel to the will and affections.'[104]

In making this assertion, the Puritans are not suggesting that the will

---

[96] Gurnall, *Christian in Complete Armour*, I:123.

[97] *WCF*, VI:III.

[98] From the primary sources, Sommerville concludes that the main difference between Puritan and Anglican literature, after the Restoration, was their understanding of human nature. The Puritans had a more radical understanding of human depravity and, therefore, a greater dependence on God's work in salvation. *Popular Religion in Restoration England* (University Press of Florida, 1977) 89-97.

[99] Calvin, *Institutes*, II:I:6.

[100] Augustine, *Enchiridion, Select Library: Vol. III*, III:XXVI.

[101] *Door of Salvation*, V:420.

[102] *Treatise of the incomparableness of God in his being, attributes, works and word: opened and applied*, IV:376.

[103] Flavel, *Pneumatologia, Works*, II:503. His italics.

[104] Sinclair Ferguson, *John Owen on the Christian Life* (Edinburgh: Banner of Truth, 1987) 38. See Owen, *Holy Spirit, Works*, III:250-252.

necessarily follows the dictates of the mind. Swinnock does not believe that the mind is the efficient cause of the will's choice. Rather, in referring to the mind as the 'supreme faculty of the soul,' he means: first, that – as created in the image of God – the will ought to follow the mind; second, that the knowledge of God always begins in the mind; and third, that the will cannot choose that which is unknown to the mind. As Baxter explains, 'The will is the first principle in men's actions *quoad exercitium*, though the intellect be the first as to specification.'[105]

This perspective echoes Calvin, who states, 'Let the office... of understanding be to distinguish between objects, as each seems worthy of approval or disapproval; while that of the will, to choose and follow what the understanding pronounces good, but to reject and flee what it disapproves.'[106] Here, Calvin describes the proper functioning of the soul as the mind directing the will. There is no suggestion, however, that the will necessarily follows the mind. On the contrary, he writes, 'It will not be enough for the mind to be illuminated by the Spirit of God unless the heart is also strengthened and supported by his power. In this matter the Schoolmen go completely astray, who in considering faith identify it with a bare and simple assent arising out of knowledge, and leave out confidence and assurance of heart.'[107] Simply put, the mind is the leading faculty, but this does not mean that the will follows by necessity.[108]

There are two main schools of thought surrounding Calvin's perspective: intellectualism and voluntarism. According to Richard Muller, these terms refer to 'the two faculties of soul, intellect and will, and to the question of the priority of the one over the other, intellectualism indicates a priority of intellect,

---

[105] Richard Baxter, *Christian Directory* (1673) in *The Practical Works of Richard Baxter, Vol. 1* (London: George Virtue, 1846; rpt., Morgan: Soli Deo Gloria, 2000) 85.

[106] Calvin, *Institutes*, I:XV:7.

[107] *Ibid.*, III:II:33.

[108] Fiering identifies three competing perspectives on the relationship between the mind and the will. (1) According to Scholastic intellectualism (or Aristotelian and Thomist intellectualism), the will always follows the mind. This idea is based upon the notion that no one can will evil as evil. In other words, the soul is always inclined toward what it perceives to be good. (2) According to Scholastic voluntarism, the will is divided, in that there is a conflict between the relative and absolute judgment. (3) According to Augustinian voluntarism, the will does not necessarily follow the mind. Therefore, sinful nature is primarily a matter of perverse will, not intellectual error. *Moral Philosophy at Seventeenth-Century Harvard*, 111-118. The Puritans follow Augustine. For an analysis of Ames' thought on this subject, see Lynne Boughton, 'Choice and Action: William Ames's Concept of the Mind's Operation in Moral Decisions,' *Church History* 56 (1987) 188-203.

voluntarism a priority of the will.'[109] Intellectualism identifies the mind as the causal faculty in the soul's approval of good whereas voluntarism identifies the will (inclination and choice). Does the will necessarily follow the intellect's proposal of the good, or does the will possess the ability to deny the known good?

Robert Kendall argues that Calvin is an intellectualist: 'The position which Calvin wants pre-eminently to establish (and fundamentally assumes) is that faith is knowledge.'[110] Kendall suggests that Calvin actually emphasizes the mind to the exclusion of the will. Dewey Hoitenga, on the other hand, believes that Calvin writes as 'an intellectualist on human nature as it was created, but a voluntarist on both its fallen and redeemed states.'[111] Given the fact, however, that Calvin attributes Adam's fall to the free choice of the will apart from the mind,[112] Hoitenga sees an inconsistency in Calvin's claim that the will necessarily follows the mind in the state of innocence.[113] For this reason, he actually portrays Calvin as an inconsistent voluntarist.[114] Muller fails to see any inconsistency in Calvin's thought, writing, 'Calvin appears to echo the voluntarist tradition insofar as he places choice in the will and does not make the intellect either efficiently or finally the cause of the will's choice... Under the terms of Calvin's ideal or philosophical definition, reason ought to announce the good and the will follow the dictates of reason, albeit freely and

---

[109] Richard Muller, '*Fides* and *Cognitio* in Relation to the Problem of Intellect and Will in the Theology of John Calvin,' *Calvin Theological Journal* 25 (Nov 1990) 211. For a detailed explanation of these terms, see Hoitenga, *John Calvin and the Will*, 28-43. For overviews of the historical development of the views surrounding the relationship between the mind and the will, see Hannah Arendt, *Two/Willing* in *The Life of the Mind* (New York: Harcourt, 1971); Vernon Bourke, *Will in Western Thought: An Historico-Critical Survey* (New York: Sheed and Ward, 1964); and Fiering, *Moral Philosophy at Seventeenth-Century Harvard*.

[110] Kendall, *Calvin and English Calvinism*, 19.

[111] Hoitenga, *John Calvin and the Will*, 45.

[112] Calvin, *Institutes*, I:XV:8.

[113] Hoitenga, *John Calvin and the Will*, 23. He attributes Calvin's apparent inconsistency to his struggle with the difference between the philosophical (or Greek) view and biblical view of human nature, stating, 'For the Greeks, right reason (or the intellect) is the defining power of the human soul... The Bible, by contrast, locates the defining origin of human thought and action in the heart.'

[114] Upon closer examination, Hoitenga's charge appears unfounded. As a remedy to Calvin's apparent inconsistency, he suggests, 'The office of reason is to distinguish between ends or objects, whether they are good or evil... Reason has no power to move us to act, for that is the function of the will; but the will depends upon the reason as the leader and governor of the soul to propose a course of action to it'. *Ibid.*, 65. Yet, there is nothing in this remedy that contradicts Calvin who states, 'In this integrity man by free will had the power, if he so willed, to attain eternal life.' *Institutes*, I:XV:8. In other words, the will always possessed the choice whether or not to follow the mind. See *Institutes*, II:III:5-10, III:II:6-8.

of its own choice.'[115] This does not mean that the will is the primary faculty, but that it is free to choose.[116] Muller makes an insightful observation when he distinguishes between *temporal* priority and *causal* priority in Calvin's thought.[117] According to the former, the mind must come first, in that the will requires an object to which it can respond. According to the latter, the will is free to respond positively or negatively to the object presented by the mind. In this paradigm, the will is dependent upon the intellect for its object, because the will is unable to choose the unknown. However, dependence is not the same as determination.

The Puritans adopt this view of the temporal priority of the mind. Perkins remarks, 'The minde must approove and give assent, before the will can choose or will: and when the minde hath not power to conceive or give assent, there the will hath no power to will.'[118] Like Calvin and Perkins, Swinnock ascribes to the temporal priority of the understanding. Prior to the fall, it was governed by the knowledge of God, and it was the vehicle by which God communicated to the soul. The affections were inclined to this knowledge. The soul willed action according to its understanding and affections. However, this priority was lost when Adam disobeyed. According to Swinnock, the understanding was 'darkened.'[119] Commenting on 1 Corinthians 2:14,[120] he writes, 'Natural light will not help a man to see spiritual objects, because there is no proportion between the faculty and the object; and because it cannot apprehend them, therefore it condemneth them as foolish and ridiculous.'[121] Charnock concurs, 'The first effect of sin was to spread a thick darkness upon Adam's understanding.'[122] For his part, Baxter remarks, 'Ignorance is the soul's blindness, and the privation of the image of God on the understanding.'[123] Bolton remarks, 'The mind was endued with a perfect actual knowledge of God, so far as the human nature may be supposed capable... Now as the clear sunshine overwhelmed with a cloud, so is the mind of man overcast with palpable darkness.'[124] Griffiths sees this same emphasis in John Owen, writing,

---

[115] Muller, '*Fides* and *Cognitio*,' 215-216.

[116] For Calvin's concept of the will, see John Leith, 'The Doctrine of the Will in the *Institutes of the Christian Religion*' in *Reformatio Perennis: Essays on Calvin and the Reformation in Honor of Ford Lewis Battles*, eds. B. A. Gerrish and R. Bendetto (Pittsburgh: Pickwick Press, 1981) 49-66.

[117] Muller, '*Fides* and *Cognitio*,' 221.

[118] Perkins, *Reformed Catholike, Works*, I:553.

[119] Eph. 4:18.

[120] 'But a natural man does not accept the things of the Spirit of God, for they are foolishness to him; and he cannot understand them, because they are spiritually appraised.'

[121] *Sinner's Last Sentence*, V:420.

[122] Charnock, *Efficient of Regeneration, Works*, III:184.

[123] Baxter, *Divine Life, Practical Works*, 149.

[124] Bolton, *Carnal Professor*, 21-22.

'The effect of the fall on humanity, then, was to invert the psychological priority within each individual; that which had formerly been an intellectual being, with the reason informing the will, became a voluntarist being with the corrupted will and affections now driving the mind.'[125]

Sin in the Affections

For Swinnock, the individual makes choices according to inclination, which is determined by the soul's affections (or passions). These affections are subject to two appetites. The first is the sensitive – that which the senses determine to be good. The second is the rational – that which the understanding determines to be good. On the basis of these two appetites, the soul chooses. The foundation for this paradigm dates back to Aristotle who writes, 'The origin of action – its efficient, not its final cause – is choice, and that of choice is desire and reasoning with a view to an end.'[126]

In innocence, the rational appetite possessed the ability to control the sensitive appetite. Reynolds believes that Adam had the power 'to excite, continue, remit, lay downe his Passions, as Reason should dictate to him.'[127] When Adam fell, the understanding lost that power. The affections were 'disjoynted from Reason;' i.e., they 'cast off the reines whereby they should be guided' and, therefore, 'there cannot be that sweet harmonie in the motion thereof, which is required to the weale of Man's Nature.'[128] Now, according to Reynolds, 'Passions are become... Beastly and Sensuall.'[129] This means the sensitive appetite governs the affections. And, in its darkened condition, the mind is powerless to do anything about it.[130]

In this state, the affections become lusts. Thomas Manton explains this transformation by way of three premises: first, 'the soul of man is chiefly and mainly made up of desires;' second, 'the bent of the soul, the most vigorous, commanding, swaying faculty of the soul, is desire;' and third, 'since the fall, man rather consulteth with his desires than with anything else, and there all action and pursuit beginneth.'[131] He adds, 'this faculty is eminently corrupted, and corrupteth and swayeth all the rest; and therefore gross lusts, the lower and baser desires, are called, "the law of the members" (Rom. 7:23); desires or lusts

---

[125] Griffiths, *Redeem the Time*, 65.

[126] Aristotle, *Nicomachean Ethics* in *The Works of Aristotle: Vol. IX*, ed. W. D. Ross (Oxford University Press, 1963) VI:2.

[127] Reynolds, *Passions and Faculties*, 61.

[128] *Ibid.*, 45.

[129] *Ibid.*, 62.

[130] According to Calvin, Adam's fall resulted in the loss of the temporal priority of the mind, and its knowledge of the greatest good. At that time, the will succumbed to the influence of the corrupted affections. *Institutes*, II:II:18,24.

[131] Thomas Manton, *An Exposition on the Epistle of James* (1693; London: Banner of Truth, 1968) 93.

giving law to the whole soul.'[132]

That is how Swinnock sees it. Having been alienated from God, the affections are no longer moved by the knowledge of God. Rather, individuals fulfil 'the desires of the flesh and of the mind.'[133] Consequently, they hate what they should love and love what they should hate. Because of this corruption of the faculties, humanity prefers 'every sensual, sinful pleasure, every foolish, perishing creature, before the beautiful image of God, the unsearchable riches in Christ, the endless happiness in heaven.'[134] In a similar vein, Bolton writes, 'They are moved unto contrary objects, for those which should be stirred up by the evilness of an object to abhor it, do in that respect embrace it and move towards it, and those which should be moved by the goodness of an object to embrace it, do in that respect abhor and shun it.'[135] This hardening of the affections means humanity has lost the ability to enjoy God. 'Thy heart,' remarks Swinnock, 'is full of enmity against God, and thy life nothing else but a walking contrary to him, and therefore thou canst have no delight or joy in him, which is the very heaven of heavens.'[136]

Sin in the Will

In his state of innocence, Adam possessed the freedom to choose what he wanted in response to his rational and sensitive appetites. In the state of apostasy, humanity still possesses this freedom. The problem, however, is that the understanding is darkened and the affections are hardened, because humanity is excluded from the life of God. Consequently, as directed by a corrupt head and heart, humanity will never choose the chief good. According to the Westminster divines, 'Man, by his fall into a state of sin, hath wholly lost all ability of will to any spiritual good accompanying salvation; so as a natural man, being altogether averse from that good, and dead in sin, is not able, by his own strength, to convert himself, or to prepare himself thereunto.'[137] The will is controlled by an understanding that prefers darkness to light and by affections that prefer evil to good. As a result, the will itself is no longer free.

As H. J. McSorley observes, the terms *freedom* and *free* have a variety of meanings. It is, therefore, crucial to define them in order to understand the meaning of the expression *freewill*. For his part, McSorley identifies three types

---

[132] *Ibid.*
[133] Eph. 2:3.
[134] *Heaven and Hell*, III:211-212.
[135] Bolton, *Carnal Professor*, 31.
[136] *Fading of the Flesh*, IV:459.
[137] *WCF*, IX:III.

of freedom.[138] First, there is natural freedom: the ability to choose what one wishes. Second, there is circumstantial freedom: the ability to achieve what one wishes. Third, there is acquired freedom: the freedom to do morally good. He demonstrates that it is possible to possess natural freedom without acquired freedom, remarking, 'Adam and his descendents did lose their freedom from sin and death as well as their freedom to do the good that is pleasing to God, as a result of the original disobedience. In our terminology, this is the loss of acquired freedom but not of natural freedom.'[139] Again:

> Man's slavery to sin... is a lack of acquired freedom. It is not a loss or lack of the first type of freedom... natural freedom. The biblical doctrine of bondage to sin has nothing to do with a doctrine of an 'unfree' will if we take 'unfree will' to mean that man no longer is able to choose or make a free decision, or that whatever he does is done by absolute necessity, and that he never has the possibility of doing other than what he actually does. If, however, we understand by 'unfree will' man's total helplessness to break free by his own efforts from the slavery to sin in which he finds himself, then man indeed, in this sense, has an 'unfree will.'[140]

McSorley affirms that this is Augustine's position, commenting, 'Although Augustine at times uses ambiguous terminology, there is never any ambiguity about the fact that he always held to the natural freedom of the will even in fallen man... As a consequence of Adam's sin, however, the human race has lost its true liberty, the liberty of acting or living rightly or justly, as one ought. Man thus has lost his acquired freedom, but never his natural freedom.'[141] For Augustine, the will is always free in the sense of natural freedom. After the fall, however, it is a captive freewill.[142] He remarks, 'When man by his own freewill sinned, then sin being victorious over him, the freedom of his will was lost.'[143]

McSorley traces the evolution of these concepts from Augustine to late Scholasticism in order to demonstrate that the Roman Church had developed an exaggerated concept of the role of the will in salvation. Luther challenges this neglect of God's grace by returning to the question of the fallen will. In so doing, he fails to preserve the distinction between natural freedom and acquired freedom. For McSorley, there are two reasons for this. First, 'Luther is greatly concerned about what we call "free" and that to which we give the name "freedom." He is not so interested in denying man's power to choose – *liberum*

---

[138] H. J. McSorley, Luther: Right or Wrong? An Ecumenical-Theological Study of Luther's Major Work, The Bondage of the Will (New York: Newman Press, 1969) 25-27.

[139] *Ibid.*, 39.

[140] *Ibid.*, 49.

[141] *Ibid.*, 64.

[142] *Ibid.*

[143] Augustine, *Enchiridion, Select Library: Vol. III*, III:XXX.

arbitrium – as he is in denying that this should be called freedom.'[144] In brief, Luther thinks the expression *freewill* confuses people by giving them the impression that salvation is their work. He states, 'For when it has been conceded and agreed that free choice, having lost its liberty, is perforce in bondage to sin and cannot will anything good, I can make no other sense of these words than that free choice is an empty phrase, of which the reality has been lost.'[145] Second, 'Luther is unable to say with the schoolmen that God moves some things necessarily and some contingently, and that even those things which happen contingently are known infallibly by God and from the point of view of God's will they are said to happen by necessity of infallibility or immutability.'[146] Despite this confusion in Luther's thought, McSorley still maintains that Luther believes in natural freedom because 'the necessity spoken of in Luther's necessitarian argument is a necessity which arises as a result of God's willing and knowing. This is the same as saying that it is a necessity which occurs on the supposition or condition that God has willed and known an event.'[147]

As for Calvin, he upholds the distinction between relative and absolute necessity, stating, 'But what God has determined must necessarily so take place, even though it is neither unconditionally, nor of its own peculiar nature, necessary.'[148] According to Anthony Lane:

> This appears to run counter to the Augustinian tradition, which maintains man's freewill (*liberum arbitrium*) even as a sinner. But Calvin took great pains to counter the idea that he was opposed to Augustine at this point. Central to his case is the distinction between necessity and coercion (*coactio*). Man sins necessarily, but this necessity is inherent and arises from his own nature. There is no external coercion or violence exercised on man from outside himself.[149]

As Lane notes, Calvin was prepared to use the expression *liberum arbitrium* as long as it did not imply free choice of that which is good in God's sight.[150] Calvin remarks, 'For we do not deny that man was created with free choice, endowed as he was with sound intelligence of mind and uprightness of will. We do declare that our choice is now held captive under bondage to sin, but how did this come about except by Adam's misuse of free choice when he had it?'[151]

---

[144] McSorley, *Luther: Right or Wrong?* 265.
[145] Luther, *The Bondage of the Will* in *Luther's Works*, ed. H. T. Lehmann (Philadelphia: Fortress Press, 1972) XXXIII:116.
[146] McSorley, *Luther: Right or Wrong?* 230.
[147] *Ibid.*, 315.
[148] Calvin, *Institutes*, I:XVI:9.
[149] Lane, 'Did Calvin Believe in Free Will?' 78.
[150] *Ibid.*, 79. See Calvin, *Institutes*, II:II:7, II:III:5.
[151] Calvin, *The Bondage and Liberation of the Will*, ed. A. N. S. Lane (Grand Rapids: Baker Books, 1996) 47.

According to Calvin, people are free to do whatever they want. The problem is that, because of the fall, they only want evil. In short, the will is in bondage to sin. He adds, 'A bound will, finally, is one which because of its corruptness is held captive under the authority of evil desires, so that it can choose nothing but evil, even if it does so of its own accord and gladly, without being driven by external impulse.'[152]

According to Berkouwer, when the Reformers denied the freedom of the will in this manner, 'most Catholic and humanist thinkers saw this as nothing less than an attack on, and indeed an annihilation of, human nature, of man's essence, which was presumed to be inconceivable without freedom as part of it.'[153] He adds, 'The Reformers' teaching on the will of man was interpreted as *coactio*, as *necessitas*, and over against this the so-called physical freedom of the will was stressed, a freedom not destroyed through the power of sin because it belonged to the essential structure of man's nature.'[154] However, it was never the Reformers' intention 'to posit compulsion as over against freedom.'[155] Their denial of the freedom of the will did not imply that God acted in a mechanical fashion. They clearly maintained that individuals are free to will; however, they do so with an enslaved will – *servum arbitrium*.

The Puritans adopt this paradigm. According to Perkins, 'man must be considered in a four-fold estate:' 'as he was created,' 'corrupted,' 'renewed,' and 'glorified.'[156] In the first, the will possessed 'libertie of nature, in which he could will either good or evill.'[157] Elsewhere, Perkins adds, 'This libertie is remaining since the fall of Adam, and is naturall to the will, from which it cannot possibly be severed.'[158] However, it 'is joined with a necessitie of sinning; because it stands in bondage under sinne: in this respect, it is fitly tearmed of Augustine, the *bond free-will*.'[159] At this point, Perkins distinguishes between the 'libertie of nature' and the 'libertie of grace.' The latter is founded in the 'goodness of integritie of the will.'[160] It was lost at the fall, however 'the libertie of nature' remained. Thus, he concludes, 'necessitie and freedome of will, may both stand together.'[161]

Lewis Bayly agrees with Perkins, affirming that 'man in his state of corruption hath free-will to evil, but not to good.'[162] For his part, Baxter argues

---

[152] *Ibid.*, 69.

[153] Berkouwer, *Man: The Image of God*, 314.

[154] *Ibid.*

[155] *Ibid.*, 315.

[156] Perkins, *Reformed Catholike, Works*, I:551.

[157] *Ibid.*

[158] Perkins, *A Treatise of Gods free Grace, and Mans Free-Will, Works*, I:709.

[159] *Ibid.*, I:703.

[160] *Ibid.*, I:710.

[161] *Ibid.*, I:704. For Charnock's thoughts on the 'necessity of infallibility,' see *Existence and Attributes of God*, I:446-451.

[162] Bayly, *Practice of Piety*, 81.

that the will is naturally free: 'It is free from violence, and it is a self-determining principle.'[163] However, he denies that it is morally free: 'It is not free from evil dispositions. It is habitually averse to God and holiness... It is enslaved by a sinful bias.'[164] Again, 'Your will is naturally free, that is, a self-determining faculty, but it is viciously inclined, and backward to do good; and therefore we see by sad experience that it hath not a virtuous moral freedom.'[165] Charnock concurs:

> Though since the fall we have such a free will left, which pertains to the essential nature of man, yet we have lost that liberty which belongs to the perfection of human nature, which was to exercise acts spiritually good and acceptable to God... In Adam, by creation we were possessed of it. In Adam, by his corruption we were stripped of it; we have not lost the physical but the moral nature of these faculties; not the faculties themselves, but the moral goodness of them.[166]

This is the tradition, in which Swinnock stands. He clearly distinguishes between the individual's natural and moral ability,[167] between what the individual 'can do' and 'will not do.'[168] The bondage of the will consists in individuals being so captivated by sin that they have no power to escape from it. Because of original sin, the will (though free in the actions it performs) is captive in its way of performing them. Griffiths provides an excellent summary, quoting Owen as follows: 'The will, in the depraved condition of fallen nature, is not only habitually filled and possessed with an aversion from that which is good spiritually... but also continually acts in opposition unto it, as being under the power of the "carnal mind," which is "enmity against God."'[169]

The Evil of Sin

In this state, humanity has lost the supernatural gifts whereby enjoyment of God is possible. Now, rather than embracing God as the chief good, humanity elevates *self* as its chief end. In the Puritan mindset, this is what makes sin so

---

[163] Baxter, *Call to the Unconverted, Practical Works*, 438.

[164] *Ibid.*

[165] *Ibid.*, 475. Baxter actually rebukes those who 'separate the natural power of a sinner from his moral impotency, and his natural freedom of will from his moral servitude, as if they were inconsistent, when they are conjunct.' *Christian Directory*, 272.

[166] Charnock, *Efficient of Regeneration, Works*, III:171-172. Also see III:175,184-187,211,238.

[167] *Sinner's Last Sentence*, V:285.

[168] *Door of Salvation*, V:244. Also see *Christian Man's Calling*, II:166; *Heaven and Hell*, III:366; and *Sinner's Last Sentence*, V:309-310.

[169] Owen as quoted by Griffiths, *Redeem the Time*, 85. For a summary of Jonathan Edwards' position, see Stephen Holmes, *God of Grace and God of Glory: An Account of the Theology of Jonathan Edwards* (Grand Rapids: Eerdmans, 2001) 150-155.

serious. Sin is the substitution of God with *self* as the chief good and, therefore, the way to happiness. Bayly comments, 'With the loss of this divine image, she lost the love of God, and the blessed communion which she has with him, wherein consists her life and happiness.'[170] According to Charnock, 'Man would be his own end and happiness in opposition to God.'[171] Such a desire is opposed to God's sufficiency for it denies that God is humanity's only source of satisfaction. In the words of Jeremiah Burroughs:

> As far as sin appears, it holds this forth before all and speaks this language: that there is not enough good in God, that is, the Blessed, Glorious, All-Sufficient, Eternal, Unchangeable Good and Fountain of all Good. Yet sin makes this profession, that there is not enough good in God to satisfy this soul, or else why does the soul depart from him in any sinful way and go to the creature for any good if there is enough in God himself?[172]

Shepard echoes this sentiment, stating, 'And hence the soul, because it never found that infinite sweetness in God himself, lusts after and delights in the creature for itself, loves pleasure for pleasure, delights in the creature for the creature, not for God... And here the soul of man cleaves night and day, committing spiritual whoredom before the face of God.'[173] From this, it naturally follows that sin is opposed to God's existence. Charnock comments, 'Sin implies that God is unworthy of a being. Every sin is a kind of cursing God in the heart; an aim at the destruction of the being of God; not actually, but virtually; not in the intention of every sinner, but in the nature of every sin.'[174] For Ralph Venning, sin 'makes the sinner wish and endeavour that there might be no God, for sinners are haters of God.'[175] For Thomas Watson, the individual 'does what in him lies to extirpate a Deity. He wishes there was no God... A wicked man would not only unthrone God, but "unbe" God. If he could help it, God would no longer be God.'[176] According to Burroughs, 'The language of sin is, "God shall not reign!" It is the setting of the will of a base, wretched creature against the will of the infinite, eternal, glorious God.'[177] Swinnock agrees wholeheartedly with his contemporaries, writing, 'Sin is incomparably malignant, because the God principally injured by it is incomparably

---

[170] Bayly, *Practice of Piety*, 32.
[171] Charnock, *Existence and Attributes of God*, I:135.
[172] Jeremiah Burroughs, *The Evil of Evils; or, The Exceeding Sinfulness of Sin* (London, 1654) 58.
[173] Thomas Shepard, *The Parable of Ten Virgins* in *The Works of Thomas Shepard* (1695; Ligoneir: Soli Deo Gloria, 1990) II:28.
[174] Charnock, *Existence and Attributes of God*, I:93.
[175] Ralph Venning, *The Sinfulness of Sin; or, The Plague of Plagues* (1669; Edinburgh: Banner of Truth, 1965; rpt., 1993) 35.
[176] Thomas Watson, *The Mischief of Sin* (1671; Pittsburgh: Soli Deo Gloria, 1994) 17.
[177] Burroughs, *Evil of Evils*, 42.

excellent.'[178] It is 'a breach of this incomparable God's law,'[179] 'a contempt of this incomparable God's authority,'[180] 'a dishonouring this incomparable God, whose name alone is excellent,'[181] and 'a destroying this incomparable God.'[182]

The Renewal of the Image

'Thy misery by thy fall,' writes Swinnock, 'is chiefly in this, that thou hast thereby lost the image of God. Thy want of conformity to him, is the cause why thou hast not communion with him.'[183] For Swinnock, the solution to this predicament is renewal, which he believes is the restoration of the image of God whereby the faculties are sanctified.[184] As Miller observes, this is the standard position among the Puritans: 'If original sin is a dislocation of the faculties, then regeneration must set them right again.'[185] Swinnock defines regeneration as 'a work of God's Spirit, whereby he doth, out of his mere good pleasure, for his own glory and the salvation of his elect, at first renew the whole man after his own image by the ministry of the word.'[186] He explains this definition according to five causes.[187]

The Efficient Cause

To begin with, Swinnock affirms that 'regeneration is a work of God's Spirit;'

---

[178] *Incomparableness of God*, IV:456.

[179] *Ibid.*, IV:457.

[180] *Ibid.*

[181] *Ibid.*, IV:458.

[182] *Ibid.*

[183] *Heaven and Hell*, III:359.

[184] For this theme in Owen's writings, see Griffiths, *Redeem the Time*, 206-218.

[185] Miller, *New England Mind*, 280.

[186] *Door of Salvation*, V:20.

[187] *Sinner's Last Sentence*, V:405. Swinnock appears to employ the framework of Aristotle's theory of causation. Aristotle groups all objects according to ten categories: substance, quantity, quality, relation, place, time, position, state, action, and affection. The last nine categories are merely properties of substance. When these properties (or form) are added to substance, it becomes something. This relationship between substance and form is foundational to Aristotle's theory of causation, in that he believes that an object may be explained according to four causes: the material cause is the object's substance; the formal cause is the subject's form; the efficient cause is the initiator of motion; and the final cause is the object's end. For a detailed description, see *Categories, Works: Vol. I*. Charnock identifies four causes of regeneration: efficient, moving (or impulsive), instrumental, and final. *Efficient of Regeneration, Works*, III:168-169,183,249-250; and *A Discourse of the Word, the Instrument of Regeneration, Works*, III:309. Baxter stresses the efficient (or principle), instrumental, and final causes. *Divine Life, Practical Works*, 130,207,228; and *Treatise on Conversion, Practical Works*, 292-293.

in other words, the Holy Spirit is 'the efficient principle cause of regeneration.'[188] Swinnock explains, 'Man cannot generate himself naturally, much less regenerate himself spiritually; they which are born of the flesh contribute nothing to their own beings, neither do they which are born of the Spirit bring anything to their new beings, unless it be a passive receptiveness, as they are reasonable creatures.'[189] Therefore, 'the birth of the new man is wholly from God; and the power wherewith he effects it is both miraculous and almighty.'[190] Swinnock maintains that regeneration is totally dependent upon God's power, because the individual is spiritually dead – excluded from the life of God. For this reason, there is an inability to respond to God. Plus, there is complete hostility toward God. He writes, 'The carnal mind, Lady Reason herself, the chief and principal faculty of man, is enmity against God: "It is not subject to the law of God, neither indeed can be" (Rom. 8:7). He who is an enemy to a man's person, will never be a friend to his precepts, much less will he who is enmity against God's life, be subject to his law.'[191]

This state, therefore, necessitates an initial work of God. In reference to John 1:13,[192] Charnock writes, 'Not of the will of the flesh, that is only corruption; nor of the will of man, that at best is but moral nature. But whatsoever the meaning of those particular expressions is, the evangelist removes all pretences nature may make to the efficiency of this regeneration, and ascribes it wholly to God.'[193] Quite simply, sinners – who are at enmity with God – are incapable of turning to God. For this reason, conversion must be God's work. For Shepard, people 'are bound hand and foot in this estate, and can not come out... for all kind of sins, like chains, have bound every part and faculty of man.'[194] With this in mind, Joseph Alleine exhorts his readers: 'Never think you can convert yourself. If ever you would be savingly converted, you must despair of doing it in your own strength. It is a resurrection from the dead, a new creation, a work of absolute omnipotence.'[195] He proceeds to identify the 'efficient cause' of conversion as God's grace and Christ's intercession,[196] emphasizing – in typical Puritan fashion – humanity's impotency and God's sovereignty.

---

[188] *Door of Salvation*, V:20. For more on God as the 'principal efficient,' see *Christian Man's Calling*, I:312,328,368, II:123. For Shepard's treatment of the efficient cause of salvation, see *The Sound Believer: A Treatise of Evangelical Conversion* in *The Sincere Convert and The Sound Believer*, 193-199.

[189] *Door of Salvation*, V:20.

[190] *Ibid.*, V:73.

[191] *Sinner's Last Sentence*, V:417.

[192] 'Who were born, not of blood nor of the will of the flesh nor of the will of man, but of God.'

[193] Charnock, *Efficient of Regeneration, Works*, III:169.

[194] Shepard, *Sincere Convert*, 35.

[195] Joseph Alleine, *A Sure Guide to Heaven; or, An Alarm to the Unconverted* (1671; Edinburgh: Banner of Truth, 1989) 26.

[196] *Ibid.*, 27.

Along with his contemporaries, Swinnock does not deny people's responsibility to choose, nor does he deny their freedom to do so. Rather, he affirms that people are free to choose whatever their understanding thinks best and their affections want most. The problem, as identified by Swinnock, is that the individual's understanding is 'enmity against God.' This means people hate God. In this state, they will never choose God. Instead, they will always choose in accordance with the condition of their understanding and affections. It is for this reason that regeneration must be a work of God's Spirit.

The Moving Cause

Next, Swinnock claims that the 'impulsive or moving cause' of regeneration is God's 'good pleasure.'[197] By this, he means regeneration is according to God's grace: 'Grace chooseth thee (Rom. 11:5)... Grace calleth (2 Tim. 1:9)... Grace distinguisheth and differenceth thee from others (1 Cor. 15:10)... Grace justifieth (Rom. 3:24)... Grace glorifieth (Eph. 2:8).'[198] Given humanity's sinful condition, people are unwilling to choose God. Thus, if anyone is to be renewed, God must intervene. Charnock puts it this way: 'We are not regenerate because our will has consented to the persuasions of grace; for that it does not do of itself; but the grace of God disarms our will of all that is capable to make resistance, and determines it to accept and rejoice in what is offered.'[199] This view of grace is found in Calvin, who affirms that humanity is unable to turn to God without an initial and continual work of God:

> The human will is of itself evil and therefore needs transformation and renewal so that it may begin to be good, but that grace itself is not merely a tool which can help someone if he is pleased to stretch out his hand to [take it]. That is, [God] does not merely offer it, leaving [to man] the choice between receiving it and rejecting it, but he steers the mind to choose what is right, he moves the will also effectively to obedience, he arouses and advances the endeavour until the actual completion of the work is attained. Then again, that [grace] is not sufficient if it is just once conferred upon someone, unless it accompanies him without interruption.[200]

Similarly, Swinnock views God's grace as sovereignly effectual and irresistible.[201] In other words, God does not work in people's lives because they take the first step. If God waited for this step, it would never happen. The reality is, however, that not everyone is regenerate. This points to the fact that God must elect some individuals whilst passing over others. This is precisely

---

[197] *Door of Salvation*, V:22.
[198] *Ibid.*
[199] Charnock, *Efficient of Regeneration, Works*, III:177.
[200] Calvin, *Bondage and Liberation of the Will*, 114.
[201] For prevenient and efficacious grace in Calvin, see *Institutes*, II:III:6-7,10,13.

what Swinnock means when he says that regeneration is according to God's 'good pleasure.' Evidently, for Swinnock, this sets the 'moving cause' of regeneration within the realm of God's eternal decree. He remarks:

> Unclasp the secret book of God's decree, and look into it as far as the word will warrant thee, and thou shalt find that in that internal work of election God had the renewing of man after his image in his eye... when all mankind was before God, he did, in his eternal thoughts, set some apart to be chosen pieces... Go from God's decree to its execution, from his inward to his outward actions, and thou shalt find thy renewing after his image to be full in his eye.[202]

Swinnock does not spend much time wrestling with the tension between the doctrine of divine sovereignty and human responsibility,[203] nor does he address what is, at times, perceived to be arbitrariness on God's part. In his own words, he unclasps 'the secret book of God's decree' and looks into it 'as far as the word will warrant.' Rather than entering into speculation, he focuses on a more pastoral issue: 'What did God foresee in thee more than in others, that he called thee by his grace?'[204] He does not become ensnared with the mechanics of election, but enthralled with the implications, asking:

> Shouldst not thou think, Lord, how is it that I, unworthy I, should be chosen, when others are rejected? that I should be called when others are neglected, that I, who came into the world with the same rage against God and godliness, and did many a day run with others to the same excess of riot, should turn about, be in love with holiness, and run the ways of thy commandments, when many others still wallow in their wickedness, and are every hour hastening unto hell? Lord, how is it that thou hast revealed thyself to me, and not to the world?[205]

The Instrumental Cause

According to Swinnock, the instrumental cause of regeneration is 'the ministry of the word.'[206] In quoting James 1:18[207] and 1 Peter 1:23,[208] he affirms that 'the word of God gives a spiritual birth and being to men and women, when there is no likelihood or possibility in nature, yea, when their natures are in flat opposition and contrariety to it... the word discovereth our diseases... applieth

---

[202] *Door of Salvation*, V:182-183.

[203] For a brief discussion, see *Sinner's Last Sentence*, V:309-311.

[204] *Ibid.*, V:254.

[205] *Ibid.*

[206] *Ibid.*, V:23.

[207] 'In the exercise of His will He brought us forth by the word of truth, so that we would be a kind of first fruits among His creatures.'

[208] 'For you have been born again not of seed which is perishable but imperishable, that is, through the living and enduring word of God.'

the medicine for our cure... killeth sin, casteth down Satan, enliveneth the soul.'[209] This is a description of the manner in which God's Spirit applies God's Word to the soul in the work of regeneration.

Charnock echoes Swinnock's view of the instrumental cause of regeneration, stating, 'The gospel is the power of God in a way of instrumentality, but the almightiness of God is the principal in a way of efficiency.'[210] To clarify the difference between the efficient and instrumental causes, he appeals to the Greek prepositions – ἐκ, ἐξ, and διά – demonstrating that the first two are always used in reference to the work of God's Spirit,[211] whereas the third is always used in reference to the work of God's Word.[212] He suggests that the prepositions ἐκ and ἐξ note the efficient cause whereas διά notes the instrument or means by which a 'thing is wrought.'[213] In other words, Scripture has no inherent power. Many people hear God's Word, yet are never born again. The reason is that the Holy Spirit must apply it to people's hearts, thereby convincing them of its truth.[214] Once, they discern that 'it is in truth, the word of God,'[215] they embrace it with their hearts. Hence, it is the instrument by which the Holy Spirit calls the elect to salvation.[216] Baxter comments:

> The same Spirit doth by this word (heard or read) renew and sanctify the souls of the elect; illuminating their minds, opening and quickening their hearts, prevailing with, changing, and resolving their wills, thus writing God's word, and imprinting his image by his word upon their hearts, making it powerful to conquer and cast out their strongest, sweetest, dearest sins, and bringing them to the saving knowledge, love, and obedience of God in Jesus Christ.[217]

In this process, Swinnock is critical of any suggestion that sinners are forced into a state of salvation. If this were the case, then they would have no awareness of their own experience. Instead, he affirms that God proceeds with individuals by steps so that they are involved in the process.[218] He describes the

---

[209] *Door of Salvation*, V:237.

[210] Charnock, *Existence and Attributes of God, Works*, II:75.

[211] See Jn. 3:5 and 1 Jn. 3:9.

[212] See 1 Pet. 1:23 and 1 Cor. 4:15.

[213] Charnock, *Instrument of Regeneration, Works*, III:309.

[214] The Puritans gravitate to the example of Lydia in Acts 16:14. Charles Cohen considers this in 'Two Biblical Models of Conversion: An Example of Puritan Hermeneutics,' *Church History* 58 (1989) 182-196.

[215] 1 Thess. 2:13.

[216] Without employing the terms *efficient* and *instrumental*, Calvin makes this same distinction. *Institutes*, IV:I:6.

[217] Baxter, *Christian Directory*, 69-70.

[218] Commenting on Perkins, Mark Shaw writes, 'His covenant theology enabled him to follow a consistent line of co-action which gave strong emphasis to God's sovereign grace in Christ as the ultimate cause of salvation while at the same time emphasizing the necessity of human response... The human psyche as created by God needed the

'whole of Christianity' as consisting in these steps: illumination, humiliation, application, and dedication.[219]

By the 'illumination' of God's Spirit, people apply God's Word to themselves thereby recognizing their 'sins and misery.'[220] 'This is first in the Spirit's operation on the soul.'[221] They then experience 'humiliation' because of their inability and inadequacy. Their heart is 'deeply and thoroughly affected.'[222] Richard Sibbes refers to such people as 'bruised reeds.'[223] By this, he means that they are conscious of their sin, mindful of their need, and aware that Christ is their only help. For Sibbes, 'This bruising is required before conversion so that the Spirit may make way for himself into the heart by levelling all proud, high thoughts, and that we may understand ourselves to be what indeed we are by nature.'[224] William Guthrie identifies this preparatory work of the Holy Spirit with the law, remarking, 'The most ordinary way by which many are brought to Christ, is by a clear and discernible work of the law, and humiliation; which we generally call the spirit of bondage.'[225] The Holy Spirit applies God's Word to sinners whereby they are convinced that it is speaking against them.

According to Guthrie, this humiliation for sin 'makes a man take salvation to heart as the one thing necessary.'[226] At this point, the individual experiences what Swinnock calls 'application.' This means the individual looks to Christ for 'pardon, grace, and salvation.'[227] 'Nothing but perfect righteousness will pacify God's anger, or satisfy his justice, please those eyes which are purer than to behold the least iniquity. And this righteousness is only in Christ, who was made sin for thee, that thou mightest become the righteousness of God in him.'[228] Aware of their sinfulness, these bruised reeds receive Christ by faith.

---

sovereignty of grace to deliver it from the condemnation it was helpless to alter while at the same time it needed to apply and respond to his grace.' 'Drama in the Meeting House: The Concept of Conversion in the Theology of William Perkins,' *Westminster Theological Journal* 45 (1983) 71. Shaw identifies Perkins's four-stage model in conversion as 'humiliation – faith – repentance – obedience.' *Ibid.*, 56.

[219] *Heaven and Hell*, III:331-361. Elsewhere, he expands these 'steps' to include illumination, conviction, anhelation, lamentation, implantation, and resolution. *Door of Salvation*, V:201-217. Shepard speaks of conviction, compunction, humiliation, and application. *Sound Believer*, 117-190.

[220] *Heaven and Hell*, III:331.

[221] *Ibid.*, III:334.

[222] *Ibid.*, III:336.

[223] Richard Sibbes, *The Bruised Reed* (1630; Edinburgh: Banner of Truth, 1998) 3.

[224] *Ibid.*, 4.

[225] William Guthrie, *A Short Treatise of The Christian's Great Interest* (1658; rpt., Edinburgh: James Watson, 1720) 35-36.

[226] *Ibid.*, 52.

[227] *Heaven and Hell*, III:348.

[228] *Ibid.*, III:349.

John Flavel identifies three components of this faith: first, the understanding of
the mind in regards to the truths of Christ as revealed in Scripture; second, the
acceptance of the heart in regards to Christ as the complete remedy for sin; and
third, the choice of the will in receiving Christ.[229] Here, Flavel equates faith
with the exercise of the three faculties of the soul. This means faith involves the
whole person. Baxter notes, 'Faith enters at the understanding; but it hath not
all its essential parts, and is not the gospel faith indeed, till it hath possessed the
will.'[230] This possession of the will is repentance. Perkins affirms, 'Repentance
is a worke of grace, arising of a godly sorrow; whereby a man turnes from all
his sinnes unto God, and brings forth fruites worthie amendment of life.'[231] For
Thomas Watson, repentance is 'a grace of God's Spirit whereby a sinner is
inwardly humbled and visibly transformed.'[232] This transformation possesses
six ingredients: sight of sin, sorrow for sin, confession of sin, shame for sin,
hatred of sin, and turning from sin.[233] In relation to this final ingredient, Alleine
maintains that 'turning from sin to God' is the essence of conversion.[234]

Illumination, humiliation, and application are followed by 'dedication,'
whereby the individual dedicates 'soul and body... unto the service and glory
of Jesus Christ.'[235] 'There is certainly,' writes Swinnock, 'if thou wilt be a
Christian indeed, a necessity of laying thy health, strength, time, estate, name,
friends, interests in the world, thy calling and comforts whatsoever, at the feet
of Christ, to be employed wholly in his service, and improved altogether for his
glory, and to be denied or enjoyed, in whole or in part, according to his call and
command.'[236]

Returning for a moment to the issue of intellectualism versus voluntarism,
Richard Muller maintains that Calvin ascribes to 'philosophical intellectualism'
before the fall and 'soteriological voluntarism' after the fall.[237] For this reason,

---

[229] John Flavel, *The Method of Grace in the Gospel Redemption*, *Works*, II:129-134.
[230] Baxter, *Directions and Persuasions*, *Practical Works*, 590.
[231] William Perkins, *Two Treatises. I. Of the nature and practice of repentance. II. Of
      the combate of the flesh and spirit*, *Works*, I:453. For Calvin, repentance is
      regeneration – the entire process by which a sinner turns to God and grows in
      holiness. Calvin, *Institutes*, III:III:5,9.
[232] Thomas Watson, *The Doctrine of Repentance* (1668; Edinburgh: Banner of Truth,
      1994) 17.
[233] *Ibid.*, 18-45.
[234] Alleine, *Sure Guide to Heaven*, 37,43.
[235] *Heaven and Hell*, III:355.
[236] *Ibid.*, III:357.
[237] Richard Muller, 'The Priority of the Intellect in the Soteriology of Jacob Arminius,'
      Westminster Theological Journal 55 (1993) 56. In this article, Muller responds to
      Kendall's assertion that Calvin was 'intellectualistic' in his doctrine of faith whereas
      later Calvinists – because of Beza and perhaps Arminius – were 'voluntaristic.'
      Muller argues that Arminius includes *notitia* (knowledge) and *assensus* (assent)
      under the 'direct act of faith' whereas he includes *fiducia* (trust) under the 'reflex act

Calvin views the regeneration of the will as a necessary prerequisite for choosing the known good.[238] The sinful will (including affections) rules individuals. For this reason, they will never submit to the known good without the regeneration of the will, namely, the reordering of the affections toward good. In other words, faith necessarily involves both the mind and will. Calvin writes, 'Now we shall possess a right definition of faith if we call it a firm and certain knowledge of God's benevolence toward us, founded upon the truth of the freely given promise in Christ, both revealed to our minds and sealed upon our hearts through the Holy Spirit.'[239] William Ames expresses this same emphasis:

> To believe signifies ordinarily an act of the understanding as it gives assent to evidence. But since as a consequence the will is wont to be moved and reach out to embrace the good thus proved, faith may rightly designate this act of the will as well... Although faith always presupposes a knowledge of the Gospel, there is nevertheless no saving knowledge in anyone... except the knowledge which follows this act of the will and depends upon it.[240]

Swinnock adopts this same conviction. Whilst the instrumental cause of regeneration is 'the ministry of the Word,' made effectual by the Holy Spirit, Swinnock believes the individual is consciously involved in the entire process – from illumination (the mind) to dedication (the will). This is, according to Swinnock, 'without question the whole of Christianity.'[241]

The Formal Cause

Swinnock claims that the formal cause of regeneration is the renewal of 'the whole man after God's own image.'[242] In this statement, he sees four 'particulars.'

---

of faith.' *Ibid.*, 61. In so doing, Arminius draws the emphasis away from *fiducia* toward *notitia*. Muller believes this opened the way in Arminius's theology for human initiative in the work of salvation. *Ibid.*, 69. Based upon his analysis, Muller concludes, 'Quite the reverse of Kendall's hypothesis, Arminius appears to have held an intellectualist and not a voluntarist view of faith: the willing that Arminius views as leading to *fiducia*, the final element of saving faith, rests on an intellectively defined "substance" of faith.' *Ibid.*, 72.

[238] Calvin, *Institutes*, II:II:26, III:XV:7-8.

[239] *Ibid.*, III:II:7.

[240] Ames, *Marrow*, I:III:2-4. Also see John Owen, *The Doctrine of Justification by Faith, Works*, V:94-102.

[241] *Heaven and Hell*, III:361.

[242] *Door of Salvation*, V:24.

The Act of Regeneration

The first is the act of regeneration: it is a renewing. Swinnock states, 'In regeneration nature is not ruined, but rectified. The convert is the same man, but new made. The faculties of his soul are not destroyed, but they are refined.'[243] Again, regeneration 'changeth the understanding by illumination, the will by renovation, and the affections by sanctification; it doth not infuse new faculties into the soul, but it doth renew the old; it turneth the same waters into another channel – they ran before after the world and the flesh, but now after God and his ways.'[244] Charnock agrees, 'Sin took not away the essence, but the rectitude; the new creation therefore gives not a new faculty, but a new quality.'[245] Again, 'He doth not change the soul by an alteration of the faculties, but by an alteration of something in them... by proposing to the understanding something to be known, and informing it of the reasonableness of his precepts, and the innate goodness and excellency of his offers, and by inclining the will to love and embrace what is proposed.'[246] Baxter also agrees, 'For though he be the same in substance and person and the natural faculties of his soul, yet not the same in disposition and practice.'[247] Torrance finds this same emphasis in Calvin, stating, 'While Calvin thinks of our natural gifts as being totally corrupted, they are not deprived of being. That is evident when he thinks of the conversion of man in which he gains a new creature, but in such a way that while it is "wholly of God," "everything essential to our original nature remains."'[248]

For the Puritans, this 'act' of renewal is the fruit of the individual's union with Christ.[249] Swinnock defines this union on the basis of the apostle Paul's assertion in Romans 6:6 that 'our old man is crucified with Him.'[250] The purpose of this crucifixion is so that 'the body of sin might be destroyed.' He explains, 'It is faith that causeth the union between Christ and the soul, and

---

[243] *Ibid.*, V:25.

[244] *Heaven and Hell*, III:300.

[245] Charnock, *Nature of Regeneration, Works*, III:91.

[246] Charnock, *Existence and Attributes of God*, I:547. Also see I:23.

[247] Baxter, *Treatise of Conversion, Practical Works*, 322.

[248] Torrance, *Calvin's Doctrine of Man*, 91. See Calvin, *Institutes*, II:III:6.

[249] Charles Partee suggests that union with Christ is the 'central dogma' of Calvin's *Institutes*. 'Calvin's Central Dogma Again,' *Sixteenth Century Journal* XVIII (1987) 191-199. A helpful overview of this aspect of Puritanism is found in Nuttall, *The Holy Spirit in Puritan Faith and Experience*. Also see R. Tudor Jones, 'Union with Christ: The Existential Nerve of Puritan Piety,' *Tyndale Bulletin* 41:2 (1990) 186-208. Curiously, Armstrong argues that the Puritan emphasis upon the mystical communion of the individual soul with God is explained by their 'strongly anti-intellectual predilection.' He adds, 'This helps account for the predominance of the uneducated lay person, and especially of women, in the movement.' 'Puritan Spirituality,' 238. The Puritans were anything but 'anti-intellectual.'

[250] Rom. 6:6. *Door of Salvation*, V:33,96.

joins them together; by virtue of which union the Christian hath communion with Christ in his merit and righteousness, that his life, and death, and burial are the Christian's, are by God imputed to him, as if performed in his own person, hence it is said that the Christian lives with Christ, is crucified with Christ, and buried with Christ (Rom. 6:4).'[251] Owen adds:

> We are crucified with him *meritoriously*, in that he procured the Spirit for us to mortify sin; *efficiently*, in that from his death virtue comes forth for our crucifying; in the way of a *representation* and *exemplar* we shall assuredly be crucified unto sin, as he was for our sin. This is that the apostle intends. Christ by his death destroying the works of the devil, procuring the Spirit for us, hath so killed sin, as to its reign in believers, that it shall not obtain its end and dominion.[252]

In Romans 6, the apostle Paul develops the consequences of this union, asking, 'Do you not know that when you present yourselves to someone as slaves for obedience, you are slaves of the one whom you obey, either of sin resulting in death, or of obedience resulting in righteousness?'[253] According to this verse, there are two masters: sin, resulting in death;[254] and righteousness, resulting in life.[255] The first master rules over those in Adam, whereas the second rules over those in Christ. The regenerate are united with Christ and, therefore, are no longer in Adam. This union means that sin's mastery over them is broken. They are freed from sin and enslaved to righteousness. The consequences of this union with Christ are central to the Puritan mindset as it implies that the old life of sin in Adam is past. The regenerate are brought from that old life, the end of which was death, into a new life, the end of which is righteousness. All of this is summarized in the words of Walter Marshall: 'If we be joined to Christ, our hearts will be no longer left under the power of sinful inclinations, or in a mere indifferency of inclination to good or evil; but they will be powerfully endowed with a power, bent, and propensity to the practice of holiness, by the Spirit of Christ dwelling in us, and inclining us to mind spiritual things and to lust against the flesh (Rom. 8:1,4-5; Gal. 5:17).'[256]

The Puritans (including Swinnock) gravitate to the marriage metaphor in Ephesians 5:21-30 to describe this union.[257] First, it is covenantal. Before the

---

[251] *Sinner's Last Sentence*, V:343. Also see *Christian Man's Calling*, III:99,230; *Door of Salvation*, V:214; and *Sinner's Last Sentence*, V:295-296,405-406.

[252] Owen, *Mortification, Works*, VI:85. His italics.

[253] Rom. 6:16.

[254] Rom. 6:16,17,20.

[255] Rom. 6:13,16,18,19.

[256] Walter Marshall, *Gospel Mystery of Sanctification* (1670; Grand Rapids: Reformation Heritage Books, 1999) 37.

[257] *Christian Man's Calling*, I:464-528. Jones comments, 'When the Puritans describe their relationship with Jesus Christ in terms of spiritual marriage, they guide us into

foundation of the world, the Father united himself to his people by way of a covenant, promising that he would be their God and they would be his people.[258] Second, it is natural. At the incarnation, the Son united himself with his people in their humanity in order to ratify the eternal covenant. He fulfilled all righteousness on their behalf. He died, rose again, and ascended to the Father on their behalf. Now, he intercedes on their behalf. Third, it is spiritual (or mystical). At the moment of regeneration, the Spirit unites his people to Christ whereby they enter into the blessings of the covenant.

For Swinnock, this union is manifested in Christlikeness. Christ declares, 'I am the vine, you are the branches.'[259] Naturally, the purpose of a branch is to bear fruit, the character of the vine actually being reproduced in the fruit of the branches. Similarly, the character of Christ is reproduced in the regenerate. In this connection, Christ promises, 'He who abides in Me and I in him, he bears much fruit, for apart from Me you can do nothing.'[260] There is, therefore, a vital, organic union between the vine and its branches; the latter drawing upon the resources of the former. In the words of Swinnock, the branches 'partake of its sap, and thereby thrive and flourish.'[261]

The Subject of Regeneration

The second 'particular' is the subject of regeneration: it is a renewing of the whole man. Swinnock contends, 'Original sin defileth the whole man, from the crown of the head to the soles of the feet; and regeneration refineth the whole man.'[262] In terms of the faculties of the soul, this renewal begins in the understanding. As created by God, the individual was to be governed by the understanding. For this reason, the darkened understanding must be illuminated. Swinnock remarks, 'It is observable, that in the covenant of grace the mind is still spoken of to be renewed before the heart (Heb. 10:8-9; Jer. 31:33). For it is by the understanding that grace slips down into the affections.' Again, 'Till the understanding of a man be enlightened to see the deformity of sin, and the beauty of holiness, he will never heartily loathe and grieve for the former, love and long for the latter.'[263] Charnock agrees, 'The first appearance of life, when God raises the soul, is in the clearness and distinctness of its knowledge of God... Our eye first sees an object before our hearts desire it, or our members move to it; so there is an apprehension of the goodness of the thing proposed, before there be any motion of our wills to it; so God begins his

---

the inner sanctum of their piety.' 'Union with Christ,' 199. See Thomas Watson, *The Godly Man's Picture* (1666; Edinburgh: Banner of Truth, 1999) 239.

[258]   Heb. 8:10-12.

[259]   Jn. 15:5.

[260]   *Ibid.*

[261]   *Door of Salvation*, V:113. Also see *Sinner's Last Sentence*, V:401.

[262]   *Door of Salvation*, V:26.

[263]   *Ibid.*, V:201-202.

work in our minds, and terminates it in our wills.'[264] Shepard also agrees, stating, 'There must precede this act of the understanding, to see Christ, before a man can close with Christ by his will.'[265]

Once the understanding is illuminated, the hardened affections are softened. For Swinnock, 'There must be a daybreak of light in the understanding, before there can be a heartbreak of sorrow in the affections.'[266] When this occurs, the affections are stirred to hate that which they formerly loved (i.e., sin) and love that which they formerly hated (i.e., God). Swinnock comments, 'But now the man loathes what formerly he loved, and loves what formerly he loathed, though sin were the luscious meat which did so exceedingly please his palate, that his teeth were always watering after it, and he rolled it as a sweet morsel under his tongue; yet, now he serves it, as Amnon did Tamar, the hatred wherewith he hates it is far greater than the love wherewith he loved it.'[267]

Once the affections are softened, the enslaved will is liberated.[268] Charnock comments, 'After the act of understanding has preceded in a serious consideration, and thorough conviction, the act of the will, by virtue of the same Spirit, follows in a delightful motion to the object proposed to it; it is conducted by light, and spirited by love; the understanding hands the object to the will, as necessary to be embraced, and the arms of the will are opened to receive it, as the eyes of the mind are to behold it.'[269] Baxter agrees, 'He first revealeth saving truth to the understanding, and affecteth the will by showing the goodness of the things revealed; and these employ the thoughts, and passions, and senses, and the whole body, reducing the inferior faculties to obedience, and casting out by degrees those images which had deceived and prepossessed them.'[270] In its corrupted state, the will cannot choose what the understanding and the affections have not found to be good. However, once the understanding is illuminated and the affections are softened, the will chooses what the affections want most; namely, God. The *WCF* summarizes this renewal as follows:

> All those whom God hath predestinated unto life, and those only, he is pleased, in his appointed and accepted time, effectually to call, by His Word and Spirit, out of that state of sin and death, in which they are by nature, to grace and salvation by Jesus Christ; enlightening their minds, spiritually and savingly, to understand the things of God; taking away their heart of stone, and giving unto them an heart of

---

[264] Charnock, *Efficient of Regeneration, Works*, III:279-280. Also see *Existence and Attributes of God*, I:574, II:283,345,385.

[265] Shepard, *Parable of the Ten Virgins*, II:120.

[266] *Heaven and Hell*, III:334.

[267] *Door of Salvation*, V:31-32.

[268] *Ibid.*, V:30.

[269] Charnock, *Efficient of Regeneration, Works*, III:283-284.

[270] Baxter, *Christian Directory*, 96.

flesh; renewing their wills, and by his almighty power determining them to that which is good.[271]

It is clear from the preceding remarks that although the head is the starting-point in regeneration, the Holy Spirit must also affect the heart. As Fiering explains, there is speculative (or notional) knowledge and sensible (or inclinational) knowledge. The first involves the mind whereas the second involves the will. In regeneration, the Holy Spirit works upon the mind to ensure that truth is 'rightly understood' and works upon the will to ensure that truth is 'warmly embraced.'[272] On its own, speculative knowledge is unable to stir the affections. For this reason, an individual may possess speculative knowledge of the truth yet act contrary to it. There must, therefore, be sensible knowledge. As Geerhardus Vos states:

> It is true, the Gospel teaches that to know God is life eternal. But the concept of 'knowledge' here is not to be understood in its Hellenic sense, but in the Shemitic sense. According to the former, 'to know' means to mirror the reality of a thing in one's consciousness. The Shemitic and Biblical idea is to have the reality of something practically interwoven with the inner experience of life. Hence 'to know' can stand in the Biblical idiom for 'to love,' 'to single out in love.'[273]

The Pattern of Regeneration

The third 'particular' is the pattern of regeneration: it is a renewing of the whole man after the image of God.[274] Calvin affirms that regeneration's 'sole purpose is to restore in us the image of God that had been disfigured and all but obliterated through Adam's transgression.'[275] The Puritans agree. Bolton comments, 'the sanctifying spirit, by the miraculous operative of saving grace, doth purge and mortify the inmost affections, plant justifying faith in the heart, renew all the powers of the soul, and reinvest them in some good measure with the blessed image of holiness and integrity which they lost in Adam.'[276] For his part, Charnock writes, 'It is a likeness to Christ; the whole human nature of Christ was holy, every faculty of his soul, every member of his body, his nature holy, his heart holy.'[277] Baxter adds, 'A renewed nature is the very image of God; Christ dwelling in us, and the Spirit of God abiding in us; it is a beam from the face of God; the seed of God remaining in us; the only inherent beauty

---

[271] *WCF*, X:I.

[272] Fiering, *Moral Philosophy at Seventeenth-Century Harvard*, 142.

[273] Geerhardus Vos, *Biblical Theology: Old and New Testaments* (Edinburgh: Banner of Truth, 1992) 8.

[274] *Door of Salvation*, V:34.

[275] Calvin, *Institutes*, III:III:9.

[276] Bolton, *State of True Happiness*, 22.

[277] Charnock, *Nature of Regeneration, Works*, III:97.

of the rational soul: it ennobles man above all nobility; fits him to understand his Maker's pleasure, do his will, and receive his glory.'[278] By 'image of God' these authors mean the faculties of the soul as characterized by knowledge, righteousness, and holiness. As Swinnock says:

> Therefore the regenerate are said to be partakers of the divine nature (2 Pet. 1:4)... The corrupt image of Satan and the old Adam is defaced; therefore it is called a putting off the old man... the pure image of God is introduced, therefore it is called a putting on the new man (Eph. 4:24); which after God is created in righteousness and true holiness; and a being holy as God is holy (1 Pet. 1:14-16). And, indeed, all these new-born children do, so far as they are regenerate, completely resemble their Father. Their godliness is nothing but god-likeness, a beam of the divine glory, a representation of God's own perfections.[279]

The Season of Regeneration

The fourth 'particular' is the season of regeneration: it is a renewing of the whole man after the image of God at first. By this Swinnock implies that regeneration occurs at a moment of time.[280] After regeneration, there is the ongoing process of renewal, known as 'sanctification.' Swinnock distinguishes between the two as follows: 'Sanctification is a constant, progressive renewing of the whole man, whereby the new creature doth daily more and more die unto sin and live unto God. Regeneration is the birth, sanctification is the growth of this babe of grace.'[281] Again, 'regeneration is a specifical change from nature to grace... sanctification is a gradual change from one degree of grace to another.'[282] Thus regeneration and sanctification are distinct, yet inseparable. They are distinct, in that the former occurs at a moment in time whereas the latter occurs over a period of time. However, they are inseparable, in that the latter is the product of the former. As Swinnock notes, 'Regeneration is the birth, sanctification is the growth of this babe of grace.'

The Final Cause

Swinnock states that the final cause of regeneration is God's 'own glory and the salvation of his elect.'[283] He believes that all things are for God's glory as the

---

[278] Baxter, *Saints' Everlasting Rest, Practical Works*, 108. For Owen, see *Holy Spirit, Works*, III:330,470,510,523,578.

[279] *Door of Salvation*, V:34.

[280] Calvin views regeneration as a life-long process. See *Institutes*, III:III:8-9, III:VI:5. This is a difference in terminology, not soteriology.

[281] *Door of Salvation*, V:34.

[282] *Ibid.*, V:35.

[283] *Ibid.*

final cause,[284] and God is most glorified when his creatures are happy in him. The renewal of the image of God is the means by which this happens, for the regenerate 'praise the greatness of God's power, the manifoldness of God's wisdom, the sweetness of God's love, the sureness of God's word, the riches of God's mercy, the freeness of God's grace, the beauty of God's image, the preciousness of God's Christ, and all this upon their own knowledge and experience.'[285] Swinnock's affinity with Calvin is again evident. As Leith notes, 'Sanctification,' for Calvin, 'is subordinated to the glory of God, and the "final" cause of salvation is the demonstration of the divine righteousness and the praise of the divine goodness.'[286]

Conclusion

In this process of renewal, it is evident that the soul's faculties are inseparable. As Swinnock remarks, 'Right knowledge, though it begin at the head, doth not end there, but falls down upon the heart to affect that, and floweth out in the life to order and regulate that.'[287] This means that the affections stand between the mind and the will. It is no surprise to discover, therefore, that Swinnock defines true religion in terms of the affections. He expresses this conviction as a pastoral concern, commenting, 'They which know experimentally what the sanctification of the Holy Ghost meaneth, are few indeed.'[288] And this is at the root of his spirituality – the conviction that people must experience an affective appropriation of grace, moving beyond intellectual assent to heartfelt 'dedication unto Christ.'[289]

---

[284] *Christian Man's Calling*, I:48. Stephen Holmes considers this emphasis in Jonathan Edwards, writing, 'Happiness is the perception of excellency, so the world is created that angels and humanity may see God's perfections and rejoice in the sight.' *God of Grace and God of Glory*, 37. This applies to the realm of creation and redemption. He writes, 'Edwards' great theme is the self-glorification, by means of self-communication, of God as the final end of all His actions.' *Ibid.*, 108.

[285] *Ibid.*, V:36-37.

[286] Leith, *John Calvin's Doctrine of the Christian Life*, 38. See Calvin, *Institutes*, III:XIV:17, III:XV:21.

[287] *Incomparableness of God*, IV:482.

[288] *Heaven and Hell*, III:205.

[289] *Ibid.*

Chapter Four

The Fear of God

Swinnock maintains that the 'chief failing' of the Pharisees was in their lack of the 'power of godliness.'[1] He states, 'Their affections were bad; their practices did not proceed from renewed and gracious principles. Whatsoever civility was without in the life, there was no real sanctity within in the heart.'[2] Avoiding this 'chief failing' is one of Swinnock's primary pastoral concerns. It is an anxiety that literally permeates his writings.[3] He believes that external morality and civility are dangerous, because they always proceed from an unregenerate heart, thereby producing a mere 'form of godliness.' Many trust in this 'form' for their salvation, yet it falls well short of God's requirements. Consequently, Swinnock is desirous that his readers appreciate that the 'power of godliness' is found in sanctified affections.[4]

---

[1] 2 Tim. 3:5.

[2] *Gods Are Men*, IV:133.

[3] Swinnock is not alone in this concern. Lovelace notes its prevalence among the Puritans: 'The problem that confronts the Puritans as they look out on their decaying society and their lukewarm church is not simply to dislodge the faithful from the slough of mortal or venial sin, but radically to awaken those who are professing but not actual Christians, who are caught in a trap of carnal security.' 'The Anatomy of Puritan Piety,' 303.

[4] For a treatment of 'affectionate' theology, see Mark Dever, *Richard Sibbes: Puritanism and Calvinism in Late Elizabethan and Early Stuart England* (Macon: Mercer University Press, 2000) 138-160. Many scholars miss the Puritan emphasis upon the affections. J. Rodney Fulcher argues that Puritanism was characterized by an internal struggle between piety and intellect, because of its adoption of faculty psychology with its emphasis upon the mind. He believes Jonathan Edwards finally 'struck a balance.' 'Puritans and the Passions: The Faculty Psychology in American Puritanism,' *Journal of the History of the Behavioural Sciences* 9 (1973) 123-139. Equally startling is Bourke's suggestion that 'Jonathan Edwards took an intellectualist position on the human will. He is not a philosopher who stresses love and affection... His *Treatise concerning Religious Affections* is more concerned with understanding and intellectually-guided willing than with what we would today recognize as affection or feeling.' *Will in Western Thought*, 141.

The Affections

According to James Packer, 'The affections are the various dispositional drives, positive and negative, with their emotional overtones – love, hope, hate, fear, and so on – which elicit choices by drawing man to or repelling him from particular objects.'[5] This definition is confirmed in Bunyan, for whom the affections are 'the Hands and Arms of the Soul... that take hold of, receive and imbrace what is liked by the Soul.'[6] Flavel notes that affections are 'originally designed and appointed for the happiness of man, in the promoting and securing its chiefest good.'[7] In full agreement, Swinnock refers to the affections as the soul's 'greatest part.'[8] According to Edward Reynolds, the affections are

> those naturall, perfective, and unstrained motions of the Creatures unto that advancement of their Natures, which they are... ordained to receive, by a regular inclination to those objects, whose goodnesse beareth a naturall conveniencie or vertue of satisfaction unto them; or by an antipathie and aversation from those, which bearing a contrarietie to the good they desire, must needs be noxious and destructive, and by consequent, odious to their natures.[9]

In other words, the affections are the inclination or disinclination of the soul to an object in accordance with the soul's perception of that object as either desirous or odious. With this basic definition, Reynolds identifies five pairs of affections.[10] The first – love and hatred – concerns the attitude of the soul to an object in its own essential nature. If the object is good, then the soul loves it; but, if the object is evil, then the soul hates it. Reynolds affirms that these 'are the two radicall, fundamentall, and most transcendent Passions of all the rest.' The second pair – desire and scorn – is the response of the soul to an object from which it is absent. If the object is good, then the soul desires it; but, if the object is evil, then the soul scorns it. The third pair is joy and sorrow. When the soul is in contact with the object, it either rejoices or grieves depending on whether the object is deemed good or evil. The fourth pair is despair and hope. The former is stirred when it is impossible to obtain a desired object whereas the latter is stirred when it is possible. The fifth pair is boldness and fear. The

---

[5] Packer, *Quest for Godliness*, 195. The terms *affection* and *passion* are used varyingly in the primary literature. (1) Passions are the emotions of the sensitive appetite, whereas the affections are the emotions of the rational appetite. (2) Affections and passions are the same, belonging to the sensitive appetite. (3) Affections and passions are the same, belonging to both the rational and sensitive appetites. Hence, humans share some affections-passions with animals whilst others are unique to them. This last position is predominant among the Puritans.

[6] Bunyan, *Greatness of the Soul, Miscellaneous Works*, IX:147.

[7] Flavel, *Pneumatologia, Works*, II:509.

[8] *Christian Man's Calling*, II:486.

[9] Reynolds, *Passions and Faculties*, 31-32.

[10] *Ibid.*, 39-40.

former occurs when avoidance of a scorned object is probable whereas the latter occurs when avoidance is improbable.

This, therefore, is Reynolds' theory of the affections. His central premise is clearly Aristotelian and Augustinian. As a matter of fact, his book is saturated with references from these two ancients.[11] Miller mentions that, in Reynolds' day, the 'groundwork' for this concept of the affections was Aristotle and that 'his *De Anima* remained the basic textbook.'[12] For his part, Aristotle identifies the passions – e.g., anger, fear, confidence, envy, joy, hatred, longing, emulation, and pity – as 'feelings' that accompany 'pleasure or pain.'[13] Aristotle believes that pleasure stimulates positive feelings whereas pain produces negative feelings. Therefore, the affections change according to the soul's perception of an object.

As for Augustine, he identifies four motions of the soul: desire, fear, joy, and sorrow.[14] Desire and joy are the 'volition of consent' to a 'loved' object: desire occurs when consent takes the form of seeking the object, and joy occurs when consent takes the form of enjoying it. On the other hand, fear and sorrow are the 'volition of aversion' from a 'hated' object: fear occurs when aversion takes the form of turning from the object, and sorrow occurs when aversion takes the form of experiencing it.[15] It is unmistakable that, in this paradigm, love and hatred ultimately determine the response of the other affections: desire is yearning for what is loved; joy is delighting in what is loved; fear is fleeing from what is hated; and sorrow is experiencing what is hated.[16] From this, Augustine argues that as long as the object of an individual's love is 'well-directed,' the affections are good. This changes, of course, if the object of an individual's love is 'ill-directed.'[17] Prior to Adam's fall, the object of humanity's love was God and, as a result, the affections were 'good.' This state, however, was terminated at the time of the fall when love for God was lost and, consequently, the affections became 'evil.' At regeneration, the individual's love is again 'well-directed,' and the affections respond accordingly. Augustine summarizes, 'The citizens of the holy city of God, who live according to God in the pilgrimage of this life, both fear and desire, and grieve and rejoice. And because their love is rightly placed, all these affections

---

[11] Reynolds includes at least 160 citations from Aristotle and at least 50 from Augustine.

[12] Miller, *New England Mind*, 244.

[13] Aristotle, *Nicomachean Ethics, Works: Vol. IX*, II:5.

[14] Augustine, *City of God, Select Library: Vol. II*, XIV:5. In *Confessions, Select Library: Vol. I*, X:14:22, Augustine refers to these 'motions' as the 'four perturbations of the mind.' He also refers to them as 'passions,' 'emotions,' or 'affections.'

[15] Augustine, *City of God, Select Library: Vol. II*, XIV:6.

[16] The Puritans agree with the priority given to love and hatred. See Shepard, *Parable of the Ten Virgins*, II:588.

[17] Augustine, *City of God, Select Library: Vol. II*, XIV:7.

of theirs are right.'[18]

Clearly, Aristotle and Augustine share the same premise; namely, that the affections change as they are attracted or repelled. Reynolds builds upon this foundation. And it is within this tradition that Swinnock stands. In his treatises, he identifies eight affections (or 'precious graces'):[19] love, desire, delight, trust, hope, fear, sorrow, and hatred.[20] Like Reynolds, he believes that these are present in an individual whether in a state of apostasy or renewal as they are the soul's natural response to its perception of an object. He shares this opinion with Charnock, who states:

> The acts of a renewed man, and the acts of a natural man, are the same in the nature of the acts, as when a man loves God and fears God, or loves man and fears man; it is the same act of love, and the same act of fear; there are the same motions of the soul, the same substantial acts simply considered; the soul stands in the same posture in the one as in the other, but the difference lies in the objects; the object of the one is supernatural, the object of the other is natural.[21]

As Charnock notes, it is the soul's perception of an object that changes as it moves from a state of apostasy to a state of renewal. In other words, 'it is not the existence of a thing that excites any of those affections, but the relation a thing bears to us in particular.'[22] Similarly, Bunyan affirms, 'These passions of the Soul are not therefore good, nor therefore evil, because they are the passions of the Soul: but are made so by two things, to wit, Principle and Object. The Principle I count that from whence they flow, and the Object that upon which they are pitched.'[23]

Along with his contemporaries, Swinnock affirms that the affections are sanctified by the soul's perception of God as 'the greatest good.'[24] For Charnock, 'The goodness of God renders God amiable. His goodness renders him beautiful, and his beauty renders him lovely... This is the most powerful attractive, and masters the affections of the soul.'[25] When this happens, these 'sanctified affections,' writes Perkins, 'are moved and inclined to that which is good, to embrace it.'[26] For Swinnock, this means the soul embraces God – 'his

---

[18]   *Ibid.*, XIV:9.

[19]   *Heaven and Hell*, III:305.

[20]   *Christian Man's Calling*, I:14,32,39; *Heaven and Hell*, III:290,295,305; *Fading of the Flesh*, III:454; *Gods Are Men*, IV:107; and *Men Are Gods*, IV:341.

[21]   Charnock, *Nature of Regeneration*, *Works*, III:92.

[22]   Charnock, *Existence and Attributes of God*, I:41.

[23]   Bunyan, *Greatness of the Soul*, *Miscellaneous Works*, IX:151. For Baxter, see *Treatise of Conversion*, *Practical Works*, 296-297.

[24]   *Christian Man's Calling*, I:4,38,71.

[25]   Charnock, *Existence and Attributes of God*, II:330.

[26]   William Perkins, *A Treatise Tending unto a Declaration, whether a man be in the estate of Damnation, or in the estate of Grace*, *Works*, I:371-372.

will chooseth him, his affections love him, his desire is after him, his delight is in him, his fear is of him, his trust is on him, his care and endeavour is to walk worthy of the Lord unto all well-pleasing.'[27] This sensible (or inclinational) knowledge of God is the fear of God.[28]

The Object of Fear

The prophet Malachi records God's rebuke of the nation of Israel – 'A son honors his father, and a servant his master. Then if I am a father, where is My honor? And if I am a master, where is My respect?'[29] According to the context, the Israelites were guilty of offering 'defiled food' upon God's altar, in that they presented the blind, lame, and sick as sacrifices in violation of his law. In order to expose their sin, God challenges them to offer such sacrifices to their provincial governor: 'Would he be pleased with you?' Offering 'defiled food' to a human leader was unimaginable, as the Israelites knew the consequences for such impudence, yet they had no difficulty in presenting these sacrifices to God. This demonstrated their lack of fear for the 'great King.' Swinnock comments, 'Petty princes may be owned and served with petty presents; but a great King, a great sovereign, must have great sacrifices.'[30]

He appeals to this text on several occasions[31] to demonstrate that there is no fear of God without 'apprehensions of God's infinite majesty.'[32] Quite simply, people cannot fear God if they do not know God. In the words of Charnock, 'When the knowledge of anything is fluctuating and uncertain, our actions

---

[27] *Door of Salvation*, V:105.

[28] Ted Campbell identifies the roots of this 'affective piety' in Perkins, who stressed hope for salvation, fear of God, contempt for worldly things, zeal for God's glory, and sorrow for sin, as the signs of the 'affective appropriation of the grace of election.' Campbell finds this same emphasis in Goodwin, Bunyan, and Baxter. As a result, he sees one expression of Puritan piety, spanning the seventeenth century. He summarizes, 'The religion of the Puritans had become a religion of the heart... the religious life had come to be centred on the changed "heart" – the will and affections convicted, converted, and sanctified by the predestining grace of God.' 'Affective Piety in Seventeenth-Century British Calvinism' in *The Religion of the Heart* (Columbia: University of South Carolina Press, 1991) 46-50,53,65-68.

[29] Mal. 1:6-14.

[30] *Incomparableness of God*, IV:471-472. For Baxter's use of Malachi, see *Directions to Weak Christians, Practical Works*, 666; and *Christian Directory*, 23. For Charnock, see *Existence and Attributes of God*, I:113-116,157,211,218,243,262-264, II:177,360,441,466. For Bayly, see *Practice of Piety*, 26,96. For Perkins, see *Cases*, 151. For Manton, see *A Description of the True Circumcision* in *The Complete Works of Thomas Manton* (Worthington: Marantha Publication) II:26,30.

[31] *Christian Man's Calling*, I:184, II:34; *Heaven and Hell*, III:215,324; *Men Are Gods*, IV:341; and *Sinner's Last Sentence*, V:393,428.

[32] *Christian Man's Calling*, I:95.

about it are careless.'[33] The affections are only stirred when the mind catches a glimpse of God's greatness: 'If God be so great a God, how greatly is he to be reverenced! Canst thou do too much service for him, or give too much glory to him? Can thy love to him be too great, or can thy fear of him be too great... God is great, and therefore greatly to be feared.'[34]

When speaking of such fear, Swinnock is careful to distinguish between 'filial' and 'servile' fear.[35] Similarly, Reynolds distinguishes between a 'feare of Admiration and Reverence' and a 'feare of Slavery and Rebellion.'[36] Gurnall speaks of 'holy' fear and 'slavish' fear.[37] Baxter contrasts 'holy' or 'godly' fear with 'slavish' fear.[38] Charnock distinguishes between 'reverential,' 'religious,' 'godly,' or 'holy' fear and 'slavish,' 'terrifying,' or 'bondage' fear.[39] According to Brian Gerrish:

> Calvin distinguishes two types of fear: a merely servile dread of God and the reverence for God that fits those who are *both* servants *and* children. The differences between the two types is plain from the fact that whereas those who lack piety (the *impii*) are frightened by the thought of divine vengeance, *fidelium timor* is fear, not of punishment, but of giving offense to the heavenly father.[40]

The Puritans agree that the difference between 'servile' and 'filial' fear is determined by the individual's view of God. Ungodly fear is the result of viewing God as a potential source of harm. It causes people to take steps to minimize the perceived threat whilst remaining steadfast in their sin. For Perkins, this 'slavish fear' occurs 'when a man onely feares the punishment, and not the offence of God, or at least the punishment more than the offence.'[41] Swinnock believes that such fear is 'a great foe to godliness,' adding, 'He who fears his skin is no friend to his soul, but will defile the latter to defend the former.'[42] In marked contrast, godly fear is the result of viewing God as the greatest good. Such a view of God's greatness and goodness causes the faculties of the soul to function in their proper sequence, resulting in changed

[33] Charnock, *Existence and Attributes of God*, I:84.
[34] *Heaven and Hell*, III:330.
[35] *Ibid.*, III:295.
[36] Reynolds, *Passions and Faculties*, 124,289.
[37] Gurnall, *Christian in Complete Armour*, I:119,222,263,372,373, II:579.
[38] Baxter, *Divine Life, Practical Works*, 146. See *Christian Directory*, 125,187.
[39] Charnock, *Existence and Attributes of God*, I:27,41,98,172,231236,254, II:107-109.
[40] Gerrish, *Grace and Gratitude*, 67 (f. 71). His italics. See Calvin, *Institutes*, III:II:26-27. According to John Murray, there is the fear that consists in being afraid. It elicits anguish and terror. There is also the fear of reverence. It elicits confidence and love. *Principles of Conduct* (Grand Rapids: Eerdmans, 1957) 233. He adds that the fear of God in us is that frame of heart and mind which reflects our apprehension of who and what God is, and this leads to total commitment to him. *Ibid.*, 242.
[41] Perkins, *Cases*, 151.
[42] *Christian Man's Calling*, II:294.

behaviour.

In order to show the distinction between godly and ungodly fear, Bunyan appeals to Moses' words to the Israelites at Mt. Sinai, 'Do not be afraid; for God has come in order to test you, and in order that the fear of Him may remain with you, so that you may not sin.'[43] Here, Moses refers to two types of fear: ungodly and godly. He forbids the first when he commands the Israelites 'Do not be afraid,' whereas he encourages the second when he states that 'God has come in order to test you, and in order that the fear of Him may remain with you, so that you may not sin.' On this basis, Bunyan concludes, 'Therefore, that fear that already had taken possession of them, was not the fear of God, but a fear that was of Satan, of their own misjudging hearts, and so a fear that was ungodly... Mark you, here is a fear and a fear, a fear forbidden, and a fear commended.'[44] The Israelites' ungodly fear was caused by their view of God as a perceived threat. They were afraid of the thunder and lightning. In other words, they regarded God as an immediate hazard to their personal well-being. Bunyan argues that this ungodly fear is the expression of selfishness, because it is exclusively concerned with self-preservation. It may cause people to leave their sin whilst the perceived threat exists. However, it falls short of making any lasting impression. Gurnall concurs, 'Thus oft we see God's judgments leave such an impression on men's spirits, that for a while they stand aloof from their sins... but when they see fair weather continue, and no clouds gather towards another storm, then they can descend to their old wicked practices, and grow more bold and heaven-daring than ever.'[45] In a similar vein, Charnock remarks, 'Many men perform those duties that the law enjoins, with the same sentiments that slaves perform their drudgery; and are constrained in their duties by no other considerations but those of the whip and cudgel. Since, therefore, they do it with reluctancy, and secretly murmur while they seem to obey, they would be willing that both the command were recalled, and the master that commands them were in another world.'[46] Charnock proceeds to argue that people actually desire the annihilation of what they fear will harm them. This means ungodly fear is tantamount to desiring the annihilation of God, whose attributes are perceived as detrimental to one's self-interest.[47]

In marked contrast, godly fear is caused by an appreciation of God himself. This may include a fear of God's wrath, but it is not limited to this; on the contrary, it focuses on God's majesty. This is what Moses encouraged at Sinai: 'God has come in order to test you, and in order that the fear of Him may remain with you, so that you may not sin.' In regards to the same incident, Swinnock writes:

---

[43] Ex. 20:20.
[44] Bunyan, *A Treatise of the Fear of God*, *Miscellaneous Works*, IX:25.
[45] Gurnall, *Christian in Complete Armour*, I:289.
[46] Charnock, *Existence and Attributes of God*, I:98.
[47] *Ibid.*, I:98-99.

> Why doth the mighty possessor of heaven and earth appear at that time in such a state and royalty and magnificence, with such a train of heavenly courtiers, with such thundering volleys of shot, with the mountain smoking under him, and trumpets sounding before him, but to assure us that he is not so contemptible, as to be slighted by any; that he is not impotent, but able to revenge himself on all that affront him; nay to teach us that he will be feared and reverenced in all them that draw nigh to him.[48]

God's 'royalty' and 'magnificence' evoke fear in those to whom he reveals himself. Again, this fear includes a dread of God's wrath, however it is not limited to this; rather, it stems from an admiration of his glory. Swinnock affirms that this 'filial' fear is synonymous with fearing God's name – the fullest revelation of his glory. To make his point,[49] he turns to Deuteronomy 28:58 where the Israelites are exhorted to fear God's name because it declares his holiness. Watson develops this same thought in his exposition of the Lord's Prayer. In regards to the first petition,[50] he asks, 'What is meant by God's name?' He answers, 'As a man is know by his name; so by his attributes of wisdom, power, holiness, and goodness, God is known by his name.'[51]

For Swinnock, God's name reveals his incomparable excellence.[52] Echoing Job, he asks,[53] 'Shall not his excellency make you afraid?'[54] This, according to Swinnock, is the distinction between ungodly and godly fear. The former is focused on a perceived threat whilst the latter is focused on the excellence of God's glory, thus making God 'the proper object of fear.'[55] Swinnock writes, 'But now between God and us there is an infinite distance, and therefore there ought to be, if it were possible, infinite reverence; he is so vastly above and beyond all others in excellency, that he alone deserves the name of excellency, therefore his name is holy and reverend (Ps. 111:9) and he is to be greatly feared. The greatest excellency calleth for the greatest reverence.'[56]

The Nature of Fear

Such 'filial fear' is, as Bunyan puts it, 'the principle from which godly affections flow.'[57] In Swinnock's view, this is the essence of worship:

---

[48] *Christian Man's Calling*, I:96.
[49] *Christian Man's Calling*, I:96-97; and *Incomparableness of God*, IV:387.
[50] Matt. 6:9.
[51] Thomas Watson, *The Lord's Prayer* (1692; 1890; Edinburgh: Banner of Truth, 1999) 38-39.
[52] *Incomparableness of God*, IV:387.
[53] *Ibid.*, IV:386.
[54] Job 13:11.
[55] *Men Are Gods*, IV:311.
[56] *Incomparableness of God*, IV:472.
[57] Bunyan, *Greatness of the Soul, Miscellaneous Works*, IX:152.

Those that worship God give him their hottest love, their highest joy, their deepest sorrow, their strongest faith, and the greatest fear... What Moses calls fearing God (Deut. 6:13), our Saviour quoting, calls worshipping God (Matt. 4:9-10) by a synecdoche, because the former is both a part and a sign of the latter. As when the guard are watching at the court-gate, or on the stairs, and examining those that go in, it is a sign the king is within; so when the fear of God stands at the door of the heart, to examine all that go in, lest the traitor should steal in slyly, it is a sign that God is within, that he sits upon the throne of the soul, and is worshipped there.[58]

From this, it is evident that Swinnock defines worship as a condition of the heart, meaning people worship when they give God their 'hottest love,' 'highest joy,' 'deepest sorrow,' 'strongest faith,' and 'greatest fear.' Charnock agrees, stating, 'Fear, in the Scripture dialect, signifies "the whole worship of God" (Acts 10:35).'[59] Swinnock affirms that 'the deeper our worship comes from the heart, the more delightful it is in God's ears.'[60] Such worship means that the fear of God stands 'at the door of the heart,' ordering (or sanctifying) the soul's affections.[61]

Love

To begin with, the fear of God sanctifies love. Perceiving God to be the greatest good, the soul makes him the object of its love. Baxter describes such love as 'the ruling affection in the sanctified.'[62] For Charnock, 'Love is a commanding affection, a uniting grace; it draws all the faculties of the soul into one centre.'[63] For this reason, Swinnock refers to it as 'the cream of our affections.'[64] As he points out, the understanding embraces God who is 'eternal truth' and the will embraces God who is 'essentially, universally, unchangeably, and infinitely good.'[65] Therefore, God draws out the greatest love from the soul. Like Swinnock, Reynolds deems love to be the 'highest affection.'

---

[58] *Christian Man's Calling*, I:31-32. Similarly, Gurnall sees 'the fear of God' and 'religious worship' as synonymous expressions. *Christian in Complete Armour*, II:470.

[59] Charnock, *Existence and Attributes of God*, I:206.

[60] *Christian Man's Calling*, I:34.

[61] For Baxter's view of the affections, see *Divine Life, Practical Works*, 127,131,152-156,165,183,191,237; *Treatise on Conversion, Practical Works*, 314-320; and *Directions to Weak Christians, Practical Works*, 651. For Bunyan, see *Greatness of the Soul, Miscellaneous Works*, IX:151-154.

[62] Baxter, *Directions and Persuasions, Practical Works*, 608. For Baxter on love for God, see *Christian Directory*, 120-124.

[63] Charnock, *Existence and Attributes of God*, I:272.

[64] *Incomparableness of God*, IV:474.

[65] *Fading of the Flesh*, IV:37.

The Master-Wheele, or first Mover in all the Regular Motions of this Passion, is the *Love of God*, grounded on the right *knowledge* of Him; whereby the Soule being ravished with the apprehension of his infinite *Goodnesse*, is earnestly drawne and *called out*, as it were, to desire an *Union, Vision*, and participation of his Glory and Presence; yeelding up it selfe unto Him... and conforming all its Affections and Actions to his Will.[66]

It is worth noting Reynolds' emphasis upon the relationship between knowledge and love: there is a mutual causality, meaning that the knowledge of God generates love whilst love spawns a desire to grow in the knowledge of God.[67] In this state, the soul is 'ravished' with the apprehension of God's 'infinite Goodnesse.' Interestingly, Reynolds depicts the expression of love in terms such as *desiring, yielding*, and *conforming*. In other words, 'a man giveth himselfe to the thing which he loves.' For this reason, the soul gives itself entirely to God. In this respect, Swinnock quotes Augustine as saying, 'He that is not zealous for God, hath no true love to God: for though love be a passion, yet it delighteth to shew itself in acting for the party beloved.'[68]

With this in mind, Swinnock differentiates between true and false love. He believes some people feign love for God simply because they are interested in acquiring his 'blessings.' He quotes Augustine as saying, 'That love is adulterous, and the love of a harlot, which is greater to the gift than the giver.'[69] For Swinnock, true love is focused upon an object's goodness, not any perceived personal benefits derived from it. He affirms, 'As nothing that a godly man giveth God content him, unless he give God himself, so nothing which God giveth a godly man will satisfy him, unless God giveth himself to him.'[70] Elsewhere, he writes, 'All true love is... a motion of the soul towards the enjoyment of God for himself.'[71] Similarly, Baxter comments, 'He loves him most of all for his infinite perfections and essential excellencies; his infinite power, wisdom, and goodness, simply in himself considered.'[72] Charnock remarks, 'To love God only for his benefits, is to love ourselves first, and him secondarily: to love God for his own goodness and excellency, is a true love of God; a love of him for himself.'[73] Shepard also agrees, 'There is a natural love to Christ, as to one that doth thee good, and for thine own ends; and spiritual, for himself, whereby the Lord only is exalted.'[74] Watson distinguishes between *amor concupiscentiae* (a love of concupiscence) and

---

[66] Reynolds, *Passions and Faculties*, 81-82. His italics.

[67] *Ibid.*, 104.

[68] *Men Are Gods*, IV:369.

[69] *Christian Man's Calling*, II:64.

[70] *Heaven and Hell*, III:249.

[71] *Christian Man's Calling*, II:251. Also see II:272,331.

[72] Baxter, *The Character of a Sound Confirmed Christian, Practical Works*, 701.

[73] Charnock, *Existence and Attributes of God*, II:333. Also see I:148-150.

[74] Shepard, *Parable of the Ten Virgins*, II:49.

amor amicitiae (a love of delight).[75] The former is 'self-love; as when we love another, because he does us a good turn… This is rather to love God's blessing than to love God.' The latter is 'the heart set upon God, as a man's heart is set upon his treasure.'

It is the fear of God that accounts for this difference between true and false love.[76] Devoid of God's glory, the soul is incapable of true love for it is not yet convinced of God's goodness. However, this affection is sanctified when the fear of God takes hold. Love is removed from self and fixed upon God, who is embraced as the greatest good. In this condition, according to Reynolds, the soul 'delighteth to shew itself in acting for the party beloved.' This means the person who loves God obeys God, not reluctantly or begrudgingly, but with delight.

Desire

This 'sanctified' love is always manifested in desire for God. Reminiscent of Augustine, Swinnock affirms, 'desire and delight are the two acts of love, distinguished only by the absence or presence of the object.'[77] Reynolds describes this first 'act' of love as 'the wing of the soule whereby it moveth, and is carried to the thing which it loveth… to feed it selfe upon it, and to be satisfied with it.'[78] Baxter states, 'When God hath once effectually touched the heart with converting grace, it leaves a secret thirsting after him in the soul.'[79] Swinnock maintains that when people know 'the blessed God… the sweetest

---

[75]   Watson, *Body of Divinity*, 6.

[76]   For Swinnock, it is impossible to love God without fearing him. This appears to be a blatant contradiction of 1 Jn. 4:18. However, Swinnock would argue that the apostle John is here speaking of 'servile' fear, not 'filial' fear. It is true that ungodly fear and love are incompatible, but the opposite is true for godly fear and love. For Swinnock, fear of God and love for God are not mutually exclusive; rather, they are inseparable – true love always flows out of 'awful apprehensions' of God's glory. Similarly, Baxter remarks, 'That fear is not filial, and of the right stamp, if love be not its companion… You may fear a thing at the same time when you hate it.' *Directions and Persuasions, Practical Works*, 607. Hesselink notes the same emphasis in Calvin, commenting, 'For Calvin, fear and love are not contradictory but are rather complementary aspects of the same attitude. The fear of God, when understood in this positive sense, like love, "includes faith, and is in fact, properly speaking, produced by faith"… There is, of course, a type of fear which is opposed to love, the servile fear of dread which is the experience of the wicked when they are confronted with God and his wrath. But this is completely different from the childlike fear or reverence which is characteristic of believers.' *Calvin's Concept of the Law*, 128. See *Institutes*, III:II:27, III:XIV:8.

[77]   *Incomparableness of God*, IV:475. Manton makes the same observation. *True Circumcision, Works*, II:38.

[78]   Reynolds, *Passions and Faculties*, 161.

[79]   Baxter, *Treatise on Conversion, Practical Works*, 315.

love, the richest mercy, the surest friend, the chiefest good, the greatest beauty, the highest honour, and the fullest happiness,' they will 'leave the colliers of this world to load themselves with thick clay, and turn merchant adventurer to the other world... for the enjoyment of God.'[80] He argues that such a longing 'for the enjoyment of God' is a sure sign of regeneration, and asks, 'In what channel doth the stream of thy desires run?'[81] If they are set on the world, then the affections are unsanctified.

At this point, Swinnock distinguishes between true and false desire by affirming that God must have 'incomparable desires, panting, longing, yea, fainting, out of vehemency of desire.'[82] This signifies that the Christian must desire God above everything else. The same sentiment is found in Reynolds: 'Desires ought not to bee faint and sluggish, but industrious and painefull.'[83] He adds, 'These affections must have life in them, which bring life after them: Dead desires are deadly desires.'[84] To underscore their importance, Swinnock asks, 'What is the calling which thou followest with greatest eagerness and earnestness?'[85] If it is not God, then there is no love for God. He adds, 'The Christian, who hath the blessed God for his portion, strives and labours, and watcheth and prayeth, and weepeth, and thinks no time too much, no pains too great, no cost enough for the enjoyment of his God.'[86] Knowing that there is no enjoyment of God without conformity to his image, the regenerate also long for holiness 'without which no one will see the Lord.'[87] He comments, 'Now a Christian is described by his hungering and thirsting, his panting and breathing after a perfect conformity to God that thereby he may be prepared for perfect communion with God; but blessed are they which now thus hunger and thirst, for then they shall be filled.'[88] The only thing that prevents the soul's uninhibited enjoyment of God is sin. Recognizing this, the soul hungers and thirsts for righteousness. It knows that this will facilitate its communion with God. From Swinnock's perspective, such an intense longing always sets true desire apart from false desire.

Delight

The second 'act' of love is delight. When the fear of God sanctifies love, the individual naturally rejoices in God. According to Reynolds, 'Delight is

---

[80] *Fading of the Flesh*, IV:28.
[81] *Ibid.*, IV:23.
[82] *Incomparableness of God*, IV:475.
[83] Reynolds, *Passions and Faculties*, 197.
[84] *Ibid.*, 198-199.
[85] *Fading of the Flesh*, IV:25.
[86] *Ibid.*, IV:25.
[87] Heb. 12:14.
[88] *Heaven and Hell*, III:250.

nothing else but the Sabbath of our thoughts, and that sweet tranquility of mind, which we receive from the Presence and Fruition of that good, wherunto our Desires have carried us.'[89] Once the soul obtains the object of its love, it is 'ravished, ecstasied in the presence and enjoyment of God.'[90] Swinnock sees this 'spiritual ecstasy' portrayed in the marriage relationship,[91] commenting, 'The love betwixt Christ and his spouse, which is so fervent that she is sick of love to him, and he died for love to her is set out by the love betwixt husband and wife, to shew how great this love is.'[92] For this reason, he has no difficulty in turning to the book of Canticles for language to describe the soul's enjoyment of God.[93] Based on Canticles 7:11-12,[94] he writes, 'Mark, there in the fields, where no eye beholdeth the sweet meeting of our lips, the close embraces of our arms, the intimate conjunction of our hearts – there I will give

---

[89]   Reynolds, *Passions and Faculties*, 199. For Baxter on delight in God, see *Christian Directory*, 138-142. For the place of joy among the Puritans, see J. Gwyn-Thomas, 'The Puritan Doctrine of Christian Joy' in *Puritan Papers: Vol. II*, ed. J. I. Packer (Phillipsburg: Presbyterian and Reformed, 2001) 119-240. Swinnock states, 'Holy alacrity and joy is not only a crown and credit to, but also a special part of, Christianity.' *Christian Man's Calling*, I:239.

[90]   *Incomparableness of God*, IV:475.

[91]   Jones views 'union with Christ' as a covenantal relationship. Believers are united to Christ by the covenant of grace. This relationship between God and his people is like a marriage covenant – a conjugal relationship. 'Union with Christ,' 194-199.

[92]   *Christian Man's Calling*, I:471-472.

[93]   *Ibid.*, 1:100,117,130,173,182,191,209,226,265,472, II:337,408; *Heaven and Hell*, III:238,355; *Gods Are Men*, IV:128; *Incomparableness of God*, IV:393,507; and *Door of Salvation*, V:149,176. For Owen's use of Canticles, see Ferguson, *John Owen on the Christian Life*, 78-86. Of particular note is Ferguson's comment that 'The Song of Solomon is for *Owen* a transcript of the affections of Christian experience.' *Ibid.*, 78. At times, Swinnock clearly takes the typology too far. By way of example, commenting on Cant. 7:2, he writes, 'By the navel expositors agree that baptism is understood, by which, as children by the navel, the members of the church are nourished... By the belly is meant the Lord's Supper.' *Christian Man's Calling*, I:182. Allegorical interpretation among the Puritans is the subject of some controversy. Paul Jewett makes a helpful distinction by noting that allegorical interpretation is not the same as the interpretation of allegories. Rather, it is concerned with interpreting a text in terms of something else. According to Jewett, there is a 'rational' basis for such allegorising as long as it 'presupposes the unity and continuity of biblical revelation.' After all, the NT authors interpret the OT in terms of Jesus' work. In so doing, however, they never undermine the historicity of the original texts. That is the test. 'Concerning the Allegorical Interpretation of Scripture,' *Westminster Theological Journal* 17 (1954) 1-20.

[94]   'Come, my beloved, let us go out into the country, Let us spend the night in the villages. Let us rise early and go to the vineyards; Let us see whether the vine has budded and its blossoms have opened, and whether the pomegranates have bloomed. There I will give you my love.'

thee my loves.'[95] For Swinnock, this physical intimacy illustrates the soul's satisfaction in God, resulting from its mystical union with Jesus.[96] By virtue of this union, it experiences all that is good in God.[97]

Yet again, Swinnock warns that there is a discernible difference between true and false delight. There are individuals who think 'fondly' of Jesus and, on this basis alone, imagine that they belong to him. Normally, the cause of this 'flashy and washy joy' is God's blessing rather than God's greatness. In highlighting this danger, Swinnock asks, 'What is the feast at which thou sittest with most delight?'[98] If the answer to this question is anything but God, then the soul has not yet embraced him as the greatest good. True delight is not caused by any prospect of heaven or hell, reward or punishment, but by an admiration of God. Swinnock maintains that it is possible to discern between the two by examining one's actions. Quite simply, false delight fails to produce any 'alteration in the man.'[99] Reynolds agrees, 'Delight whetteth and intendeth the actions of the Soule towards the thing wherein it delighteth; it putteth forth more force, and more exactnesse in the doing of them, because it exonerateth the mind of all those dulling Indispositions which unfitted it for Action.'[100] Similarly, Shepard writes, 'The false spirit, having given a man comfort and peace, suffers a man to rest in that state; but the true Spirit, having made the soul taste the love of the Lord, stirreth up the soul to do and work mightily for the Lord.'[101]

True delight manifests itself in putting 'forth more force' in experiencing its object of delight. With this in mind, Swinnock exhorts, 'Speak thyself, whether thou prayest, readest, hearest, singest from the divine nature within, from love

---

[95]   *Christian Man's Calling*, II:408.

[96]   It is imperative to observe the difference between the Puritan concept of 'union with God' and what is normally called 'mysticism.' As Lovelace notes, 'Medieval mysticism shares with Platonic mysticism a common structure: that of a threefold path to God, consisting of purification, contemplation, and final union.' 'The Anatomy of Puritan Piety,' 318. The Puritans, on the other hand, begin with union and stress the mortification of sin, not the purification of the senses.

[97]   Jones demonstrates that from Perkins to Bunyan, the Puritans stress 'union with Christ.' He finds it present in earlier Protestantism; e.g., Calvin who insisted that there is no benefit unless the Holy Spirit engrafts us into Christ. In this union, the mind contemplates God, the affections are centred on God, and the will embraces God. 'In other words,' says Jones, 'there is no part of the believer's human personality that is not affected by the beneficial consequences of union with Christ.' 'Union with Christ,' 186-188. Howard Hageman argues that mystical union with Christ is the 'starting-point' for Calvin's spirituality. 'Reformed Spirituality' in *Protestant Spiritual Traditions*, ed. F. C. Senn (New York: Paulist, 1986) 61.

[98]   *Fading of the Flesh*, IV:24.

[99]   *Door of Salvation*, V:67.

[100]   Reynolds, *Passions and Faculties*, 220.

[101]   Shepard, *Sincere Convert*, 87.

to the infinitely amiable God, from the delight thou takest in communion with him in duties.'[102] Charnock agrees, 'If there is no delight in the means that lead to God, there is no delight in God himself.'[103] In addition, true delight, says Swinnock, expresses itself in delighting 'greatly in his commandments.'[104] In other words, the soul that delights in God also delights in obeying God.[105] In this regard, Kevan rightly concludes that, for the Puritans, 'Only the heart that can say, "I delight to do thy will, O my God" (Ps. 40:8), can be adjudged to be truly converted and godly.'[106]

Trust

When the soul perceives God to be the greatest good – an unchanging good – it trusts in the object of its love. Therefore, says Swinnock, 'God must have our surest love and firmest faith.'[107] As usual, he reminds his readers of the need to distinguish the true from the false. In speaking of 'deceiving' and 'saving' faith, he affirms that the difference 'doth not consist in the strength of persuasion, but in the ground of it.'[108] True faith is the acceptance of God as the greatest good. As with the other renewed affections, it is manifested in action; above all else, it causes the soul to conquer sin. As Swinnock observes, 'When faith brings much fuel, the fire of love will be great. Faith will not suffer a man to live without repentance. The eye of faith which beholds a Christ crucified for sin, affects the heart with sorrow for, and indignation against, those sins that crucified him.'[109] A 'deceiving' faith has no interest in this struggle against sin, thus demonstrating that the fear of God has not yet gripped the affections.

On this basis, Swinnock exhorts his readers to 'draw nigh to God with a humble faith and confidence... as also with a cheerful reverence and awfulness, as to a God infinite in his being and in all his perfections, between whom and thee, a poor worm, there is an infinite distance.'[110] When the knowledge of God is impressed upon the soul, there is an awareness of the 'infinite distance' between the creature and the Creator. This results in drawing nigh to God, the greatest good, 'with a humble faith.' To underscore the connection between trust and the fear of God, Swinnock refers to Psalm 5:7 where David declares, 'I will enter Your house, At Your holy temple I will bow in reverence for You.' From this, Swinnock concludes, 'The Christian, like a net, must have both the

---

[102] *Heaven and Hell*, III:295.

[103] Charnock, *Existence and Attributes of God*, I:151. Also see I:235.

[104] *Door of Salvation*, V:107.

[105] For more on this, see Manton, *Several Sermons Upon the CXIX Psalm*, *Works*, VII-IX.

[106] Kevan, *Grace of Law*, 183.

[107] *Incomparableness of God*, IV:475.

[108] *Door of Salvation*, V:59-60.

[109] *Sinner's Last Sentence*, V:344.

[110] *Ibid.*, V:385.

lead of a holy fear, and the cork of a lively faith… if the cork of faith was without the lead of fear, the net would lie too high; if the lead of fear were without the cork of faith, the net of the soul would fall too low, and so nothing would be caught; but both together lay in the likest place for a good draught.'[111] Watson arrives at the same conclusion, arguing that 'fear' must be 'joined with faith.' He comments, 'Faith and fear go hand in hand. When the soul looks at God's holiness, he fears. When he looks at God's promises, he believes. A godly man trembles, yet trusts.'[112]

Hope

The next affection is hope, which Reynolds defines as 'an earnest and strong inclination and expectation of some great good apprehended as *possible* to be obtained, though not by our owne strength, nor without some intervenient *Difficulties.*'[113] The soul loves God, consequently it desires him, delights in him, and trusts in him. Despite all this, there is an expectation of more. There is the prospect of 'some great good' in the future. In expounding Philippians 1:21,[114] Swinnock identifies this 'great good' as the 'full and immediate fruition of God… the apex of the saint's happiness,'[115] also known as the 'beatifical vision.'[116] At present, the regenerate's greatest desire and delight is God. However, their enjoyment of God is limited by their capacities, the remnants of sin still impairing the perfect functioning of the faculties of the soul. When they are glorified, these restrictions will be removed. At that moment, their desire and delight in God will eclipse anything they have experienced this side of heaven.

In his treatment of this affection, Swinnock warns against false hope; or, what he calls, 'presumption.'[117] Its focus is on a place rather than a person and, consequently, it falls short of true hope, in that it never leads people to a diligent pursuit of that which is good. As with the previous affections, such a pursuit means: first, seeking God through his appointed means; and, second, obeying God's commandments. With this in mind, Reynolds refers to hope as 'an exciting Passion, which moveth every Principle to its proper and speedy operation for gaining that perfection which the Mind so earnestly breathes after.'[118] False hope produces no such thing.

---

[111] *Christian Man's Calling*, I:95.
[112] Watson, *Godly Man's Picture*, 178. He has Heb. 11:7 in mind.
[113] Reynolds, *Passions and Faculties*, 237-238. His italics.
[114] 'For to me, to live is Christ and to die is gain.'
[115] *Heaven and Hell*, III:247.
[116] *Ibid.*, III:248.
[117] *Ibid.*, III:265.
[118] Reynolds, *Passions and Faculties*, 260.

Fear

As evident from the foregoing discussion, the first five affections – when sanctified by the fear of God – are positive responses of the soul toward God. In Swinnock's judgment, the remaining affections are negative inclinations of the soul toward that which infringes upon its enjoyment of God. For starters, there is fear. At this point, a distinction must be made between the fear of God and the fear of sin. For Swinnock, the former refers to the sanctification of the affections by the knowledge of God, thus resulting in obedience. The latter is simply one of the affections. At times, the two are confused. For example, Kevan writes, 'This dread of "impiety," and the realization of their relation to the holy Law of God, engendered that godly fear within the Puritans which has ever been regarded as one of their outstanding characteristics. William Perkins teaches that among the sanctified affections "is the fear of God, a most excellent and wonderful grace of God," and Richard Rogers, likewise, speaks of "fearing most of all to offend God."'[119] Here, Kevan treats the 'fear of God' and the 'fear of sin' as synonymous concepts. For Swinnock, they are not the same thing. Whilst it is impossible to have one without the other, the latter is always the product of the former.

In the words of Reynolds, fear 'is a Griefe, Trouble, Flight, Aversation of some approaching Evill apprehended, either as destructive, or as burthensome to our nature, and not easily resistable by our strength.'[120] Having embraced God as the greatest good, the soul's primary fear is any 'approaching evil' that will disrupt its delight in God. It fears 'lest some or other evil should disturb the peace, or violate the purity of what we love.'[121] According to Swinnock, 'When the new creature's heart leaps with hope of heaven, he is then fullest of fear lest he should displease God.'[122] This fear of sin is not to be confused with the fear of sin's consequences. Swinnock is very clear on this, warning, 'Like the burnt child thou mayest dread the fire of sin, not because it soots and blacks thee, but because it scorches and burns thee.'[123] This echoes Calvin, who writes, 'This mind restrains itself from sinning, not out of dread of punishment alone; but, because it loves and reveres God as Father, it worships and adores him as Lord. Even if there were no hell, it would still shudder at offending him alone.'[124]

In avoiding sin, some people are merely motivated by the horror of sin's repercussions such as suffering or sorrow. For Swinnock, this reveals that, although sin is avoided, it is still loved. It also reveals that there is no true appreciation of sin's malignity or God's majesty. As Bunyan explains, 'If in its own nature it be desirable to thy mind, and only therefore shunned, for fear of

---

[119] Kevan, *Grace of Law*, 176.
[120] Reynolds, *Passions and Faculties*, 278.
[121] *Ibid.*, 105.
[122] *Door of Salvation*, V:32.
[123] *Ibid.*, V:69.
[124] Calvin, *Institutes*, I:II:2. Also see I:III:2.

punishment, that attends the Commission of it: without a doubt thou art none of them that do depart from it.'[125] In referring to the example of Felix in Acts 24:25,[126] Swinnock remarks, 'The sting of sin to the unregenerate is punishment, and the sting of punishment to the regenerate is sin. To fear sin, as it bringeth a heavy rod, usually proceeds from nature; but to fear sin, as it is a wandering from a holy rule, can proceed only from grace.'[127] True fear is exemplified in Joseph's cry when tempted by Potiphar's wife: 'How then could I do this great evil and sin against God?'[128] Joseph feared sin, because his soul perceived it as against a glorious God. In Swinnock's estimation, this is the only acceptable reason for fearing sin. He points out that such fear is never discernible from an individual's 'public' actions when motives are swayed by others, but from 'private' actions when God alone is witness.

Sorrow

When the soul experiences that which it fears (i.e., sin), there is sorrow.[129] Reynolds defines sorrow as 'a perturbation and unquietnesse wrought by the pressure of some *present evill*, which the mind in vaine strugleth with, as finding it selfe alone too impotent for the conflict.'[130] According to Swinnock, it 'springeth from the consideration that thou hast sinned against so good, so pure, so perfect a God, in conformity to whom, and communion with whom, all thy happiness consisteth.'[131] Again:

> The worth and dignity of the object doth exceedingly heighten and aggravate the offence. How horrid then is sin, and of how heinous a nature, when it offendeth and opposeth not kings, the highest of men, not angels, the highest of creatures, but God, the highest of beings; the incomparable God, to whom kings and angels, yea, the whole creation is less than nothing... Sin is incomparably malignant, because the God principally injured by it is incomparably excellent.[132]

Here, Swinnock speaks of the 'worth and dignity' of God whom sin 'offendeth and opposeth.' Seeing this, the soul views sin as 'heinous' and sorrows for it.

---

[125] John Bunyan, *A Holy Life: The Beauty of Christianity, Miscellaneous Works*, IX:274.

[126] 'But as he was discussing righteousness, self-control and the judgment to come, Felix became frightened and said, "Go away for the present, and when I find time I will summon you."'

[127] *Door of Salvation*, V:69-70.

[128] Gen. 39:9.

[129] For Baxter on sorrow for sin, see *Christian Directory*, 293-296.

[130] Reynolds, *Passions and Faculties*, 223. His italics.

[131] *Heaven and Hell*, III:341. By way of illustration, Swinnock refers to two 'famous' examples: Peter and Mary. *Christian Man's Calling*, I:188.

[132] *Incomparableness of God*, IV:456.

Swinnock describes several ways in which sin 'offendeth and opposeth' God. Most notably, it opposes his attributes: 'unrighteousness' opposes his justice; 'folly,' his wisdom; 'murmuring,' his patience; 'weakness,' his power; 'unthankfulness,' his mercy; and 'ignorance,' his knowledge. 'In all these,' says Swinnock, 'sin disgraceth his holiness, which is his glory, and the glory of all his attributes.'[133] He also affirms that sin opposes God's existence, remarking, 'Truly, sin is such a monster, such a devil, that were its power equal to its spite, and its strength to its malice, the living God should not live a moment... all sin is God-murder.'[134] Shepard conveys a similar sentiment, stating, 'Thou has sinned, and that grievously, against a great God... First, in every sin thou dost strike God, and fling a dagger at the heart of God. Second, in every sin thou dost spite against God... Third, in every sin thou dost disthrone God, and settest thyself above God.'[135] For Swinnock, and his contemporaries, this antagonistic relationship between God and sin leads the regenerate to comprehend their personal enmity towards God, and to sorrow accordingly. He declares:

> Oh how odious, how loathsome, how abominable is sin, that breaks the law, slights the authority, dishonours the name, and to its utmost dethrones and destroys the being of this incomparable God, this self-sufficient, independent, absolutely perfect, eternal, incomprehensible, infinite being, which alone deserves the name of being, and to which all other beings are no beings! Reader, should this God of glory appear to thee... and shew thee a glimpse of his excellent glory, that is above the heavens... what wouldst thou then think of sin? Oh, what wouldst thou then think of thyself for thy sins? Shouldst thou not have other thoughts of sin, and of thyself for sin, than ever yet thou hast had? Wouldst thou not even loathe thyself for being so base, so vile, so unworthy, yea, so mad as to offend and affront, and fight against such a God?[136]

When people catch a glimpse of the 'incomparable God,' they begin to appreciate 'how odious, how loathsome, how abominable sin is.' These thoughts of sin are the direct result of proper thoughts of God. In this, Swinnock's emphasis on the understanding as the starting-point for the 'fear of God' is again evident. When the knowledge of God enters the mind, it embraces the affections thereby sanctifying them. This fear of God, says Swinnock, is expressed in an attitude of true (or 'evangelical') humiliation, which consists 'partly in mourning for sin, partly in turning from sin.'[137]

This 'mourning' and 'turning' distinguishes godly sorrow from ungodly sorrow. Swinnock explains, 'There are two words used by the Holy Ghost for

---

[133] *Ibid.*, IV:458.

[134] *Ibid.*, IV:458-459. Also see *Door of Salvation*, V:178.

[135] Shepard, *Sincere Convert*, 94.

[136] *Incomparableness of God*, IV:459.

[137] *Christian Man's Calling*, I:187.

repentance μεταμελεία (Matt. 27:3) and μετανοία (2 Tim. 2:25); the former signifieth sorrow for a fault committed, the latter after-wit, a change of the mind, or making wise for the future. The former may be in the unregenerate.'[138] They never experience godly sorrow, because they never feel the burden of their sin as committed against a glorious God. They have not embraced God as the 'cream of their affections,' therefore their heart never breaks on account of their sin. And, consequently, there is no change in behaviour. After betraying Jesus, Judas 'felt remorse,' yet he 'went away and hanged himself.'[139] From this, Swinnock concludes that it is possible to 'repent' without having one's heart melted for sinning against God.

In marked contrast, godly sorrow is expressed in 'lamenting sin' and 'leaving sin.' Swinnock comments, 'The Christian who hath truly repented is so sensible of the weight of sin and wrath of God, that he is resolved never more to meddle with those burning coals; alas! they are too heavy for him.'[140] He is not alone in making this distinction. Shepard states that 'true humiliation is ever accompanied with hearty reformation,' thus distinguishing it from 'cold,' 'hypocritical,' or 'legal' repentance.[141] He adds, 'In their obedience, the one takes up duties out of love to Christ, to have him; and hence he mourns daily, because Christ is no greater gainer by him; the other out of love to himself, merely to save his own soul; and hence he mourns for his sins, because they may damn him.'[142] In the same way, Burroughs writes:

> There are many who are struck with many fears and terrors for sin, but these are never humbled for sin aright... Why? Because the humiliation for sin that is right must be a humiliation for it as it is the greatest evil of all; and it is the greatest evil as it is against God himself... This is not the thing that usually takes the hearts of men and women in their trouble for sin. It is the fear of the wrath of God, the fear of hell, and an accusing conscience that flashes the very fire of hell in their faces... There can be no humiliation deep enough unless the soul is humbled for sin because it has sinned against God.[143]

For Burroughs, the connection between the apprehension of sin's severity and God's holiness is paramount to the development of godly sorrow. Gurnall concurs, 'Thus we might say to such selfish mourners, "We perceive that if thou couldst but save the life of thy soul from eternal death and damnation, though the glory of God miscarried, thou couldst be pleased well enough." But

---

[138] *Door of Salvation*, V:68.

[139] Matt. 27:3-5. For similar examples, see Cain (Gen. 4:13-16) and Saul (1 Sam. 26:21; 28:7). For Calvin on true and false repentance, see *Institutes*, III:III:4.

[140] *Christian Man's Calling*, I:189.

[141] Shepard, *Sincere Convert*, 36,60.

[142] *Ibid.*, 23.

[143] Burroughs, *Evil of Evils*, 85.

know, that a gracious soul's mourning runs in another channel.'[144]

Hatred

The last affection is hatred. When the fear of God embraces the whole man, sin becomes the object of the soul's loathing because it is the object of God's loathing. Swinnock states, 'There is an antipathy in his nature against the smallest sin, as sin is contrary to his being, law, and honour. Though he is so perfect a God that no sin can be hurtful to him, yet he is so pure a God that every sin is hateful to him.'[145] Reynolds explains that sin is unchangeable, therefore our hatred of it must be continual; sin is impudent, therefore our hatred of it must be resolved; and sin is intense, therefore our hatred of it must be unrelenting.[146] This detestation of sin is the direct result of that knowledge which enters the mind and embraces the affections. Swinnock observes, 'They who know the holiness of God... know that sin is loathsome to him, because contrary to his holy nature, and therefore they hate it.'[147] Again, 'He only hath hateful thoughts of sin, and self-loathing apprehensions because of it, who hath seen the great and glorious, the good and gracious God, whose authority is condemned, whose law is violated, whose name is dishonoured, whose image is defaced, and whose love is abused by it.'[148] Baxter agrees, 'You can no further know what sin is than you know what God is, whom you sin against.'[149]

In general, the Puritans go to great lengths to unmask the gravity of sin in order to create sensitivity toward it. They expect this sensitivity to produce hostility. This approach is captured in the words of Ralph Venning: 'It cannot but be extremely useful to let men see what sin is: how prodigiously vile, how deadly mischievous, and therefore how monstrously ugly and odious a thing sin is. Thus a way may be made... for hating sin, and repenting for and from it, thereby taking a holy, just and good revenge on it and ourselves.'[150] The focus of this 'good revenge' is summarized in the term 'abhorrence.' The Puritans maintain that a true awareness of humanity's sinfulness and God's holiness always fosters an attitude of disgust toward sin. Their agreement with Calvin is again evident. He writes:

Primal worthiness cannot come to mind without the sorry spectacle of our foulness and dishonour presenting itself by way of contrast, since in the person of the first man we have fallen from our original condition. From this source arise abhorrence and displeasure with ourselves, as well as true humility; and thence is

---

[144]   Gurnall, *Christian in Complete Armour*, I:429.

[145]   *Ibid.*, II:473.

[146]   Reynolds, *Passions and Faculties*, 132-133.

[147]   *Christian Man's Calling*, III:155.

[148]   *Incomparableness of God*, IV:377.

[149]   Baxter, *Christian Directory*, 90.

[150]   Venning, *Sinfulness of Sin*, 18.

kindled a new zeal to seek God, in whom each of us may recover those good things which we have utterly and completely lost.[151]

Here, Calvin equates self-abhorrence with 'true humility.' For him, it is the product of a deep conviction concerning the severity of sin. In commenting on 2 Corinthians 7:10,[152] he notes that the apostle Paul 'calls it "sorrow... according to God" when we not only abhor punishment but hate and abominate sin itself, because we know that it displeases God.'[153] The Puritans agree. Watson comments, 'A sinner is well-conceited of himself while he dresses himself by the flattering glass of presumption. But if he knew how loathsome and disfigured he was in God's eye, he would abhor himself in dust.'[154] Charnock writes, 'True piety is to hate ourselves, deny ourselves, and cleave solely to the service of God.'[155] Again, 'A love of holiness cannot be without a hatred of everything that is contrary to it.'[156] Similarly, in Swinnock's thinking, this hatred of sin invariably turns people upon themselves. Recognizing the corruption of their nature, they hate their own unholiness: 'As for man, he is a sink of sin, a sty of filth, overspread from head to foot with the leprosy of sin (Gen. 6:5); and therefore, instead of comparing with God for holiness, is bound to abhor himself for his unholiness.'[157] Again, 'Truly this poor sinner, beholding himself in the glass of law, and viewing those hellish spots of sin all over his soul and body, he abhorreth himself in dust and ashes.'[158] Swinnock affirms that those who fear God avoid sin because they hate it. The knowledge of God and self has penetrated the affections, impressing upon them the severity of sin by virtue of its animosity to God – the object of their love.

It is this loathing that makes a divorce between sin and the soul, thus differentiating true and false hatred. Reynolds expresses this difference as follows: 'If hee doth still retaine some privy exceptions, some reserved and covered delights... this is rather a personated than a true hatred, a meteor of the braine, than an affection of the Soule.'[159] Swinnock is in full agreement, asking, 'Does thou hate and fight against sin as sin, and so against every sin? for all true hatred is against the whole kind. Dost thou loathe it as much when it riseth in thy heart, as when it rageth in thy life? In thy dearest friends, as in thy bitterest enemies?[160] This hatred is expressed in fighting against 'every sin.' In

---

[151] Calvin, *Institutes*, II:I:2.
[152] 'For the sorrow that is according to the will of God produces a repentance without regret, leading to salvation, but the sorrow of the world produces death.'
[153] Calvin, *Institutes*, III:III:7.
[154] Watson, *Mischief of Sin*, 5.
[155] Charnock, *Existence and Attributes of God*, I:121.
[156] *Ibid.*, II:118.
[157] *Incomparableness of God*, IV:404.
[158] *Door of Salvation*, V:205.
[159] Reynolds, *Passions and Faculties*, 143.
[160] *Door of Salvation*, V:101-102.

other words, there is a desire to identify and mortify sin wherever it is found. Baxter remarks, 'In every truly converted man, the chief bent of his heart and life is against sin, and his chief desire and endeavour is to destroy it.'[161]

The Effect of Fear

Having perceived God to be the greatest good, the soul embraces him as the object of the cream of its affections. In this state of renewal, the affections function correctly. Love for God replaces love for self. Fear of sin replaces desire for sin. Sorrow for sin replaces delight in sin. Hatred of self replaces hatred of God. As far as Swinnock is concerned, this impartation of the fear of God – the proper ordering of the affections – is holiness. In this state, the regenerate cleanse themselves 'from all defilement of flesh and spirit, perfecting holiness in the fear of God.'[162] Like many Puritans, Gurnall sees this 'holiness in the fear of God' exemplified in Job.'[163] Evidently, Job apprehended something of God's majesty. This made him aware of the evil of sin, which, in turn, led him to abhor it. For this reason, Job is described as a man 'fearing God and turning away from evil.'[164] The proper ordering of the affections is always evident in such an earnest desire for holiness. Baxter writes, 'If you had the fear of God, it would rouse you out of your slothfulness.'[165]

In Swinnock's opinion, this 'perfecting holiness in the fear of God' has both a positive and negative expression, in that it includes avoiding what is forbidden and practicing what is commanded. He challenges his readers: 'Consider, if thou art a believer, thy predominant new nature inclines thee to positive as well as negative holiness.'[166] Again, 'Consider, sanctification, repentance, or sound, saving conversion, consisteth in positive as well as negative holiness; nay, more especially and principally in positive holiness, as that which consummateth and perfecteth the work.'[167] Swinnock gives greater importance to positive holiness, because it corresponds to what he calls 'sins of omission,' which 'are the ground of, and make way for, sins of commission.'[168] He proceeds to explain the difference between the two by affirming that 'in every command there is a precept and a prohibition... a precept enjoining some duty, and a prohibition forbidding the contrary.'[169] When people neglect to do what the precept 'enjoins,' they are guilty of sins of omission. When they fail to

---

[161] Baxter, *Treatise on Conversion, Practical Works*, 330.
[162] 2 Cor. 7:1. See *WCF*, XIII:3.
[163] Gurnall, *Christian in Complete Armour*, I:419
[164] Job 1:1,3; 42:5-6.
[165] Baxter, *Saints' Everlasting Rest, Practical Works*, 44.
[166] *Sinner's Last Sentence*, V:405.
[167] *Ibid.*, V:400.
[168] *Ibid.*, V:328.
[169] *Ibid.*, V:319. Charnock makes the same distinction. *Existence and Attributes of God*, I:25,93.

do what the precept 'forbids,' they are guilty of sins of commission. The latter proceeds from the former, thereby indicating that actual sins are the fruit of unsanctified affections. He explains:

> All sin springeth from this, the departure of the heart from God (Jer. 2:5; Heb. 3:12), and the want of true love to, and fear of, his majesty (1 Jn. 5:3; Jn. 15), which are sins of omission. Where there is no love to God, there is no care to forbear what he forbids... and where there is no fear of God, all manner of wickedness will abound (Ps. 36:1-2). David concludes a wicked man's omission from his sins of commission... His scandalous practices, and sins of commission, tell me that he is guilty of inward omissions, that there is no fear of God before his eyes.[170]

Here, Swinnock identifies the origin of 'all sin' as 'the want of true love to, and fear of God's majesty.' In other words, sins of commission are the result of not loving him, trusting him, and desiring him. With the affections misplaced, the will chooses amiss, thereby resulting in actual sins.

Elsewhere, Swinnock asserts that living 'without the love and fear of God, without delight in him, and communion with him... may be a greater sign of the reign of sin, and thereby of an unregenerate state, than the commission of some gross actual transgressions.'[171] For this reason, Swinnock is more concerned with positive holiness than negative holiness. He desires to address the root problem; namely, the fact that sinners rob 'God of that love, and fear, and trust which they owe him in their hearts.'[172] This necessarily means 'that a negative religion, or negative Christianity, is not enough,' 'that nothing short of practical godliness will speak a man's estate safe,' and 'that the condition of men merely civil, and negatively religious, will be woeful at that day.'[173] In short, holiness is forsaking evil (i.e., negative holiness) because of the fear of God (i.e., positive holiness), the former depending upon the latter. For this reason, 'God will not be put off with the body, without the soul of religion;'[174] i.e., obeying the will of God 'with reverence, humility, faith, love, joy.'[175] In such positive holiness, 'God takes most pleasure.'[176]

Conclusion

This chapter's purpose was to demonstrate that the sanctification of the affections is pivotal to Swinnock's concept of the 'fear of God.' He writes,

---

[170] *Ibid.*, V:325-326.
[171] *Ibid.*, V:342.
[172] *Ibid.*, V:337.
[173] *Ibid.*, V:352-370.
[174] *Ibid.*, V:377.
[175] *Ibid.*, V:324.
[176] *Ibid.*, V:412.

'Before conversion, hope and fear, joy and grief, humility and resolution, were repugnant to each other; but regeneration makes them good friends.'[177] By renewal after God's image, 'the affections are wound up accordingly, and so make a complete harmony of the whole.'[178] In this way, the fear of God becomes the governing principle in the soul. As described by John Flavel, 'This fear is a gracious habit or principle planted by God in the soul, whereby the soul is kept under an holy awe of the eye of God, and from thence is inclined to perform and do what pleaseth him, and to shun and void whatever he forbids and hates.'[179]

---

[177] *Door of Salvation*, V:32.

[178] *Ibid.*

[179] John Flavel, *A Practical Treatise on Fear: Its Varieties, Uses, Causes, Effects and Remedies, Works*, III:252.

Chapter Five

Obedience: The Expression of Love for God

At the foundation of Swinnock's spirituality is a teleological understanding of the image of God in humanity that is based upon faculty-humour psychology. This means Swinnock views sanctification as the proper ordering of the soul's faculties after the image of God. How is this expressed in experience? The starting-point is obedience. As noted in the previous chapter, the distinguishing feature of positive holiness is delight in God's law. Swinnock declares, 'If thou art a Christian indeed, the image of God is imprinted on thee; now this image consisteth in knowledge, righteousness, and true holiness. Righteousness conforms thy heart to the whole second table of the moral law; holiness conforms it to the whole first table, and knowledge completes this conformity to both.'[1] Charnock concurs, 'It is a renewing in the heart that law which was written in the heart of Adam… holiness towards God, which includes the duties of the first table; righteousness, including the duties of the second table.'[2]

The Fear of God and the Law

Traditionally, Protestant theologians have identified three uses of the law.[3] First, there is the *usus civilis* or *politicus*. In the words of Donald MacLeod, 'This refers to its function as an instrument of civil government for the preservation and promotion of civil order.'[4] He adds, 'On this, Luther and Calvin are in complete agreement.'[5]

Second, there is the *usus spiritualis* or *theologicus*. In this capacity, as MacLeod notes, the law 'is disciplinary and educative, a mirror of sins, inducing repentance and creating and sustaining the sense of spiritual need out of which faith is born.'[6] Once again, he observes that 'here is something on

---

[1] *Door of Salvation*, V:107-108.
[2] Charnock, *Nature of Regeneration*, *Works*, III:119.
[3] The following definitions are taken from W. R. Godfrey, 'Law and Gospel' in *New Dictionary of Theology*, eds. S. B. Ferguson, D. F. Wright, and J. I. Packer (Downers Grove: Inter-Varsity Press, 1988) 379.
[4] Donald MacLeod, 'Luther and Calvin on the Place of the Law' in *Living the Christian Life* (London: Westminster Conference, 1974) 5.
[5] *Ibid.*
[6] *Ibid.*, 7-8.

which Luther and Calvin are in complete agreement.'[7] For his part, Luther writes, 'Now when a man has learned from the commandments, and perceived his own incapacity, then he will be anxious to know how to keep the commandment, for unless he fulfils the commandment he will be damned. This will take away all his pride, and he will become as nothing in his own eyes; he will find nothing in himself to make him acceptable to God.'[8] Similarly, for Calvin, 'The law is like a mirror. In it we contemplate our weakness, then the iniquity arising from this, and finally the curse coming from both – just as a mirror shows us the spots on our face. For when the capacity to follow righteousness fails him, man must be mired in sins.'[9]

Third, there is the *usus in renatis*. Here, the law is viewed as directing the regenerate in holy living. It is at this point that Calvin and Luther appear to disagree. This disagreement is explained by Calvin's positive view of the law as opposed to Luther's negative view. Luther is so focused on the antithesis between the law (a righteousness of works) and the gospel (a righteousness of grace) that he loses sight of the fact that they are actually two modes in the same plan of salvation. John Hesselink remarks, 'Luther... following the negative strictures of the apostle Paul in his controversies against the Judaizers, saw the law primarily as a corollary of sin.'[10] Edward Dowey adds, 'Luther's apprehension of law as a curse and a killer, from Scripture in correlation with his own experience as a monk and a priest, made it forever impossible for him to consider a third, positive use for the Law, the *usus in renatis*, in the life of the believer. It is precisely here that the great debate with Calvin and Calvinism begins.'[11]

The Bible indeed points to an antithetical relationship between the law and the gospel, however Calvin affirms that this must be interpreted in terms of the threefold relationship between the two.[12] First, there is a unity of substance. Second, there is a distinction in the form of administration. Third, there is an antithesis of letter and Spirit.[13] Concerning Calvin's interpretation of the latter, Hesselink remarks:

> What separates the law from the gospel like fire and water is the matter of justification. There are two kinds of promises and two kinds of righteousness: legal promises and evangelical promises, the righteousness of works and the

---

[7]   *Ibid.*
[8]   Luther, *The Freedom of a Christian in Reformation Writings of Martin Luther* (London: Lutterworth Press, 1952) I:361. Also see *Bondage of the Will, Works*, XXXIII:128,133-134.
[9]   Calvin, *Institutes*, II:VII:7.
[10] Hesselink, *Calvin's Concept of the Law*, 255.
[11] Edward Dowey, 'Law in Luther and Calvin,' *Theology Today* 41 (1984) 151.
[12] Hesselink, *Calvin's Concept of the Law*, 160-187.
[13] For this antithesis in the Bible, see Jn. 1:17; Rom. 4:15, 5:20; 2 Cor. 3:6; Gal. 3:19-20; and Heb. 12:18-20.

righteousness of faith... These are two opposing systems, which are totally irreconcilable... When the law is separated from the promises and the gospel, where it is viewed according to its distinctive properties in contrast to those of the gospel, the antithesis is profound and radical.[14]

For Calvin, therefore, the antithesis is not between an accurate interpretation of the law and the gospel, but between an inaccurate interpretation of the law and the gospel. When the law is viewed as a ladder to heaven (a righteousness of works), then it stands in an antithetical relationship to the gospel (a righteousness of grace). Calvin refuses to allow this antithetical relationship to detract from his positive view of the law, as an expression of God's eternal will.[15] For Calvin, the law is not a reaction to humanity's fall nor is it merely an aspect of Israel's religion. On the contrary, in the words of Hesselink, 'for Calvin, the law is something primary, basic, and permanent in the wisdom and plan of God.'[16] He adds, 'When the law is viewed and experienced according to its original purpose, i.e., as a gift and guide to God's children, then it is a peculiar organ of the Holy Spirit for renewing and reforming people in the image of God. Hence its chief function is for those who have been regenerated by the Spirit of God.'[17] According to Calvin, the law is useful to the regenerate, in that: first, it gives a clearer understanding of God's will for their lives; and second, it continues to convict, thereby cultivating a sense of need within them.[18]

Contrary to popular misconception, this emphasis on the third use of the law does not lead to legalism.[19] As Hesselink observes, Calvin is careful to guard against this: 'He does not hesitate to remind his readers of God's high demands. But preceding the imperative, "thou shalt" is the indicative, "I am." The grace of God does not render superfluous but rather makes possible the imperative. God gives before he commands. And in his covenant he gives nothing less than himself.'[20] Again, 'To obey the law means to testify gratefully to God's salvation. The only obedience acceptable to him is that which issues spontaneously and cheerfully from a new heart. We should delight to do his will and yield ourselves willingly to him.'[21] In the New Covenant, Jeremiah

---

[14] Hesselink, *Calvin's Concept of the Law*, 195-196.

[15] Calvin, *Institutes*, I:XVII:2, II:VIII:5,59, II:IX:4.

[16] Hesselink, *Calvin's Concept of the Law*, 19.

[17] *Ibid.*, 251.

[18] Calvin, *Institutes*, II:VII:12.

[19] The misuse of the third use of the law usually leads to one of two extremes. The first is antinomianism; that is, the Christian is free from the law as a governing principle in life. See Kevan, *Grace of Law*, 22-28. The second is neonomianism (or moralism); that is, the Christian's obedience becomes a constituent element of justifying faith. See *Ibid.*, 203-207.

[20] Hesselink, *Calvin's Concept of the Law*, 107.

[21] *Ibid.*

speaks of God's putting his law within the people[22] whereas Ezekiel speaks of God's putting his Spirit within them.[23] An appreciation of this relationship between the law and the Spirit is pivotal. Because of the new birth, the regenerate love God with all their heart, soul, and mind, thereby fulfilling the law.[24] Therefore, as Hesselink remarks, 'Law and love are corollaries, not contraries.'[25]

The Puritans are in agreement with Calvin.[26] According to the Westminster divines, justification is the act of God justifying sinners 'by imputing the obedience and satisfaction of Christ unto them, they receiving and resting on him and his righteousness by faith; which faith they have not of themselves, it is the gift of God.'[27] However, having been justified by faith, they are still bound to obey the law.[28] This duty is not 'contrary to the grace of the gospel,' because it is 'the Spirit of Christ subduing and enabling the will of man to do that freely and cheerfully which the will of God, revealed in the law, requireth to be done.'[29] For the Puritans, therefore, there is no antithesis between law and gospel. As a matter of fact, as Young Song observes, the law is the point of

---

[22] Jer. 31:31-33.

[23] Ezek. 36:26-27.

[24] Matt. 22:37-40. See Lev. 19:18; Deut. 6:3-5, 10:12-13; and Rom. 10:13.

[25] Hesselink, *Calvin's Concept of the Law*, 108.

[26] Holmes Rolston argues that the Puritans distort Calvin's concept of God's grace by defining humanity's relationship with God in legal terms. *John Calvin Versus the Westminster Confession* (Richmond: John Knox Press, 1972) 36. Also see Rolston, 'Responsible Man in Reformed Theology: Calvin Versus the Westminster Confession,' *Scottish Journal of Theology* 23 (1970) 129-155. For a similar position, see McGiffert, 'The Perkinsian Moment of Federal Theology,' 118-148. According to these authors, the prelapsarian covenant of works resulted from the Puritans' concept of people as legal creatures, whose relationship with God is defined in terms of moral obedience. Accordingly, Puritan federal theology focuses on the conditional covenant in Adam rather than the unconditional covenant in Christ. For Rolston and McGiffert, this entire schema is foreign to Calvin. For the opposite view, see Peter Lillback, *The Binding of God: Calvin's Role in the Development of Covenant Theology* (Grand Rapids: Baker Books, 2001). David McWilliams critiques Rolston's thesis in 'The Covenant Theology of the *Westminster Confession of Faith* and Recent Criticism,' *Westminster Theological Journal* 53 (1991) 109-124. For him, Rolston's view is explained by his denial of the historicity of Adam. *Ibid.*, 113. In addition, he argues that Rolston's basic problem with federalism arises from his commitment to universalism: 'The existential discontent with federalism is the fruition of a basic antagonism to a fundamental element of Reformed theology, namely, *particularism.*' *Ibid.*, 115. For further discussion on the relationship between Calvin and the *WCF*, see David Weir, *The Origins of the Federal Theology in Sixteenth-Century Reformation Thought* (Oxford University Press, 1990).

[27] *WCF*, XI:I.

[28] *WCF*, XIX:V.

[29] *WCF*, XIX:VII.

contact between the covenant of works and the covenant of grace since obedience is fundamental to both covenants.[30] However, the focus shifts from the obedience of the Christian to the obedience of Christ – the covenant of works having been fulfilled in the covenant of grace. Peter Lillback explains, 'It is really God who keeps the covenant for his people, since he enables them in Christ's righteousness to receive the blessings for keeping the covenant. This is why the covenant emphasizes obedience, but never allows room for meritorious works.'[31]

For the Puritans, therefore, the regenerate are not free from obeying the law, but free to obey it in accordance with the New Covenant. Again, this emphasis often results in the erroneous charge of 'legalism.' However, as Kevan rightly acknowledges, 'Legalism is the abuse of the Law as a means of obtaining a meritorious standing before God; it is the use of the Law "as pharisaically conceived," and an employment of it in its outward form without regard to its inward demands... The "legalism" of Puritanism is a "bogey" constructed by prejudiced imagination from the popular caricature of the God-fearing Puritan and from ignorance of what he taught.'[32] As is evident in Swinnock, obedience is not an attempt to obtain a meritorious standing before God; rather, it is the effect of the fear of God, which inclines the regenerate to positive holiness. He comments, 'Indeed, the gospel is a law of liberty, but not a law of licentiousness (Jas. 1:25). It freeth us from the curse, but not from the commands, of the law. A true Christian is not ἄνομος, without law, but ἔννομος, under the law to Christ (1 Cor. 9:21).'[33]

The Fear of God and the Sermon on the Mount

Swinnock warns, 'There is much counterfeit coin in the world, that goeth current among men, as if it were as good as the best; so there is a great deal of counterfeit holiness in the world, a great deal of civility, of morality, of common grace, which is taken for (or rather mistaken) by men for true saving grace; much fancy is taken for faith, presumption for hope, self-love for saint-love, and worldly sighs for godly sorrow.'[34] Swinnock quotes Jesus' words, in the Sermon on the Mount, as a warning against this error: 'For I say to you that unless your righteousness surpasses that of the scribes and Pharisees, you will

---

[30] Young Song, *Theology and Piety in the Reformed Federal Thought of William Perkins and John Preston* (Lewiston: Edwin Miller Press, 1998) 50.

[31] Lillback, *Binding of God*, 195.

[32] Kevan, *Grace of Law*, 259.

[33] *Pastor's Farewell*, IV:95. Antinomianism was a constant fear among the Puritans. For the controversy in New England, see William Stoever, 'Nature, Grace and John Cotton: The Theological Dimension in the New England Antinomian Controversy,' *Church History* 44 (1975) 22-33.

[34] *Heaven and Hell*, III:287.

not enter the kingdom of heaven.'[35] In this sermon, Jesus demonstrates that the Pharisees were rigorous in their observance of the law,[36] plus conscientious in their giving, praying, and fasting.[37] In Swinnock's view, they 'were famous for gifts and parts,' yet 'infamous for profaneness.' On the basis of Jesus' warning in Matthew 7:22-23,[38] Swinnock cautions that it is possible to 'pray like a saint, to preach like an angel, and yet to practice like a devil.'[39] In simple terms, the Pharisees' problem was that 'there was in them... one thing wanting, and that was the regeneration of their natures.'[40] Swinnock says that 'their practices were seemingly good, but their principles really bad. The tree was corrupt, and therefore could not bring forth good fruit (Matt. 7:17).'[41] In brief, they served the wrong master, because God was not the object of their love.[42]

Consistent with his contemporaries, Swinnock views the Sermon on the Mount as the definitive statement concerning the nature of that righteousness which belongs to Jesus' followers.[43] It is the fruit of regeneration as evidenced in sanctified affections. For Swinnock, this is clearly portrayed in the beatitudes as found in Matthew 5:3-10.[44] As Don Carson explains, the beatitudes constitute a stylistic devise known as 'inclusion,' meaning that everything bracketed between the first and last beatitudes can be included under the same theme.[45] In the first beatitude, Jesus declares, 'Blessed are the poor in spirit, for theirs is the kingdom of heaven.'[46] In the last beatitude, he declares, 'Blessed are those who have been persecuted for the sake of righteousness, for theirs is the kingdom of heaven.'[47] Hence, the inclusion is marked by the phrase 'kingdom of heaven.' This is important, as Lloyd-Jones observes, for it makes the beatitudes a single unit. In them, there is a 'description of what every

---

[35] Matt. 5:20. *Christian Man's Calling*, III:17; *Heaven and Hell*, III:218; *Door of Salvation*, V:55; and *Sinner's Last Sentence*, V:358.
[36] Matt. 5:21-48.
[37] Matt. 6:1-18.
[38] 'Many will say to Me on that day, "Lord, Lord, did we not prophesy in Your name, and in Your name cast out demons, and in Your name perform many miracles?" And then I will declare to them, "I never knew you; DEPART FROM ME, YOU WHO PRACTICE LAWLESSNESS."'
[39] *Door of Salvation*, V:53-54.
[40] *Heaven and Hell*, III:218.
[41] *Door of Salvation*, V:55.
[42] Matt. 6:21-24.
[43] There are well over one hundred citations from the Sermon on the Mount (Matt. 5-7), permeating Swinnock's works. He quotes more than fifty percent of the Sermon.
[44] *Christian Man's Calling*, 1:40,187,206,II:190; *Incomparableness of God*, IV:508; *Door of Salvation*, V:44,94,144; and *Heaven and Hell*, III:250.
[45] Don Carson, *The Sermon on the Mount* (Grand Rapids: Baker Books, 1978) 16.
[46] Matt. 5:3.
[47] Matt. 5:10.

Christian is meant to be.'[48] Thus, the beatitudes constitute a whole, portraying the essence of repentance and its corresponding righteousness.[49]

This is Swinnock's approach to the beatitudes. He believes that they provide a composite picture of an individual who truly fears God. To begin with, the individual is 'poor in spirit.' For Swinnock, this has nothing to do with physical poverty; rather, the 'poor in spirit' are the 'broken-hearted' who possess a 'hungry soul.'[50] They recognize that they are without moral virtues adequate to commend themselves to God. In this state, they are utterly dependent upon God's grace. Furthermore, their poverty of spirit causes them to 'mourn,' that is, they are troubled by the very nature of sin.[51] They perceive sin's opposition to God, and grieve because of it. In turn, this sorrow cultivates meekness – humility in God's presence. Their proper self-assessment obliterates their self-assurance and self-reliance. In this condition, they 'hunger and thirst after righteousness.' In respect to this verse, Swinnock writes, 'Now a Christian is described by his hungering and thirsting, his panting and breathing after a perfect conformity to God, that thereby he may be prepared for perfect communion with God; but blessed are they which now thus hunger and thirst, for then they shall be filled.'[52] When people perceive the seriousness of their sin, they long to mortify it. In the words of Lloyd-Jones, 'If only we saw the things of which we are guilty so continually in the sight of God, and in the sight of utter holiness, we should hate them even as God himself does. That is a great reason for hungering and thirsting after righteousness – the hatefulness of sin.'[53] To this point, the beatitudes focus on people's awareness of their need. The remaining beatitudes are concerned with the disposition that results from this awareness.

The expression *fear of God* is not found in the beatitudes. Nevertheless, it is enshrined therein. Consequently, Jesus' words provide a standard by which people may determine if they fear God. This is particularly true of the first beatitude. For Swinnock, poverty of spirit is a sure sign of the fear of God because it issues from a correct view of sin. In defining the poor in spirit,

---

[48]   Martyn Lloyd-Jones, *Studies in the Sermon on the Mount* (Grand Rapids: Eerdmans, 1962) I:33.

[49]   Returning to Swinnock's teleological understanding of the image of God, it is apparent that the beatitudes are the key to happiness. Humanity's capacity to enjoy God was lost at the fall when Adam's faculties were corrupted. By regeneration, the soul is again united to God. The affections are properly ordered, meaning the soul once again finds its enjoyment in God. This soul is characterized by poverty of spirit, sorrow, meekness, and longing for righteousness. Therefore, this God-fearing soul is 'blessed.' Bolton conveys this reality as follows: 'To fear God... is the only way to be possessed of true happiness.' *State of True Happiness*, 8.

[50]   *Christian Man's Calling*, I:206.

[51]   *Ibid.*, I:187.

[52]   *Heaven and Hell*, III:250.

[53]   Lloyd-Jones, *Studies in the Sermon on the Mount*, I:93.

Watson refers to 'those who are brought to the sense of their sins, and seeing no goodness in themselves, despair in themselves and sue wholly to the mercy of God in Christ. Poverty of spirit is a kind of self-annihilation. Such an expression I find in Calvin. The poor in spirit (says he) are they who see nothing in themselves, but fly to mercy for sanctuary.'[54] Shepard echoes this sentiment,[55] as does Walter Marshall:

> We must know, that our old state, with its evil principles, continueth still in a measure, or else we shall not be fit for the great duties of confessing our sins, loathing ourselves for them, praying earnestly for the pardon of them, a just sorrowing for them with a godly sorrow, accepting the punishment of our sins, and giving God the glory of his justice, and offering to him the sacrifice of a broken and contrite spirit, being poor in spirit, working out our salvation with fear and trembling.[56]

For Swinnock, then, the beatitudes reveal the right 'principles' by which people may determine the state of their heart. As expected, this raises the entire issue of assurance in Swinnock's thought. According to the *WCF*, assurance is founded upon: first, 'the divine truth of the promises of salvation;' second, 'the inward evidence of those graces unto which these promises are made;' and third, 'the testimony of the Spirit of adoption witnessing with our spirits that we are the children of God.'[57] Watson explains this threefold ground of assurance as follows:

> Assurance consists of a practical syllogism, in which the word of God makes the major, conscience the minor, and the Spirit of God the conclusion. The Word says, 'He that fears and loves God is loved of God;' there is the major proposition; then conscience makes the minor, 'But I fear and love God;' then the Spirit makes the conclusion, 'Therefore thou art loved of God;' and this is what the apostle calls 'The witnessing of the Spirit with our spirits, that we are his children.'[58]

Essentially, this means that the Holy Spirit impresses the reality of the marks of grace upon Christians, thereby assuring them that they are partakers in the promises of Scripture.[59] In commenting on the Puritan understanding of

---

[54] Thomas Watson, *The Beatitudes* (1660; Edinburgh: Banner of Truth, 1994) 42.

[55] Shepard, *Sincere Convert*, 63.

[56] Marshall, *Gospel Mystery of Sanctification*, 169.

[57] *WCF*, XVIII:II. For views on the Puritan position, see Joel Beeke, 'Personal Assurance of Faith: The Puritans and Chapter 18.2 of the Westminster Confession,' *Westminster Theological Journal* 55 (1993) 1-30; R. Hawkes, 'The Logic of Assurance in English Puritan Theology,' *Westminster Theological Journal* 52 (1990) 247-261; and Packer, *Quest for Godliness*, 179-189.

[58] Watson, *Body of Divinity*, 174.

[59] The Puritans were agreed as to the first two grounds of assurance, but not the third. Beeke identifies three schools of thought. (1) Those who viewed the testimony of

Romans 8:16,[60] Packer writes, 'The Puritans identified "our spirit" with the Christian's conscience, which, with the Spirit's aid, is able to discern in his heart the marks which Scripture specifies as tokens of the new birth and to conclude from them that he is a child of God.'[61] In this paradigm, the Holy Spirit both provides the evidence (i.e., marks of grace) and empowers the individual's reason to evaluate it. Appealing to 2 Peter 1:10,[62] therefore, the Puritans urge Christians to examine their lives to see both the internal (mystical syllogism) and external (practical syllogism) evidence of God's work. This self-examination is known as 'the reflex act of faith.'[63]

---

the Holy Spirit as referring exclusively to the practical and mystical syllogisms. (2) Those who distinguished the Holy Spirit witnessing with the Christian's spirit by syllogism from his witnessing to the Christian's spirit by direct applications of the Word. (3) Those who believed that the witness of the Holy Spirit was an immediate impression which marked the zenith of the experimental life – often equated with the 'sealing of the Spirit' (Eph. 1:13). 'Personal Assurance of Faith,' 25-27.

[60] 'The Spirit Himself testifies with our spirit that we are children of God.'

[61] Packer, *Quest for Godliness*, 183.

[62] 'Therefore, brethren, be all the more diligent to make certain about His calling and choosing you; for as long as your practice these things, you will never stumble.'

[63] For a typical treatment, see Thomas Brooks, *Heaven on Earth: A Treatise on Christian Assurance* (1654) in *The Works of Thomas Brooks: Vol. I-VI* (Edinburgh: Banner of Truth, 1980). There is considerable controversy surrounding the relationship between Calvin and the Westminster divines' articulation of the doctrine of assurance. Kendall ignited much of this debate by asserting that the *WCF* departs from Calvin's belief that 'faith is *knowledge*... merely witnessing what God has already done in Christ' and that assurance is 'the *direct* act of faith.' *Calvin and English Calvinism*, 19-20,25. His italics. For a similar position, see Basil Hall, 'Calvin Against the Calvinists' in *John Calvin: A Collection of Distinguishing Essays*, ed. G. E. Duffield (Grand Rapids: Eerdmans, 1966) 19-37. Kendall locates the primary cause of this departure in Theodore Beza's doctrine of limited atonement, for it 'makes Christ's death that to which the decree of election has particular reference and that which makes the elect's salvation efficacious.' *Calvin and English Calvinism*, 29. Similarly, Brian Armstrong argues that there are 'two very different intellectual traditions' operative in the seventeenth century: scholasticism and humanism. The latter is consistent with the teaching of Calvin whereas the former – although known as Calvinism – actually departs from Calvin. *Calvinism and the Amyraut Heresy: Protestant Scholasticism and Humanism in Seventeenth-Century France* (University of Wisconsin Press, 1969) xix. Armstrong points to Amyraut as standing against the tide of scholasticism by faithfully articulating Calvin's humanistic emphasis, whereas he points to Beza as the one most responsible for the propagation of scholasticism within Protestantism. *Ibid.*, 38. Richard Muller challenges this view in *Christ and the Decree: Christology and Predestination in Reformed Theology from Calvin to Perkins* (Grand Rapids: Baker Books, 1986) 11. Returning to Kendall, he argues that William Perkins adopted Beza's distortions of Calvin's teaching, and his legacy ensured their inclusion at the Westminster Assembly where they received 'creedal sanction.' *Calvin and English*

Often times, the secondary literature portrays the quest for assurance as the

---

Calvinism, 76. On this basis, Kendall concludes that the *WCF* 'hardly deserves to be called Calvinistic.' *Ibid.*, 212. Gordon Keddie makes the same argument in 'Unfallible Certenty of the Pardon of Sinne and Life Everlasting: The Doctrine of Assurance in the Theology of William Perkins (1558-1602),' *Evangelical Quarterly* 48 (1976) 242-243. For the opposite opinion, see Richard Muller, 'Perkins' *A Golden Chain*: Predestination System or Schematized Ordo Salutis,' *Sixteenth Century Journal* 9 (1978) 69-81. For critical reviews of Kendall's thesis, see Paul Helm, 'Calvin, English Calvinism and the Logic of Doctrinal Development,' *Scottish Journal of Theology* 34 (1981) 179-185; Anthony Lane, 'Review of R. T. Kendall's *Calvin and English Calvinism to 1649*,' *Themelios* 6 (1980) 29-31; and W. Stanford Reid, 'Review of R. T. Kendall's *Calvin and English Calvinism to 1649*,' *Westminster Theological Journal* 43 (1980) 155-164. Also see Robert Letham, 'Faith and Assurance in Early Calvinism: A Model of Continuity and Diversity' in *Later Calvinism: International Perspectives*, ed. W. F. Graham (Kirksville: Sixteenth Century Journal, 1992) 355-388; and Hawkes, 'The Logic of Assurance,' 247-261. Opponents levy two major criticisms. First, Kendall's assertion that Calvin believed in universal atonement is not conclusive. For the various views, see Roger Nicole, 'John Calvin's View of the Extent of the Atonement,' *Westminster Theological Journal* 47 (1985) 197-225; M. Charles Bell, 'Calvin and the Extent of the Atonement,' *Evangelical Quarterly* 55 (1983) 115-123; Hans Boersma, 'Calvin and the Extent of the Atonement,' *Evangelical Quarterly* 64 (1992) 333-355; W. Robert Godfrey, 'Reformed Thought on the Extent of the Atonement to 1618,' *Westminster Theological Journal* 37 (1975) 133-171; and Stephen Strehle, 'The Extent of the Atonement and the Synod of Dort,' *Westminster Theological Journal* 51 (1989) 1-23. For an extensive treatment of this subject, see G. Michael Thomas, *The Extent of the Atonement: A Dilemma for Reformed Theology from Calvin to the Consensus (1536-1675)* (Bletchley: Paternoster, 1997). Second, Kendall's assertion that Calvin defines faith exclusively as an act of the mind is inadequate. Both Lane and Reid argue that Calvin never restricts faith to the mind; rather, he believes that faith begins in the mind and proceeds to the heart where it provokes a response. Joel Beeke adopts an entirely different view from Kendall in regards to the relationship between Calvin and the *WCF*, commenting, 'The difference between Calvin and the Calvinists is substantial and developmental, but *not* antithetical as Hall and Kendall advocate.' *Assurance of Faith: Calvin, English Puritanism, and the Dutch Second Reformation* (New York: Peter Lang, 1991) 20. Also see Paul Helm, *Calvin and the Calvinists* (Edinburgh: Banner of Truth, 1982) 25-26. Beeke responds to Kendall's thesis by arguing that, although the Puritans gave practical and mystical syllogisms a more intrinsic role than Calvin, they continued to regard the promises of God as the primary ground for assurance. Plus, they distinguished between an initial act of faith and a fully developed assurance whilst insisting that the latter proceeds from the former. In this respect, Hawkes observes that, for the Puritans, 'full assurance grows out of an assurance implicit in the first act of faith.' 'The Logic of Assurance,' 250. For more on Calvin's position, see Anthony Lane, 'John Calvin: The Witness of the Holy Spirit' in *Faith and Ferment* (London: Westminster Conference, 1982) 1-17.

all-encompassing theme in Puritan spirituality. It is highly significant that Swinnock rarely mentions it. The impetus behind his preaching and writing is not the desire to impart assurance to troubled souls, but to undermine presumption in confident ones.[64] Evidently, he views the second group as more reflective of his audience. This emphasis in no way alleviates Swinnock of all potential criticism. In his attempt to undermine 'morality' and 'civility' whilst encouraging assurance on the basis of warm affections, he opens the door to three potential dangers. The first is introspection.[65] Swinnock frequently compels his readers to examine themselves. Andrew Davies sees the danger, commenting, 'Whilst their stress on self-examination was a healthy corrective to those who were in danger of hypocrisy, it was an unhelpful emphasis for those who were given to introspection.'[66] The second danger is despair.[67] Whilst affirming the need for warm affections, Swinnock acknowledges that many people suffer from cold affections. By way of solution, he proposes that dissatisfaction with one's lack of affection is a sign of affection.[68] Such reasoning can easily lead to a vicious cycle whereby anxiety becomes a mark of piety. The third danger is moralism. Swinnock's emphasis upon 'marks' is a small step away from a works-oriented concept of salvation. When detailed prescriptions for obedience become central, grace is always threatened.[69]

---

[64] See *Heaven and Hell*, III:205,289; and *Door of Salvation*, V:109-116.

[65] Baird Tipson considers this danger in the context of the church. 'Invisible Saints: The "Judgment of Charity" in the Early New England Churches,' *Church History* XLIV (1975) 460-471. Traditionally, Protestantism determined church membership on the basis of the 'judgment of charity.' This means 'the visible church could not... presume to second-guess God's revealed will by speculating about his secret, predestinating will.' *Ibid.*, 462. Tipson believes that New England Puritanism (e.g., John Cotton) departed from the 'judgment of charity,' looking instead to inward signs of regeneration as requirements for church membership. For more on this, see Morgan, *Visible Saints*, 63,112.

[66] Andrew Davies, 'The Holy Spirit in Puritan Experience' in *Faith and Ferment* (London: Westminster Conference, 1982) 25.

[67] John Stachniewski deals with this subject at some length, maintaining that the doctrines of election and reprobation led the Puritans to establish detailed ways of knowing one's spiritual state. This inevitably fostered despair. *The Persecutory Imagination: English Puritanism and the Literature of Religious Despair* (Oxford: Clarendon Press, 1991) 26-27.

[68] At one point, he encourages his readers 'to weep over thy tears, to be ashamed of thy shame, and to abhor thyself for thy self-abhorrency.' *Christian Man's Calling*, I:190.

[69] An example of this is Baxter. See C. F. Allison, *The Rise of Moralism: The Proclamation of the Gospel from Hooker to Baxter* (New York: Seabury Press, 1966). Allison identifies a 'classical' position within the Church of England regarding the doctrine of justification. It views 'the formal cause' of justification as 'the righteousness of Christ *imputed* to us when we are incorporated in Christ.' *Ibid.*, 3. His italics. This differs from the Council of Trent, according to which justification

Divorced from its larger context, Swinnock's spirituality may appear to be on the brink of succumbing to these three dangers. However, his repeated emphasis upon the covenant of grace safeguards against it.

The Fear of God and the Covenant

Swinnock informs his readers that the door of their happiness 'hangs on these two hinges': first, 'the merit of Christ without thee, and its acceptation with God for the justification of thy person;' and, second, 'the Spirit of Christ within thee, and its operation for the sanctification of thy nature.'[70] In speaking of 'nature,' Swinnock affirms that everyone is under 'the covenant of works.'[71] In it, God promises life to all those who obey his law. However, everyone has broken this covenant and, therefore, everyone is 'liable to the curse of the Law.'[72] For this reason, Swinnock encourages his audience to embark on 'another vessel,' i.e., 'the covenant of grace.'[73] This covenant was 'promised to Adam, believed by the patriarchs, shadowed in the sacrifices, foretold by the prophets, and witnessed in the Scriptures.'[74] He explains, 'Since man's apostasy, and impossibility thereby of attaining happiness by his own works, God hath been pleased to accept of the perfect obedience of Jesus Christ, on the behalf of the believing, penitent Christian; which act of infinite grace being revealed in the gospel, it is most fitly called the word of his grace.'[75] In short, people are incapable of pleasing God by their 'own works,' however God has accepted Christ's 'perfect obedience' thereby graciously accepting all those united to Christ. Thus, Christ has fulfilled the covenant of works on behalf of those who believe in him.

In this, Swinnock echoes the federal theology of the *WCF*,[76] which David

---

is 'the inherent righteousness of a regenerate person infused into him.' *Ibid.* Owen stands in the 'classical' tradition. *Ibid.*, 174-177. Baxter, however, departs from it. Allison explains, 'Baxter takes the position that Christ himself fulfilled the conditions of the old covenant, and thereby purchased for us easier terms within the new covenant. On account of Christ's righteousness, our own righteousness (faith and repentance) is accounted, or imputed, as acceptable righteousness. We are, in other words, justified by our own righteousness *on account of* the righteousness of Christ.' *Ibid.*, 156-7. His italics. This view gave rise to the 'new moralism.' *Ibid.*, 192,207.

[70] *Fading of the Flesh*, III:454.
[71] *Pastor's Farewell*, IV:61.
[72] *Fading of the Flesh*, III:455.
[73] *Ibid.*
[74] *Christian Man's Calling*, I:173.
[75] *Pastor's Farewell*, IV:61.
[76] For a summary of the rise of the two covenants in English theology, see Michael McGiffert, 'Grace and Works: The Rise and Division of Covenant Identity in Elizabethan Puritanism,' *Harvard Theological Review* 75 (1982) 463-505.

Weir defines as a specific type of covenant theology, characterized by a prelapsarian and postlapsarian covenant schema centred on the first Adam and the last Adam.[77] According to the *WCF*, the prelapsarian covenant refers to the life that 'was promised to Adam, and in him to his posterity, upon condition of perfect and personal obedience.'[78] In failing to keep this covenant as humanity's federal head, Adam brought condemnation upon his posterity. For this reason, there was a need for a postlapsarian covenant – the covenant of grace wherein God 'freely offered unto sinners life and salvation by Jesus Christ, requiring of them faith in him that they may be saved, and promising to give unto all those that are ordained unto life his Holy Spirit, to make them willing and able to believe.'[79]

In support of this system, the Puritans appeal to Romans 5:12-20, affirming that God in his dealings with humanity has appointed two representatives: the first Adam and the last Adam.[80] In the garden, the first Adam stood in the place of his descendants. As their head, he was given a specific commandment. When he sinned, God counted his sin as his posterity's sin, his guilt as his posterity's guilt, and his punishment as his posterity's punishment. Watson explains, 'Adam being a representative person, while he stood, we stood; when he fell, we fell. We sinned in Adam; so it is in the text, "In whom all have sinned."'[81] Here, Watson refers to Romans 5:12, where the apostle Paul speaks of a single act in which all humanity participated, namely, Adam's sin. He makes the point that 'death reigned from Adam until Moses,' however 'sin is not imputed when there is no law.' In other words, the law was not given until Sinai yet death reigned until that time; therefore, humanity must be guilty of breaking the law in Adam.

Having thus explained humanity's position in Adam, the apostle Paul states that Adam 'is a type of Him who was to come.'[82] This means that the first Adam has a counterpart – the last Adam (or Christ). Just as Adam is the head of the old creation, Christ is the head of the new creation. From here, the apostle Paul contrasts the work of Adam and Christ. To begin with, he contrasts the result of their work. The 'transgression' of Adam resulted in death and condemnation whereas the 'free gift' of Christ resulted in life and

---

[77] Weir, *Origins of the Federal Theology*, 3.

[78] *WCF*, VII:II.

[79] *WCF*, VII:III. For further discussion of the various views, see Mark Karlberg, 'The Original State of Adam: Tensions Within Reformed Theology,' *Evangelical Quarterly* 87 (1987) 291-309.

[80] *Door of Salvation*, V:243-244. See Charnock, *Existence and Attributes of God*, I:355-356,568-575, II:275-276,291-292. Charnock subscribes to a third covenant: the covenant of redemption. *Ibid.*, II:288. Flavel agrees. *Fountain of Life, Works*, I:52-62. This is also Owen's position, according to Ferguson, *John Owen on the Christian Life*, 25-27.

[81] Watson, *Body of Divinity*, 101.

[82] Rom. 5:14.

justification.[83] Next, he contrasts the quality of their work. Adam's work was an act of 'transgression' whereas Christ's work was an act of 'righteousness.'[84] Finally, the apostle Paul contrasts the nature of their work. Adam disobeyed ('through the one man's disobedience the many were made sinners'), but Christ obeyed ('through the obedience of the One the many will be made righteous').[85] According to the Westminster divines (and Swinnock), Christians are no longer in Adam (under the covenant of works) because they have been united with Christ (under the covenant of grace), who has fulfilled the covenant of works on their behalf. Again, in the words of Swinnock, 'God hath been pleased to accept of the perfect obedience of Jesus Christ, on the behalf of the believing, penitent Christian.'[86]

---

[83] Rom. 5:15-17.
[84] Rom. 5:18.
[85] Rom. 5:19.
[86] *Pastor's Farewell*, IV:61. For Robert Letham's thesis that covenant theology emerged from factors present within Reformed theology from the very start, see 'The *Foedus Operum*: Some Factors Accounting For Its Development,' *Sixteenth Century Journal* XIV (1983) 457-467. Some scholars argue that covenant theology is absent from Calvin. See Charles Ryrie, *Dispensationalism Today* (Chicago: Moody Press, 1965) 180. Perry Miller popularized the notion that it was the Puritans who actually developed covenant theology in response to perceived deficiencies in Calvin's theology. By 'deficiencies,' Miller has in mind Calvin's concept of God's absolute sovereignty, which fails to provide individuals with any motive for moral behaviour or any ground for personal assurance. *New England Mind*, 366-374. The Puritans remedied these 'deficiencies' by creating a covenant theology that stressed human duty. According to Miller, Calvin knew nothing of any such system. For a similar view, see Hill, *Society and Puritanism*, 474; and Norman Pettit, *The Heart Prepared: Grace and Conversion in Puritan Spiritual Life* (Middletown: Wesleyan University Press, 1989). For the opposite view, see Anthony Hoekema, 'The Covenant of Grace in Calvin's Teaching,' *Calvin Theological Journal* 2 (1967) 133-161; Lillback, *Binding of God*, 126-158; and George Marsden, 'Perry Miller's Rehabilitation of the Puritans: A Critique' in *Reckoning With the Past: Historical Essays on American Evangelicalism from the Institute for the Study of American Evangelicals*, ed. D. G. Hart (Grand Rapids: Baker Books, 1995). As for the precise relationship between Calvin and the federal theology of the *WCF*, there are three main schools of thought. (1) Some scholars argue that the *WCF* departs from Calvin. Whilst not denying the presence of covenant theology in Calvin, they affirm that Calvin's teaching represents one of two conflicting movements: the Genevan Reformer expounds an unconditional (or unilateral) covenant with the emphasis on God's sovereignty whilst the Zurich-Rhineland Reformers expound a conditional (or bilateral) covenant with the emphasis on human responsibility. Trinterud's thesis is that Puritan federal theology followed the Zurich-Rhineland tradition as opposed to the Genevan tradition. 'The Origins of Puritanism,' 37-57. For more on the two traditions theory, see Everett Emerson, 'Calvin and Covenant Theology,' *Church History* 25 (1956) 136-144; McGiffert, 'The Perkinsian Moment of Federal Theology,' 117-148; and Jens Moller, 'The Beginnings of Puritan Covenant

According to the covenant of grace, God requires 'faith in Christ,' yet he promises 'to give unto all those that are ordained unto life his Holy Spirit, to make them willing and able to believe.'[87] Hence, the covenant is conditional upon an individual's faith, which is unconditionally produced by the work of the Holy Spirit in those who are 'ordained unto life.' Therefore, the covenant of grace requires human duty whilst affirming God's sovereignty in salvation. Charnock writes, 'He puts a condition to his covenant of grace, the condition of faith, and he resolves to work that condition in the hearts of the elect.'[88] For his part, Swinnock maintains that the covenant of grace is conditional, in that people are required to fear God, and unconditional, in that God promises, 'I will make an everlasting covenant with them, that I will not turn away from

Theology,' *Journal of Ecclesiastical History* 14 (1963) 46-67. (2) Many scholars challenge this interpretation, insisting that there is fundamental agreement between Calvin and the Zurich-Rhineland Reformers and, by consequence, a basic unity between Calvin and the Puritans. See Lyle Bierma, 'Federal Theology in the Sixteenth Century: Two Traditions?' *Westminster Theological Journal* 45 (1983) 304-321; and Bierma, 'The Role of Covenant Theology in Early Reformed Orthodoxy,' *Sixteenth Century Journal* XXI (1990) 453-462. With slight variations, Hoekema and Lillback share this view. Bierma believes that the notion of a 'bilateral' versus 'unilateral' understanding of the covenant is misleading. It is true that both Zwingli and Bullinger teach that God expects obedience as a covenantal response to his grace. However, this does not mean that God's favour is based upon that response. It is also true that Calvin emphasizes God's sovereignty in regards to the covenant. However, he also stresses the individual's response in faith and obedience. These are not the fruit of one's effort, but of the Holy Spirit working within. (3) Still other scholars recognize both the similarities and differences between Calvin and the Zurich-Rhineland Reformers in their approaches to the covenant. Song refers to this as the 'Diversity within Unity Theory.' *Theology and Piety*, 11. He acknowledges the diversity within the Reformed covenant tradition, yet denies that this stems from a theological division between God's grace and human duty. Rather, he sees the diversity as resulting from a methodological distinction between logical (Calvin) and historical (Zurich-Rhineland Reformers) approaches to the covenant. *Ibid.*, 19. The latter emphasizes a dispensational view of God's covenant revelation whereas the former applies the covenant concept to the *ordo salutis*, thereby developing a systematic view of God's covenant dealings with his people. *Ibid.*, 27.These are not contradictory, but complimentary, approaches. Similarly, John Von Rohr recognizes the federalist tradition in distinction from the Calvinist tradition. *The Covenant of Grace in Puritan Thought* (Atlanta: Scholars Press, 1986) 31-32. However, he is careful to affirm that they merely represent two different emphases; namely, human responsibility and divine sovereignty. Again, these are not in contradiction. Like Song, Von Rohr insists that the Puritans never opted for one at the expense of the other. Instead, they conjoined the two in the covenant of grace. *Ibid.*, 33. Also see Von Rohr, 'Covenant and Assurance in Early English Puritanism,' *Church History* 34 (1965) 195-203.

[87]   *WCF*, VII:III.
[88]   Charnock, *Existence and Attributes of God*, I:355.

them, to do them good; but I will put my fear in their hearts, that they shall not depart from me.'[89] In other words, the fear of God is a condition that God himself graciously fulfils in sinners by the renewing of their affections.

Conclusion

Swinnock asks, 'When God intends that his people should walk in his statutes, keep his judgments, and do them, what doeth he for them to prepare them and enable them thereunto?' He answers, 'Truly this: he regenerates them, and changeth them, and putteth a new principle into them: "I will give them a new heart and a new spirit" (Ezek. 36:26).'[90] Obedience, therefore, is not an attempt to obtain a meritorious standing before God. It is the effect of the fear of God, inclining the regenerate to positive holiness. Kevan provides an excellent summary: 'The Puritans believed that the highest spirituality was to be seen in a life that rejoices to be commanded. They held that, far from involving the believer in legalistic bondage, it gave expression to his desire to please God, from which, as a subjective motive such an obedient life sprang. The spiritual man has such "a true love and liking of the Law of God" that "absence of a delight is a sign of unspirituality."'[91]

---

[89] Jer. 32:40.
[90] *Sinner's Last Sentence*, V:421.
[91] Kevan, *Grace and Law*, 249. Here, Kevan quotes Edward Elton.

Chapter Six

Godliness: The Christian Man's Calling

Swinnock's *Christian Man's Calling* constitutes almost half of his literary output. In the opinion of James Nichol, it is 'one of the best exhibitions of the gospel in its application to the ordinary affairs of life.'[1] In it, Swinnock's goal 'is to discover and direct how religion, the great end for which we are born, and the great errand upon which we are sent into the world, may be made our principal business.'[2] To achieve this, he expounds the apostle Paul's words in 1 Timothy 4:7 – 'Exercise thyself unto godliness.'[3] By *godliness*, Swinnock means 'worshipping God in the inward motions of the heart, and the outward actions of the life.'[4] Regarding the latter, he affirms, 'Whether a Christian be eating or drinking, or buying or selling, or ploughing or sowing, or riding or walking, whatever he be doing, or wherever he be going, he must be always in the fear of the Lord... Thy duty is to "pass the whole time of thy sojourning here in fear" (1 Pet. 1:17).'[5] For Swinnock, this duty is achieved by exercising self-control in all of life.[6]

The Nature of Self-Control

As seen in the previous chapter, *filial* fear and *servile* fear differ in their object. According to William Gouge, filial fear 'ariseth from faith in the mercy and goodness of God.' When the soul feels 'a sweet taste of Gods goodnesse' and finds 'that in his favour only all happinesse consisteth, it is stricken with such an inward awe and reverence.'[7] On the other hand, servile fear 'ariseth from diffidence: For when mans heart doubteth of Gods mercy, and expecteth nothing but vengeance, the very thought of God striketh an awe or rather dread into him.'[8] These two fears also differ in their effect. For Gouge, 'A sonne

---

[1]   Nichol in *Works of George Swinnock*, V:xiv.
[2]   *Christian Man's Calling*, I:8-9.
[3]   *Ibid.*, I:27.
[4]   *Ibid.*, I:33. This is a common distinction among the Puritans. See Baxter, *Christian Directory*, 547,553.
[5]   *Christian Man's Calling*, I:85.
[6]   *Ibid.*, I:86,393, II:187.
[7]   William Gouge, *Of Domesticall Duties: Eight Treatises* (London, 1622) 8.
[8]   *Ibid.*

feareth simply to offend or displease his father: so as it is accompanied with love. A bondslave feareth nothing but the punishment of his offence; so as it is joined with hatred.'[9] For this reason, filial fear results in 'a carefull endevour to please God' and 'a carefull avoiding of such things as offend the Majesty of God.'[10] Furthermore, it 'maketh us more respect what God requireth and commandeth, than what our corrupt heart desireth and suggesteth: It subdueth our unruly passions, and bringeth them within compasse of dutie: It maketh us deny our selves and our owne desires.'[11]

For the Puritans, this subjection of 'unruly passions' is the essence of self-control. They share this conviction with Calvin. According to Peter Leithart, Calvin inherited it – at least in part – from the Stoics.[12] Leithart believes the Stoic notion of man's innate rationality led Calvin to qualify his doctrine of original corruption.[13] Calvin insists that sin enslaves the whole man, including reason. 'As a consequence,' writes Leithart, 'it seems clear that Calvin could not exhort men to follow nature or natural reason.'[14] However, when speaking of the image of God, Calvin distinguishes between spiritual and natural gifts. The former were destroyed at the fall, whereas the latter were merely corrupted. For this reason, people are incapable of discerning 'heavenly' truth, yet capable of discerning 'earthly' truth. For Leithart, this paradigm leads to the question of 'whether Calvin did justice to the noetic effects of sin within the realm of

---

[9] *Ibid.*, 9.

[10] *Ibid.*, 8.

[11] *Ibid.*, 12.

[12] Leithart presents his arguments in three articles: 'Stoic Elements in Calvin's Doctrine of the Christian Life – Part I: Original Corruption, Natural Law, and the Order of the Soul,' *Westminster Theological Journal* 55 (1993) 31-54; 'Stoic Elements in Calvin's Doctrine of the Christian Life – Part II: Mortification,' *WTJ* 55 (1993) 191-208; and 'Stoic Elements in Calvin's Doctrine of the Christian Life – Part III: Christian Moderation,' *WTJ* (1994) 59-85. The Stoics believed that everyone possesses impulses – inclinations toward or away from objects. As long as reason is in control, these impulses are no problem. However, when they exceed the bounds of reason, they become passions: fear, sorrow, pleasure, and desire. The external factors that cause these passions are without virtue; thus, the passions themselves are irrational. Virtue is a state of moderation (ἀπάθεια) attained when people become indifferent toward externals, thereby freeing themselves from passions. According to Fiering, 'The Stoics revived the extreme intellectualist doctrine of Socrates that founded virtue on knowledge alone. Where the passions seemed to have an influence leading to vice, they were treated for the most part as a species of intellectual error or false judgment that had to be eliminated for the sake of virtue.' *Moral Philosophy at Seventeenth-Century Harvard*, 82-83. For more on the history of Stoicism, see *Encyclopaedia of Religion and Ethics*, ed. James Hastings (Edinburgh: T & T Clark, 1913) XI:860-864.

[13] Leithart, 'Part I,' 33.

[14] *Ibid.*, 35-36.

earthly things.'[15] Leithart raises this question, because 'Calvin... assumed a universal consensus of morality that is in a general way consistent with biblical norms... a set of general moral principles that are affirmed by all men in all cultures.'[16] For Leithart, this 'moral knowledge' means 'Calvin failed to do full justice to the radical antithesis between the regenerate and unregenerate, and he did so under the influence of the Stoic idea of universal reason.'[17]

From here, Leithart analyses Calvin's view of the impact of sin upon the inner workings of the soul, summarizing, 'Sin brings disorder to the soul both by filling the mind with evil thoughts and by weakening the reason, rendering the latter incapable of exercising its hegemony over the other faculties.'[18] From this, he infers, 'Calvin was a rationalist in the sense that he considered reason to be inherently superior to other faculties of the soul.'[19] Leithart believes this parallels the Stoic doctrine of εὐπάθεια or 'rational impulses,' commenting, 'Calvin often explained that passions are sinful precisely because they are against reason.'[20] Leithart concludes his analysis, stating, 'Our God is no Stoic sage. Calvin was certainly correct to emphasize that our passions and desires are corrupt, but one cannot conclude from the scriptural evidence that our corruption consists in "immoderation." Rather, as Augustine put it, our corruption consists in the fact that our desires and passions are wrongly directed. Christians should strive not for moderate passions, but for strong God-directed passions.'[21]

Leithart is correct in his assessment of Augustine, who criticizes the Stoics for their assertion that 'the fool can do no more than desire, rejoice, fear, be sad.'[22] Augustine believes Christians 'both fear and desire, and grieve and rejoice. And because their love is rightly placed, all these affections of theirs are right.'[23] In other words, they 'follow the guidance of right reason.'[24] This emphasis upon 'right reason' does not mean Augustine is a Stoic. On the contrary, he remarks, 'If that is to be called apathy, where the mind is the subject of no emotion, then who would not consider this insensibility to be worse than all vices?' Again, 'If some... have become enamored of themselves because they can be stimulated and excited by no emotion, moved or bent by no affection, such persons rather lose all humanity than obtain true tranquility. For

---

[15]   *Ibid.*, 38.

[16]   *Ibid.*, 44.

[17]   *Ibid.*, 44-45. It is difficult to see how Calvin's concept of a 'universal consensus of morality' stems from 'the Stoic notion of man's innate rationality' as opposed to his exposition of Rom. 2:14-15. Leithart is not very convincing on this point.

[18]   *Ibid.*, 45.

[19]   *Ibid.*, 47.

[20]   *Ibid.*, 51. Also see 53.

[21]   Leithart, 'Part III,' 85.

[22]   Augustine, *Confessions, Select Library: Vol. I*, XIV:8.

[23]   *Ibid.*, XIV:9.

[24]   *Ibid.*

a thing is not necessarily right because it is inflexible, nor healthy because it is insensible.'[25]

Whilst correct in his assessment of Augustine, Leithart fails to demonstrate that Calvin actually disagrees with Augustine's assertion that 'Christians should strive not for moderate passions, but for strong God-directed passions.' It appears far more likely that Calvin's concept of 'immoderation' is based upon the 'object' – not the 'measure' – of the affections. He writes:

> We do not condemn those inclinations which God so engraved upon the character of man at the first creation... but only those unbridled impulses which contend against God's control. Now, all men's faculties are, on account of the depravity of nature, so vitiated and corrupted that in all his actions persistent disorder and intemperance threaten because these inclinations cannot be separated from such lack of restraint... we teach that all human desires are evil, and charge them with sin – not in that they are natural, but because they are inordinate.[26]

For Calvin, 'unbridled impulses' are 'inordinate' affections, because they are misplaced affections – 'they tend against God's control.' In other words, they are not God-directed affections.

Returning to the Puritans, Daniel Doriani argues that their high view of moderation 'conformed to prevailing ideas,'[27] received from Aristotle through Aquinas, namely: (1) 'self-control with regard to the senses and sensual pleasures;' (2) 'modesty or dignity in conduct, so that one does not show extreme emotion, enthusiasm or devotion to anything;' and (3) 'the general avoidance of passion.'[28] Doriani agrees with the first idea, but views the other two as unbiblical. To prove this, he appeals to numerous Scriptures that commend 'zeal.' In addition, he argues that 'moderation... is not an absolute value.'[29] It 'may be good, bad, or indifferent, depending on the object of the passion, the manner of its expression, and the nature of the situation in which the passion might be expressed.'[30] Doriani believes the Puritans succumb to a distorted view of self-control, owing to their failure 'to distinguish the two senses of lust: (1) strong desire, as a neutral thing depending on its object; and (2) inordinate passion, especially for something forbidden.'[31]

---

[25] *Ibid.*

[26] Calvin, *Institutes*, III:III:12.

[27] Daniel Doriani, 'The Puritans, Sex, and Pleasure,' *Westminster Theological Journal* 53 (1991) 140.

[28] *Ibid.*.

[29] *Ibid.*, 141.

[30] *Ibid.*

[31] *Ibid.* Levin Schucking describes Puritan 'sobriety' as 'full emotional control' by 'reason.' Interestingly, he suggests that this accounts for the 'reserved' English character. *The Puritan Family: A Social Study from the Literary Sources* (London: Routledge & Kegan Paul, 1969) 7-8.

There are two problems with Doriani's thesis. First, in making 'zeal' and 'passion' synonymous terms,[32] he infuses a meaning into 'passion' that is foreign to the Puritans. They most certainly are not opposed to zeal. On the contrary, they view zeal (i.e., spiritual heat, resulting from the stirring of the soul's affections) as a necessary requirement to the true worship of God. Wilson defines zeal 'as the earnestness and increase of all the affections, liking or disliking, as love and hatred, grief and joy, desires, delights, fears, and anger, boiled to the highest degree, and to the hottest temper and intention.'[33]

Second, in suggesting that the Puritans embrace self-control as an 'absolute value' without any regard for its object, Doriani ignores the Puritan consensus. The object of their self-control is not 'strong' desire, but 'inordinate' desire. Perkins defines self-control (or 'temperance') as a 'vertue, that moderateth appetite or lust.'[34] This virtue arises when the soul's 'affection' is 'tempered and allayed with the feare of God.'[35] Aristotle defines virtue as the 'mean' between two extremes. Perkins rejects this, stating:

> Some learned Philosophers… taught, that the very nature of Vertue standeth in a meane, or mediocritie of affections. This that they say is true in part, but not wholly. For the mediocritie, of which they speak, without renovation of affections, is nothing: and therefore all virtues, that are not joined with a renovation and change of the affections, are no better than sinnes.[36]

The Puritans never uphold moderation as an absolute value. Rather, they view it as a virtue that controls inordinate desire, which arises when the object of the soul's love is evil. This concept of self-control is best understood in the context of humanity's three-fold state. In innocence, the soul is directed by a 'true self-love.'[37] According to Gouge, this 'good and commendable self-love' is natural, in that it is 'the very instinct of nature.'[38] It is also spiritual, for it 'is that which is supernaturally wrought in man by Gods Spirit: whereby he is both inlightned to discerne what is most excellent, and best for him, and also moved to choose the same.'[39] In innocence, the soul loves itself; therefore, it desires its own happiness. Perceiving God to be 'most excellent,' it loves and pursues God. The more the soul loves itself (its own happiness), the more it loves

---

[32] Doriani, 'The Puritans, Sex, and Pleasure,' 140.

[33] Wilson, *David's Zeal for Zion*, 2.

[34] Perkins, *Cases*, 305.

[35] *Ibid.*, 349.

[36] *Ibid.*, 163.

[37] *Christian Man's Calling*, I:219,459. A century later, Jonathan Edwards articulates this concept of self-love in unparalleled fashion. For a summary of his position, see *Charity and Its Fruits: Christian Love as Manifested in the Heart and Life* (1852; rpt., Edinburgh: Banner of Truth, 2000) 157-166.

[38] Gouge, *Domesticall Duties*, 81.

[39] *Ibid.*, 82.

God.[40] In apostasy, however, the soul is directed by a false self-love.[41] For Gouge, this self-love errs in its 'object,' being 'cast upon our corruptions, our lusts, and evill humors.'[42] It also errs in its 'measure,' being 'wholly and only cast upon our selves.'[43] Because the soul is alienated from God, it views itself as the source of its happiness. Bolton comments:

> For... the worldly minded man, wanting utterly the eie of faith, and having his eie of reason dimmed with mists, that rise from his tumultuous and fierie passions, grosse ignorance, and wilfull malice, so that he onely lookes upon the honoures, riches and pleasures of this life with a carnall and sensual eie, may seeme to see in them, some glimmerings of happiness, and thereafter conforme and proportion his desires, endevours and projects; because he hath his portion onely in this life.[44]

As a result of its alienation from God, the soul pursues objects for itself.[45] By 'objects,' Swinnock means wealth, recreation, sleep, food – anything that gratifies the sensitive appetite. There is nothing wrong with these objects in themselves. However, when the soul views them as its happiness apart from God, they become idols. It will crave them immoderately and abuse them unthinkingly.[46] As Manton states, 'Carnal self-love maketh idols, and sets up

---

[40]   Baxter maintains that there is no conflict between the pursuit of God's glory (love for God) and the pursuit of one's happiness (love for self). On the contrary, they are mutually dependent. He writes, 'I cannot possibly do any thing for one, that doth not equally promote the other, if I do them rightly, preferring God before myself, in my inward estimation, love, and intention.' *Christian Directory*, 158.

[41]   Charnock describes a three-fold self-love: 'natural' – a desire to seek our good; 'carnal' – a desire to be superior to God; and 'gracious' – a desire to fulfil our end, that is, to glorify God. *Existence and Attributes of God*, I:136. Manton identifies a four-fold self-love: carnal, natural, spiritual, and glorified. *A Practical Exposition of the Lord's Prayer*, *Works*, I:67-69.

[42]   Gouge, *Domesticall Duties*, 82.

[43]   *Ibid.*, 83.

[44]   Bolton, *State of True Happiness*, 13. For more of Bolton's thoughts on this subject, see *Carnal Professor*, 9-59.

[45]   *Christian Man's Calling*, I:54-55.

[46]   In *Christian Man's Calling*, there are at least thirty-six quotations from Seneca – mostly illustrative. In one place, Swinnock quotes him as saying, 'He may defy earth and hell, and be happy in spite of both, who hath but a heart weaned from the earth, and placed in heaven' (II:72). Prior to this, Swinnock writes, 'According to the price we set upon things, such is our pleasure and joy in their presence, and our pain and sorrow in their absence.' Here, he mentions the four passions. He explains the need to prepare for adversity by rating 'the world according to its worth.' He exhorts, 'Love heaven as thy paradise, and look on earth but as the place of thy pilgrimage, then thou wilt cheerfully travel in all ways, whether fair or foul' (II:73). In all this, he never suggests that the passions are irrational. He encourages the subjection of the passions to reason, because they are set upon the wrong object – earth. It is this

other gods instead of the true God.'[47] In this condition, says Charnock, the individual acts 'as if something below God could make him happy without God, or that God could not make him happy without the addition of something else.'[48] Baxter is most insightful on this point. Regarding the senses, he writes:

> Sin made its entrance by them, and by sin they are now corrupted and vitiated with the body, and are grown inordinate, violent, and unruly in their appetite; and the rational powers having lost and forsaken God, their proper end and chiefest object, have hired or captivated themselves to the sensitive appetite, to serve its ends. And so the sensitive appetite is become the ruling faculty in the unsanctified, and the senses the common entrance of sin, and instruments of Satan: and though the work of grace be primarily in the rational powers, yet secondarily the lower powers themselves also are sanctified, and brought under the government of a renewed mind and will, and so restored to their proper use... We see that temperance and chastity do not only restrain, but take down the appetite from the rage and violence which before it had: not the natural appetite, but the sensitive, so far as it is sinful.[49]

Earlier, Baxter defines love 'as the complacency of the appetite in apprehended good.'[50] Individuals possess sensitive and rational appetites. Consequently, 'sensitive' love is 'the complacency of the sensitive appetite in sensible good' whereas 'rational' love is 'the complacency of the rational appetite in that which reason apprehendeth as good.'[51] Baxter builds on this, defining self-love as a 'love of happiness, and self-preservation, which God did put into innocent Adam, and hath planted in man's nature as necessary to his government.'[52] As in the case of love, Baxter maintains that self-love is both 'sensitive' and 'rational.'[53] The former is the love of 'life.'[54] The latter extends beyond the love of life to 'extrinsic good.'[55] He explains:

> God is good... the dirigent and ultimately ultimate cause of all created good; as making and directing all things for himself. Therefore it is the duty of the intellectual creature to love God totally, without any exceptions or restrictions, with all the power, mind, and will, not only in degree above ourselves and all the

---

misdirection that makes them excessive. If people love heaven as their paradise, there is no immoderation.

[47] Manton, *True Circumcision, Works*, II:53.

[48] Charnock, *Existence and Attributes of God*, I:143. For his description of how 'sin hath turned man's affections wholly to himself,' see I:89-175.

[49] Baxter. *Christian Directory*, 301.

[50] *Ibid.*, 154.

[51] *Ibid.*

[52] *Ibid.*, 126.

[53] *Ibid.*, 154.

[54] *Ibid.*, 155.

[55] *Ibid.*

world, but also as God, with a love in kind transcending the love of every creature.[56]

In innocence, self-love directs the soul to God – the greatest good. In apostasy, this is not the case, as the soul has turned from God to self.[57] In this state, self-love is 'carnal, inordinate... the chiefest enemy to the love of God.'[58] Consequently, it falls under the control of the sensitive appetite. Reynolds describe this change as follows:

> *Appetite* was in *Beasts* onely made to be governed by a *sensitive knowledge*: But in *Man*, Sense ought not to have any commanding or moving Power, but onely *Instrumentall*, Ministeriall, and Conveying, in respect of the object. The Action of *sense*, was not from the first Institution, ordain'd to touch the *Affection*, but to present it selfe primarily to the *Understanding*; upon whose determination and conduct, the *Passions* were to depend... The *Corruption* then of *Passion* in this respect, is the independence thereof upon its true Principle: when it stayeth not to looke for, but anticipates and prevents the Discourses of *Reason*; relying onely on the judgement of *sense*, wherewith it retaines an undue correspondence.[59]

Baxter maintains that the sensitive appetite is 'predominant' to such an extent that 'reason is voluntarily enslaved to... sense: so that even the intellectual appetite, contrary to its primitive and sound nature, loveth chiefly the sensitive life and pleasure.'[60] He adds, 'The thing therefore that every carnal man would have, is an everlasting, perfect, sensual pleasure; and he apprehendeth the state of his soul's perfection mostly as consisting in this kind of felicity.'[61] Again, 'Indeed the state of sin lieth both in man's fall from God to self, and in the mistake of his own felicity, preferring even for himself a sensible good before a spiritual, and the creature before the Creator.'[62] In this state, the affections

> are too easily and violently moved by the sensitive interest and appetite; and are habitually prone to such carnal, inordinate motions, running before the understanding and will... The sin of the sensitive appetite consisteth in the inordinate rage or immoderateness to its object, which causeth it to disobey the commands of reason, and to become the great inciter of rebellion in the soul; violently urging the mind and will to consent to its desires.[63]

[56] *Ibid.*
[57] *Ibid.*, 868.
[58] *Ibid.*, 126.
[59] Reynolds, *Passions and Faculties*, 43-44. His italics.
[60] Baxter, *Christian Directory*, 157.
[61] *Ibid.*
[62] *Ibid.* Also see 64,76,93.
[63] *Ibid.*, 86. Also see 223.

In a word, 'Reason is dethroned by sin; and the will is left unguided and unguarded to the rapes of sensual violence.'[64] For Baxter, it is only through regeneration that 'the inordinate love of sensual pleasure' and 'the inordinate love of self' is 'destroyed,' and 'lawful and just self-love' is subjected to 'the highest, purest love of God.'[65] This is 'a purified, cleansed soul,' in which the sensitive appetite is subjected to the rational, and the rational 'illuminated' and 'rectified' by faith.[66]

Whilst not as detailed in his explanation as Baxter or Reynolds, Swinnock certainly adheres to the same model. In his many 'directions,' governing the use of sensitive pleasures, his chief concern is that his readers put God before self, thereby avoiding idolatry. He encourages them to delight in natural pleasures, echoing the words of the apostle Paul – 'Whether, then, you eat or drink or whatever you do, do all to the glory of God.'[67] For Swinnock, this is the essence of self-control. In apostasy, the affections serve the sensitive appetite. In renewal, the affections are caught between the sensitive and rational appetites as the image of God is restored. In this condition, the individual's goal is to subdue the sensitive. For Swinnock, 'It is an abominable shame to a saint to be a slave to the beast in him, his sensitive appetite. "He that striveth for the mastery, is temperate in all things."'[68] This striving for the 'mastery' is the rational appetite exercising control over the sensitive. This is reminiscent of Augustine, who writes, 'I call wise only those men whose life is controlled by the mind and who are at peace with themselves by their complete mastery over every unlawful desire.'[69] A person can only be at peace with himself when the rational and sensitive appetites agree in their response to an object. The problem, therefore, according to Swinnock, is not 'passion' in the Stoic sense,[70] but 'unruly passions' or 'unlawful desires.' Self-control is the moderation of these, according to the fear of God.

The Fear of God in All Actions

For Swinnock, self-control must touch every area of life. 'Whether a Christian be eating or drinking, or buying or selling, or ploughing or sowing, or riding or walking, whatever he be doing, or wherever he be going, he must be always in the fear of the Lord. Godliness must be his guide, his measure, and his end...

---

[64] *Ibid.*, 301.

[65] *Ibid.*, 161.

[66] *Ibid.*, 21. For similar statements, see 229,248,284,295.

[67] 1 Cor. 10:31.

[68] *Christian Man's Calling*, I:271. Also see II:411.

[69] Augustine, *The Free Choice of the Will* in *The Fathers of the Church: Vol. LIX* (Washington: Catholic University of America Press, 1968) 91 (I:IX).

[70] For Reynolds's critique of Stoicism, see *Passions and Faculties*, 46-50. For Gouge, see *Domesticall Duties*, 83,362.

Every moment must be devoted to God; and as all seasons, so all actions must be sacred.'[71]

Natural

Beginning with natural actions, he remarks, 'A scribe instructed for the kingdom of heaven, is heedful not only that the weightiest actions of God's immediate worship, but also that the meaner passages of his life, be conformable to God's law.'[72]

In terms of eating, this implies the regenerate must differ from those who 'feed without fear.'[73] Simply put, 'piety or holiness to the Lord must be written upon their pots.'[74] This is achieved by adhering to three duties.[75] First, they must 'eat and drink sacredly'[76] by 'begging a blessing' before meals, employing 'holy expressions and affections' during meals, and 'returning thanks' after meals.[77] Second, they must 'eat and drink soberly'[78] by watching the 'quantity' and 'quality'[79] of their diet, for 'a lack of temperance' wrongs the body, estate, and soul.[80] Third, they must 'eat and drink seasonably,' remembering that 'as there is a season for spiritual actions, when they are most profitable, so there is a season for natural actions, when they are most proper… the body's place is after, not before the soul.'[81]

In terms of dressing, Swinnock acknowledges that it is 'of less concernment than some other subjects,' yet – even in small things – he believes 'we must walk by the rule of God's word.'[82] He gives three guidelines to help the regenerate 'manifest grace' in their apparel. First, the 'ends of' apparel 'must be minded.' This means they must remember that clothes exist to cover

---

[71]   *Christian Man's Calling*, I:85.

[72]   *Ibid.*, I:260.

[73]   *Ibid.*, I:262.

[74]   *Ibid.*, I:261.

[75]   There is nothing particularly noteworthy about Swinnock's three duties. Bayly summarizes them in one directive: 'Eat, therefore, to live, but live not to eat.' *Practice of Piety*, 149-152. For Perkins on food and drink, see *Cases*, 319-327. Peter Beale provides a summary of the Puritan approach to meals in 'Sanctifying the Outer Life' in *Aspects of Sanctification* (London: Westminster Conference, 1981) 68.

[76]   *Christian Man's Calling*, I:262.

[77]   *Ibid.*, I:263-265.

[78]   *Ibid.*, I:270.

[79]   *Ibid.*, I:273.

[80]   *Ibid.*, I:271-272.

[81]   *Ibid.*, I:276.

[82]   *Ibid.*, I:277. For Perkins on apparel, see *Cases*, 333-342. For Baxter, see *Christian Directory*, 391-394.

nakedness, defend and adorn the body, and distinguish sexes.[83] Second, the 'sins about' apparel 'must be avoided.' The principal sin is 'pride.'[84] Others include 'prodigality,' 'curiosity,' and 'wasteful expense of time.'[85] Third, the 'virtues in' apparel 'must be manifested:' modesty, gravity, and ability.[86]

As for sleeping, 'three things are principally to be minded.'[87] First, the regenerate must mind 'the quantity of it,'[88] remembering 'the discommodities of immoderate sleep' – it wastes time, injures the soul, wrongs the body, and threatens one's estate.[89] Second, they must mind the 'season of it'[90] – 'some considerable time after a moderate supper.'[91] Third, they must mind the 'end of it'[92] – 'Sleep is given us by God, not for the solution or weakening, but for remission and refreshing of nature, which would be not only wearied, but quite tired out by continual labour. The effects of moderate sleep will speak its ends. Sleep will, if taken seasonably, and not in excess, help digestion, recreate thy mind, repair thy spirits, comfort the whole body.'[93]

Recreational

Closely related to natural actions is recreation, which Swinnock describes as the 'spending of some time in delightful exercise, for the refreshing of my body and mind.'[94] The regenerate must keep their bodies in 'the best plight and health, vigour, and liveliness' for their souls' sake.[95] If they are constantly occupied in their 'general' and 'particular' callings, then 'the wings of devotion' will 'flag.'[96] Unsurprisingly, Swinnock forbids 'vain and sinful recreations' – 'those sports which are of evil report amongst the saints, or which thou hast experienced to be bellows to blow up the fire of thy passion, or fuel to thy covetousness.'[97] Furthermore, he warns against those recreations that are 'dishonourable to God' or 'disadvantageous to thy neighbour.'[98] Swinnock

---

[83] *Christian Man's Calling*, I:277-278.
[84] *Ibid.*, I:278-279.
[85] *Ibid.*, I:280-281.
[86] *Ibid.*, I:281-282.
[87] *Ibid.*, I:283. For Bayly on sleep, see *Practice of Piety*, 133-135.
[88] *Ibid.*
[89] *Ibid.*, I:283-284.
[90] *Ibid.*, I:284.
[91] *Ibid.*, I:284-285.
[92] *Ibid.*, I:285.
[93] *Ibid.*
[94] *Ibid.*, I:299. For Perkins on recreation, see *Cases*, 343-349. For Baxter, see *Christian Directory*, 386-390. Also see Beale, 'Sanctifying the Outer Life,' 74.
[95] *Christian Man's Calling*, I:289.
[96] *Ibid.*
[97] *Ibid.*, I:290.
[98] *Ibid.*, I:291.

refrains from mentioning specific examples, choosing rather to encourage his audience to think of the apostle Paul's 'rule'[99] – 'All things are lawful for me, but all things are not profitable.'[100]

This rule means the regenerate must 'mind moderation,' remembering that recreation is not their occupation.[101] It also means they must look to its 'end.' Simply put, 'the Christian may allow his mind moderate release, he may afford the ground of his outward man some rest; but his end must be, that when it comes again to be sowed, to be employed, it may be the more serviceable to God and his soul.'[102] Finally, it means they must 'have an eye to the season' of their recreation – not 'when God and men's families are neglected,' 'on a Lord's-day,' or 'in times of public calamities.'[103] Swinnock concludes his discussion of recreation, stating, 'I wish... that I may never abuse this favour which my Master affordeth me... to make me unfit for his work, but may be so conscientious in observing those cautions about it, which his law prescribeth, that my vigour and strength thereby repaired, I may after it follow his business with the more alacrity and ability.'[104]

Puritan Asceticism

In his numerous (and, at times, tedious) directions concerning the use of sensitive delights, Swinnock calls repeatedly for 'moderation.' This emphasis among the Puritans has given rise to the notion of Puritan asceticism. In describing the Puritans as ascetics, Max Weber states, 'Asceticism turns all its force... against one thing in particular: the *uninhibited enjoyment* of life and of the pleasures it has to offer.'[105] Today, the term *puritan* is often used to designate an individual, who is hostile to pleasure. This, however, is a misnomer. Jesus says to his disciples, 'If anyone wishes to come after Me, he must deny himself, and take up his cross and follow Me.'[106] Here, two aspects of discipleship are delineated: denying self and following Jesus.[107] If asceticism is a synonym for such discipleship, then Swinnock is certainly an ascetic. However, the term *asceticism* is often used to describe the 'purification of the

---

[99] *Ibid.*

[100] 1 Cor. 6:12.

[101] *Christian Man's Calling*, I:291.

[102] *Ibid.*, I:293-294.

[103] *Ibid.*, I:295-297.

[104] *Ibid.*, I:299.

[105] Max Weber, *The Protestant Ethic and the 'Spirit' of Capitalism*, ed. P. Baehr, trans. G. C. Wells (New York: Penguin Books, 2002) 112-113. His italics.

[106] Mk. 8:34.

[107] This is how Calvin defines mortification: denying self and following Jesus (or bearing the cross). Self-denial is inward mortification whereas following Jesus is outward mortification. Self-denial involves the subduing of passions whereas following Jesus involves the suffering of afflictions. *Institutes*, III:VII:1-10.

soul from its passions' as 'a necessary means for loving God more perfectly and for attaining to contemplation.'[108] This 'purification of the soul' is achieved by 'external exercises' such as 'abstinences, fasts, and vigils,'[109] which serve to dull the senses. This system of thought stems from a dualistic view of the universe, in which the material (including the body) is evil and the spiritual is good. It is for this reason that abstinence from certain natural actions is viewed as a necessary step to a deeper spirituality. In this sense of the term, Swinnock is most certainly not an ascetic.

Whilst it is true that the Puritans hold to a bi-partite view of humanity in which the soul is superior to the body, it is false to suggest that they regard the body as inherently evil. For this reason, the concept of 'Puritan asceticism' lacks substance. Undoubtedly, misplaced zeal led some to adopt ascetic practices.[110] However, this should not be seen as normative. As Keeble rightly notes, 'The main thrust of Puritan thought was that the way to perfection lay not through abstinence and asceticism, but through the right admission and moderate utilization of the world and the flesh. The Puritan neither under-valued nor over-valued them: he sanctified them.'[111] Lovelace arrives at a similar conclusion: 'It is clear that the Puritans were extremely worried about this sort of amalgam and that they took pains to emphasize the fact that the biblical *sarx* did not mean the body but the totality of sin affecting the personality; that progress in holiness and approach to God were effected by mortification of sin and not of the senses.'[112]

This view is clearly evident in Swinnock, who writes, 'Godliness does not deny us our natural delights, only rectify and regulate them, lest we should surfeit them.'[113] He entertains no thought of abstaining from 'natural delights' in order to mortify the senses in an attempt to purify the soul. On the contrary, he writes:

> The merciful God is pleased, out of his bounty, not only to allow his creatures what is for *necessity*, but also what is for *delight*. Christian, it is more than God requireth of thee to be always pondering and poring on such subjects as make thy heart sad, whereby thou thyself art disadvantaged, banishing that cheerfulness

---

[108] *Oxford Dictionary of the Christian Church* (hereafter *ODCC*), ed. F. L. Cross (Oxford University Press, 1966) 93.

[109] *Ibid.* For more on the history of asceticism, see *Encyclopaedia of Religion and Ethics*, II:63-80.

[110] At times, it is possible to find ascetic practices in Baxter. To curb 'filthy lusts,' he recommends, (1) 'Eat no breakfasts nor suppers;' (2) 'Drink no wine or strong drink;' (3) 'Eat no hot spices;' (4) 'Let blood;' and (5) 'Oft bathe in cold water.' *Christian Directory*, 335. However, such comments should not be construed as representing his entire approach.

[111] Keeble, 'Puritan Spirituality,' 326.

[112] Lovelace, 'The Anatomy of Puritan Piety,' 318.

[113] *Christian Man's Calling*, III:185.

from thee, which is an ornament to Christianity; and others discouraged, supposing that all who walk in heaven's way, must needs be, as thou art, mopish and melancholy. Piety doth regulate, but not extirpate our pleasures.[114]

Swinnock's assertion that God has given us 'not only... what is for *necessity*, but also what is for *delight*' is extremely significant. It sets his 'directions' and 'duties' in a much broader context. This is also true of Perkins, who comments, 'We may use these gifts of God... not sparingly alone, and for meere necessitie, to the satisfying of our hunger, and quenching of our thirst; but also freely and liberally, for Christian delight and pleasure. For this is that liberty, which God hath granted to all beleevers.'[115] Clearly, the Puritans have no problem in deriving pleasure from the created order. To demonstrate this, Swinnock appeals to 1 Timothy 4:4, where the apostle Paul declares, 'For everything created by God is good, and nothing is to be rejected if it is received with gratitude.'[116] Earlier in the chapter, the apostle Paul warns of false teachers who pay attention to 'deceitful spirits and doctrines of demons,' in that they 'forbid marriage and advocate abstaining from foods.'[117] As William Hendriksen observes, these false teachers 'had in common *Asceticism*, the renunciation of the comforts of life with a view to attaining happiness and perfection.'[118] The apostle responds to this false teaching by affirming that God has created these things to be 'gratefully shared in by those who believe and know the truth.'[119] God created all things, and declared all things to be good. This fact undermines the notion that the physical is inherently evil. Therefore, for Swinnock, the way to holiness is not found in abstaining from God's good gifts, but in carefully enjoying them. The regenerate must not over-value natural delights according to their sinful inclination; rather, they must moderate their use of them according to the fear of God. He says, 'Godliness will cause thee to enjoy the creatures in God, the fountain of them, and thereby they will be pleasant to thee.'[120]

Baxter reveals the same mindset, affirming, 'You know not what it is to be a man, if you know not that God hath made all the senses to be the inlets of objects, and so of holy pleasures into the soul... It is therefore a foolish pretence of spirituality, to dream of acting without our senses, or avoiding those delights, which may and must be, sanctified to us.'[121] Elsewhere, he states,

---

[114] *Ibid.* My italics.

[115] Perkins, *Cases*, 321. Also see 342.

[116] *Christian Man's Calling*, I:263,267.

[117] 1 Tim. 4:1-3.

[118] William Hendriksen, *A Commentary on 1 & 11 Timothy and Titus* (London: Banner of Truth, 1964) 146. His italics. He sees an incipient Gnosticism behind these beliefs.

[119] 1 Tim. 4:3.

[120] *Christian Man's Calling*, I:262.

[121] Baxter, *Christian Directory*, 704-705.

'mere natural pleasing of the senses is in itself no moral good or evil.'[122] Rather, 'The delight of the flesh or senses is a natural good; and the natural desire of it in itself... is neither vice nor virtue: but when this little natural good is preferred before the greater spiritual, moral, or eternal good, this is the sin of carnal minds.'[123] Baxter urges his readers to keep in mind the 'difference' between: (1) 'the appetite itself;' (2) 'the violence and unruly disposition of the appetite;' and (3) 'the actual obeying and pleasing of the appetite.' The first was in 'innocency;' the other two are the result of the fall.[124]

Like Swinnock, Baxter rejects the idea that 'all love of the creature' is sin, for 'the works of God are all good, as such; and all goodness is amiable.'[125] The problem arises when the creature turns the soul from God, resulting in 'inordinate pleasure.'[126] This can happen with 'honour, greatness, authority, praises, money, houses, lands, cattle, meat, drink, sleep, apparel, sports, friends, relations, and life itself.'[127] This danger in no way nullifies the legitimate use of these sensitive pleasures. Baxter states, 'If it be such a love to the creature as exceedeth not its worth, and is intended ultimately for God, and maketh you not love him the less but the more, it is not it that I am speaking against, or persuading you to mortify.'[128] Baxter is well aware that some may take his exhortations to an extreme. Thus, he warns of the 'over-scrupulous person,' who is 'afraid of every bit they eat, or of all they possess, or wear, or use, and sometimes of their very children and relations,' adding 'It is a very hard thing for us to write or preach to one party, but the other will misapply it to themselves, and make an ill use of it.'[129]

In short, Baxter's concern is that God occupy first place: 'When you delight in God, your creature delight will be sanctified to you, and warrantable in its proper place.'[130] Therefore, he says, 'Let all lawful, natural mirth be taken in, as animated and sanctified by this holy delight and joy; and know that this natural, sanctified mirth is not only lawful, but a duty exceeding congruous and comely for a thankful believer in his way to everlasting joy.'[131] Yet again, 'So far as we can make use of a delight in friends, or food, or health, or habitations, or any accommodations of our bodies, to further our delight in God, or to remove those melancholy fears or sorrows, which would hinder this spiritual delight, it is not only lawful, but our duty to use them, with that moderation as tendeth to

---

[122] *Ibid.*, 78. Also see 276,303.

[123] *Ibid.*, 224. Also see 227,275.

[124] *Ibid.*, 228.

[125] *Ibid.*, 214.

[126] *Ibid.*, 78. For Baxter's seven 'qualifications' for the 'lawful' pleasing of the senses, see 225.

[127] *Ibid.*, 275.

[128] *Ibid.*, 276.

[129] *Ibid.*, 277.

[130] *Ibid.*, 140.

[131] *Ibid.*, 281.

this end.'[132]

In their approach to sensitive delights, the Puritans stand with Calvin.[133] As Lucien Richard demonstrates, Calvin was no ascetic. He begins his analysis by looking at the Brethren of the Common Life, who understood 'inner devotion' as a 'deep consciousness of a personal relationship with God and a perpetual striving to direct all... work, prayer and spiritual exercise to Him.'[134] This *Devotio Moderna* emerged into 'a systematic method of private meditative prayer which wielded a wide and profound influence... This movement of ordered and meditative prayer was woven into the traditional doctrine of the three ways or stages of the spiritual life, the purgative, the illuminative, and the unitive.'[135] Related to this was the practice of asceticism. However, as Richard explains, 'The spirituality of Calvin represents a complete break from the monastic type and so differs radically from the spirituality of the *Devotio Moderna*... For Calvin, contempt of this world was achieved through comparison with the future life.'[136] He adds, 'The term "inner-worldly asceticism" can be used to describe the spirituality of John Calvin. His ideal was not withdrawal from the world, but the conquest of the world for the glory of God.'[137] For Calvin, 'Piety is not contempt for created reality but the understanding that man's inner life is what matters, a life which is dependent upon God. Created reality has a value, but it is a relative value; it has autonomy, but a relative autonomy.'[138]

In his discussion of the present life, Calvin acknowledges his disapproval of 'some good and holy men,' who only 'allowed man to use physical goods in so far as necessity required.'[139] Whilst applauding their concern to curb 'wantonness,' he rejects their strictness, commenting, 'To them necessity means to abstain from all things that they could do without.'[140] He has no interest in such asceticism, emphatically stating, 'Away, then, with that

---

[132]   *Ibid.*, 141. Also see 112,124.

[133]   As George Yule demonstrates, Luther attacked medieval ascetic practices, because they encouraged 'legal repentance.' Luther believed this aberration had entered the church through Tertullian, who translated the Greek *metanoia* into the Latin *poenitentium agitur* – 'to do penance.' Through Jerome's Latin Bible, this notion permeated the church. 'Luther and the Ascetic Life' in *Monks, Hermits and the Ascetic Tradition: Studies in Church History, Vol. XXII*, ed. W. J. Sheils (Basil Blackwell, 1985) 229-230.

[134]   Richard, *Spirituality of John Calvin*, 12.

[135]   *Ibid.*, 30.

[136]   *Ibid.*, 125. Gleason acknowledges some similarity between Calvin and the *Devotio Moderna*, in that Calvin adopts the movement's 'individualistic style of spirituality.' *John Calvin and John Owen on Mortification*, 47.

[137]   Richard, *Spirituality of John Calvin*, 126.

[138]   *Ibid.*, 127.

[139]   Calvin, *Institutes*, III:X:1.

[140]   *Ibid.*

inhuman philosophy which, while conceding only a necessary use of creatures, not only malignantly deprives us of the lawful fruit of God's beneficence but cannot be practiced unless it robs a man of all his senses and degrades him to a block.'[141] In contrast, Calvin gives only one 'principle' to guide people in their use of pleasures – 'that the use of God's gifts is not wrongly directed when it is referred to that end to which the Author himself created and destined them for us, since he created them for our good, not for our ruin.'[142] This is the essence of moderation. He writes, 'And we have never been forbidden to laugh, or to be filled, or to join new possessions to old or ancestral ones, or to delight in musical harmony, or to drink wine. True indeed. But where there is plenty, to wallow in delights, to gorge oneself, to intoxicate mind and heart with present pleasures and be always panting after new ones – such are very far removed from a lawful use of God's gifts.'[143] He adds, 'Away, then, with uncontrolled desire, away with immoderate prodigality, away with vanity and arrogance – in order that men may with a clean conscience cleanly use God's gifts.'[144] For Calvin, 'This is spiritual sobriety, when we use this world so sparingly and temperately that we are not entangled with its allurements.'[145]

Swinnock's view of self-control is entirely in keeping with Calvin. The issue is not food, drink, or any other delight. Swinnock has no qualms with 'outward pleasures,' affirming, 'moderate delight in creatures is allowed and commanded.'[146] They are good, because God ordained them. The issue is abuse, whereby the soul seeks its satisfaction in these things apart from God. The regenerate must moderate such inordinate desire. They do so by enjoying sensitive delights in an attitude of thanksgiving, according to God's design. As Richard Schlatter observes, 'The Puritan was determined to make earthly things divine, not by forbidding them, but by infusing them with holiness.'[147]

The Fear of God in All Vocations

Self-control must also be evident in one's calling, which Perkins defines as 'a certaine kind of life, ordained and imposed on man by God, for the common good.'[148] It is 'the execution of some particular office, arising of that distinction

---

[141] *Ibid.*, III:X:3.

[142] *Ibid.*, III:X:2.

[143] *Ibid.*, III:XIX:9.

[144] *Ibid.*

[145] Calvin, *Commentary on the First Epistle to the Thessalonians, Calvin's Commentaries* (Grand Rapids: Baker Books, 2003) XXI:288.

[146] *Christian Man's Calling*, I:288.

[147] Richard Schlatter, *The Social Ideas of Religious Leaders, 1660-1688* (New York: Octagon Books, 1971) 11.

[148] William Perkins, *A Treatise of the Vocations; or, Callings of men, with the sorts and kinds of them, and the right use thereof, Works,* I:727.

which God makes betweene man and man in every societie.'[149] This 'distinction' is of two 'sorts:' 'such as be of the essence and foundation of any society' – family, commonwealth, and church;[150] and 'such as serve onely for the good, happy, and quiet estate of a society' – employment.[151] Regarding the second, Swinnock writes, 'As religion must be our business in our spiritual and natural, so also in our civil actions and particular callings... Godliness must be the key to open thy shop; godliness must be the whip to drive thy cart; godliness must be the cock to call thee up to thy work; godliness must be the clock to call thee off thy work; godliness must be the principle, the rule, and the end of thy work.'[152] Gurnall concurs, 'The Christian must express the power of holiness in his particular calling... The Christian man is not to buy and sell, as a mere man, but as a Christian man... wherever the Christian is, whatever he is adoing, he must keep his religion on – I mean, do it holily.'[153]

Foundational to Swinnock's view of work is his dismissal of the notion that the sacred refers to anything under the church's control whereas the secular refers to anything not under the church's control.[154] For Swinnock, work is sacred, because it is a means by which people serve God. Perkins comments, 'We must consider the maine end of our lives, and that is, to serve God in the serving of men in the workes of our callings.'[155] According to Charnock, 'Though our callings are our work, yet they are by God's order, wherein we are to be faithful to our great Master and Ruler.'[156] Beale expresses the significance of this view as follows: 'Whether his calling was an exalted or a humble one, the Puritan worker sought to glorify God by the way in which he worked, knowing that he had a Master in heaven.'[157] For Swinnock, this means the regenerate must approach their calling in the fear of God.[158] Carnal self-love

---

[149] *Ibid.*, I:731.

[150] In *Christian Man's Calling*, Swinnock never addresses the impact of godliness upon one's calling within the commonwealth. He saves this for his treatises on magistracy: *Gods Are Men* and *Men Are Gods*. For Charnock on magistracy, see *Existence and Attributes of God*, II:301,444-445. For Baxter, see *Christian Directory*, 741-769.

[151] Perkins, *Vocations, Works*, I:735.

[152] *Christian Man's Calling*, I:300-301.

[153] Gurnall, *Christian in Complete Armour*, I:435.

[154] For Luther, this separation between the sacred and secular was the first of 'three walls' constructed by the Romanists. He writes, 'It is pure invention that pope, bishop, priests, and monks are called the spiritual estate while princes, lords, artisans, and farmers are called the temporal estate. This is indeed a piece of deceit and hypocrisy.' *To the Christian Nobility of the German Nation Concerning the Reform of the Christian Estate, Works*, XLIV:127.

[155] Perkins, *Vocations, Works*, I:734.

[156] Charnock, *Existence and Attributes of God*, II:420-421.

[157] Beale, 'Sanctifying the Outer Life,' 72.

[158] For Perkins on this subject, see *Vocations, Works*, I:743-753.

may lead to laziness, for, as Baxter explains, 'Sloth is an averseness to labour, through a carnal love of ease, or indulgence to the flesh.'[159] It may also lead to idolatry whereby work becomes a god. Swinnock tells such ones to be 'diligent'[160] and 'deal righteously.'[161] They must not permit their calling to steal away their 'heart' or 'time.'[162] As Gurnall affirms, a person's calling must 'not turn the edge of his affections, and leave a bluntness upon his spirit as to holding communion with God.'[163] Above all, Swinnock exhorts them to work for contentment – 'a holy composedness.'[164]

Much has been made of the Puritan concept of 'calling.' According to Max Weber, it is responsible for today's capitalism.[165] He argues that the doctrine of election caused the Puritans to focus upon assurance. Given their concept of work as God-ordained, they urged *tireless labor in a calling... as the best possible means of attaining* this self-assurance.'[166] This resulted in an emphasis upon 'ceaseless, constant, systematic labor in a secular calling' as 'the surest and most visible proof of regeneration and the genuineness of faith.' And this, according to Weber, 'was inevitably the most powerful lever imaginable with which to bring the spread of that philosophy of life which we have here termed the "spirit" of capitalism.'[167] Weber's thesis has generated a large body of literature. Some scholars question the legitimacy of Weber's distinction between a particularly Puritan and generally Protestant work ethic.[168] Even more serious is Weber's notion of a direct link between the Puritan doctrine of assurance and the rise of capitalism. He places far too much emphasis upon a

---

[159] Baxter, *Christian Directory*, 378.

[160] *Christian Man's Calling*, I:301.

[161] *Ibid.*, I:304.

[162] *Ibid.*, I:306. For this thought in Gurnall, see *Christian in Complete Armour*, I:437.

[163] Gurnall, *Christian in Complete Armour*, I:438.

[164] *Christian Man's Calling*, I:314. For more on this, see Paul Seaver, *Wallington's World: A Puritan Artisan in Seventeenth-Century London* (Stanford University Press, 1985); and Seaver, 'The Puritan Work Ethic Revisited,' *Journal of British Studies* 19 (1980) 35-53.

[165] Weber, *Protestant Ethic*, 13. His italics. For similar views, see Schlatter, *Social Ideas of Religious Leaders*, 186; and Hill, *Society and Puritanism*, 135-138.

[166] Weber, *Protestant Ethic*, 77-78. His italics.

[167] *Ibid.*, 116. His italics.

[168] See Timothy Breen, 'The Non-Existent Controversy: Puritan and Anglican Attitudes on Work and Wealth,' *Church History* 35 (1966) 273-287. From his examination of the primary literature, Breen identifies three common beliefs among Protestants: (1) they 'referred to God's placing of each man in the social order as the "particular" or personal calling;' (2) they 'aggressively attacked idleness;' and (3) they 'thought that wealth was neither good nor evil in itself.' C. John Sommerville adopts an entirely different approach, arguing that Anglicanism – not Puritanism – stressed 'worldly enterprise.' 'The Anti-Puritan Work Ethic,' *Journal of British Studies* 20 (1981) 73. This was the case, because 'moralistic Anglican piety' viewed labour at an earthly calling as 'one part of earning salvation.' *Ibid.*, 78.

perceived tendency among the Puritans to equate economic prosperity with God's favour.[169] In actual fact, the Puritans stress God's inscrutability when it comes to economic prosperity. They are well aware that many times the unregenerate prosper whilst the regenerate experience adversity. As for Swinnock, he never seeks to explain the economic prosperity of the unregenerate as a sign of assurance.[170]

The Fear of God in All Relations

Swinnock defines the family as 'a natural and simple society of certain persons, having mutual relation one to another, under the private government of one head or chief.'[171] This 'society' consists of three main relationships: parents and children, husbands and wives, masters and servants.[172] In this society, self-control is essential, for, as Baxter notes, 'It is the pernicious subversion of all societies, and so of the world, that selfish, ungodly persons enter into all relations with a desire to serve themselves there, and fish out all that gratifieth their flesh, but without any sense of the duty of their relation... All their

---

[169] Like Weber, Robert Michaelsen argues that the Puritan concept of calling released the economic drives of Western man. 'Changes in the Puritan Concept of Calling or Vocation,' *The New England Quarterly* 26 (1953) 315-336. Following the Reformers, the early Puritans developed a religious doctrine of vocation. However, the later Puritans moved to a more secular doctrine – 'When the late Puritans talked about the general calling they thought chiefly of particular *acts* which might be called religious acts, rather than an overwhelming experience of the grace of God in Jesus Christ.' *Ibid.*, 326. He includes Swinnock within this group: 'Religion, conceived as a series of pious acts, was regarded by Swinnock as man's primary business.' *Ibid.*, 327 (f. 37). These later Puritans gave more power to the natural man by minimizing the doctrine of original sin and maximizing the role of good works in salvation. *Ibid.*, 328. This shift led to a stress upon industry, prudence, diligence, and orderliness. 'It is not a great step,' claims Michaelsen, 'from the blessing of industry and prudence as the best exercises for the soul to the blessing of these virtues in themselves, or the blessing of the material wealth gained by them.' *Ibid.*, 332.

[170] *Christian Man's Calling*, I:58.

[171] *Ibid.*, I:329-330.

[172] The only mention of Swinnock's family is found in his 'Epistle Dedicatory' to George Bates, 'Physician in Ordinary to his Excellent Majesty Charles the Second.' *Ibid.*, I:368. There is nothing original in Swinnock's approach to the family. Most of his directions are found in Gouge's *Domesticall Duties* – a popular treatise on household duties. Gouge's approach is found even further back in Heinrich Bullinger's *The Christen State of Matrimonye*, trans. Myles Coverdale (1541; rpt., Amsterdam: Theatrum Orbis Terrarum, 1974) chapters xvii-xxii. According to Ronald Frye, it is 'the first important Protestant formulation on marriage to be published in English,' having 'gone through nine issues or editions by 1575.' 'The Teaching of Classical Puritanism on Conjugal Love,' *Studies in the Renaissance* 2 (1955) 149.

thought is, what they shall have, but not what they shall be and do.'[173]

Parents and Children

Beginning with parents, Swinnock encourages them to raise their children 'in the fear of the great God.'[174] Regarding their children's 'temporal' estate, they must provide food, apparel, and education, train them in some calling, arrange for their marriage, and leave them an inheritance.[175] Regarding their children's 'spiritual' estate,[176] they must dedicate them to God by baptism, instruct them in the 'word and will of God,' acquaint them with the works of God so that they will 'fear, love, and trust him,' pray earnestly for them, correct them, and set a good example for them.[177] Swinnock warns, 'Children will observe their fathers' courses and carriage, and sooner follow their poisonous patterns, than their pious precepts.'[178]

Turning to children, Swinnock appeals to Obadiah's example,[179] stating, 'This poor child that is wise – i.e., that feareth God, and keepeth his commandments – doth infinitely outweigh, and is exceedingly more worth than, an old king that is wicked.'[180] With this in mind, he exhorts children to 'fear the Lord' in their youth,[181] remembering that 'early piety' is profitable, 'delays are dangerous,' God deserves their youth, and they will give 'an account' for their youth.[182] By way of duties, he maintains that children are to be known for their reverence, obedience, submission, affection, and gratitude.[183] Swinnock concludes with a child's good wish – 'that the fear of my God may take such early possession of my soul that when Satan, the world, and youthful lusts shall hereafter sue for my service, they may be wholly prevented in their projects, and disappointed of my heart, that presence-chamber being taken up beforehand.'[184]

---

[173] Baxter, *Christian Directory*, 431.
[174] *Christian Man's Calling*, I:395. For Baxter on parents, see *Christian Directory*, 449-454. For Gouge, see *Domesticall Duties*, 497-588.
[175] *Christian Man's Calling*, I:418-425.
[176] Swinnock gives several motives to 'quicken' parents. *Ibid.*, I:399-403.
[177] *Ibid.*, I:404-415.
[178] *Ibid.*, I:416. For the Puritans on 'the education of children,' see Schlatter, *Social Ideas of Religious Leaders*, 31-59.
[179] 1 Kgs. 18:12.
[180] *Christian Man's Calling*, I:438. For Baxter on children, see *Christian Directory*, 454-457. For Gouge, see *Domesticall Duties*, 427-496.
[181] *Christian Man's Calling*, I:445.
[182] *Ibid.*, I:439-445.
[183] *Ibid.*, I:447-455.
[184] *Ibid.*, I:458-459.

Husbands and Wives

Swinnock defines marriage as 'the lawful conjunction of one man and one woman for the term of their natural lives, for the generation of children, the avoiding of sin, or the comfort of mutual society.'[185] He affirms that 'matrimony and sanctity are not inconsistent,'[186] pointing out that marriage is a 'divine institution,' established in 'man's estate of innocency.' Thus, 'how abominable is it to call that impure which God hath cleansed; or to make the holy God the author of a sinful ordinance... Surely those popish doctors who term it filthiness and pollution do not consider that it was ordained before man's fall and corruption.'[187] Once again, it is evident that Swinnock is no ascetic.[188] For him, the fact that God created Adam and Eve, declared that they should not be alone, and brought them together (all prior to the fall), is sufficient evidence that marriage is good.

Despite this biblical evidence, the view of celibacy as a means to spirituality entered the church at an early date. Beginning in the second century, many allowed dualistic philosophies[189] to influence their beliefs regarding sex. They held that lust taints all sexual activity. For many, this implied that virginity was superior to marriage.[190] For some, it meant that second marriages were unacceptable.[191] These convictions even contributed in part to the emulation of the Virgin Mary.[192] Without question, the most influential thinker of the time period was Augustine, who argues that sex 'practically paralyses all power of deliberate thought.'[193] Prior to the fall, Adam and Eve were unashamed, because 'no desire stirred their organs in defiance of their deliberate decision.'[194] This means 'passion had no place before they sinned; it was only after the fall, when their nature had lost its power to exact obedience from the sexual organs, that they fell and noticed the loss and, being ashamed of their lust, covered these unruly members.'[195] For Augustine, Adam and Eve would

---

[185] *Ibid.*, I:464. For Baxter on marriage, see *Christian Directory*, 394-409,422-449. For Puritan views in general, see Schlatter, *Social Ideas of Religious Leaders*, 1-30. Much of his analysis is based upon Baxter's *Christian Directory*.

[186] *Christian Man's Calling*, I:465.

[187] *Ibid.*, I:466-467.

[188] For the Puritans in general, see Packer, *Quest for* Godliness, 259-266. Schucking identifies Baxter as an exception to the rule, in that he 'shows signs of reverting to the basic Catholic point of view.' *The Puritan Family*, 24. This is debatable.

[189] E.g., Manichaeism and Gnosticism.

[190] E.g., Cyprian, 'Treatises Attributed to Cyprian' in *The Ante-Nicene Fathers* (Grand Rapids: Eerdmans, 1951) V:589.

[191] E.g., Tertullian, 'On Monogamy' in *Ante-Nicene Fathers*, III:59-72.

[192] E.g., Irenaeus, 'Irenaeus Against Heresies' in *Ante-Nicene Fathers*, I:547; and Gregory, 'Four Homilies' in *Ante-Nicene Fathers*, VI:62-63.

[193] Augustine, *City of God, Select Library: Vol. II*, XIV:16.

[194] *Ibid.*, XIV:17.

[195] *Ibid.*, XIV:21.

have produced children in the garden 'by deliberate choice and not by uncontrollable lust.'[196] Hence, procreation of children is 'both legally right and morally good,'[197] yet involves a passion that is shameful, because it is 'roused counter to the commands of the rational will.'[198] As Henry Chadwick remarks, for Augustine, 'in human nature as it now is the sexual impulse is the supreme symptom or expression of the irrational, the uncontrollable, the obsessive condition of the human psyche in its fallen condition. The physiology of the impulse was at war with will and reason.'[199]

From this premise, the church of the Middle Ages acknowledged two reasons for marriage: the procreation of children and the avoidance of fornication.[200] These notions remained prominent within the church until the Reformers departed from the accepted tradition by adding a third reason for marriage, namely, mutual society. Heinrich Bullinger, for example, criticizes 'cyrtayne spirituall men and women of the spirituality' who deny due benevolence 'thynkyng therby to be very holy clene and spirituall.'[201] He insists that 'holy wedlok was instituted... in the paradise and garden of pleasure... before the fall of man... of God himselfe, doutlesse to mans greate comforte and helpe.'[202] He explains that God instituted marriage 'even to the intent that they maye lyve honestly and friendly the one with the other, that they maye avoyde unclennesse, that they maye bring up children in the feare of God, that the one maye helpe and comforte the other.'[203]

Despite this advancement, Levin Schucking believes the Reformers fell short of affirming that sex is good in itself. He remarks, 'The essentially ascetical spirit of Christianity had in this case been too powerful. The teaching of St Augustine, which clearly implied that sexuality was really the original sin, had so poisoned men's minds that it was impossible for the cleansing effects of the Reformation immediately to assert themselves.'[204] This is evident to some extent in Bullinger, who believes 'God hath geven and ordened mariage to be a remedy and medicine unto our feble and weake flesh, to swage the disquietnesse thereof.'[205] This points to some uncertainty concerning the state

---

[196] *Ibid.*, XIV:24.

[197] *Ibid.*, XIV:18.

[198] *Ibid.*, XIV:19.

[199] Henry Chadwick, 'The Ascetic Ideal in the History of the Church' in *Monks, Hermits and the Ascetic Tradition: Vol. 22*, ed. W. J. Sheils (Basil Blackwell, 1985) 19.

[200] Schucking, *Puritan Family*, 22.

[201] Bullinger, *Christen State of Matrimonye*, xxiiiv.

[202] *Ibid.*, i.

[203] *Ibid.*, iv. For Bullinger's full treatment of the three reasons for marriage, see xxiii-xxvii.

[204] Schucking, *Puritan Family*, 45. This is a slight overstatement, in that Augustine never 'implied that sexuality was really the original sin.'

[205] Bullinger, *Christen State of Matrimonye*, xxv.

of the body in innocence. Why did God ordain marriage as a remedy for feeble and weak flesh when it was neither feeble nor weak? Similarly, Calvin makes some ambiguous statements such as: 'The honorableness of matrimony covers the baseness of incontinence.'[206] In other words, married men and women are guilty of 'baseness,' however they are not condemned because matrimony covers their 'baseness.' This is confusing. Calvin appears to teach that sex is disgraceful, yet not shameful because of marriage.

Schucking believes it was the Puritans who finally freed marriage from such lingering doubts.[207] Doriani challenges this view, stating, 'The Puritans... formulated so many warnings and restrictions that their protestations of the goodness and purity of sexuality lost their force.'[208] According to Doriani, the Puritans maintain that marriage and sex are pure, that God requires couples to communicate their bodies to each other, and that sexual relations have beneficial products. However, he believes they fail to rid themselves of 'the Greek and Roman Catholic idea that lust taints the procreative act so that it is shameful.'[209] Therefore, their 'vague discomfort with passion and pleasure descends from the Greek and Catholic dualism with its denigration of and antipathy toward the body. The godly brethren found it very difficult to make a complete break with that tradition, even over several generations.'[210]

There is undoubtedly some truth to Doriani's conclusion; however, it is difficult to speak categorically for all Puritans. As for Swinnock, he affirms – like the Reformers before him – three 'ends' for marriage. However, he reverses the order: 'the procreation of children,' 'the comfort of mutual society' (or 'the benefit of a good companion'), and 'the avoiding of fornication.' He makes it clear that the third 'end' has only existed 'since the fall.'[211] Procreation and companionship, therefore, are God's good gifts. The need to avoid fornication only exists, because sin exists. In this, Swinnock demonstrates no 'antipathy toward the body.'[212] He simply believes it is necessary to guard

---

[206] Calvin, *Institutes*, II:VIII:44. Also see II:VIII:41-42.

[207] For an overview of Puritan views of sexuality, see Doriani, 'The Puritans, Sex, and Pleasure,' 125-143; and Frye, 'The Teachings of Classical Puritanism,' 149-155. For the common charge of Puritan prudery, see L. Koehler, *A Search for* Power (University of Illinois Press, 1980) 10; and L. Stone, *The Family, Sex and Marriage in England, 1500-1800* (New York: Harper & Row, 1977) 499,523. For the opposite view, see L. Ryken, *Worldly Saints: The Puritans as They Really Were* (Grand Rapids: Zondervan, 1986) 43-45; Edmund Leites, 'The Duty to Desire: Love, Friendship, and Sexuality in Some Puritan Theories of Marriage,' *Journal of Social History* 15 (1982) 383-403; and Schlatter, *Social Ideas of Religious Leaders*, 8-9;

[208] Doriani, 'The Puritans, Sex, and Pleasure,' 133.

[209] *Ibid.*

[210] *Ibid.*, 142.

[211] *Christian Man's Calling*, I:464.

[212] He comments, 'Jerome, whom Pope Syricius followed, in his passionate love of virginity, did make a blot in his exposition of Romans 8:8. They that are in the flesh,

against 'inordinate' passion. To do so, he suggests several duties, beginning with 'amity.'[213] Quite simply, husbands and wives are to love each other. This manifests itself in mutual respect. There should also be 'fidelity' in their estates, names, and bodies.[214] The last 'consisteth in giving to each the seasonable moderate use of the other's body and denying it to all others.'[215] Swinnock's call for moderation does not stem from some residual dualistic tendencies in his thinking, but from his conviction that people are prone to abuse God's good gifts.[216] Thus, they must exercise self-control in the fear of God.

Gouge shares these sentiments, openly encouraging due benevolence.[217] He states, 'As the man must be satisfied at all times in his wife, and even ravisht with her love; so must the woman be satisfied at all times in her husband, and even ravisht with his love.'[218] Again, 'This *due benevolence...* is one of the most proper and essentiall acts of marriage... it must be performed with good will and delight, willingly, readily and cheerfully.'[219] For Gouge, 'there are two extremes contraie to this dutie.' The first is a 'defect' – 'when in the case of need it is not required, or being required by one, it is not yielded by the other.' The second is 'excess' in the measure or time.[220]

Neither Swinnock nor Gouge demonstrate what Doriani calls a 'vague discomfort with passion and pleasure.' Speaking of the Puritans in general, Frye observes that 'their fear was of an immoderate love, whose very violence precluded it from maintaining the stability necessary for the marriage relationship, and whose intensity of attachment was likely to burn itself out and die.'[221] He adds, 'Man's humanity... consisted in his living according to the divine plan, in his existential expression of God's will rather than self-will. To assign prior importance, before God, to anything under God was idolatry.'[222] On this basis, the Puritans consider lust to be idolatry. 'Thus,' says Frye, 'the Puritan warnings were not concerned with any sin involved in physical love itself... Two things were feared: lust as unstable sexual foundation for marriage in this world, and lust as idolatrous preventative of happiness in the world to

---

i.e., qui inserviunt officio conjugali, that is, saith he, those that are married, cannot please God, when man pleased God by taking a wife, before ever he displeased God by hearkening to his wife. God would never have said, "It is not good for man to be alone," if it had been evil for him to have had such a companion.' *Ibid.*, I:467.

[213] *Ibid.*, I:471.

[214] *Ibid.*, I:475.

[215] *Ibid.*, I:476.

[216] For Baxter on this theme, see *Christian Directory*, 431.

[217] Gouge, *Domesticall Duties*, 365-366.

[218] *Ibid.*, 217.

[219] *Ibid.*, 222. His italics.

[220] *Ibid.*, 222-223.

[221] Frye, 'The Teachings of Classical Puritanism,' 156.

[222] *Ibid.*, 158.

come.'[223] From his analysis of the primary literature, Edmund Leites concludes, 'This sensuous love is not simply permitted, given the existence of a higher, holier, "spiritual" relation between man and wife, nor is it allowed only to forward the other purposes of marriage. It is required as a constituent and intrinsic element of a good marriage. This sensual affection and delight must continue unabated, with the full intensity of youthful desire throughout the whole of married life.'[224]

The Role of Husbands

As for specific duties, Swinnock begins with husbands, stating that there must be 'affection.'[225] He appeals to the example of Jesus' love for the church – it is 'chaste,' 'constant,' and 'fervent.'[226] There must also be 'instruction.'[227] Finally, there must be 'provision' of food, apparel, and cohabitation (or the right of bed).[228] In short, Swinnock exhorts husbands, 'love thy wife cordially... instruct her constantly, and... provide for her competently... all out of conscience to God's command.'[229]

Swinnock places a tremendous emphasis upon the husband's responsibility to love his wife, stating, 'They are one body, one flesh, and so should have but one soul, one spirit; they have one bed, one board, one house, and therefore should be one in heart. The love betwixt Christ and his spouse, which is so fervent that she is sick of love to him, and he died for love to her (Cant. 2:4; Jn. 15:13) is set out by the love betwixt husband and wife, to shew how great this love is, or at least ought to be.'[230] This is no mere sentimentality. Swinnock writes, 'So the word προσκολληθὲναι in the Greek also signifieth, shall cleave to his wife (Matt. 19:51), be glued to his wife, importing a conjunction so near as nothing can come between, and so firm that nothing can dissolve it.'[231] With this in mind, he exhorts husbands, 'Be thou ravished with her love (Prov. 5:19).'[232] Again, 'Do thou err in thy love... and so affectionately to desire her,

---

[223] *Ibid.*.

[224] Leites, 'The Duty to Desire,' 388.

[225] *Christian Man's Calling*, I:489. For Gouge on husbands, see *Domesticall Duties*, 349-426.

[226] *Ibid.*, I:499-500.

[227] *Ibid.*, I:492.

[228] *Ibid.*, I:495.

[229] *Ibid.*, I:496.

[230] *Ibid.*, I:472. At this point, it is worth commenting on the perception that the Puritans encourage wife beating. Swinnock writes, 'Surely if Scripture will not allow thee to be bitter to thy wife, it will not allow thee to beat her... Socrates could say, For a man to beat his wife was as great a sacrilege as to profane the most holy things in the world.' *Ibid.*, I:491. For Gouge, the husband who beats his wife is 'worse then the venomous viper' – a 'beast' rather than a 'man.' *Domesticall Duties*, 389-390.

[231] *Christian Man's Calling*, I:473.

[232] *Ibid.*, I:492.

and to delight in her, that others may think thee to doat on her.'[233] There is nothing wrong with strong 'desire' and 'delight.' As Edmund Leites remarks, 'an outward fulfillment of the duties of marriage was not enough; the proper intentions and feelings toward your spouse must also exist.'[234]

The Role of Wives

As for wives, they must honour their husband's person,[235] further their husband's good,[236] love their husband above all others,[237] and endeavour their husband's spiritual welfare.[238] Swinnock concludes with a wife's good wish – 'Lord, unite my heart to fear thy name, and let the dread of thy majesty be as a bridle to prevent my wanderings from thy covenant, and to preserve me in the way of thy commandments. I wish that this fear of my God may be evidence to myself and others by my fear of my husband.'[239]

Swinnock clearly teaches that wives are to submit to their husbands.[240] He explains that this 'dominion... is not that of a master over his slave, but such as the soul hath over the body; not for its hurt, but for its help, to further its welfare.'[241] He gives seven reasons why it is necessary:[242] (1) 'the woman was made after the man, therefore she should not go before the man;' (2) 'the woman was made of man;' (3) 'the woman was made for man... that which serveth to any end, is less than the end to which it serveth;' (4) 'the woman was first in sin;' (5) 'the man is the head of the woman;' (6) 'the man is the image and glory of God... The woman is the image and glory of God, according to her original creation... but not according to her personal relation to her husband;' and (7) 'God hath given the man dominion over his wife.' Many argue that such a position necessarily stems from a low view of women. And, on occasion, Swinnock makes statements that seem to confirm this – e.g., 'Every woman, as a woman, is inferior to man.'[243] However, in such cases, he is referring to a positional (not an intrinsic) inferiority. He declares:

---

[233] *Ibid.*

[234] Leites, 'The Duty to Desire,' 383.

[235] *Christian Man's Calling*, I:504-505. For Gouge on wives, see *Domesticall Duties*, 267-348.

[236] *Ibid.*, I:511.

[237] *Ibid.*, I:518.

[238] *Ibid.*, I:519.

[239] *Ibid.*, I:524.

[240] For Swinnock, the wife's duty to submit comes before the husband's duty to love: 'First, Because the duty of a wife is most difficult... Secondly, Because the love of a husband doth very much depend upon the subjection of a wife.' *Ibid.*, I:503. Swinnock's reasoning is open to criticism. Is it not as true to say that a wife's subjection does 'very much depend' upon a husband's love?

[241] *Ibid.*, I:492.

[242] *Ibid.*, I:507-508.

[243] *Ibid.*, I:505.

Though the philosopher tells us that woman is only σφάλμα φύσεως, the aberration of nature, and many vilify them as persons of no worth, yet Scripture, the word of truth, dignifieth them as consisting of the same essential parts, and capable of the same celestial perfections, with men. How highly doth God commend them when they are holy! And for aught any man can tell, a woman, next the human nature of Christ, hath the greatest place of any creature in heaven.[244]

Gouge articulates a similar understanding.[245] He speaks of women as 'inferior'[246] and as 'the weaker sex.'[247] Yet, he clarifies:

But if man and woman be compared together, we shall finde a neere equality... they are both made after the same image, redeemed by the same price, partakers of the same grace, and heires together of the same inheritance. *Quest.* What is then the preferment of the male kinde? What is the excellency of the husband? *Answ.* Only outward and momentary. *Outward,* in the things of this world only: for *in Christ Jesus are both one. Momentary,* for the time of this life only: for *in the resurrection they neither marie, nor are given in marriage, but are as the Angels of God in heaven*: then all subjection of wives to husbands ceaseth.[248]

There is no doubt that some Puritans view women as intrinsically inferior.[249] However, this attitude is difficult to detect in Swinnock, for whom subjection is no gauge of worth.[250] He believes there are God-ordained roles in the marriage relationship. Carnal self will corrupt these roles. Thus, the regenerate must moderate their inordinate self-love. For the husband, this means he must love his wife as Christ loves the church. For the wife, this means she must submit to her husband as the church submits to Christ.

---

[244] *Ibid.*, 1:504.

[245] Gouge admits that his sermons on this subject earned him the censure of many as 'an hater of women.' 'Epistle Dedicatory' in *Domesticall Duties.*

[246] *Ibid.*, 22,27.

[247] *Ibid.*, 23,276,350.

[248] *Ibid.*, 423. His italics.

[249] See Baxter, *Christian Directory,* 399. Some theologians argue that women are inherently inferior, based on the apostle Paul's statement in 1 Tim. 2:14. However, as Susan Foh demonstrates, the apostle Paul is simply stating an historical fact – 'Paul speaks of the difference in the manner of sinning: the man was not deceived (implying he knew what he was doing), but the woman was thoroughly deceived.' *Women and the Word of God: A Response to Biblical Feminism* (Phillipsburg: Presbyterian and Reformed, 1979) 127.

[250] Unsurprisingly, this subject has generated much debate. For an extensive bibliography, see William Webb, *Slaves, Women, and Homosexuals: Exploring the Hermeneutics of Cultural Analysis* (Downers Grove: InterVarsity Press, 2001).

Masters and Servants

The last household relationship is that of masters and servants.[251] By servants, the Puritans mean employees such as domestic workers, apprentices, labourers, and shop assistants.[252] Under normal circumstances, these lived as members of their employer's family. Swinnock gives masters several motives to 'quicken' them in their duty.[253] They are to remember that they are 'made of the same earth,' 'heirs of the same heaven,' and accountable to the 'same master.'[254] Swinnock appeals to Job as an example – 'The fear of God, not any human affection, made him faithful to the meanest of his family.'[255] When governed by such fear, masters will seek the welfare of their servants, provide what is 'just and convenient' for them, command them 'nothing but what is fit and lawful,' teach them their calling, exercise discipline toward them, encourage them, and 'set a good pattern before them.'[256] Swinnock adds, 'I wish that the fear of My master above may make me faithful to my servant here below... If the presence and awe of a king make a judge righteous to his subjects, shall not the omnipresence and dread of a God make me just to my servants?... Lord, though I could abuse my servant without any fear of man, let me not dare to rule with rigour, out of the fear of thee.'[257]

Turning to servants,[258] they must be reverent, obedient, diligent, and faithful.[259] Swinnock is adamant that 'he hath no fear of his Maker, who doth not fear his master.'[260] He concludes with a good wish – 'Enable me to be subject to my master according to the flesh, with fear and trembling, in singleness of heart, as unto Christ, not with eye-service, as a man-pleaser, but as the servant of Christ, doing the will of God from the heart: with good will

---

[251] For Puritan views on masters and servants, see Schlatter, *Social Ideas of Religious Leaders*, 60-86.

[252] Swinnock never comments on the ethics of slavery. Baxter, on the other hand, is very strong in his condemnation of the practice: 'To go as pirates and catch up poor negroes or people of another land, that never forfeited life or liberty, and to make them slaves, and sell them, is one of the worst kinds of thievery in the world; and such persons are to be taken for the common enemies of mankind; and they that buy them and use them as beasts, for their mere commodity, and betray, or destroy, or neglect their souls, are fitter to be called incarnate devils than christians.' *Christian Directory* 462.

[253] For Baxter on masters, see *Christian Directory*, 460-463. For Gouge, see *Domesticall Duties*, 646-693.

[254] *Christian Man's Calling*, II:5-8.

[255] *Ibid.*

[256] *Ibid.*, II:10-21.

[257] *Ibid.*, II:24.

[258] For Baxter on servants, see *Christian Directory* 458-460. For Gouge, see *Domesticall Duties*, 589-645.

[259] *Christian Man's Calling*, II:34-37.

[260] *Ibid.*, II:34.

doing service, as to the Lord, and not to men.'[261]

The Puritan Home

As Edmund Morgan observes, 'The order of society,' for the Puritans, 'consisted in certain dual relationships, most of them originating in agreements between the persons related and all arranged in a pattern of authority and subjection.'[262] This emphasis is developed from Ephesians 5:22-6:9 and Colossians 3:18-4:1. In the first text, the apostle Paul prefaces his remarks with a general exhortation: 'Be subject to one another in the fear of Christ.'[263] He then applies this to the three household relationships. John Stott notes, 'The emphasis throughout is on submission. Thus, wives are addressed before their husbands and are told to *be subject* to them... children are mentioned before their parents and are told to *obey* them... and slaves are addressed before their masters and are told to *be obedient* to them.'[264] The success of these relationships is made contingent upon obedience to the first command: 'Be subject to one another in the fear of Christ.' This fear is evident in the moderation of 'inordinate passions' and 'unruly desires' – the rational appetite exercising the mastery over the sensitive. This, in turn, produces a willingness to subject oneself to others. And this is required to govern carnal self-love, which always seeks to exert itself to the detriment of household relationships.

Building on this, Swinnock sees the man (husband, father, and master) as a governor, seeking to cultivate godliness in his household. He writes, 'Every master of a family is a priest, and his whole family should be a royal priesthood.'[265] Commenting on this emphasis within Puritanism, Schucking remarks, 'It may well be said that the whole Puritan movement has its roots in the family and that we cannot even begin to understand it if we leave the family out of account. Religion is for the Puritan family religion. Divine worship is, not incidentally but primarily, family worship.'[266]

There is some debate as to the origin of this emphasis within Puritanism. Margo Todd challenges any notion of a Puritan 'spiritualized household,' arising from Protestant theology.[267] She argues that the exaltation of marriage,

---

[261] *Ibid.*, II:42.

[262] Edmund Morgan, *The Puritan Family: Religion and Domestic Relations in Seventeenth-Century New England* (New York: Harper & Row, 1956) 28. His assessment is of American Puritanism, however it is also true of English Puritanism.

[263] Eph. 5:21.

[264] John Stott, *The Message of Ephesians: God's New Society* in *The Bible Speaks Today*, eds. J. A. Motyer and J. Stott (Downers Grove: Intervarsity Press, 1986) 215. His italics.

[265] *Christian Man's Calling*, I:337.

[266] Schucking, *The Puritan Family*, 56.

[267] Margo Todd, 'Humanists, Puritans and the Spiritualized Household,' *Church History* 49 (1980) 18. Kathleen Davies also disputes the suggestion that Puritanism

the creation of the family church, the rise of religious education, the practice of disciplinary duties, and the recognition of spiritual equality emerged from 'classical ideas transmitted to the Puritans by humanism.'[268] These views were common to Puritans, Roman Catholics, and Anglicans alike until the last two groups rejected the humanist tradition. Roman Catholicism desired 'parochial conformity' and, therefore, 'saw the practice of religious education and discipline in the household as liable to threaten the spiritual authority of the hierarchy by replacing it with the priestly position of parents.'[269] For this reason, the Council of Trent condemned parental teaching as unauthorized teaching.[270] As for Anglicanism, it desired 'doctrinal and liturgical uniformity,' thus Laud attempted 'to replace the spiritual autonomy of families with a clerically dominated conformist religion.'[271] This departure from the humanist tradition left Puritanism by itself, thereby accounting for the erroneous concept of 'Puritan household theory.'[272] She concludes, 'Social theory is not as dependent on theological stance as historians of Puritanism have thought. Christian humanism, not English Calvinism, laid the foundation of the spiritualized household.'[273]

Todd rightly acknowledges the similarities between Puritans and humanists, stemming from their shared 'biblicism.'[274] However, she fails to address the fundamental difference between the two groups. At the foundation of the Puritan 'spiritualized household' is not the promotion of 'civic-mindedness' as articulated by Aristotle, Plato, or any other classical author, but the promotion of godliness. William Hendriksen dismisses any comparison between the New Testament household codes and the 'maxims of stoics and other moral philosophers,' highlighting three main differences.[275] First, 'Christianity… supplied the *power* to carry out the commands, that power being the grace of God.' Second, 'Christianity… presented a new *purpose*. That purpose was *not*

---

represents 'a very different and more elevated view of family life from that presented in pre-Reformation or early Protestant views of marriage.' 'The sacred condition of equality – how original were Puritan doctrines of marriage?' *Social History* 2 (1977) 563. For the opposite view, see Frye, 'The Teachings of Classical Puritanism,' 149-155; and Schucking, *The Puritan Family*.

[268] Todd, 'Humanists, Puritans, and the Spiritualized Household,' 22.

[269] *Ibid.*, 31-32.

[270] *Ibid.*, 32.

[271] *Ibid.*, 33. Todd's comparison of Puritanism with Anglicanism is problematic. At this stage, the term *Anglican* is anachronistic. The Puritans cited on these pages – Swinnock, Bayly, Gurnall, and Perkins – represent diverse ecclesiastical and political convictions, yet similar views on household theory.

[272] *Ibid.*

[273] *Ibid.*, 34.

[274] *Ibid.*, 19.

[275] William Hendriksen, *Exposition of Colossians and Philemon* in *New Testament Commentary* (Grand Rapids: Baker Books, 1975) 167-168. His italics.

simply "to try to live in agreement with Nature," but "to do everything to the glory of God" (1 Cor. 10:31).' Third, 'Christianity, as originating in Christ, supplied the only true *pattern* for God-glorifying conduct on the part of the very groups here discussed.'

There is a clear antithesis between the Aristotelian and the Christian concept of virtue. The former is external, whereas the latter is internal. In other words, Christian virtue issues from love. As Fiering notes, 'Aristotle showed little apparent concern for the purity of motive behind the act' and, for the Christian, this is 'the most serious deficiency in Aristotle's ethics.'[276] For the Puritans, the intention of the heart is the essence of virtue.[277] This means the deeds of the unregenerate may be good in their material form yet still sinful because they issue from a corrupt heart. Their affections must be changed. This is the goal of the Puritan household, and this is a far cry from Aristotle's virtuous man.

In promoting the spiritual household, Swinnock is concerned with the cultivation of godliness. For him, the family is the basic unit of society; hence, 'the way to make godly parishes, and godly countries, and godly kingdoms, is to make godly families.'[278] Bayly agrees:

> If every householder were thus careful, according to his duty, to bring up his children and family in the service and fear of God in his own house, then the house of God should be better filled, and the Lord's table more frequented every Sabbath day, and the pastors' public preaching and labour would take more effect than it doth; – the streets of towns and cities would not abound with so many drunkards, swearers, whoremongers, and profane scorners of true piety and religion; – our courts would not be so full of contentions, wrangling suits, and unchristian debates; – and the prisons would not be every session so full of thieves, robbers, traitors, murderers.[279]

Similarly, Gurnall comments, 'Much, though not all, of the power of godliness lies within doors, to those that God hath there related us unto. It is in vain to talk of holiness, if we can bring no letters testimonial from our holy walking with our relations.'[280] The responsibility for cultivating such godliness in the home falls in large measure upon its 'governor.' Perkins writes, 'Governours of families must teach their children, and servants, and their whole houshold the doctrine of true religion, that they may know the true God, and walke in all his waies in doing righteousnesse and judgement.'[281]

With this in mind, Swinnock imparts several directions.[282] (1) 'Be careful

---

[276] Fiering, *Moral Philosophy at Seventeenth-Century Harvard*, 102.
[277] See Ames, *Marrow*, II:II:21-26. Calvin makes the same point. *Institutes*, III:VII:7.
[278] *Christian Man's Calling*, I:330.
[279] Bayly, *Practice of Piety*, 144.
[280] Gurnall, *Christian in Complete Armour*, I:439.
[281] Perkins, *Creede of the Apostles*, *Works*, I:173.
[282] Gurnall echoes many of these. *Christian in Complete Armour*, I:439-442.

whom thou admittest into thy family,'[283] for 'one man may pull down that house, which many, with much care, cost, and pains, did set up.'[284] (2) 'Mind holy performances in thy family.'[285] (3) 'Set a good pattern to thy family,'[286] for 'if godliness be written in the book of thy life... it may invite thy children and servants to read and like it.'[287] (4) 'Be careful and diligent that thy whole family may sanctify the Lord's-day.'[288] (5) 'Let discipline be set up in thy family.'[289] (6) 'Take care that all in thy family be well employed.'[290] (7) 'Maintain peace and love in thy family.'[291] 'In a word,' says Swinnock, 'I wish I may, like Cornelius, fear the Lord with all my house; so govern it, according to God's law, that all in it may be under the influence of his love, and heirs of everlasting life.'[292]

Good and Evil Company

For Swinnock, 'True godliness payeth its dues to men, as well as its duty to God; nay, it cannot do the latter without the former.'[293] Similarly, Gurnall comments, 'The power of holiness is to appear to others, must not stay within doors, but walk out into the streets, and visit thy neighbours round.'[294] There is, however, a problem. As Baxter explains, 'selfishness or inordinate self-love' is an 'enemy to Christian love... for this will make men love no one heartily, but as they serve, or love, or honour them, and according to the measures of their selfish interest.'[295] For this reason, Swinnock encourages his readers to manifest meekness in all 'companies.' 'This meekness,' he explains, 'is a virtue by which we moderate our passions, and keep them in subjection, lest we should wrong our neighbours.' It bears three marks. As for its 'manner,' it is 'righteous'[296] in 'works'[297] and 'words;'[298] it is also 'courteous'[299] and 'meek.'[300]

---

[283] *Christian Man's Calling*, I:334.
[284] *Ibid.*
[285] *Ibid.*, I:337-338.
[286] *Ibid.*, I:342.
[287] *Ibid.*, I:342-343.
[288] *Ibid.*, I:345.
[289] *Ibid.*, I:347.
[290] *Ibid.*, I:349.
[291] *Ibid.*, I:351.
[292] *Ibid.*, I:362.
[293] *Ibid.*, II:187-188.
[294] Gurnall, *Christian in Complete Armour*, I:444.
[295] Baxter, *Christian Directory*, 877.
[296] *Christian Man's Calling*, II:194.
[297] *Ibid.*
[298] *Ibid.*, II:205.
[299] *Ibid.*, II:209.
[300] *Ibid.*, II:211.

As for its 'principle,' it proceeds from 'obedience to God's command.'[301] As for its 'end,' it is focused upon God's glory and others' spiritual good.[302] In a word, 'The true Christian's righteousness towards men proceedeth from the fear of his God.'[303] For this reason, Swinnock prays, 'Oh, let the fear of thy God ever possess thee, that the love of this world may never pollute thee! Manifest thy love to thy Saviour, by loving thy neighbour as thyself.'[304] Again, 'I wish that those beautiful children of righteousness, courtesy, and meekness in my carriage, may have the Spirit of God for their parent; I mean, that the fear of my God may be the principle from which they flow.'[305]

The Fear of God in All Conditions

For Swinnock, 'life is a mixture of mercies and miseries... a house of mourning or mirth.'[306] Simply put, it is marked by prosperity and adversity. 'Both,' says Swinnock, 'have their snares and temptations.'[307] For this reason, he adopts Agur's prayer: 'Give me neither poverty nor riches; Feed me with the food that is my portion. That I not be full and deny You and say, "Who is the LORD?" Or that I not be in want and steal, And profane the name of my God.'[308] Swinnock's desire for moderation is again evident.

Prosperity and Adversity

The first condition, prosperity, 'consisteth in the fruition of outward good things, as health, strength, friends, riches, honours, and the like.'[309] Swinnock seeks to 'persuade' his readers to make prosperity 'profitable' to their souls by considering that it is 'a grievous sin... not to serve God in the enjoyment of mercies,'[310] that prosperity will 'try' them 'to purpose,'[311] and 'that prosperity most commonly is abused to profaneness.'[312] Charnock describes this abuse as a 'treachery' to God's 'goodness' – 'to make his benefits serve for an end quite contrary to that for which he sent them.'[313] In terms of 'contrary' ends,

---

[301] *Ibid.*, II:216.

[302] *Ibid.*, II:217.

[303] *Ibid.*

[304] *Ibid.*, II:227.

[305] *Ibid.*, II:232.

[306] *Ibid.*, II:46.

[307] *Ibid.*, II:47.

[308] Prov. 30:8-9.

[309] *Christian Man's Calling*, II:47. For Perkins on 'the Moderation of Appetite in the use of Riches,' see *Cases*, 305-315.

[310] *Christian Man's Calling*, II:49.

[311] *Ibid.*

[312] *Ibid.*, II:51.

[313] Charnock, *Existence and Attributes of God*, II:322-323.

Charnock means 'pride' – vaunting it 'loftily' above others; 'ease' – spending time in 'idleness;' 'security' – 'turning the grace of God into wantonness;' and 'sensuality' – 'resolving to live like beasts.'[314] God prospers individuals with the stipulation that they use 'for his glory' what he has bestowed 'by his bounty.'[315] When they fail to do so, they abuse his goodness. Baxter believes that people 'have far more cause to be afraid of prosperity, than of adversity,' for 'it must be something that seemeth good, that must entice men from the chiefest good.'[316] For this reason, the 'corrupted nature is apter to abuse prosperity and earthly delights, than any other state, to the diverting of the heart from God.'[317]

Swinnock sees many dangers in prosperity, remarking, 'Truly, thus too many serve the blessed God; if poverty, or disgrace, or sickness surprise them, then none but God... but when their afflictions are removed, and estates, or honour, or health restored, then they can do well enough without him, and banish him their hearts and souls.'[318] With this danger before him, Swinnock provides directions to help the regenerate mind their 'carriage' in prosperity. They are to watch for those sins that accompany prosperity,[319] value the eternal over the temporal, give God the glory for outward mercies, love God the more for his mercies, serve God out of their abundance, and make provision for adversity.[320] Swinnock appends his 'good wish' with the following: 'Oh that... I may fear the Lord and his goodness, and the goodness of my God may lead me to repentance... Godliness in prosperity will best speak my sincerity. The day of light and comforts is a fitter season to discover the colour and complexion of the soul than the night of darkness and sorrows.'[321]

The second condition is adversity, which Swinnock describes as 'the want of outward good things, and presence of outward evil things, as sickness, disgrace, poverty, imprisonment, and the like.'[322] He begins with a discussion of adversity's causes. The efficient is God.[323] The meritorious is sin. 'Indeed,' says Swinnock, 'every affliction is not for sin; yet every affliction is from sin.'[324] The formal is the 'absence of something necessary' or the 'presence of something troublesome.'[325] The final is 'either to prove or purify.'[326] Charnock

---

[314] *Ibid.*, II:323.

[315] *Ibid.*, II:436.

[316] Baxter, *Christian Directory*, 78.

[317] *Ibid.*, 141.

[318] *Christian Man's Calling*, II:54.

[319] He means atheism 'in general;' and pride, carnal confidence, and senselessness of other people's miseries 'in particular.' *Ibid.*, II:56-58.

[320] *Ibid.*, II:53-67.

[321] *Ibid.*, II:74-75.

[322] *Ibid.*, II:82.

[323] *Ibid.*

[324] *Ibid.*, II:83.

[325] *Ibid.*

also points to God as the 'efficient cause' of adversity, stressing the fact that God's goodness is behind affliction: 'If it be "good for us to be afflicted," for which we have the psalmist's vote (Ps. 119:71), then goodness in God is the principal cause and orderer of the afflictions.'[327] Charnock believes that 'by afflictions' God 'snaps asunder those chains which fettered us,' 'quells those passions which ravaged us,' 'sharpens our faith,' and 'quickens our prayers.'[328] With all this in view, he asks, 'What can we fear from the conduct of Infinite Goodness?'[329] Like Charnock, Swinnock wants his readers to understand these causes so that they may see God's hand in adversity, submit to his will, wait for his deliverance, rejoice in him, and contemplate his purpose.[330] The last is 'the first and chiefest of all.'[331]

The Mystery of God's Providence

Contemplation of God's purpose in adversity raises a popular Puritan motif – the mystery of God's providence. For Swinnock, God is 'incomparable' in his providence, namely, in his works of 'preservation' and 'gubernation' (governance).[332] Swinnock's understanding of the latter rests upon his concept of Christ's kingdom. There is his 'spiritual' kingdom 'whereby he ruleth by his Spirit and word in the hearts of his people. In this respect he is called King of saints.' And there is his 'providential' kingdom 'whereby he ruleth in the world, disposing of all things therein; in this respect he is called King of nations.'[333] As for the link between the two, Christ 'ordereth his providential kingdom for the advancement of his spiritual kingdom... as may be most for the welfare of his people.'[334] Similarly, the *WCF* states: 'As the providence of

---

[326] *Ibid.*

[327] Charnock, *Existence and Attributes of God*, II:309. Also see II:451-452.

[328] *Ibid.*, II:310.

[329] *Ibid.*, II:342.

[330] *Christian Man's Calling*, II:92-111.

[331] *Ibid.*, II:111.

[332] *Incomparableness of God*, IV:427-428.

[333] *Christian Man's Calling*, II:133.

[334] *Ibid.*, II:134. This concept of providence may lead people to view history as part of God's special revelation. Berkouwer warns, 'It is often forgotten that we have not been given a norm for explaining the facts of history, and that in the absence of a norm only an untrustworthy plausibility remains. Otherwise one must take refuge in religious intuition or divination, which, it has been claimed, is capable of discerning God's finger in the panorama of history. This would introduce a second source of Divine information.' *Studies in Dogmatics – The Providence of God* (Grand Rapids: Eerdmans, 1974) 171-172. Ronald VanderMolen considers this tendency among the Puritans in 'Providence as Mystery, Providence as Revelation: Puritan and Anglican Modifications of John Calvin's Doctrine of Providence,' *Church History* 47 (1978) 27-47. He writes, 'According to Calvin, even though all events are the result of

God doth, in general, reach to all creatures, so, after a most special manner, it taketh care of his Church, and disposeth all things to the good thereof.'[335] Two main tenets emerge from this view of God's providence.

God Controls all Things

The first is this: Christ's 'kingdom... ruleth over all.' This means there is nothing that falls outside of the parameters of his control.[336] Jesus confirms this in Matthew 10:29-30, asking, '"Are not two sparrows sold for a cent?" And yet not one of them will fall to the ground apart from your Father.' Based on these words, Swinnock remarks, 'Sparrows seem to fly at liberty, and to fall casually; but even their flight is directed by God, and their fall ordered by him: they neither fly nor fall accidentally, but providentially.'[337] This all-encompassing view of providence often produces three objections.

First, it appears to make God the author of sin. If nothing falls outside the parameters of God's control, then he must be responsible for sin. Swinnock's answer to this charge is the doctrine of concurrence. As Chares Hodge explains, two theories of providence were popular among the Reformers. The first is 'Entire Dependence.'[338] Proponents maintain that God, as an absolute and infinite being, is the only efficient cause. Therefore, second causes are without efficiency. The second is 'Concursus.'[339] Adherents propose that in the production of every effect there is an efficiency of two causes: first and second.[340] According to Paul Helm, Zwingli is representative of the first theory whereas Calvin is representative of the second.[341] Helm writes:

God's actions, only God knows the ultimate meanings of those events... Thus, Calvin avoided any interpretation of providence which made God's action in history contingent upon human behaviour.' *Ibid.*, 31-32. VanderMolen believes many Puritans depart from Calvin by turning 'mysterious providence' into a form of divine revelation. *Ibid.*, 33. He explains, 'By teaching that earthly rewards and punishments revealed God's actions and God's dispositions as well, Puritan historiography provided a means by which social, political, and economic activity could be predicated on earthly success.' *Ibid.*, 47. VanderMolen is careful to acknowledge that not all Puritans adopt this approach. *Ibid.*, 45. It is difficult to find in Swinnock. For Calvin's view, see *Institutes*, I:XVIII:9.

[335] *WCF*, V:VI. This is also reminiscent of Calvin. *Institutes*, I:XVII:1. For more on Calvin's view, see Etienne de Peyer, 'Calvin's Doctrine of Divine Providence,' *Evangelical Quarterly* 10 (1938) 30-44.

[336] *Incomparableness of God*, IV:428-437.

[337] *Ibid.*, IV:429.

[338] Charles Hodge, *Systematic Theology* (Peabody: Hendrickson, 2001) I:592-593.

[339] *Ibid.*, I:593-605.

[340] *Ibid.*, I:600.

[341] Some scholars challenge the belief that Calvin accepted secondary causes. See C. J. Kinlaw, 'Determinism and the Hiddenness of God in Calvin's Theology,' *Religious Studies* 24 (1988) 497-510. He believes Calvin is committed to a 'radical divine

This difference can be starkly illustrated from the perspective attitudes of Calvin and Zwingli to the distinction between primary and secondary causes... Calvin (with the aid of the scholastics) strives to preserve that distinction because it is the way in which the biblical testimony that God is both holy and the author of sinful actions can be preserved. In Zwingli's case, God's power is, for a priori reasons, so supreme that the idea of there being any distinct causal agency apart from God disappears.[342]

The Westminster divines adopt the doctrine of concurrence, stating, 'Although in relation to the foreknowledge and decree of God, the first cause, all things come to pass immutably and infallibly, yet by the same providence he ordereth them to fall out, according to the nature of second causes, either necessarily, freely, or contingently.'[343] Swinnock stands in this tradition, affirming, 'It is impossible for the creation, or any part of it, to bear up a moment, if God should forget it, and deny his actual concurrence to it... God is to the world as the soul to the body, which alone can actuate and move it, without which it cannot stir at all, but is as a dead corpse.'[344] Swinnock affirms the free acts of second causes whilst insisting that God actuates and moves them to act. This is God's 'over-ruling providence.'[345] God decrees all that comes to pass, including evil. However, he is not responsible for evil, because he actuates and moves second causes to act in accordance with their desires.

Swinnock provides no defence for this position; however, Charnock does.[346] He argues that people are dependent upon God for their 'creation' and 'action.'[347] As for the latter, there is a distinction between 'substance' and 'viciousness.' Simply put, 'No act, in regard of the substance of it, is evil,' because it is merely 'the efficacy of the faculty, extending itself to some outward object.'[348] It only becomes evil when it 'consists in a privation of that comeliness and righteousness which ought to be in an action.'[349] Thus, Charnock concludes that an action's substance and viciousness 'have two distinct causes... Though the action be from God as a concurrent cause, yet the

---

determinism' – 'everything issues necessarily, immediately, and concretely from God's all-encompassing will.' *Ibid.*, 501.

[342] Paul Helm, 'Calvin (and Zwingli) on Divine Providence,' *Calvin Theological Journal* 29 (1994) 404. Helm's conclusions are based upon his analysis of Calvin's *Defence of the Secret Providence of God* and Zwingli's *On Providence*. Schaff also notes Zwingli's denial of the efficiency of second causes. *Creeds of Christendom*, I:370.

[343] *WCF*, V:II.

[344] *Incomparableness of God*, IV:428.

[345] *Christian Man's Calling*, II:85.

[346] Charnock, *Existence and Attributes of God*, II:139-171.

[347] *Ibid.*, II:156.

[348] *Ibid.*, II:157.

[349] *Ibid.*, II:158.

ill quality of the action is solely from the creature with whom God concurs.'[350] This is the case, because 'God doth no more when he leaves a man to sin... but leave him to his natural inclination.'[351] This 'is not an action, but a denial of action, and therefore cannot be the cause of the evil actions of men.'[352] In brief, God simply permits evil.[353] Perkins is helpful on this point, distinguishing between God's 'permission' and 'operative permission.'[354] By the first, God effectually produces all good things. By the second, God willingly permits evil things.[355] Charnock agrees, 'This act of permission is not a mere and naked permission, but such an one as is attended with a certainty of the event.'[356]

Second, Swinnock's view of providence appears to destroy human liberty. He affirms that God commands people's 'hearts' and 'hands;'[357] furthermore, 'No man is master of himself, so much as of his thoughts.'[358] Such statements seem irreconcilable with human liberty. Swinnock's solution to this quandary rests upon his understanding of faculty psychology. He does not believe the will is free to act contrary to all motives. Rather, it is determined by whatever the understanding and affections (rightly or wrongly) view as good. This paradigm does not undermine self-determination, because it maintains a difference between 'constraining' and 'non-constraining' causes. Simply put, people are free when their choices are their own. This position does, however, undermine the notion that the will itself possesses self-determination (or arbitrary power). Swinnock believes people are free in the choices they make, because they possess understanding, affections, and will. He also believes these faculties are corrupt, and the will – without any external constraint – chooses accordingly. This is how he reconciles God's sovereignty and human liberty.

Augustine anticipates a further objection to this paradigm: 'If God foreknows that man will sin, then you will say that he must sin, and if this has to happen, there is no freedom of the will in the act of sinning, but rather an

---

[350] *Ibid.*, II:159.

[351] *Ibid.*, II:168.

[352] *Ibid.*, II:147.

[353] *Ibid.*, II:150. The Bible abounds with examples of this. God used the Assyrian invasion (Is. 10:12-16), Joseph's enslavement (Gen. 45:5-8, 50:20), Samson's sin (Jgs. 14:4), the Babylonian invasion (Hab. 3:17-19), Judas's betrayal (Matt. 27:15-26), and Jesus' crucifixion (Acts 2:23-24) to accomplish his will. In each instance, he permitted second causes (free agents) to act according to their desires. For Charnock's use of biblical examples, see *Existence and Attributes of God*, I:447, II:145-146,161,167-168.

[354] Perkins, *Golden Chain*, *Works*, I:15.

[355] Perkins again speaks of 'operative permission' in *Creede of the Apostles*, *Works*, I:160.

[356] Charnock, *Existence and Attributes of God*, II:149.

[357] *Incomparableness of God*, IV:428.

[358] *Ibid.*, IV:429.

inevitable and unbending necessity.'[359] He calls such reasoning 'sheer folly,'[360] adding:

> Since God has foreknowledge of our will, its future will be such as He foreknows it. It will be a will precisely because He foreknows it as a will, and it could not be a will if it were not in our power. Hence God also has foreknowledge of our power over it. The power, then, is not taken from me because of His foreknowledge, since this power will be mine all the more certainly because of the infallible foreknowledge of Him who foreknew that I would have it.[361]

Perkins agrees, 'Gods foreknowledge in it selfe, is not a cause why things are, but as it is conjoyned with his decree. For things do not therefore come to passe, because that God did foreknow them; but because he decreed and willed them, therefore they come to passe.'[362] Charnock also adopts Augustine's position, affirming, 'God's foreknowledge of man's voluntary actions doth not necessitate the will of man.'[363] This is so, because there is a distinction between a necessity of compulsion and a necessity of immutability (or infallibility). The former takes away free will whereas the latter does not.[364] Charnock acknowledges, 'The will cannot be compelled, for then it would cease to be the will.'[365] The point is: God's foreknowledge does not compel. It is not 'the cause of anything.'[366] Charnock affirms, 'Though the foreknowledge of God be infallible, yet it doth not necessitate the creature in acting... they voluntarily run into such courses, not by any impulsion.'[367] Baxter concurs, 'Suppose God either to decree, or but to foreknow the freest, most contingent act, and there will be a logical impossibility in order of consequence, that it should be otherwise than he so decreeth or foreseeth. But that inferreth no natural impossibility in the thing itself.'[368] By way of example, Charnock appeals to Jesus' death as described in Acts 4:27-28,[369] stating, 'God did not only foreknow, but determine the suffering of Christ... It did infallibly secure the event, but did not annihilate the liberty of the action, either in Christ's

---

[359] Augustine, *The Free Choice of the Will, Fathers of the Church: Vol. LIX*, 170 (III:III).

[360] *Ibid.*, 172 (III:III).

[361] *Ibid.*, 173 (III:III).

[362] Perkins, *Golden Chain, Works*, I:15.

[363] Charnock, *Existence and Attributes of God*, I:446.

[364] *Ibid.*, I:446.

[365] *Ibid.*, I:447.

[366] *Ibid.*, I:448.

[367] *Ibid.*, II:145.

[368] Baxter, *Christian Directory*, 513.

[369] 'For truly in this city there were gathered together against Your holy servant Jesus, whom You anointed, both Herod and Pontius Pilate, along with the Gentiles and the peoples of Israel, to do whatever Your hand and Your purpose predestined to occur.'

willingness to suffer, or the crime of the Jews that made him suffer.'[370]

Third, Swinnock's view of providence appears to make God in favour of evil. If nothing falls outside the parameters of God's control, then he necessarily wills sin. Swinnock dispels this notion by upholding the distinction between God's secret and revealed wills.[371] The first refers to the rule of God's actions (decrees) whereas the second refers to the rule of man's actions (precepts). Scripture appears to support such a distinction. Joseph's brothers sinned when they sold him as a slave. This was not God's revealed will (disposition). However, it was his secret will (decree), for Joseph says to his brothers, 'It was not you who sent me here, but God.'[372] The Jews sinned when they crucified Jesus. Again, this was not God's revealed will (disposition). However, it was his secret will (decree), for the apostle Peter declares, 'This Man, delivered over by the predetermined plan and foreknowledge of God, you nailed to the cross by the hands of godless men and put Him to death.'[373]

Calvin recognizes such a distinction, writing, 'Moses proclaims that the will of God is to be sought not far off in the clouds or in the abyss, because it has been set forth familiarly in the law (Deut. 30:11-14), it follows that he has another hidden will which may be compared to a deep abyss.'[374] Calvin anticipates an objection to this dichotomy, namely, 'There are in him two contrary wills, because by his secret plan he decrees what he has openly forbidden by his law.'[375] He responds, 'But even though his will is one and simple in him, it appears manifold to us because, on account of our mental incapacity, we do not grasp how in divers ways it wills and does not will something to take place... For it would not be done if he did not permit it; yet he does not unwillingly permit it, but willingly.'[376] Charnock builds on this: 'To say God doth will sin as he doth other things, is to deny his holiness; to say it entered without anything of his will, is to deny his omnipotence.'[377] By way of solution, he affirms, 'God wills good by a positive decree, because he hath

---

[370] Charnock, *Existence and Attributes of God*, II:146.

[371] *Christian Man's Calling*, I:79. This distinction is based upon Deut. 29:29. For Charnock, see *Essence and Attributes of God*, II:147-155. For Perkins, see *Of Gods free grace and mans free will, Works*, I:705.

[372] Gen. 45:5-8; 50:20.

[373] Acts 2:23.

[374] Calvin, *Institutes*, I:XVII:2. Calvin refers to this 'hidden will' as God's 'secret plan,' 'secret providence,' 'secret judgments,' 'incomprehensible plans,' 'secret command,' and 'secret direction.' *Ibid.*, I:XVI:2,3,6,9, I:XVII:1,2, I:XVIII:1,2,4. It is 'a certain and deliberate will.' *Ibid.*, I:XVI:3.

[375] *Ibid.*, I:XVIII:3.

[376] *Ibid.* At times, it appears Calvin rejects the notion of God's permissive will – 'They babble and talk absurdly who, in place of God's providence, substitute bare permission – as if God sat in a watchtower awaiting chance events, and his judgments thus depended upon human will.' *Ibid*, I:XVIII:1, III:XXIII:8.

[377] Charnock, *Existence and Attributes of God*, II:148.

decreed to effect it. He wills evil by a private decree, because he hath decreed not to give that grace which would certainly prevent it,'[378] adding, 'That which is permitted by him, is in itself, and in regard of the evil of it, hateful to him: but as the prospect of that good which he aims at in the permission of it is pleasing to him, so that act of his will, whereby he permits it, is ushered in by an approving act of his understanding.'[379] By an act of his will, therefore, God effects good and permits evil. This is his secret will (decree). When he willingly permits evil, he does not contradict his revealed will (i.e., his disposition toward evil), for he does not approve of it, but approves of 'that good which he aims at in the permission of it.'

God Controls all Things for the Good of his People

The second main tenet in Swinnock's understanding of God's providence is this: Christ's 'kingdom, which ruleth over all, shall be disposed as may be most for the welfare of his people.' According to Thomas Watson, there are two kinds of providence: first, that which God overrules for good on behalf of the godly; and second, that which God overrules for evil on behalf of the ungodly. In the case of the former, 'All the various dealings of God with his children do by a special providence turn to their good.'[380] Like Watson, Swinnock sees a clear difference between 'the punishments God inflicts on sinners' and 'the afflictions he brings on saints.'[381] First, they differ in 'manner.'[382] God punishes his enemies with joy whereas he afflicts his children with compassion. Second, they differ in 'measure.'[383] God punishes his enemies with no regard for what they can endure whereas he afflicts his children according to what they are able to suffer. Third, they differ in 'end.'[384] God punishes his enemies to satisfy his offended judgment whereas he afflicts his children to sanctify their polluted hearts. In a word, God governs all things (including evil) for the welfare of his people.

For support, Swinnock gravitates to the apostle Paul's words in Romans 8:28 – 'And we know that God causes all things to work together for good to those who love God, to those who are called according to His purpose.' This means they are never in the grip of blind forces. Rather, everything that happens to them is divinely planned. This includes 'all things, not only thy comforts, but also thy crosses; not only the love of God, but also the hatred of

---

[378] *Ibid.*

[379] *Ibid.*, II:149.

[380] Thomas Watson, *All Things for Good; or, A Divine Cordial* (1663; Edinburgh: Banner of Truth, 1986: rpt., 1994) 11. This is an excellent treatment of the subject. For another, see John Flavel, *Divine Conduct; or, The Mystery of Providence: A Treatise upon Psalm 57:2, Works*, IV:339-497.

[381] *Christian Man's Calling*, II:127.

[382] *Ibid.*

[383] *Ibid.*, II:128.

[384] *Ibid.*, II:129.

the world, and the malice of hell.'[385] With this awareness, 'A godly man should be like a rock, immoveable, though high winds and boisterous waves of providence blow and beat upon him.'[386] According to Perkins:

> Such as professe the knowledge of the true God, must better acquaint themselves with this providence and goodnes of God, and labour to feele it, as well in sicknes as in health, in want as in wealth, in persecution as in libertie and peace. And when we can in some good measure doe this, experience of divine providence will breede and bring forth contentation.[387]

Burroughs defines such contentment as 'that sweet, inward, quiet, gracious form of spirit, which freely submits to and delights in God's wise and fatherly disposal in every condition.'[388] He provides ten 'considerations to content the heart in any afflicted condition;' the last being 'the experience that God does good to us in afflictions.'[389] All of this is reminiscent of Calvin, who writes, 'In times of adversity believers comfort themselves with the solace that they suffer nothing except by God's ordinance and command, for they are under his hand.'[390] Again, 'His solace, I say, is to know his Heavenly Father so holds all things in his power, so rules by his authority and will, so governs by his wisdom, that nothing can befall except he determine it.'[391] As Horton Davies notes, 'The more one studies Calvin's doctrine of Providence, the clearer it becomes that his interest in it is not so much theoretical or philosophical, as wholly pastoral.'[392] The same is true of Swinnock.

Moderation

According to Derek Thomas, the 'doctrine of God's incomprehensibility' is Calvin's interpretive key for understanding God's providence.[393] He explains that, for Calvin, 'the key to Christian piety in general, is submission to a sovereign and incomprehensible God,'[394] for this 'submission' results in the moderation of the affections. Thomas writes, 'Taming what Calvin calls "the

---

[385] *Ibid.*, II:122. For ten 'thoughts which may quiet and compose the heart in all occurents,' see III:160-164.

[386] *Ibid.*, I:315.

[387] Perkins, *Vocations, Works*, I:745.

[388] Jeremiah Burroughs, *The Rare Jewel of Christian Contentment* (1648; Edinburgh: Banner of Truth, 1964: rpt., 1987) 19.

[389] *Ibid.*, 213.

[390] Calvin, *Institutes*, I:XVI:3.

[391] *Ibid.*, I:XVII:11.

[392] Davies, *Vigilant God*, 98.

[393] Derek Thomas, *Proclaiming the Incomprehensible God: Calvin's Teaching on Job* (Ross-shire: Christian Focus, 2004) 17.

[394] *Ibid.* Calvin, *Institutes*, I:V:1, I:XIII:21.

affections" is a prerequisite to living the Christian life... Calvin confesses... "there is nothing more hard than to moderate a mans selfe in suche wise, as we may keepe rule and compasse." "Our affections," he adds later, "are like wyld beastes: which dash us against God."[395] Such moderation is only achieved by acknowledging God's incomprehensibility in providence. As Thomas explains, Calvin finds this truth in Job's example:

> Understanding Job as a model, Calvin differentiates godly fear from servile fear. Godly fear... is a response to the goodness of God as much as it is to his majesty... Such fear involves having a right understanding of God and his works, a mind and heart that are not given over to speculation. Godly fear in response to God's providence ought, writes Calvin, to 'shut our mouths,' cause us to renounce ourselves, prevent us from presumption, 'over-boldness' and 'vanitie,' and result in true joy.[396]

Swinnock shares this mindset, believing like Calvin in an incomprehensible God. As the *WCF* states, 'There is but one only, living and true God, who is infinite in being and perfection, a most pure spirit, invisible, without body, parts, or passions; immutable, immense, eternal, incomprehensible, almighty, most wise, most holy, most free, most absolute.'[397] Since God is incomprehensible, his providence is ultimately a mystery. And it is this awareness that causes the regenerate to fear him, thereby exercising moderation in the midst of suffering. Adversity kindles 'inordinate' and 'unruly' passions by depriving the sensitive appetite of the objects of its desire. Carnal self-love responds selfishly. However, for Swinnock, the regenerate exercise self-control, fearing the incomprehensible God of providence.

Conclusion

'I wish,' writes Swinnock, 'that I may never waste that precious season, which is given me for the working out of my salvation, about needless affairs, but mind the one thing necessary, and pass the whole time of my sojourning here in the fear of my God.'[398] As seen in this chapter, he believes this is achieved by exercising self-control. Prior to regeneration, 'the affections were... carried out inordinately after objects that were lawful... when he joyed in the creatures he would overjoy, and turn thereby his mirth into madness; when he loved his relations he would over-love them, and change thereby his love to them into

---

[395] *Ibid.*, 52. See Thomas for references from Calvin's sermons on the book of Job.

[396] *Ibid.*, 231.

[397] *WCF*, II:I.

[398] *Ibid.*, II:511. For Baxter's directions on 'how to spend every ordinary day of the week,' see *Christian Directory* 466-469. For the Puritans in general, see E. Braund, 'Daily Life Among the Puritans' in *Puritan Papers: Vol. I*, ed. D. M. Lloyd-Jones (Phillipsburg: P & R Publishing, 2000) 156-161.

self, or soul hatred.'[399] By regeneration, the affections are sanctified, thereby facilitating moderation.

Based on Titus 2:11-12,[400] Swinnock remarks, 'The body of godliness parteth itself into these three principal members: godliness – our duty towards God; soberness – our duty towards ourselves; and righteousness – our duty towards other men.'[401] Gurnall arrives at the same conclusion, stating that our duty toward God is 'piety,' our duty toward ourselves is 'sobriety,' and our duty toward others is 'righteousness.'[402] Commenting on the same text, Calvin points out that the apostle Paul

> limits all actions of life to three parts: soberness, righteousness, and godliness. Of these, soberness doubtless denotes chastity and temperance as well as a pure and frugal use of temporal goods, and patience in poverty. Now righteousness embraces all the duties of equity in order that to each one be rendered what is his own (Rom. 13:7). There follows godliness, which joins us in true holiness with God when we are separated from the iniquities of the world. When these things are joined together by an inseparable bond, they bring about complete perfection.[403]

Interestingly, the term *soberness* is the Greek adverb σωφρόνως, and in Mark 5:15, the healed demoniac is described as being 'in his right mind' (σωφρονέω). Thus, to be 'sober' is to be in one's 'right mind.' It is what Hendriksen calls 'self-mastery'[404] – for Swinnock, the rational appetite exercising the 'mastery' over the sensitive. Such sobriety means the affections are removed from sinful objects and moderated toward earthly objects, because they are sanctified by the fear of God.

---

[399] *Door of Salvation*, V:32.
[400] 'For the grace of God has appeared, bringing salvation to all men, instructing us to deny ungodliness and worldly desires and to live sensibly, righteously and godly in the present age.'
[401] *Christian Man's Calling*, I:394.
[402] Gurnall, *Christian in Complete Armour*, I:444.
[403] Calvin, *Institutes*, III:VII:3.
[404] Hendriksen, *I & II Timothy and Titus*, 372.

Chapter Seven

Discipline: The Pursuit of the Means of Grace

The moderation of the sensitive appetite is no easy task, given the fact that carnal self-love remains in some measure in the regenerate until glorification. For this reason, there is a need to heed the apostle Paul's command to 'lay aside the old self.'[1] For Swinnock, this means the regenerate must constantly mortify carnal self-love. He makes it clear that they are incapable of effecting this in their own strength, yet they are capable of applying themselves to those means by which the Holy Spirit effects it. Consequently, he places tremendous emphasis upon the 'means of grace.'[2] With a similar paradigm in view, Bayly affirms that the essence of spirituality is 'to join together, in watching, fasting, praying, reading the Scriptures, keeping his Sabbaths, hearing sermons, receiving the holy Communion, relieving the poor, exercising in all humility the works of piety to God, and walking conscionably in the duties of our calling towards men.'[3]

Spiritual Duties

This commitment to the means of grace is directly related to the Puritans' teleological understanding of the image of God. By regeneration, individuals are renewed in the image of God, thereby restoring their enjoyment of God. The Holy Spirit works through means to draw them into closer communion with the object of their delight. Naturally, therefore, the regenerate delight in these means. Bolton explains:

> Here is no greater encouragement, or stronger motive, to stirre a man to an eager, and earnest pursuite of the meanes, then to purpose unto him an end, wherein at

---

[1]   Eph. 4:22-24.

[2]   In *Christian Man's Calling*, Swinnock refers to the means of grace as 'sacred duties' (I:87), 'religious duties' (I:19,36,87,90,91,222), 'religious exercises' (I:40), 'spiritual performances' (I:87), 'religious actions' (I:87), 'sacred ordinances' (I:242), 'holy duties' (I:101,222,225), 'holy performances' (I:226), and 'religious ordinances' (I:227).

[3]   Bayly, *Practice of Piety*, 163. According to E. Glenn Hinson, this statement sums up 'the whole Puritan platform.' 'Puritan Spirituality' in *Protestant Spiritual Traditions*, ed. F. C. Senn (New York: Paulist Press, 1986) 165.

length his heart may repose, as in a concurrence of all comforts and contentments... What ingenuous mind would not be inflamed with zeale, to the prosequution of those meanes, which leade unto an end as full of happiness, as the Sunne is full of light, and the Sea of waters?[4]

According to Bolton, 'the highest perfection of blisse' is found in God. The regenerate's realization of this stirs them to a zealous pursuit of those 'means' that lead to God. As a matter of fact, a neglect of these 'means' reveals that there is no true desire for the 'end' – God. Shepard writes, 'Truly, beloved, you can have but little evidence you do desire the Lord Jesus' company in heaven at the last day, that long not vehemently after him in his ordinances now.'[5] Again, 'Your practice in the habitual neglect of means is a clear and manifest witness, like the day, against you, that you do not desire sincerely the end (as you think) in having so little respect to the means that conduce thereunto.'[6] The Puritans' commitment to spiritual duties, therefore, arises from the conviction that these are the only means by which the soul communes with the object of its delight.

By the expression *means of grace*,[7] Swinnock has in view those 'secret, private, and public duties'[8] through which God works in the individual's soul.[9] Simply put, they are 'conduit-pipes whereby the water of life is derived from Christ in the hearts of Christians.'[10] In full agreement, Shepard exhorts his readers, 'Labour to be near the Lord in all his ordinances also, both privately and publicly, for there is his presence.'[11] As for the duties themselves, Swinnock primarily focuses on praying, hearing and reading God's Word, receiving the Lord's Supper, and keeping the Lord's Day.[12]

---

[4]   Bolton, *State of True Happiness*, 1-2.

[5]   Shepard, *Parable of the Ten Virgins*, 168.

[6]   *Ibid.*, 246.

[7]   *Christian Man's Calling*, I:101.

[8]   *Fading of* the Flesh, III:416; and *Door of Salvation*, V:237.

[9]   Don Whitney provides a modern-day perspective of the Puritan understanding of the means of grace, explaining that they are 'like channels of God's transforming grace. As we place ourselves in them to seek communion with Christ, his grace flows to us and we are changed.' *Spiritual Disciplines for the Christian Life* (Colorado Springs: NavPress, 1991) 18-19. Also see Wallace, *The Spirituality of the Later English Puritans*, xxv-xxxii; and C. John Hambrick-Stowe, 'Puritan Spirituality in America' in *Christian Spirituality III*, eds. L. Dupré and D. E. Saliers (New York: Crossroad Publishing, 1989) 343.

[10] *Christian Man's Calling*, I:102. Sceats notes that 'the concrete imagery of water-pipes is a characteristic Puritan metaphor.' 'The Experience of Grace,' 15.

[11] Shepard, *Parable of the Ten Virgins*, 547.

[12] *Christian Man's Calling*, I:86. These four are not an exhaustive list; however, they are pre-eminent in Swinnock's thinking. Elsewhere, he includes fasting, watching, and singing psalms. *Ibid.*, I:65.

Praying

Swinnock defines prayer as 'a humble lifting up the heart, or pouring out the soul to God in the name of Christ.'[13] For the Christian, it is the place where 'Christ and his soul converse together.'[14] With this communion in view, Swinnock affirms that prayer 'is the chief duty, wherein all the graces meet.'[15] Baxter shares this belief, commenting, 'Christians, who are much in secret prayer and contemplation, are men of greatest life and joy, because they have all more immediately from God himself... the fullness of joy is in God's immediate presence.'[16] For this reason, Baxter maintains that private prayer is the mark of a person's spiritual condition. In reference to 'formal professors,' he comments, 'They will preach, or hear, or read, or talk of heaven, or pray in their families, and take part with the persons or causes that are good, and desire to be esteemed among the godly; but you can never bring them to the more spiritual duties, – as to be constant and fervent in secret prayer and meditation.'[17]

With the importance of prayer before him, Swinnock identifies two 'antecedents' – 'those things which must go before prayer.'[18] First, the regenerate must pursue that which promotes prayer. This is done through meditation – 'meditation is the best beginning of prayer, and prayer is the best conclusion of meditation.'[19] Baxter concurs, 'We need the one as well as the other, and therefore we shall wrong ourselves by neglecting either. Besides, the mixture of them, like music, will be more engaging; as the one serves to put life into the other.'[20] Swinnock affirms that the regenerate must meditate on their sins, wants, and mercies.[21] This assists in prayer, because an appreciation of sins leads to confession with shame and sorrow, an appreciation of wants leads to petition with faith and fervency, and an appreciation of mercies leads to thanksgiving with admiration and delight.[22] This 'stirring up of the graces' enables the individual to pray meaningfully.[23] Gurnall agrees, 'Now, to preserve thy affections in prayer warm and lively, let it be thy care to chase and stir up the natural heat that is undoubtedly in thee, if a Christian, by the serious

---

[13]   *Ibid.*, I:107. For Bunyan on prayer, see *I will pray with the Spirit, and I will pray with the Understanding also; or, A discourse touching prayer from 1 Corinthians 14:15, Miscellaneous Works*, II:235-275.

[14]   *Heaven and Hell*, III:246.

[15]   *Christian Man's Calling*, I:105.

[16]   Baxter, *Saints' Everlasting Rest, Practical Works*, 16.

[17]   *Ibid.*, 41.

[18]   *Christian Man's Calling*, I:111.

[19]   *Ibid.*, I:112.

[20]   Baxter, *Saints' Everlasting Rest, Practical Works*, 103.

[21]   *Christian Man's Calling*, I:112-115.

[22]   *Ibid.*, I:112.

[23]   *Ibid.*, I:117.

consideration of thy sins, wants, and mercies. While thou art pondering on these, thine eye will affect thine heart.'[24] Second, the regenerate must refuse those things that hinder prayer.[25] Quoting Psalm 66:18,[26] Swinnock affirms that prayer is ineffectual whilst sin is in the heart. He remarks, 'Prayer will not be healing and prevalent till sin, in regard of love and delight, be taken out of the soul.'[27] Until the individual does this, 'the wide mouth of sin outcrieth the voice of his prayers.'[28] Perkins agrees, stressing that prayer must necessarily follow repentance, reconciliation with other believers, and preparation 'in heart and mind, as one that is to speak familiarly with God.'[29]

In terms of 'concomitants' – 'those things which must accompany prayer,'[30] Swinnock makes three recommendations. First, there is the matter of a person's prayers. In brief, 'God's word and will must be the rule of our prayers... Divine precepts, what God commandeth us to act; divine promises, what God engageth himself to do for us; and divine prophecies, what God hath foretold shall come to pass, are to be the bounds of our prayers: he wandereth to his loss, that in his requests goeth beyond these limits.'[31] This means, in the words of Perkins, that 'every petition must be grounded upon the Word of God.'[32] Second, there is the character of the person who prays. Quite simply, 'The petitioner must be a justified and regenerate person, or the prayer will never be prevalent.'[33] Perkins concurs, 'The petition must proceed from saving and true justifying faith.'[34] Third, there are the properties of a person's prayers: they must be humble – 'Prayer is one of our nearest approaches to God on this side heaven; in it we speak to God mouth to mouth, and therefore must be poured out with much humility;'[35] they must be hearty – 'God looketh not so much to the elegancy of thy prayers, how neat they are, nor to the geometry of thy prayers, how long they are, but to the sincerity of thy prayers, how hearty they are;'[36] they must be fervent – 'When thou art begging grace and purity, with what earnestness shouldst thou pray! believing how destructive sin is to thy precious soul, and how offensive to the jealous, just, and almighty God, and in what absolute necessity thou standest in of holiness, without which thou canst never see

---

[24] Gurnall, *Christian in Complete Armour*, II:324.
[25] *Christian Man's Calling*, I:118.
[26] 'If I regard wickedness in my heart, The Lord will not hear.'
[27] *Christian Man's Calling*, I:119.
[28] *Ibid.*, I:118.
[29] Perkins, *Cases*, 154-155.
[30] *Christian Man's Calling*, I:111.
[31] *Ibid.*, I:121.
[32] Perkins, *Cases*, 155.
[33] *Christian Man's Calling*, I:122.
[34] Perkins, *Cases*, 155. See 155-157.
[35] *Christian Man's Calling*, I:123.
[36] *Ibid.*, I:124-125.

God;'[37] and they must be constant – 'A Christian's prayer may have an intermission, but never a cessation.'[38]

Turning to consequents – 'those things which must follow after prayer,'[39] Swinnock urges the regenerate to watch for an answer.'[40] Perkins calls this 'a particular faith, whereby he that prayeth, must be assured that his particular request shall be granted.'[41] In addition to watching, the regenerate must work for an answer. Swinnock instructs, 'Thy duty is to pray, as knowing assuredly that thou canst do nothing of thyself, and yet to work as if thou wert to do all by thine own power. He that doth not endeavour, in a lawful use of those means which God affordeth him, to attain the mercies he needeth and asketh, doth tempt, not trust God, and may expect a rod sooner than relief.'[42] Likewise, Perkins states, 'A man must do and practice that, which he prays for; and he is not only to pray for blessings, but also to use all the lawful means he can, whereby the blessings he asketh, may be obtained.'[43]

Hearing and Reading God's Word

The next spiritual duty is hearing and reading God's Word. The Puritans insist that the Bible is the primary means through which the Holy Spirit stirs the affections, thereby enabling the regenerate to progress in holiness.[44] For Swinnock, this makes the Bible a 'special treasure,' which God has deposited 'into the hands of the children of men.'[45] For this reason, it merits their unrivalled devotion. In a word, they must hear it and read it 'in the fear of God.'[46]

In terms of antecedents, Swinnock affirms that the regenerate must be

---

[37]   *Ibid.,* I:126.
[38]   *Ibid.,* I:129.
[39]   *Ibid.,* I:111.
[40]   *Ibid.,* I:134.
[41]   Perkins, *Cases,* 157.
[42]   *Christian Man's Calling,* I:136-137.
[43]   Perkins, *Cases,* 157-158.
[44]   For the Puritans, study begins with Scripture and extends to various kinds of devotional literature including spiritual treatises, allegories, and biographies. The last two depict the Christian's struggle in sanctification. The reader's goal is to identify with the characters in these books and apply the lessons accordingly. Regarding these treatises, Watkins comments, 'It was a genre that became popular with Puritan readers in the second half of the seventeenth century, and was the outcome of conditions that were distinctively English, notably the contribution made to reformed theology by the English puritan divines in their doctrine of divine grace.' *The Puritan Experience,* 2.
[45]   *Christian Man's Calling,* I:141.
[46]   *Ibid.,* I:97. For Baxter's directions on hearing the Word, see *Christian Directory,* 473-478.

diligent in the 'matter'[47] and 'manner'[48] of hearing and reading God's Word. To begin with, they must empty their hearts of 'evil frames' and 'prejudice.'[49] Perkins calls this 'disburdening ourselves of all impediments, which may hinder the effectual hearing of the Word.'[50] Second, they must labour to effect their hearts with the Bible's inestimable worth. Swinnock speaks of its: necessity – it 'is absolutely necessary to my spiritual and eternal good;'[51] excellency – 'it is the voice of God, and not of man;'[52] and efficacy – it 'will work one way or other; if it work not for thy salvation, it will work for thy damnation.'[53] Third, the regenerate must entreat God to bless the Bible to them. Swinnock remarks, 'There is a thick film in thine ears naturally, which hindereth thine hearing; thine ears are stopped that sermons can have no passage. Now God alone can with his syringer dissolve the wax congealed there, and break through the skin, whereby thou mayest come to hear and live.'[54] Fourth, they must desire to please God and profit their soul.[55] Finally, they must leave their worldly thoughts behind them.[56]

Regarding the regenerate's 'carriage' whilst reading and hearing God's Word, Swinnock provides three guidelines. First, they must set themselves seriously as in the presence of God. He asks, 'God setteth before thee in his word, and offereth to thee life or death, blessing or cursing, his infinite favour or fury, heaven or hell; and, friend, are these things to be jested with?'[57] Burroughs affirms that to fear God is to fear his Word, because God's Word reveals God's name which, in turn, reveals God. He declares, 'O the Word has more of God's name in it than all the world besides.'[58] Bunyan echoes this sentiment:

This therefore teacheth us how to judge who feareth the Lord; they are those that learn, and that stand in awe of the word: those that have by the holy word of God the very form of it self engraven upon the face of their souls, they fear God (Rom. 6:17). But on the contrary, those that do not love good doctrine, that give not place to the wholesome truths of the God of Heaven revealed in his testament, to

---

[47] 'Take care what you listen to' (Mk. 4:24).
[48] 'Take care how you listen' (Lk. 8:18).
[49] *Christian Man's Calling*, I:145.
[50] Perkins, *Cases*, 170. Bayly also speaks of repentance as a necessary antecedent. *Practice of Piety*, 192.
[51] *Christian Man's Calling*, I:149.
[52] *Ibid.*, I:150.
[53] *Ibid.*, I:151.
[54] *Ibid.*, I:153.
[55] *Ibid.*, I:153-154.
[56] *Ibid.*, I:154-155.
[57] *Ibid.*, I:156. See Perkins, *Cases*, 171.
[58] Jeremiah Burroughs, *Gospel Fear* (London, 1674) 9.

take place in their souls, but rather despise it, and the true professors of it, they fear not God.[59]

Second, the regenerate must apply the Bible to their lives.[60] Whether it is the curses of the law, the commands of the law, or the comforts of the gospel, they must be applied by faith. For this reason, Perkins exhorts his readers to 'hear with judgment,' adding, 'Every hearer must have care that the Word of God be rooted and grounded in his heart, like good seed in good ground.'[61] Similarly, Bayly writes, 'In hearing, apply every speech as spoken to thyself, rather by God than by man... and labour not so much to hear the words of the preacher sounding in thine hear, as to feel the operation of the Spirit working in thy heart.'[62] Third, the regenerate must permit the Bible to come with authority to their conscience. Swinnock explains, 'When the word of God cometh like a mighty rushing wind, rooting up the tall trees of thy sins, bringing down high thoughts, overturning all before it; when as fire it burneth within thee, consuming thy lusts, and turning thee into its own likeness, making thee holy, spiritual, and heavenly; oh this is excellent hearing, this is hearing to

---

[59]   Bunyan, *Fear of God, Miscellaneous Works*, IX:58.

[60]   *Christian Man's Calling*, I:157-159. Armstrong argues that 'there are two poles at the heart of Puritan spirituality – the Bible as the living word of God, and a lively sense or experience of the Spirit of God.' He maintains that these two poles are actually inseparable. The Puritans turned to the 'living Word,' believing this was the place where 'God encounters man.' Armstrong's observation is sound, however he concludes from it that study and doctrine receive very little emphasis among the average Puritan because 'the important matter... was how the Bible affected his life.' 'Puritan Spirituality,' 240,244,245. This assertion is difficult to defend. Armstrong appears to take his lead from Nuttall, who analyses Puritanism as a broad spectrum from Presbyterianism to Quakerism, based upon their pneumatology. *The Holy Spirit in Puritan Faith and Experience*, 242. Richard Greaves shares the same approach, commenting, 'The essence of Puritanism is not to be found in matters of polity, theological dogma, principles of authority, or class orientation, but, as Geoffrey Nuttall has shown us, in the deeply spiritual experience which Puritans and many sectaries shared and recognized in others.' 'The Nature of the Puritan Tradition' in *Reformation, Conformity and Dissent: Essays in Honour of Geoffrey Nuttall*, ed. R. B. Knox (London: Epworth Press, 1977) 257. Following Nuttall, Greaves is working with a very broad definition of Puritanism. Swinnock does not share a 'deeply spiritual experience' with 'sectaries' such as the Quakers. This raises doubts concerning Armstrong's emphasis on Puritan subjective experience. Thomas Lea rightly contends that Puritan pastors 'aimed at instructing the mind so that faith and obedience could become possible... They rejected an appeal for religious feeling without knowledge or instruction.' 'The Hermeneutics of the Puritans,' *Journal of the Evangelical Theological Society* 39 (1996) 284.

[61]   Perkins, *Cases*, 192.

[62]   Bayly, *Practice of Piety*, 197-198.

purpose!'[63]

As for consequents, Swinnock asserts that there must be prayer.[64] There must also be practice – 'He heareth a sermon best who practiseth it most.'[65] Perkins expands on this, stating, 'the doctrine delivered, must be treasured up in the heart and practiced in life,'[66] 'a man must meditate on the Word which he hath heard, with lifting up his heart unto God,'[67] 'he must have experience of the Word of God in himself,'[68] 'he is to examine himself,'[69] and 'he must be obedient unto it.'[70] Without this corresponding practice, the hearing and reading of God's Word is pointless. Swinnock is adamant that the individual who is renewed into the image of God will be an 'effectual doer' – not a 'forgetful hearer' – of the Word.[71] In this, Thomas Lea sees 'the most characteristic feature of Puritanism,' namely, 'its respect for Scripture and its desire to know and carry out all its prescriptions.'[72]

Swinnock concludes his treatment of this means of grace[73] with a 'good wish' – 'My prayer is, that the gospel may come to me, not in word only, but in power also... Oh that I might behold the Lord so effectually in that glass as to be changed into his image, from glory to glory!'[74] Swinnock believes that reading the Bible is the means by which the Holy Spirit illuminates the understanding. This opening of the spiritual eyes extends to the affections and will so that speculative knowledge becomes sensible knowledge, thereby strengthening the soul in its struggle against sin. For Swinnock, this process is intensified when God's Word is preached.[75] Baxter's thoughts on this are particularly helpful:

> The *reading* of the word of God, and the explication and application of it in good books, is a means to possess the mind with sound, orderly, and working

---

[63] *Christian Man's Calling*, I:159.

[64] *Ibid.*, I:163.

[65] *Ibid.*, I:166.

[66] Perkins, *Cases*, 173.

[67] *Ibid.*

[68] *Ibid.*, 174.

[69] *Ibid.*

[70] *Ibid.*

[71] Jas. 1:22-25.

[72] Lea, 'The Hermeneutics of the Puritans,' 273.

[73] Lewis confirms the prevalence of Swinnock's threefold approach among the Puritans. He focuses on (1) preparation necessary for hearing the Word preached, (2) behaviour necessary when hearing the Word preached, and (3) duties after hearing the Word preached. *The Genius of Puritanism*, 53-59. There are scattered references to Swinnock's *Christian Man's Calling*.

[74] *Christian Man's Calling*, I:171.

[75] For a description of the role of the preacher, see Paul Cook, 'The Life and Work of a Minister According to the Puritans' in *Puritan Papers: Vol. I*, ed. M. Lloyd-Jones (Phillipsburg: P & R Publishing, 2000) 177-189.

apprehensions of God, and of his holy truths: so that in such reading our understandings are oft illuminated with a heavenly light, and our hearts are touched with a special delightful relish of that truth; and they are secretly attracted and engaged unto God and all the powers of our souls are excited and animated to a holy obedient life. The same word *preached...* hath a greater advantage for the same illumination and excitement of the soul.[76]

This view of preaching is axiomatic among the Puritans, as Watkins explains:

A harmonious combination of the faculties could be achieved only by a simultaneous seizure of them all by divine grace, accompanied by a rational apprehension of the truth... The spoken word was the one agency by which, on the plane of nature, the innermost faculties could be reached, and this is why the sermon was regarded as the most effective channel of grace... Preaching, then, was the most important of the means appointed by God to bring men out of their bondage to sin and call together those who were to be His people.[77]

Lewis arrives at the same conclusion, quoting Richard Sibbes: "'The Word of God preached... is not altogether to teach us, but [exists that] the Spirit going with it" might "work grace necessary to strengthen us in the inward man (2 Cor. 4:16)... Let us therefore set a price upon God's ordinance."'[78]

This view of preaching as 'the most effective channel of grace' stems from Calvin's concept of the 'sacramental word.'[79] Commenting on Romans 10:17,[80] Calvin writes, 'This is a remarkable passage with regard to the efficacy of preaching; for he testifies that by it faith is produced... when it pleases the Lord to work, it becomes the instrument of his power.'[81] Gerrish explains Calvin's thought as follows: 'The word is not simply information about God; it is the instrument through which union with Christ is effected and his grace imparted. The word of God, in Calvin's thinking, assumes the function that medieval theology ascribed to the sacraments.'[82] Hageman agrees, 'For Calvin the reading and preaching of the Word is the way in which Christ comes to us and shares himself with us... Because the Word is the instrument through which

---

[76] Baxter, *Divine Life, Practical Works*, 195. My italics.

[77] Watkins, *The Puritan Experience*, 6.

[78] Richard Sibbes, *The Complete Works of Richard Sibbes*, V:508, as quoted in Lewis, *The Genius of Puritanism*, 41. Lewis's analysis of Puritan preaching is most helpful. It is divided into five sections: the Dignity of Preaching, the Necessity of Preaching, the Demands of Preaching, the Character of Preaching, and the Content of Preaching.

[79] Calvin, *Institutes*, IV:XIV:4.

[80] 'So faith comes from hearing, and hearing by the word of Christ.'

[81] Calvin, *Commentaries on the Epistle of the Apostle Paul to the Romans* in *Calvin's Commentaries*, XIX:401.

[82] Gerrish, *Grace and Gratitude*, 76.

Christ is given to us, it stands at the very centre of the life of the Church and at the very centre of the life and growth of the Christian.'[83] The Puritans adopt Calvin's view, stressing the efficacy of the Word, preached in the power of the Holy Spirit.

This high regard for preaching is evident in the structure of Puritan services.[84] J. A. Caiger develops this insight in his analysis of the order of service in the *Westminster Directory for Public Worship*. The service begins with a brief prayer, the reading of the Scriptures, the singing of a psalm, and the great public prayer. According to Caiger, 'All this... is by way of preparation of the congregation for the preaching of the Word which immediately follows.'[85] The service concludes with a prayer and the singing of a psalm. From this order, Caiger notes, 'Set within the framework of the singing of the psalms come the two prayers, the first of which prepares the people for the preaching of the Word and leads up to it; the second follows the preaching and seeks the blessing of God upon its matter and its message. The preaching of the Word was therefore, to the Puritans, central to the whole structure of praise and prayer in the public worship of God.'[86] Lewis shares this conclusion: 'The Puritans regarded the sermon as the climax of public worship... they regarded proclamation of the Word and instruction from the Word, accompanied by the power of the Holy Spirit, as the principal mediating instrument of the power of God unto salvation and sanctification.'[87]

This high regard for preaching is also evident in the structure of Puritan sermons. [88] By and large, the Puritans adopt Perkins's four-step approach: read the text, expound the text, derive several points of doctrine, and apply the doctrine to all of life. Perkins defines this last step as 'that whereby the doctrine rightly collected is diversely fitted according as place, time and person do

---

[83]   Hageman, 'Reformed Spirituality,' 66.

[84]   For an overview of the nature of Puritan preaching, see Harry Stout, *The New England Soul: Preaching and Religious Culture in Colonial New England* (Oxford University Press, 1988).

[85]   J. A. Caiger, 'Preaching – Puritan and Reformed' in *Puritan Papers: Vol. II*, ed. J. I. Packer (Phillipsburg: P & R Publishing, 2001) 165.

[86]   *Ibid.*, 165.

[87]   Lewis, The Genius of Puritanism, 53.

[88]   Packer maintains that four axioms underlay all Puritan thought about preaching. The first is the primacy of the intellect. The Puritans believed that all grace enters through the understanding. The second is the importance of preaching. In Packer's words, the sermon was 'the liturgical climax of public worship.' The third is the life-giving power of the Scripture. In other words, the Bible does not merely contain the Word of God, but it is the Word of God. The fourth is the sovereignty of the Holy Spirit. The Puritans insisted that the ultimate effectiveness of preaching is out of man's hands. *Quest for Godliness*, 281-284.

require.'[89] Bayly adopts this approach, encouraging his readers to listen carefully to the sermon by marking the explication of the text, the chief sum or scope of the Holy Ghost in the text, the division or parts of the text, and the doctrines – 'the proofs, the reasons, and the uses thereof.'[90] For Bayly, this is the practice of 'all faithful pastors, who desire to edify their people in the knowledge of God.'[91]

Like his contemporaries, Swinnock employs Perkins's method of preaching. All of Swinnock's treatises are structured according to exposition of the text, explanation of doctrines arising from the text, and application of those doctrines by way of uses. For him, this 'plain preaching' is best designed for 'convincing the judgment, and working upon the affections.'[92] As Davies rightly observes, 'Plain the Puritan sermon might be... it was purposefully streamlined. It proceeded from informing the mind and stirring up the affections to effect the transformation of the will.'[93] In the same way, Sceats states, 'Doctrine and use were the twin poles of the Puritan homiletic technique. They arose from the conviction that the Spirit worked by means, and that therefore the sermon needed to be as well fitted as possible to bringing the understanding of the hearers into vital contact with the meaning of the word for them.'[94] Again, 'They wanted to preach in such a way as to enter the hearts and souls of their hearers. They would do so through the understanding, but their aim was to engage the affections, stir the emotions and, in the end, to move the whole person to respond.'[95]

In summary, for Swinnock, preaching is 'a calling above all others of greatest weight,'[96] because it is the primary channel by which the Holy Spirit imparts grace to the regenerate. In reflecting upon his own preaching ministry, Swinnock declares, 'I wish, that... I may lay the foundation of sound doctrine, raise it up strong pillars of convincing reasons, and cover it with useful and powerful application.'[97] He adds, 'Oh that I might not only preach prudently, but also powerfully; that my sermons may be delivered, not as prologues to a play, as matter of sport or pastime, but as the message of a herald, with all imaginable seriousness and fervency, as containing conditions of life and death.'[98]

---

[89] William Perkins, *Arte of Prophesying; or, A treatise concerning the sacred and onely true manner and methode of preaching*, Works, II:341.

[90] Bayly, *Practice of Piety*, 198.

[91] *Ibid.*

[92] *Christian Man's Calling*, I:147.

[93] Davies, *Worship and Theology*, 165.

[94] Sceats, 'The Experience of Grace,' 17.

[95] *Ibid.*, 11.

[96] *Christian Man's Calling*, I:319.

[97] *Ibid.*, I:321.

[98] *Ibid.*, I:326.

Receiving the Lord's Supper

Turning to the Lord's Supper, Swinnock urges his readers to prepare themselves 'solemnly.'[99] By this, he means there must be a serious examination of 'graces.'[100] The purpose of this self-examination is to determine the state of the soul for 'men must have spiritual life, before they can eat spiritual meat.'[101] Swinnock proceeds to make an important distinction in explaining that their hearts must be 'clean, not with a legal cleanness, which denieth the being of sin in them... but with an evangelical cleanness, which denieth the dominion of sin over them.'[102] In other words, they are not to look for perfection, but sanctification. In addition to examining 'graces,' the regenerate must examine 'corruptions.'[103] Bayly exhorts his readers to consider their own 'unworthiness.'[104] For Swinnock, the result of such a 'thorough search' is humiliation,[105] consisting of 'mourning for sin' and 'turning from sin.'[106] He remarks, 'As thy duty is to wash thy soul in godly sorrow, so also to put off thy sinful affections, before thou enterest into God's house to partake of this ordinance.'[107]

Having done this, they are ready to partake of the Lord's Supper. Whilst 'at the sacrament,' Swinnock urges them to mind the 'subjects' that are being considered and to observe the 'graces' that are being exercised.[108] The first subject is Christ's passion.[109] The second is Christ's affection.[110] And the third is humanity's corruption.[111] Meditation upon these subjects results in the exercise of three 'special graces:' Christ's passion stirs faith; Christ's affection stirs love; and humanity's corruption stirs repentance.[112] Regarding the regenerate's duty 'after the sacrament,' Swinnock exhorts them to be thankful and faithful. He states, 'Surely, reader, if thou didst but find the Saviour in the sacrament, thou canst not but fear sin after the sacrament... Truly, if nothing

---

[99]   *Ibid.*, I:180.

[100] *Ibid.*, I:181.

[101] *Ibid.*, I:182.

[102] *Ibid.*, I:183.

[103] *Ibid.*, I:185.

[104] Bayly, *Practice of Piety*, 238.

[105] *Christian Man's Calling*, I:186.

[106] *Ibid.*, I:188.

[107] *Ibid.*

[108] *Ibid.*, I:192. For Bayly's thoughts on meditation at the Lord's Supper, see *Practice of Piety*, 245-250. Simon Chan rightly observes, 'Perhaps in no other public exercise was meditation more assiduously applied than in the sacrament of the Lord's Supper.' *The Puritan Meditative Tradition, 1599-1691: A Study of Ascetical Piety* (Unpublished PhD dissertation at Cambridge University, 1986) 98.

[109] *Christian Man's Calling*, I:192-197.

[110] *Ibid.*, I:197-201.

[111] *Ibid.*, I:201-202.

[112] *Ibid.*, I:202-211.

will dissuade thee from sin, yet this consideration, that it is a trampling upon thy blessed Saviour, should prevail with thee.'[113]

Swinnock's understanding of the nature of the Lord's Supper is set within the framework of the covenant of grace as articulated in the *WCF*.[114] God established this covenant with the last Adam – Christ. It is expressed in the Adamic, Noahic, Abrahamic, Mosaic, and Davidic Covenants until it reaches its climax in Christ's crucifixion and resurrection – the New Covenant. For Swinnock, this covenant is the 'cream' of Scripture.[115] And he believes that the Lord's Supper is its 'sign and seal.'[116]

Further to this, Swinnock views the covenant in terms of a marital relationship between Christ and his bride – the church. In this context, the Lord's Supper is the place where the husband chooses to commune in a special way with his wife. Swinnock clarifies:

> At the Lord's Table Christ kisseth his spouse with the sweetest kisses of his lips, and ravisheth her heart with his warmest love. In other ordinances he wooeth her; in this he marrieth her. In other ordinances she hath from him the salutes of a loving friend; but in this the embraces of a husband; other duties are pleasant and wholesome food, but this is the costly, delightful feast. In this Christ bringeth his beloved 'into his banqueting house,' a storehouse of all sweet delights, of variety of delicacies, 'and his banner over her is love' (Cant. 2:4).[117]

From Swinnock's language, it is apparent that he views the Lord's Supper as a very real encounter between Christ and his 'spouse.' It is a 'banqueting house' and 'delightful feast,' at which Christ offers himself to 'his beloved.' Baxter agrees:

> No where is God so near to man as in Jesus Christ: and no where is Christ so familiarly represented to us, as in this holy sacrament. Here we are called to sit with him at his table... to feed upon his very flesh and blood; that is, with our mouths upon his representative flesh and blood, and with our applying faith upon his real flesh and blood, by such a feeding as belongs to faith. The marriage covenant betwixt God incarnate, and his espoused ones, is there publicly sealed, celebrated, and solemnized.[118]

This 'feeding' and 'feasting' on Christ must not be confused with the doctrine of transubstantiation – the belief that the bread and wine, without changing in appearance, literally become Christ's body and blood at the Lord's

---

[113] *Ibid.*, I:215. For Bayly, see *Practice of Piety*, 256,260. For Perkins, see *Cases*, 203.

[114] *Christian Man's Calling*, I:16,71,135,172; *Fading of the Flesh*, III:406,429,454-458; *Pastor's Farewell*, IV:61; and *Gods Are Men*, IV:134.

[115] *Christian Man's Calling*, I:172.

[116] *Ibid.*, I:173.

[117] *Ibid.*

[118] Baxter, *Divine Life, Practical Works*, 196.

Supper. Swinnock rejects transubstantiation, yet upholds Christ's real presence
in the bread and wine. His understanding of this places him in the vicinity of
Calvin's view of the sacrament.[119] Calvin makes it very clear that the
sacraments do not have any intrinsic value, affirming, 'We must beware lest
we... think that a hidden power is joined and fastened to the sacraments by
which they of themselves confer the graces of the Holy Spirit upon us... they
are of no further benefit unless the Holy Spirit accompanies them. For it is he
who opens our minds and hearts and makes us receptive to this testimony.'[120]
This last statement is crucial to Calvin's view of Christ's presence in the bread
and wine. In his opinion, the Holy Spirit 'nourishes faith spiritually through the
sacraments.'[121] This means Christ gives spiritual nourishment from his glorified
body through the Holy Spirit to those who partake of the Supper. Christ is not
physically present in the bread and wine, because his glorified body is in
heaven. There is, therefore, an immeasurable distance between Christ and those
who partake of his Supper. However, Christ comes down to the regenerate, at
his Supper, through the Holy Spirit. For Calvin, therefore, the body and blood
of Christ are truly present in the bread and wine. This means that when the
regenerate partake of the Lord's Supper, they consume Christ spiritually.[122]
This, in turn, gives them spiritual nourishment and brings them closer to Christ.

For Calvin, this is the seal of the covenant. As Lillback explains, 'For this
covenant blessing to be truly realized, there must be an actual participation with
Christ Himself in the Supper. This spiritual union of the believer results from
the "bond" of the Holy Spirit. Christ's body being truly human is limited by all

---

[119] When it comes to the Reformers, there are three main viewpoints concerning the
nature of Christ's presence in the elements. They are usually identified with Luther,
Zwingli, and Calvin. For a summary of the various views, see Brian Gerrish, 'The
Lord's Supper in the Reformed Confessions,' *Theology Today* 23 (1966) 224-243.
For a brief overview of Luther's position, see Philip Eveson, 'Martin Luther and his
Sacramental Teaching' in *Union and Communion, 1529-1979* (London:
Westminster Conference, 1979) 7-21. For an extensive treatment of Luther, see
Herman Sasse, *This is My Body: Luther's Contention for the Real Presence in the
sacrament of the Altar* (Lutheran Publishing House, 1977). For Luther, see *An
Admonition Concerning the Sacrament of the Body and Blood of our Lord, Works,*
XXXV:102-132; *The Babylonian Captivity of the Church, Works,* XXXVI:29-34;
*That these Words of Christ – 'This is My Body' – Still Stand Firm Against the
Fanatics, Works,* XXXVII. For a brief overview of Zwingli's position, see Derek
Moore-Crispin, '"The Real Absence:" Ulrich Zwingli's View of the Lord's Supper?'
in *Union and Communion* (London: Westminster Conference, 1979) 22-33. For
Zwingli, see *Commentary on True and False Religion,* eds. S. M. Jackson and C. N.
Heller (Durham: Labyrinth Press, 1981) 233-235.
[120] Calvin, *Institutes,* IV:XIV:17.
[121] *Ibid.,* IV:XIV:12.
[122] Joseph Tylenda demonstrates Calvin's preference for the word *true* as opposed to
real in regard to Christ's presence in the Supper. 'Calvin and Christ's Presence in
the Supper – True or Real,' *Scottish Journal of Theology* 27 (1974) 65-75.

of the limitations of space that encumber normal human life. These limitations however are bridged by the Holy Spirit through His work in the sacrament, uniting Christ and the communicant.'[123] Similarly, John Nicholls explains that, for Calvin, the regenerate can only participate in Christ's life if they are brought into union with his human nature. This is accomplished through the Lord's Supper when they commune with the body and blood of Christ through the Holy Spirit.[124] Gerrish agrees, 'The believer's participation in the humanity of Christ is not an option that he or she could equally well have declined: it is a gift given by the Spirit through the efficacious power of the word proclaimed and made visible in the sacraments.'[125]

By and large, the Puritans follow Calvin's lead.[126] They too reject the doctrine of transubstantiation. Perkins remarks, 'That doctrine of transubstantiation, which teacheth, that the bread is turned into the very body of Christ, and the wine into his blood, is a very fable... The like may be said of the Lutherans consubstantiation, whereby they bear men in hand that there is a coexistence, by which the body of Christ, is either in, or with, or under the bread.'[127] Like Calvin, the Puritans stress Christ's true presence in the bread and wine, in that the regenerate partake of his body and blood by the Holy Spirit. Bayly believes that the Lord's Supper is 'a most effectual sign and pledge of our communion with Christ,'[128] adding, 'of all other times this union is best felt, and most confirmed, when we duly receive the Lord's Supper: for then we shall sensibly feel our hearts knit unto Christ, and the desires of our souls drawn by faith and the Holy Ghost, as by cords of love, nearer and nearer to his holiness.'[129] Bayly affirms that Christ is actually present in the bread and wine by a double union. The first is a spiritual union between Christ and the regenerate. The second is a sacramental union between Christ's body and blood and the outward signs in the sacrament. He explains:

> It is a spiritual conjunction of the earthly signs, which are bread and wine, with the heavenly graces, which are the body and blood of Christ, in the act of receiving: as if, by a mutual relation, they were but one and the same thing. Hence it is, that in the same instant of time that the worthy receiver eats with his mouth the bread and wine of the Lord, he eateth also with the mouth of his faith the very

[123] Lillback, *Binding of God*, 259-260. See Calvin, *Institutes*, IV:XVII:12,33.
[124] John Nicholls, "'Union with Christ:' John Calvin on the Lord's Supper' in *Union and Communion* (London: Westminster Conference, 1979) 35-53.
[125] Gerrish, *Grace and Gratitude*, 158.
[126] For an overview of the Puritan position, see Hywel Roberts, "'The Cup of Blessing:' Puritan and Separatist Sacramental Discourses' in *Union and Communion* (London: Westminster Conference, 1979) 55-71. For Owen and the dynamic view, see Ferguson, *John Owen on the Christian Life*, 221-222.
[127] Perkins, *Golden Chain*, *Works*, I:76.
[128] Bayly, *Practice of Piety*, 228.
[129] *Ibid.*, 229.

body and blood of Christ: not that Christ is brought down from heaven to the sacrament, but that the Holy Spirit by the sacrament lifts up his mind unto Christ.[130]

The Westminster divines clearly echo their predecessors:

Worthy receivers, outwardly partaking of the visible elements in this sacrament, do then also inwardly by faith, really and indeed, yet not carnally and corporally, but spiritually, receive and feed upon Christ crucified, and all the benefits of his death: the body and blood of Christ being then not corporally or carnally in, with, or under the bread and wine; yet as really, but spiritually, present to the faith of believers in that ordinance, as the elements themselves are, to their outward senses.[131]

This is the tradition in which Swinnock stands. The body and blood of Christ are 'really, but spiritually, present to the faith of believers.' Consequently, when 'God the Son cometh down in the likeness of bread and wine; he himself is eaten and drunk by faith.'[132] For Swinnock, this is when 'Christ kisseth his spouse with the sweetest kisses of his lips.' In this, Swinnock clearly distinguishes between the 'elements' and the 'sacrament',[133] stating, 'It is one thing to *take* the supper of the Lord, and another thing to *taste* the supper of the Lord.'[134] With this in mind, he says that a 'threefold act of faith' must be 'put forth at the sacrament.'[135] First, the regenerate must 'look out for Christ' – 'Consider that Jesus Christ is the very soul of the sacrament; without him it is but the carcase of an ordinance.'[136] This means they must look beyond the bread and the wine to the Holy Spirit, who presents Christ to the soul. Second, they must 'look up to Christ for grace' – 'Look up to Christ as a treasury of grace for the supply of all thy necessities, and put thy hand of faith into this treasury, and thou shalt take out unsearchable riches.'[137] Third, they must 'receive Christ, and apply him to the soul' – 'When thou puttest forth the hand of thy body to take the bread and wine, do thou put forth the hand of faith to receive the body and the blood of Christ.'[138]

For Swinnock, then, this is Christ's 'special presence' at the 'sacred ordinance'.[139] The Supper is a means by which Christ visits the regenerate unlike at any other time. As Davies observes, this view of the Lord's Supper

---

[130] *Ibid.*, 233.
[131] *WCF*, XXIX:VII.
[132] *Christian Man's Calling*, I:174.
[133] *Ibid.*, I:174-175,203.
[134] *Ibid.*, I:175. His italics.
[135] *Ibid.*, I:203.
[136] *Ibid.*
[137] *Ibid.*, I:204.
[138] *Ibid.*
[139] *Ibid.*, I:218.

'runs constantly through Puritanism... The presence of Christ is mystical and spiritual, not carnal or local, and it represents, presents, and applies to the believers the benefits of the covenant of grace, which it seals and authenticates to their faith by the power of the Holy Spirit.'[140]

Keeping the Lord's Day

The final means of grace is the observance of the Lord's Day. In the words of Irvonwyn Morgan, this 'is one of the great frames of the Puritan movement, and no appreciation of Puritanism is possible without some understanding of the Puritan love for and respect for the Sabbath day.'[141] Davies shares this sentiment, stating, 'For the Puritan there was only one festival of the Church, and that a weekly one. The Lord's day was the single red-letter day in his calendar. The Lord had decreed that one day out of every seven should be spent in religious exercises.'[142]

The Market Day for the Soul

As for the Puritans themselves, Richard Greenham describes the 'Sabbath day' as 'the schoole day, the faire day, the market day, the feeding day of the soule.'[143] Again, 'In this day wee should grow in love towards God, and tender affection to our brethren... wee keepe the Sabbath aright, when wee use it to that ende for which it was ordained, that is, when we use... those exercises, whereby we may be the more sanctified, and God the more glorified.'[144] Greenham speaks of 'private' and 'publike' exercises. By the former, he means examination and meditation.[145] By the latter, he means 'the word read and preached,' 'prayers fervently made,' 'singing of the Psalms,' and 'reverend administration of the Sacraments.'[146] For his part, Bayly declares, 'The Sabbath is God's market-day... He is not far from true piety, who makes conscience to keep the Sabbath-day; but he who can dispense with his conscience to break the Sabbath for his own profit or pleasure, his heart never yet felt what either the fear of God or true religion means.'[147] Bolton speaks of 'a heavenly hungry heart' feeding and filling itself 'upon the Lord's day, when showers of spiritual blessings are accustomed to fall from the throne of grace all the day long upon

---

[140] Horton Davies, *Worship and Theology in England from Andrewes to Baxter and Fox, 1603-1690* (Princeton University Press, 1975) 317.

[141] Irvonwyn Morgan, *Puritan Spirituality* (London: Epworth Press, 1973) 42.

[142] Davies, *Worship of the English Puritans*, 75.

[143] Richard Greenham, *A Treatise of the Sabbath* in *The Works of Richard Greenham* (London, 1612) 129.

[144] *Ibid.*, 156.

[145] *Ibid.*, 157-159.

[146] *Ibid.*, 156.

[147] Bayly, *Practice of Piety*, 170-171.

those who sincerely endeavour to consecrate it as glorious unto him.'[148]

As for Swinnock, he affirms that the Lord's Day is 'the queen of days,'[149] 'the special time for religious duties,'[150] and 'the market-day for the soul.'[151] In his estimation, the other means of grace are made more effectual on the Sabbath.[152] Undoubtedly, he learned this lesson from his uncle, Robert Swinnock, concerning whom he writes, 'The Sabbath he dedicated wholly to God's service, and did not only himself, but took care that all within his gate should spend the day in secret and private duties, and in attendance on public ordinances.'[153] His uncle's desire was that 'the Lord's day should be conscientiously observed, and devoted to the dearest Redeemer by secret, private, and public duties.'[154] Sharing his uncle's conviction, Swinnock gives eight directions to help the regenerate make full use of the Sabbath.[155] First, they must make preparation by 'removing the filth of sin' and 'awakening grace.'[156] Second, they must impress their souls with the greatness of their privilege, 'because therein we enjoy all the means of communion with God, in the highest degree and measure, without interruption.'[157] Third, they must consider the opportunity that is theirs to increase and improve grace.[158] Fourth, they must esteem the public ordinances as their chief work of the day.[159] Swinnock explains, 'Private duties are beautiful, and in season every day; but public ordinances are never so lovely and beautiful, because never so much in

---

[148] Robert Bolton, *The Four Last Things: Death, Judgement, Hell, and Heaven* (1633; Religious Tract Society, 1830; rpt., Morgan: Soli Deo Gloria, 1994) 75-76.

[149] *Christian Man's Calling*, I:231,297.

[150] *Ibid.*, I:222.

[151] *Ibid.*, I:226. For a discussion of the 'market-day' figure, see Morgan, *Puritan Spirituality*, 46-47. Hill's suggestion that the Puritan commitment to the Sabbath was motivated by social and economic necessity is difficult to find in Swinnock. *Society and Puritanism*, 145-218. For a brief critique of Hill's view, see Keith Sprunger, 'English and Dutch Sabbatarianism and the Development of Puritan Social Theology,' *Church History* 51 (1982) 36-38.

[152] According to Hambrick-Stowe, 'The practice of private devotion lay at the heart of Puritan spirituality.' 'Puritan Spirituality in America,' 346. There is no question that the Puritans place tremendous importance upon the practice of private duties, however these do not 'lay at the heart' of their spirituality. This place is reserved for the Sabbath. Morgan rightly observes that 'even the private duties of religion... were undertaken to prepare the heart to profit by the public exercise of religion on the Sabbath.' *Puritan Spirituality*, 45. This is confirmed in Swinnock.

[153] *Fading of the Flesh*, III:409.

[154] *Ibid.*, III:416.

[155] For Baxter's directions, see *Christian Directory*, 470-473.

[156] *Christian Man's Calling*, I:228.

[157] *Ibid.*, I:231.

[158] *Ibid.*, I:232-234.

[159] *Ibid.*, I:234-239.

their prime and season, as on a Lord's day.'[160] Fifth, they must tune their hearts to spiritual delight in observing the day.[161] Sixth, they must not permit any duty to satisfy them without communion with God.[162] Seventh, they must sanctify the whole day to God's service.[163] Swinnock encourages his readers to rise early in the morning and retire late at night in order 'to employ the whole day in God's worship,' adding, 'Be either praying, or reading, or hearing, or singing, or meditating, or discoursing with others about the works or word of God. Be always taken up either with public, private, or secret duties.'[164] Finally, they must meditate on the word and works of God.[165]

The Nature of Sabbatarianism

From the aforementioned, it is clear that Swinnock subscribes to what is known as Sabbatarianism. Patrick Collinson defines Sabbatarianism as 'the doctrinal assertion that the fourth commandment is not an obsolete ceremonial law of the Jews but a perpetual, moral law, binding on Christians.'[166] According to Keith Sprunger, it consists of a 'package of three parts:' the ordination of the Sabbath (now Sunday) by God; the cessation of work on Sunday; and the prohibition of frivolous recreation and sports on Sunday.[167] Similarly, John Primus identifies three essential components to Sabbatarianism: the moral nature of the fourth commandment; Sunday absolutism; and strict Sabbath observance.[168] Primus' thesis is of particular interest. He writes:

> While high Sabbath views were widespread in English Protestantism from the earliest years of the Reformation and were shared by conservative conformists and more radical Puritans alike, this consensus broke down in the 1580s and 1590s when there was a marked increase in the publication of Sabbath treatises, a more radical insistence on strict Sabbath observance, and a narrowing of the deuteronomic principle to the view that all the failures of the realm were

---

[160] *Ibid.*, I:235.

[161] *Ibid.*, I:239-242.

[162] *Ibid.*, I:242-243.

[163] *Ibid.*, I:243-246.

[164] *Ibid.*, I:245.

[165] *Ibid.*, I:246-249. For an additional twenty directions for sanctifying the Lord's Day, see I:249-255.

[166] Patrick Collinson, *Godly People: Essays on English Protestantism and Puritanism* (London: Hambledon Press, 1983) 429. For a defence of the *WCF*'s position, see John Murray, 'The Moral Law and the Fourth Commandment' in *Collected Writings* (Edinburgh: Banner of Truth, 1982) I:193-228. He defends the central motif of Sabbatarianism – the Decalogue is the 'epitome of the Moral Law' and, therefore, perpetual.

[167] Sprunger, 'English and Dutch Sabbatarianism,' 26.

[168] John Primus, *Holy Time: Moderate Puritanism and the Sabbath* (Macon: Mercer University Press, 1989) 11.

attributable to Sabbath breaking. All of this led to the emergence of a genuine Sabbatarianism that reached its doctrinal apotheosis in Sunday absolutism – the view that the Old Testament Sabbath is continued in the New Testament first day of the week.[169]

In his analysis of this development, Primus begins with John Hooper and his contemporaries,[170] concluding that whilst they share 'strong Sabbath views,' 'the most distinctive element of Sabbatarianism is missing.'[171] According to Primus, Perkins marks the advent of fully developed Sabbatarianism,[172] because he 'addresses the issues of prime importance in Sabbatarianism: the moral versus ceremonial dimensions of the fourth commandment, and the shift from the seventh day to the first.'[173] He remarks:

> Perkins's views on the Sabbath are extremely significant. His stature as an early moderate Puritan theologian and the widespread circulation of his writings, as well as his treatment of the Sabbath in cases of conscience demonstrates beyond dispute that the early consensus about the Sabbath had broken down. The central issues of the day of worship and the authority to change that day had become matters that troubled many consciences. In his long argument about the Sunday Sabbath, Perkins reflects the heart of genuine Sabbatarianism.[174]

The first mark of this 'genuine Sabbatarianism' is the moral perpetuity of the Sabbath.[175] Having described what is ceremonial in the Sabbath, Perkins explains what is perpetual: first, 'that there should be a day of rest, in which man and beast might be refreshed after labour;' second, 'that this day should be

---

[169] *Ibid.*, 12-13.

[170] *Ibid.*, 18-23.

[171] *Ibid.*, 26. In summarizing the positions of this time period, James Dennison identifies six features of Sabbath keeping: (1) a significant protest against the abuse of Sunday and other holy days; (2) civil and ecclesiastical statutes enjoining spiritual duties on the Lord's day; (3) Sabbath sanctification promoted by church and state for the sake of worship and order in the establishment; (4) identification of the Sabbath of the fourth commandment with a day, the observance of which is binding upon Christians; (5) a theological distinction between spiritual and external Sabbath; and (6) a litany which requires worshippers to beseech God for the inclination to keep the Sabbath commandment. *The Market Day of the Soul* (Lanham: University Press of America, 1983) 13.

[172] See Perkins, *Golden Chain*, *Works*, I:17-18,46-49,59-60; and *Cases*, 438-458.

[173] Primus, *Holy Time*, 68. See Perkins, *Golden Chain*, *Works*, I:102-103.

[174] *Ibid.*, 72. After Perkins, Primus believes that the three elements of Sabbatarianism are most clearly articulated in Nicholas Bound's *The Doctrine of the Sabbath*. *Ibid.*, 80. Sprunger makes the same observation. 'English and Dutch Sabbatarianism,' 26. Errol Hulse comments, 'The basic approach used by Bownde became standard in all Puritan works thereafter.' 'Sanctifying the Lord's Day: Reformed and Puritan Attitudes' in *Aspects of Sanctification* (London: Westminster Conference, 1982) 85.

[175] For a brief summary, see Packer, *Quest for Godliness*, 236-240.

sanctified; that is, set apart to the worship of God;' and third, 'that a seventh day should be sanctified to an holy rest, and that this holy rest should be observed in a seventh day.'[176] The main reason the Sabbath is moral, in Perkins's estimation, is the fact that it 'was instituted and appointed by God in Paradise, before the fall of man, and the revealing of Christ.'[177] Bayly concurs:

> To sanctify, then, the Sabbath on the seventh day is not a ceremonial law abrogated, but the moral and perpetual law of God perfected; so that the same perpetual commandment which bound the Jews to keep the Sabbath on that seventh day, to celebrate the world's creation, binds Christians to solemnize the Sabbath on this seventh day, in memorial of the world's redemption; for the fourth commandment being a moral law, requires a seventh day to be kept holy for ever.[178]

Bayly builds on this, providing ten proofs of the moral nature of the fourth commandment. First, 'God placed this commandment in the midst of the two tables, because the keeping of it is the best help to the keeping of all the rest.'[179] Second, 'It was commanded of God to Adam in his innocency... A Sabbath, therefore, of the seventh day cannot be simply a ceremony, but an essential part of God's worship.'[180] Third, 'It is one of the commandments which God spake with his mouth, and twice wrote with his own fingers... All that God wrote, were moral and perpetual commandments, and those are reckoned ten in number.'[181] Fourth, 'Christ professes, "that he came not to destroy the moral law."'[182] Fifth, 'All the ceremonial law was enjoined to the Jews only, and not to the Gentiles; but this commandment of the holy Sabbath, as matrimony, was instituted of God in the state of innocency, when there was but one state of all men.'[183] Sixth, 'The secret unwillingness of good men to sanctify sincerely the Sabbath, sufficiently demonstrates that the commandment of the Sabbath is spiritual and moral.'[184] Seventh, 'He ordained in the church on earth, the holy Sabbath to be not only the appointed season for his solemn worship, but also the perpetual rule and measure of time.'[185] Eighth, 'The whole church, by an universal consent, ever since the time of the apostles, have still held the

---

[176] Perkins, *Cases*, 259

[177] *Ibid.* For similar arguments, see Greenham, *Treatise of the Sabbath, Works*, 132-156; and Thomas Shepard, *The Doctrine of the Sabbath* (London, 1650) I:1-182.

[178] Bayly, *Practice of Piety*, 169.

[179] *Ibid.*, 170.

[180] *Ibid.*, 171.

[181] *Ibid.*

[182] *Ibid.*

[183] *Ibid.*, 173.

[184] *Ibid.*, 174.

[185] *Ibid.*

commandment of the Sabbath to be the moral and perpetual law of God.'[186] Ninth, 'The Lord himself expounded the end of the Sabbath, to be a sign and document for ever.'[187] Tenth, 'The examples of God's judgments on Sabbath-breakers, may sufficiently seal to them whose hearts are not seared, how wrathfully Almighty God is displeased with them who are willful profaners of the Lord's day.'[188]

The second mark of 'genuine Sabbatarianism' is the change of the Sabbath from Saturday to Sunday. Perkins provides the following justification for this change:[189] 'the Sabbath day of the New Testament, is called the Lord's day;' 'the church of Corinth every first day of the week made a collection for the poor;' 'Christ and his Apostles kept the first day of the week as the Sabbath... Christ rose again the first day of the week, and appeared to his disciples;' 'the Lord's day was prefigured in the eighth day, wherein the children of the Jews were circumcised;' and 'God is Lord of times and seasons, and therefore in all equity, the altering and disposing thereof is in his hands, and belongs to him alone.'

Bayly asks the question: 'Why do not we Christians under the New, keep the Sabbath on the same seventh day on which it was kept under the Old Testament?'[190] He responds, 'Because our Lord Jesus, who is the Lord of the Sabbath... did alter it from that seventh day to this first day of the week on which we keep the Sabbath.'[191] Obviously, Christ's resurrection and ascension took place on the first day of the week. Bayly maintains that, between these two great events, Christ appeared to the apostles on the first day of every week, instructing them – among other things – to 'change the Sabbath to the Lord's day.'[192] Bayly provides additional reasons for this change: (1) 'there is wrought a new spiritual creation of the world' by Christ's resurrection; (2) 'in respect of this new spiritual creation, the Scripture saith, "That old things are passed away, and all things are become new" (2 Cor. 5:17)... therefore of necessity there must be... a new Sabbath-day;' (3) 'on this day Christ rested from all the sufferings of his passion, and finished the glorious work of redemption,' thereby meriting 'a sabbath, for the perpetual commemoration of it;' (4) 'it was foretold in the Old Testament that the Sabbath should be kept under the New Testament on the first day of the week;' and (5) 'according to the Lord's mind and commandment, and the direction of the Holy Ghost... the apostles...

---

[186] *Ibid.*, 178.

[187] *Ibid.*, 180.

[188] *Ibid.*, 181. Swinnock employs many of these 'proofs.' *Christian Man's Calling*, I:222,224,232.

[189] Perkins, *Cases*, 260-262. For Shepard's argument, see *Doctrine of the Sabbath*, II:1-31.

[190] Bayly, *Practice of Piety*, 159.

[191] *Ibid.*

[192] *Ibid.*, 160.

ordained that the Christians should keep the holy Sabbath upon the seventh day.'[193]

The third mark of 'genuine Sabbatarianism' is a strict observance of the Sabbath. For Perkins, 'there are two things required; a Rest, and a Sanctification of the same rest to an holy life.'[194] Likewise, Bayly insists on two things. First, 'in resting from all servile and common business pertaining to our natural life;' e.g., works of our calling, carrying burdens, keeping fairs or markets, studying any books of science, all recreations and sports, gross feeding and liberal drinking, and all talk of worldly things.[195] Second, 'in consecrating that rest wholly to the service of God, and the use of those holy means that belong to our spiritual life.'[196]

These three marks of Sabbatarianism became enshrined in the *WCF*. Regarding the first, it states that the commandment to keep the Sabbath 'is a positive, moral, and perpetual commandment, binding all men in all ages.'[197] Regarding the second, it affirms that the Sabbath 'from the beginning of the world to the resurrection of Christ, was the last day of the week; and, from the resurrection of Christ, was changed into the first day of the week.'[198] Regarding the third, it declares that the Sabbath is to be 'kept holy unto the Lord, when men... are taken up the whole time in the public and private exercises of his worship, and in the duties of necessity and mercy.'[199]

As Primus notes, the motifs of creation, resurrection, and sanctification 'functioned powerfully' in the development of these three marks of Sabbatarianism – 'It was essentially these motifs, respectively, that provided the answers, to the three most hotly disputed aspects of Sabbatarianism: the institution, alteration, and celebration of the Sabbath.'[200] Regarding the institution of the Sabbath, it is prelapsarian, 'etched indelibly on the human heart at Creation just as all the other moral laws were, observed by the patriarchs before the time of Moses, and simply reiterated or given written form at Sinai because of the sinfulness and weakness of humankind.'[201] Regarding the alteration of the Sabbath, 'By reason of Christ's Resurrection and in memory of that great event, the apostles altered the day of worship to the first day of the week.'[202] Regarding the celebration of the Sabbath, its main purpose is sanctification. According to Primus, 'The Sabbath itself held sacramental significance, for if the preached Word was regarded as the primary sacrament,

---

[193] *Ibid.*, 162-164.
[194] Perkins, *Cases*, 265.
[195] Bayly, *Practice of Piety*, 187-191.
[196] *Ibid.*, 191-206.
[197] *WCF*, XXI:VII.
[198] *Ibid.*
[199] *WCF*, XXI:VIII.
[200] Primus, *Holy Time*, 148.
[201] *Ibid.*
[202] *Ibid.*, 153. For Swinnock on this, see *Christian Man's Calling*, I:232.

or the primary means of grace, the Sabbath was regarded as the primary means of that means of grace.'[203] Again, 'The Sabbath was the primary means for the promotion of all righteousness and obedience in the lives of the people.'[204] Primus summarizes these three motifs as follows: 'God the Father established the Sabbath when he created the world; by his Resurrection God the Son reestablished the Sabbath as the Lord's Day; and God the Holy Spirit uses the Sabbath as the chief means of sanctification.'[205]

Swinnock embraces this paradigm, stating, 'Blessed art thou among days, from henceforth all generations shall call thee blessed. Blessed be *the Father who made thee*, blessed be *the Son who bought thee*, blessed be *the Spirit who sanctifieth thee*, and blessed are all they that prize and improve thee.'[206] Again, 'Hail thou that art highly favoured of God, thou map of heaven, thou golden spot of the week, thou market-day of souls, thou day-break of eternal brightness, thou queen of days, the Lord is with thee, blessed art thou among days... *the Father ruleth thee, the Son rose upon thee, the Spirit overshadowed thee.*'[207] For Swinnock, the Triune God has ordained the Sabbath as the 'market day of the soul,' whereby the regenerate may especially commune with the object of their soul's delight through his appointed means.

The Origin of Sabbatarianism

As for the origin of Sabbatarianism, Primus traces it to Calvin.[208] This is not to suggest that the three marks of Sabbatarianism are found in Calvin's writings. Packer notes that, in terms of their understanding of the Sabbath, 'the Puritans advanced on the Reformers.'[209] As for Calvin specifically, his view is

---

[203] *Ibid.*, 176.

[204] *Ibid.*, 178.

[205] *Ibid.*, 163.

[206] *Christian Man's Calling*, I:232. My italics.

[207] *Ibid.*, I:258. My italics.

[208] For treatments of Calvin's view, see R. Gaffin, *Calvin and the Sabbath* (Fearn: Mentor, 1998); and John Primus, 'Calvin and the Puritan Sabbath: A Comparative Study' in *Exploring the Heritage of John Calvin*, ed. D. E. Holwerda (Grand Rapids: Baker Books, 1976) 40-75. For a brief summary of the Continental Reformers' views, see Hulse, 'Sanctifying the Lord's Day,' 80-85.

[209] Packer, *Quest for Godliness*, 236. Richard Bauckham makes the same point. 'Sabbath and Sunday in the Protestant Tradition,' *From Sabbath to Lord's Day: A Biblical, Historical and Theological Investigation*, ed. D. A. Carson (Grand Rapids: Zondervan, 1982) 312. He also notes that, despite their repudiation of Sabbatarianism, the Reformers hold to certain 'theological principles' from which Sabbatarianism arose. (1) The Decalogue was the essence of Christian morality. (2) The Decalogue was the revealed summary of natural law. (3) The Law was divided on the basis of 'moral' and 'ceremonial.' (4) There was little attempt to establish a

summarized in three points: first, the Sabbath is a figure of spiritual rest in Christ; second, the Sabbath serves as a day for public worship; and third, the Sabbath serves as a day of rest for servants and animals.[210] There is nothing here that approaches the Sabbatarianism of the English Puritans. When Primus maintains that Sabbatarianism has its roots in Calvin, he is not speaking of Calvin's view of the Sabbath in particular but his view of the law in general:

> One of Calvin's greatest theological accomplishments was the inclusion of a significant place for law and good works within his theology of sovereign grace... by assigning the law a 'third use;' by emphasizing human responsibility in the covenant of grace; and by a doctrine of sanctification so intimately tied to justification that the one cannot be considered apart from the other. The ultimate effect of all three was to raise the visibility of law in Reformed thought.[211]

For Primus, 'These three strands of Calvin's thought provided the broader context in which moral theology in general, and Sabbatarianism in particular, flourished.[212] Having adopted Calvin's view of the relationship between law and grace, the Puritans also adopt his proposed third use of the law. This includes the fourth commandment. For them, the logical outcome is that keeping the Sabbath is as much an expression of love for God as observing any of the other commandments. On this premise, they develop their Sabbatarianism.

This reasoning is seen, for example, in Shepard's *The Doctrine of the Sabbath*. In defending Sabbatarianism, he appeals to the moral nature of the Decalogue. He does so by making a distinction between 'largely or generally morall' laws and 'strictly or specially morall' laws. He believes the former include 'every law of God,' because all are an expression of 'the sovereigne will of God,' whereas the latter include only those that concern 'the manners of all men.'[213] In short, 'generally morall' laws are only good because God commanded them whereas 'specially morall' laws are 'inwardly good.'[214] From this premise, he concludes, 'Because morall precepts are of such things as are

---

basis for Christian weekly worship in New Testament exegesis. (5) The principle of a day of rest for worship was upheld. *Ibid.*, 312-313.

[210] Calvin, *Institutes*, II:VIII:28-34. Gaffin criticizes Calvin for failing to reckon adequately with the Sabbath institution as a 'creation ordinance.' *Calvin and the Sabbath*, 146. In addition, he maintains that Calvin's view of the fourth commandment makes sin an integral element in one of God's eternal and immutable principles for governing his creation. *Ibid.*, 148. Calvin believes that the fourth commandment addressed a typological ceremony foreshadowing the believer's rest in Christ. Now that Christ is come, the type is cancelled in accordance with Paul's word in Col. 2:16. *Institutes*, II:VIII:29.

[211] Primus, *Holy Time*, 105. Collinson agrees with this assessment. *Godly People*, 433.

[212] *Ibid.*, 108.

[213] Shepard, *Doctrine of the Sabbath*, I:6.

[214] *Ibid.*, I:7.

good in themselves, they are therefore perpetuall and unchangeable... hence also they are universall.'[215] Years earlier, Greenham made a similar distinction, stating, 'That I call morall, which doth informe mens manners, either concerning their religion to God, or their duties unto man: that I meane figurative, which is added for a time in some respect, to some persons, for an helpe to that which is morall.'[216]

Perceiving that some may struggle in discerning the difference between 'generally morall' and 'specially morall' laws, Shepard gives four rules 'whereby we may know when a law is... good in itself.'[217] First, 'specially morall' laws 'flow from natural relation, both between God and man, as well as between man and man.'[218] Second, they 'are drawn from the imitable Attributes and Works of God.'[219] Third, 'mans reason may see, either by innate light, or by any other externall helpe and light to bee just and good and fit for man to observe.'[220] Fourth, they were 'once writ upon mans heart in *pure nature*.'[221] On this basis, Shepard concludes that the Decalogue is 'specially morall,' for 'there is no one law in it, which is therefore good only because 'tis commanded, but is therefore commanded, because it is good and suitable to human nature.'[222] His reasoning is widely followed among the Puritans.

That is not to say that all Puritans adhere to this position. Like his fellow Puritans, Bunyan places tremendous importance upon the observance of the Lord's Day. In a word, it is 'to be set apart for holy Duties,'[223] because it is 'the principal Manna-day.'[224] However, Bunyan does not adhere to Sabbatarianism, in that he denies that Sabbath-keeping is a part of natural law.[225] He gives three main arguments in support of his position. First, God gave the Seventh-day-Sabbath as a precept at Sinai.[226] Second, God gave it to the Jews, not Gentiles.[227] Third, God gave it as part of Jewish ceremonialism.[228] These details prove that the Sabbath 'as to the sanction of it, is not Moral, but rather

---

[215] *Ibid.*, I:13.

[216] Greenham, *Treatise of the Sabbath*, *Works*, 132.

[217] Shepard, *Doctrine of the Sabbath*, I:15.

[218] *Ibid.*

[219] *Ibid.*, I:16.

[220] *Ibid.*, I:19.

[221] *Ibid.*, I:20. His italics.

[222] *Ibid.*, I:25.

[223] John Bunyan, *Questions about the Nature and Perpetuity of the Seventh-Day-Sabbath. And Proof, that the First Day of the Week is the true Christian-Sabbath, Miscellaneous Works*, IV:374

[224] *Ibid.*, IV:385.

[225] *Ibid.*, IV:336-337.

[226] *Ibid.*, IV:340-345. According to Bunyan, God did not give any precept concerning the 'Sabbath' in the Garden.

[227] *Ibid.*, IV:345-347.

[228] *Ibid.*, IV:348-355.

Arbitrary, to wit, imposed by the will of God upon his people, until the time he thought fit to change it for another day.'[229] This other day is Sunday.[230] Bunyan writes, 'Christ began it on THAT day: Then the Holy Ghost seconded it on THAT day: Then the Churches practiced it on THAT day. And to conclude, the Apostle by the command now under consideration, continues the sanction of THAT day to the Churches to the end of the world.'[231] Therefore, Bunyan believes that keeping the Lord's Day is moral, not because it is part of the natural law or the Decalogue, but because God has commanded the church to do so.

The Zeal of Mr. Thomas Wilson

According to Irvonwyn Morgan, zeal is 'an act by which formality in religion is turned into affection for religion, a kind of spiritual heat which God gives to those who are baptized "with the Spirit and with fire."'[232] It is the putting forth of all the affections upon an object. As Baxter explains, 'Zeal is the fervour or earnestness of the soul: its first subject is the will and affections, excited by the judgment; and thence it appeareth in the practice. It is not a distinct grace or affection, but the vigour and liveliness of every grace, and their fervent operations.'[233] From David's example in Psalm 69:9,[234] Swinnock speaks of the need for such zeal in the performance of spiritual duties.[235] Flavel agrees, 'To shuffle over religious duties with a loose and heedless spirit, will cost no great pains; but to set thyself before the Lord, and tie up thy loose and vain thoughts to a constant and serious attendance upon him: this will cost thee something.'[236] Similarly, Shepard writes:

---

[229] *Ibid.*, IV:339.

[230] For his arguments, see IV:357-370.

[231] *Ibid.*, IV:374. By 'command now under consideration,' he means 1 Cor. 16:1-2.

[232] Morgan, *Puritan Spirituality*, 63. This is a central motif among the Puritans. Seaver demonstrates that it was not restricted to the Puritan clergy, but was common among 'the ordinary urban Londoner'. Based on the writings of Nehemiah Wallington (a Puritan artisan), Seaver comments, 'As he was to discover over and over again, the desire to live a life of holy obedience and the capacity to live according to God's holy will were two quite different things. The gap between desire and accomplishment could be narrowed by a great struggle but never closed in life.' *Wallington's World*, 35. Wallington sought to narrow this through a zealous devotion to spiritual duties. *Ibid.*, 36-40.

[233] For Baxter's ten 'signs of holy zeal,' see *Christian Directory*, 383.

[234] 'For zeal for Your house has consumed me, And the reproaches of those who reproach You have fallen on me.'

[235] *Christian Man's Calling*, I:26,235-242,326; and *Men Are Gods*, IV:364.

[236] John Flavel, *Saint Indeed; or, The Great Work of a Christian, Opened and Pressed*, *Works*, V:428.

What an easy matter it is to come to church! They hear (at least outwardly) very attentively an hour and more, and then to turn to a proof, and to turn down a leaf: here is the form. But now to spend Saturday night, and all the whole Sabbath day morning, in trimming the lamp, and in getting oil in the heart to meet the bridegroom the next day, and so meet him in the word, and there to tremble at the voice of God, and suck the breast while it is open; and when the word is done, to go aside privately, and there to chew upon the word, there to lament with tears all the vein thoughts in duties, deadness in hearing, this is hard, because this is the power of godliness, and this men will not take up: so for private prayer; what an easy matter is it for a man to say over a few prayers out of some devout book, or to repeat some old prayer, got by heart since a child, or to have two or three short-winded wishes for God's mercy in the morning and at night! This form is easy. But now to prepare the heart by serious meditation of God and man's self, before he prays, then to come to God with a bleeding, hunger-starved heart, not only with a desire, but with a warrant, I must have such or such a mercy, and there to wrestle with God, although it be an hour or two together for a blessing, this is too hard; men think none do thus, and therefore they will not.[237]

In short, the effective use of the means of grace necessitates zeal. Swinnock's belief in this is made clear in his biography of Thomas Wilson.[238] By way of introduction, he writes, 'I do here present to thy view in this Treatise, a great example of godliness, one that did not only divide the word aright, but also ordered his conversation aright,'[239] adding, 'O what a lively pattern of zeal, love, faith, humility, heavenly-mindedness, courage for, and constancy in the truth did he set before you.'[240] When speaking of Wilson's zeal, Swinnock is primarily referring to his devotion to secret, private, and public duties on the Lord's Day,[241] stating, 'He was one that abundantly discovered his zeal for God in embracing all opportunities to do him service, in his great care wherever he came for the strict observation, and right sanctification of the Lord's Day.'[242]

Prior to ministering at Otham, Wilson preached at Penroth, Cumberland, where he convinced the local citizens to move their market day from Sunday to Saturday. After which, according to Swinnock, 'for many years, the people did

---

[237] Shepard, *Sincere Convert*, 66-67.

[238] This is also evident in E. Bagshawe's biography of Robert Bolton in which he commends Bolton for his piety, gravity, zeal, wisdom, and charity. *Life and Death of Mr. Robert Bolton*, 23-28. In describing Bolton's zeal, he comments, 'He wholly sacrificed himself and all his studies to the honour of God.' *Ibid.*, 26. This biography was well known to Swinnock. See *Christian Man's Calling*, III:50,60,65; and *Heaven and Hell*, III:217,247.

[239] *Life and Death of Mr. Wilson*, A-4.

[240] *Ibid.*, A-4.

[241] *Ibid.*, 30.

[242] *Ibid.*, 44.

forbear to sell any thing on the Lord's Day in that town.'[243] After moving to Otham, Wilson had a similar experience, in that he convinced the owners of local mills to close down on the Lord's Day.[244] He also demonstrated his zeal for the Sabbath by refusing to read the king's 'Declaration' for sports on Sundays.[245] Later, in Maidstone, he again prevailed with the people to observe the Sabbath. In the words of Swinnock, 'Maidstone was formerly a very profane town, insomuch that I have seen Morrice dancing, Cudgel playing, Stool-ball, Crickets, and many other sports openly and publicly on the Lord's Day.'[246] Wilson put an end to this.

According to Swinnock, Wilson was so zealous for the Sabbath because he believed that 'the sanctification of that day is exceeding useful to keep up the power of godliness in our hearts and lives... God on that day bestoweth great blessings on them, that humbly and reverently worship him on that Queen of days, that Market day of our souls.'[247] Consequently, Wilson observed the day with great diligence. Swinnock notes that his devotion began on Saturday night when he stayed in his study until midnight 'to prepare himself the better for his task on the Lord's Day.'[248] After a few hours sleep, he returned to his secret duties. Then, he joined his family for reading, singing, and praying. 'About nine a Clock he repaired to the Church,' and preached from an Old Testament text.[249] Upon returning home, he gathered his family to hear from them the truths that he had expounded at church. Once again, he retired to his study for secret duties. Later, he returned to the church, and preached from a New Testament text. In the late afternoon, his neighbours gathered at his house. At that time, he heard from them the truths that he had expounded at church, concluding with a Psalm and a prayer. After Supper, he repeated the process, ending the day with prayer about ten a clock at night. 'Thus he sanctified the Lord's Day, spending nine or ten hours in public and private worship, beside what time he spent in secret duties... so that the Sabbath... was a day of great pains and labour to him, yet is was easy, yea delightful to him.'[250]

In Wilson, Swinnock finds a man who exemplified Psalm 69:9. He comments, 'And truly such a man was Mr. Wilson... as hot as fire in the cause

---

[243] *Ibid.*, 7-8.

[244] *Ibid.*, 11.

[245] At the end of the biography, Swinnock annexes 'the articles objected against Mr. Wilson in the Archbishop's court, with his answers to them.' Article VI concerns his refusal to read the king's 'Declaration' for sports on Sundays. He gives a detailed response, arguing that it is against the testimony of the Law, the Church, the Scriptures, the Councils, the Divines (both ancient and modern), and the Schoolmen. *Life and Death of Mr. Wilson*, 74-81.

[246] *Ibid.*, 40.

[247] *Ibid.*, 41.

[248] *Ibid.*, 26.

[249] *Ibid.*

[250] *Ibid.*, 30.

of his God. The zeal of God's house burned him up.'[251] Interestingly, Wilson once preached a sermon on Psalm 69:9, entitled, *David's Zeal for Zion*. In it, he says that zeal 'is not any single affection, but the earnestness and increase of all the affections, liking or disliking, as love and hatred, grief and joy, desires, delights, fears, and anger, boiled to the highest degree, and to the hottest temper and intention.'[252] It is set against evil – 'all that which opposeth God's will and glory' – and it is carried towards good. Wilson encourages his readers, 'Receive the words of exhortation, all that be thoroughly religious, to be truly zealous; Rest not in knowledge, and good principles, but be heated with good affection, as well as taught; With good light have good fire, have grace with your knowledge, and zeal with religion; witty heads, and zealous hearts, as we are commanded.'[253] This zeal is: (1) personal – 'Let every man be a burnt offering unto the Lord, let zeal eat up all corrupt affections in us, consume our sins, and inflame our hearts toward him;' (2) celestial – 'it is a supernatural work to have such raised affection and fervent mind for the house of the Lord;' (3) regular – 'zeal is bold, but not blind, it is not rash or indiscreet, but wisely discerning things that differ;' (4) impartial – it 'layeth aside all partial affection, or respect of persons, great or small;' (5) superlative – 'it overcomes great discouragements;' and (6) constant – 'zeal is a fire' that 'should never go out.'[254]

Grace and Duty

Swinnock embraces whole-heartedly Wilson's conviction that a person must be 'truly zealous' in order to be 'thoroughly religious.' Consequently, his commitment to the means of grace is not merely an exercise of the head, but a pursuit of the heart. This emphasis upon zeal in spiritual duties (particularly the keeping of the Lord's Day) raises the entire question of the relationship between grace and duty in the Puritan mindset.[255] At first glance, there appears to be an inconsistency. Swinnock, following Wilson's lead, affirms that the Holy Spirit stirs the affections by working through the means of grace. Yet, Swinnock also affirms that the regenerate must exercise zeal in the use of the means of grace.[256] In essence, they must have their affections stirred to perform spiritual duties properly so that their affections might be stirred. This presents a quandary concerning the relationship between grace and duty in his spirituality.

As Swinnock notes, 'There must be lifting up the heart, lending the ears,

---

[251] *Ibid.*, 45.

[252] Wilson, *David's Zeal for Zion*, 2.

[253] *Ibid.*, 23.

[254] *Ibid.*, 30-33.

[255] For a good overview of this subject, see G. J. McGrath, 'Grace and Duty in Puritan Spirituality,' *Grove Spirituality Series* 37 (1991) 3-23.

[256] *Christian Man's Calling*, I:26.

seeking, searching, begging, digging, attention of the outward, intention of the inward man, before men can "understand the fear of the Lord, and find the knowledge of God" (Prov. 2:3-5).'[257] For Swinnock, this call to duty should come as no surprise seeing as 'Christ would never have commanded men to strive, as to an agony, to enter in at the strait gate (Matt. 7:13); to work out their salvation with fear and trembling (Phil. 2:12); to labour for the food which endureth to everlasting life (Jn. 6:27), if it had been such an easy thing to have reached heaven.'[258] In brief, the regenerate are to discipline themselves for the purpose of godliness. Swinnock mentions that the term *discipline* signifies 'strip thyself naked,' noting, 'It is a metaphor from runners or wrestlers, who being to contend for the prize, and resolved to put forth all their strength and power, lay aside their clothes which may hinder them, and then bestir themselves to purpose.'[259] By comparison, the regenerate 'contend for a prize,' in that they pursue godliness. They must 'strip themselves' of anything that hinders them so that they can devote 'all their strength and power' to those 'means' that will further their goal. In brief, they must make spiritual duties their chief business: they must be 'heedful' and 'watchful' over themselves whilst they are participating in duties; they must seek to 'act grace' in duties; and they must perform duties in order to give glory to God and to receive grace from God.[260]

Despite this emphasis upon human effort, Swinnock is careful to stress that spiritual duties are ineffectual apart from the sovereign work of the Holy Spirit. He comments, 'Men and means may be instrumental and subservient, but their efficacy and success dependeth on God.'[261] Again, 'God must give us fresh supplies of his Spirit in every duty, or they cannot be rightly performed.'[262] Yet again, 'The Christian hath no natural power for these spiritual performances, but God gives them his Spirit for this purpose, that he might be enabled to do sacred duties, with suitable graces... The Christian... pulls and hales at his own heavy heart in a duty, to perform the duty aright, and yet makes nothing of it till the Spirit comes and helps him, and then he goes along comfortably through the duty.'[263] According to Gurnall, 'There must be life in the soul before there can be life in the duty.'[264] For Charnock, 'What is good in any duty, is merely from his grace and Spirit, and not from ourselves.'[265]

Simply put, the regenerate must apply themselves to the practice of spiritual

---

[257] *Ibid.*, I:61. For more on 'striving,' see I:18-19,29,39-40,60-62.

[258] *Door of Salvation*, V:72.

[259] *Christian Man's Calling*, I:27.

[260] *Ibid.*, I:91-100.

[261] *Heaven and Hell*, III:366.

[262] *Pastor's Farewell*, IV:75.

[263] *Christian Man's Calling*, I:94.

[264] Gurnall, *Christian in Complete Armour*, II:478.

[265] Charnock, *Existence and Attributes of God*, I:259.

duties whilst depending upon the Holy Spirit to reward their efforts. As Flavel notes, 'A natural man hath no power, a gracious man hath some, though not sufficient; and that power he hath, depends upon the exciting and assisting strength of Christ.'[266] Baxter comments, 'Pray, and meditate, and hear, and read, and do your best, and expect his blessing. Though your ploughing and sowing will not give you a plentiful harvest without the sun, and rain, and the blessing of God, yet these will not do it neither, unless you plough and sow.'[267] For this reason, the regenerate must not view themselves as striving independent of the Holy Spirit. They have 'no power' to effect any change. On the other hand, they must not view themselves as entirely passive in the Holy Spirit's work of renewal. Instead, they must understand that he has supplied the ability they lack in order to apply themselves to the means of grace.

Kevan explains it this way: 'The common Puritan view is that the believer's sanctification in the eyes of God is both active and progressive.'[268] He adds, 'The concurrence of the Divine and human in the realm of spiritual activity is another of the paradoxes of Christian experience... There is thus a kind of passive-activity or active-passivity in the believer's acts of godliness.'[269] G. J. McGrath also addresses this relationship. Drawing from the writings of Owen and Baxter, he elucidates three elements of Puritan teaching in regards to the relationship between grace and duty. First, the regenerate perform the grace-prompted gospel duties through the work of the Holy Spirit. In other words, 'the Holy Spirit creates the necessary willingness in believers to do the works and duties of holy living.' Second, they perform duties through practical and identifiable means of grace. For McGrath, these means are instrumental causes, deriving value only as a consequence of the work of the Holy Spirit. Third, gospel duties are secondary to one's union with Christ and affection for God, that is, they flow out of love for God. His conclusion is that 'we must not make too sharp a distinction between grace and duty. They were mutually dependent. Grace came in order that duty might exist, which would in turn prove and further God's work of grace.'[270] To sum up, Daniel Webber rightly affirms, 'If we are not to distort their teaching, the Puritan balance between duty and supernatural grace must be preserved.'[271]

Conclusion

From the foregoing discussion, it is evident that – for Swinnock – a diligent use

---

[266] Flavel, *Saint Indeed, Works*, V:424.

[267] Baxter, *Christian Directory*, 71.

[268] Kevan, *Grace of Law*, 220.

[269] *Ibid.*, 222.

[270] McGrath, 'Grace and Duty in Puritan Spirituality,' 16-21.

[271] Daniel Webber, 'Sanctifying the Inner Life' in *Aspects of Sanctification* (London: Westminster Conference, 1981) 44.

of the means of grace is essential for on-going renewal. For this reason, the regenerate must discipline themselves for the purpose of godliness by zealously applying themselves to praying, reading and hearing God's Word, receiving the Lord's Supper, and keeping the Lord's Day. For some critics of Puritanism, such an emphasis appears legalistic. However, as Lovelace observes, 'It is customary to refer to this type of piety as legalistic; this is as good a way as any to escape the obligation of imitating it. However, this is not legalism in the Pauline sense of the term, since it clearly distinguishes the functions of Law and Gospel.'[272]

It is important to remember that for Swinnock, and his contemporaries, the spiritual duties are not an end in themselves; rather, they are a means to an end – communion with the greatest good. Swinnock would agree wholeheartedly with Shepard's admonition: 'Now Jesus Christ is a Christian's gain (Phil. 1:21) and hence a child of God asks himself after sermon, after prayer, after sacrament, What have I gained of Christ? Have I got more knowledge of Christ, more admiring of the Lord Jesus? Now, a carnal heart, that rests in his duties, asketh only what he hath done, as the Pharisee.'[273] Herein lies the difference between Law and Gospel. The regenerate are not satisfied by their performance of spiritual duties, but with their fellowship with God in them. With precisely this in mind, Baxter warns, 'Look not so much to the time it spends in the duty, as to the quantity and quality of the work that is done.'[274]

---

[272] Lovelace, 'Puritan Spirituality,' 308.

[273] Shepard, *Sincere Convert*, 103.

[274] Baxter, *Saints' Everlasting Rest, Practical Works*, 110.

Chapter Eight

Meditation: The Gateway between Head and Heart

For Swinnock, meditation occupies the place of distinction among the spiritual duties by virtue of the fact that it is practised in conjunction with all of them, and ultimately determines their success. This cause-and-effect relationship is entrenched in the Puritan mindset. As Joel Beeke observes, 'Meditation was a daily duty that enhanced every other duty of the Puritan's Christian life.'[1] This is the case, because meditation stirs the affections, thereby promoting zeal. As mentioned in the last chapter, zeal is crucial to the successful performance of the means of grace. The reality is, however, that the regenerate regularly struggle with their lack of zeal. For Swinnock, meditation is the solution to this quandary. He writes, 'When thine heart is like wax hardened, bring it by meditation to the warm beams of this sun, and they will soften it... when thy heart is dull and dead... if thou wouldst but ply it with the meditation of the infinite love and goodness of God... it would be a sovereign means to quicken and revive it.'[2] Again, 'Meditation to the word is what fire is to water; though water be naturally so cold, yet put fire under it, and it will make it hot and boiling; so, though thine heart be cold in regard of affection to the word, put but this fire under it, and it will boil with love to it.'[3] Simply put, meditation is the principal means by which the Holy Spirit quickens the affections for the zealous performance of the other spiritual duties. McGrath expresses this Puritan motif as follows: 'If the saints would only remind themselves of God's character, mercy, love and power then duties would flow naturally and suitably.'[4]

A Definition

Sceats affirms that, according to the Puritans, 'All grace is mediated through the understanding.'[5] Packer writes, 'Man was made to know good with his

---

[1]   Joel Beeke, *Puritan Reformed Spirituality* (Grand Rapids: Reformation Heritage Books, 2004) 75. Baxter, for example, maintains that meditation is 'that duty by which all other duties are improved.' *Saints' Everlasting Rest, Practical Works*, 91.

[2]   *Christian Man's Calling*, I:248-249.

[3]   *Ibid.*, I:249.

[4]   McGrath, 'Grace and Duty in Puritan Spirituality,' 21.

[5]   Sceats, 'The Experience of Grace,' 9.

mind, to desire it, once he has come to know it, with his affections, and to cleave to it, once he has felt its attraction, with his will; the good in this case being God, his truth and his law. God accordingly moves us, not by direct action on the affections or will, but by addressing our mind with his word, and bringing to bear on us the force of truth.'[6] This conviction necessarily stems from the Puritan view of the mind as the leading faculty of the soul. Related to this, Reynolds insists that 'all appetite (being a blind Power) is dependant upon the direction of some Knowledge.'[7] Again:

> For the *Will* alone is a blind Faculty; and therefore as it cannot see the right Good it ought to affect without the Assistance of an *Informing* Power. So neither can it see the right way it ought to take for procuring that Good without the direction of a *Conducting* power... So that all the Acts of the Will necessarily presuppose some precedent guiding Acts in the Understanding, whereby they are proportioned to the Rules of right Reason.[8]

For Reynolds, the understanding has two 'actions:' *ad extra*, in regard of an object; and *ad intra*, in regard of the will.[9] In terms of the latter, the understanding serves as a 'counselor.' As such, it possesses a 'regulating and directing' power over the will, but not a 'constraining and compulsive' power.[10] This 'regulating and directing' power is exercised by a 'double act' of the understanding. First, it 'proposeth to the Will *Felicity*, as an Absolute and Eternall *Good*, which cannot but be desired.'[11] Second, it presses upon the will 'the weight of consideration' by proposing 'circumstances' and 'consequents' of choosing the 'absolute and eternal good.'[12] Because the will is corrupt, it will not naturally surrender to the first 'act.' Therefore, the second is essential in order to make the will 'more inclinable.'[13]

Swinnock agrees with Reynolds's claim that the will (including the affections) requires 'the assistance of an informing power' and 'the direction of a conducting power' – the understanding. Swinnock states, 'Knowledge is the eye of the soul, to direct it in its motions; it is the lamp, the light of the soul, set

---

[6] Packer, *Quest for Godliness*, 195. Packer's assertion that God never moves us 'by direct action on the affections or will' is somewhat ambiguous. He appears to be saying that God never bypasses the mind to affect the will. Presumably, God's 'bringing to bear on us the force of truth' is a direct act upon the will. This is consistent with Puritan thought on the subject.

[7] Reynolds, *Passions and Faculties*, 32.

[8] *Ibid.*, 461-462. His italics.

[9] *Ibid.*, 461.

[10] *Ibid.*, 462.

[11] *Ibid.*, 466. His italics.

[12] *Ibid.*, 467.

[13] *Ibid.*

up by God himself to guide it in its actions.'[14] When it comes to choosing God, this necessarily means that there must be some 'precedent' knowledge of God. Swinnock asks, 'Is it possible to love one whom we are ignorant of? Did ever any fear an unknown evil, or desire or delight in an unknown good?'[15] In other words, the mind must know God before the will chooses him. For Swinnock, this is a 'practical knowledge.'

> Reader, knowledge is the excellency of a man, whereby he is usually differenced from a brute. The knowledge of Christ is the excellency of the Christian, whereby he is differenced from a heathen; a *practical knowledge* is the excellency of the true Christian, whereby he is known from a false one... The spring of this knowledge may be in the head, and its rise in the understanding; but it slideth down into the heart, breaketh out into the life, and so floweth along in the channel of grace and holiness, till at last it lose itself in the ocean of glory.[16]

With this framework in place, Swinnock contends that 'practical knowledge' is the cause of all godliness. This conviction naturally leads him to stress the need for serious thinking about God.[17] He is not alone in this. Charnock refers to the mind as the 'noblest faculty' that 'should be employed about the most excellent object.'[18] According to Manton, 'The greatest things do not work unless we think of them, and work them into our hearts. The natural way of operation is, that objects stir up thoughts, and thoughts stir up affections.'[19] Baxter affirms that 'the Spirit makes use of our understandings for the actuating of our wills and affections.'[20] Again, 'Knowledge must be the means to reclaim your perverse, misguided wills.'[21] Baxter has in view an 'affective practical knowledge,'[22] 'a deep, effectual, heart-changing knowledge,'[23] 'a spiritual, powerful, and practical knowledge,'[24] and a 'true, practical, saving knowledge.'[25]

For the Puritans, this 'practical knowledge' is the product of a structured life

---

[14] *Incomparableness of God*, IV:481.
[15] *Sinner's Last Sentence*, V:425. According to Gerrish, this is Calvin's view – 'There is no religion where truth does not reign: if the end of life is to serve God's glory, knowledge of God must come first. Calvin by no mean belittles confidence in God, or love for God either; rather, he holds tenaciously to the axiom that there cannot be either one where the character of God is misperceived.' *Grace and Gratitude*, 64.
[16] *Christian Man's Calling*, I:373. My italics.
[17] *Incomparableness of God*, IV:488.
[18] Charnock, *Existence and Attributes of God*, I:88.
[19] Manton, *True Circumcision, Works*, II:41.
[20] Baxter, *Divine Life, Practical Works*, 197.
[21] *Ibid.*, 207-208.
[22] *Ibid.*, 126
[23] *Ibid.*, 232.
[24] Baxter, *Directions and Persuasion, Practical Works*, 539.
[25] Baxter, *Mischiefs of Self-Ignorance, Practical Works*, 755.

of meditation. Charnock laments, 'Many truths, though assented to in our understandings, are kept under hatches by corrupt affections, and have not their due influence, because they are not brought forth into the open air of our souls by meditation.'[26] For this reason, Gurnall exhorts his readers to 'retire often to muse on some soul-awakening meditations.'[27] Packer describes this meditation as:

> an activity of holy thought, consciously performed in the presence of God, under the eye of God, by the help of God, as a means of communion with God. Its purpose is to clear one's mental and spiritual vision of God, and to let His truth make its full and proper impact on one's mind and heart... Its effect is ever to humble us, as we contemplate God's greatness and glory, and our own littleness and sinfulness, and to encourage and reassure us... as we contemplate the unsearchable riches of divine mercy displayed in the Lord Jesus Christ.[28]

Here, Packer states that the purpose of meditation is to enable God's truth to 'make its full and proper impact on one's mind and heart.' In the context of Puritan meditation,[29] he describes this 'impact' as follows:

> Knowing themselves to be creatures of thought, affection, and will, and knowing that God's way to the human heart (will) is via the human head (the mind), the Puritans practiced meditation, discursive and systematic, on the whole range of biblical truth as they saw it applying to themselves. Puritan meditation on Scripture was modeled on the Puritan sermon; in meditation the Puritan would seek to search and challenge his heart, stir his affections to hate sin and love righteousness, and encourage himself with God's promises, just as Puritan preachers would do from the pulpit.[30]

Once again, the Puritan predilection for the soul's faculties steps to the forefront. The goal of Puritan meditation is to apply Scripture (and other types of devotional literature) successively to the faculties of understanding, affections, and will. According to Davies, it is 'moving from intellectual issues to exciting the heart's affections in order to free the will for conformity to God.'[31] In a similar vein, Peter Toon states, 'In meditation a channel is somehow opened between the mind, heart, and will – what the mind receives

---

[26] Charnock, *Existence and Attributes of God*, II:102.

[27] Gurnall, *Christian in Complete Armour*, II:507.

[28] James Packer, *Knowing God* (London: Hodder and Stoughton, 1975) 20.

[29] For brief overviews of Puritan meditation, see Beeke, *Puritan Reformed Spirituality*, 73-100; Hinson, 'Puritan Spirituality,' 170-176; and Wallace, *The Spirituality of the Later English Puritans*, xxix-xxxii.

[30] Packer, *Quest for Godliness*, 24.

[31] Davies, *Worship and Theology in England*, 119.

enters the heart and goes into action via the will.'[32] In terms of the affections specifically, he states, 'Meditation was seen as a divinely appointed way of stimulating or raising the affections toward the glory of God.'[33] All together then, meditation begins in the mind with serious thoughts of God. These thoughts stimulate 'the affections toward the glory of God.' In turn, the will goes 'into action' based upon the affections.

This view of meditation is entirely consistent with Swinnock, who remarks, 'Oh what a work, a gracious sanctifying work, doth the knowledge of God make in the soul! It makes the understanding to esteem him above all, the will to choose him before all, the affections to desire him, to delight in him, more than all; the whole man to seek him, to serve him, to honour and praise him beyond all in heaven and earth.'[34] Baxter reveals the same mindset, writing, 'We must think of God, that we may love him, do his service, trust him, fear and hope in him, and make him our delight.'[35] Again, 'So it is not the most excellent truths in the world that will change your hearts, if you let them not down to your hearts, and keep them not there by meditation till they are digested and turned into spiritual life.'[36]

Throughout his treatises, therefore, Swinnock exhorts his readers to mind 'solemn and set meditation,'[37] which he believes is 'the womb of... actions.'[38] He defines it as 'a serious applying the mind to some sacred subject, till the affections be warmed and quickened, and the resolution heightened and strengthened thereby, against what is evil, and for that which is good.'[39] Swinnock himself notes 'five things in this description.'[40] First, meditation is 'applying the mind' – 'If the mind be not stirring, the affections will be nodding.'[41] Second, meditation is a 'serious applying the mind.' Here, he distinguishes between 'set' and 'occasional' meditation, commenting 'short glances do little good.'[42] Third, meditation is focused upon 'some sacred subject.'[43] Fourth, meditation results in the affections being 'warmed and quickened.'[44] Fifth, meditation results in the resolution of the will being

---

[32] Peter Toon, *From Mind to Heart: Christian Meditation Today* (Grand Rapids: Baker Books, 1987) 18.

[33] *Ibid.*, 94.

[34] *Christian Man's Calling*, III:155.

[35] Baxter, *Divine Life, Practical Works*, 217.

[36] Baxter, *Directions and Persuasions, Practical Works*, 542.

[37] *Christian Man's Calling*, II:424.

[38] *Ibid.*, II:471.

[39] *Ibid.*, II:425.

[40] *Ibid.*

[41] *Ibid.*

[42] *Ibid.* Baxter distinguishes between 'solemn' and 'transient' meditation. *Saints' Everlasting Rest, Practical Works*, 91.

[43] *Christian Man's Calling*, II:426.

[44] *Ibid.*

'strengthened... against what is evil, and for that which is good.'[45] Swinnock groups the first three 'things' under the banner of 'cogitation.' The other two are designated 'application' and 'resolution.' Together, they embrace the three faculties of the soul.[46]

The Art of Divine Meditation

With this definition, Swinnock places himself in a meditative tradition that dates back to Joseph Hall's *The Art of Divine Meditation.* F. L. Huntley describes this tradition as a 'militantly Protestant mode' that 'came into being at the beginning of the seventeenth century in direct conflict with the *Spiritual Exercises* of St. Ignatius when fear and hatred of the Jesuits was at its height.'[47] Huntley maintains that Hall's approach to meditation is 'completely independent' of Ignatius 'in theory and practice,'[48] in that it is marked by Platonic philosophy, Augustinian psychology, Calvinist theology, a homiletic thrust, and an emphasis upon the three books of God – the Creatures, the Scriptures, and the Soul.[49]

Huntley's rigid division between 'protestant' and 'catholic' meditation is an oversimplification of a complex issue, however his acknowledgment of fundamental differences between Hall and Ignatius is essentially correct. When it comes to meditation, they share some similarities in terms of their subject matter. They also share a common concern for the stirring of the affections. For his part, Ignatius writes, 'For it is not knowing much, but realizing and relishing things interiorly, that contents and satisfies the soul'.[50] However, in terms of their approach to meditation, they are noticeably different. Hall stresses the three faculties of the soul whereas Ignatius' depends primarily upon sense data in order to stimulate the imagination. This tendency in Ignatius is evident, for example, in his meditations on hell. He writes of the need 'to see with the sight of the imagination the great fires, and the souls as in bodies in fire,' 'to hear with the ears wailings, howlings, cries,' 'to smell with the smell smoke, sulphur, dregs and putrid things,' 'to taste with the taste bitter things,' and 'to touch with the touch; that is to say, how the fires touch and burn the souls.'[51] To arrive at this experience, he encourages his readers 'to chastise the

---

[45] *Ibid.*, II:427.

[46] *Ibid.*, II:429.

[47] F. L. Huntley, *Bishop Joseph Hall and Protestant Meditation in Seventeenth Century England: A Study with the Texts of the Art of Divine Meditation (1606) and Occasional Meditations (1633)* (Binghamton: Centre for Medieval and Early Renaissance Studies, 1981) 3.

[48] *Ibid.*, 43.

[49] *Ibid.*, 5-10.

[50] Ignatius, *The Spiritual Exercises of St. Ignatius of Loyola*, trans. E. Mullan (New York: P. J. Kennedy & Sons, 1914) second annotation.

[51] *Ibid.*, fifth exercise.

flesh, that is, giving it sensible pain, which is given by wearing haircloth or cords or iron chains next to the flesh, by scourging or wounding oneself, and by other kinds of austerity.'[52] Such an approach is completely foreign to Hall, who is primarily concerned with exciting the affections via the understanding.

Due to the place given to the understanding in Hall's methodology, some have suggested that he represents one of two competing meditative traditions within English Puritanism. According to Milo Kauffman, Hall 'began the process of meditation with the understanding and chose to exploit the familiar and time-worn categories for artificial argumentation in order to insure a thorough examination of the topic at hand, before the affections were worked upon.'[53] In so doing, he left no room for the senses and imagination in meditation. For Kauffman, the second tradition preserves the imagination as a 'faculty worthy of respect.'[54] He finds such an emphasis in the likes of Sibbes, Baxter, and Bunyan.[55] Kauffman's theory is problematic. He suggests that Hall never employs the senses and imagination in meditation, yet a casual reading of Hall's works clearly reveals that he has a place for both.[56] Hall never elevates the understanding at the exclusion of the imagination and senses; rather, he stresses the priority of the understanding over the imagination and senses. This is entirely consistent with later Puritan authors such as Baxter and Bunyan.

Louis Martz proposes a slightly different 'two-tradition' theory. Like Kauffman, he affirms that Hall's approach is primarily focused upon the understanding. He believes Hall's methodology was dominant among the Puritans until the middle of the seventeenth century when a second tradition emerged with Baxter's *The Saints' Everlasting Rest*.[57] At this point, Martz distinguishes himself from Kauffman, in that he views this tradition as a re-discovery of Ignatian meditation. According to Martz, Baxter criticizes his contemporaries for their neglect of this meditation.[58] They had done away with it by insisting that the spiritual life was totally dependent upon God.[59] For

---

[52] *Ibid.*

[53] U. Milo Kauffman, *The Pilgrim's Progress and Traditions in Puritan Meditation* (Yale University Press, 1966), 124.

[54] *Ibid.*, 135.

[55] Beeke believes that Kauffman's assessment 'has grains of truth' whilst overemphasizing the place of imagination in Baxter and underemphasizing it in Hall. *Puritan Reformed Spirituality*, 77. Huntley also rejects Kauffman's thesis. *Bishop Joseph Hall and Protestant Meditation*, 43-50.

[56] Joseph Hall, *Art of Divine Meditation*, XXI, XXIV; and *Occasional Meditations*, XXIII, XLVII, XCIII. These treatises are found in F. L. Huntley, *Bishop Joseph Hall and Protestant Meditation in Seventeenth Century England: A Study with the Texts of the Art of Divine Meditation (1606) and Occasional Meditations (1633)*.

[57] Louis Martz, *The Poetry of Meditation: A Study in English Religious Literature of the Seventeenth Century* (Yale University Press, 1962) 154.

[58] *Ibid.*, 156.

[59] *Ibid.*, 156-157.

Martz, Baxter purposefully sets out to recover for the Puritans 'some of these devotional practices' which had disappeared as a result of their 'Calvinist thinking.'[60] Without entering into a full debate, it is important to note that Martz's theory is open to criticism.[61] For starters, he draws a false antithesis between Baxter and his fellow Puritans in regards to their understanding of the Reformed theology of grace.[62] Furthermore, he seems unacquainted with the meditative tradition of which Baxter is a product, not a trendsetter. Related to this, he fails to see the similarity between Hall and Baxter in terms of their meditative approach. Finally, he makes an unjustifiable comparison between Baxter and Ignatius. Whilst it is true that Baxter employs the senses and imagination in meditation, he does so without ever surrendering the priority of the understanding.

In brief, the search for two traditions in Puritan meditation seems futile. Hall clearly sets the tone for the entire movement by placing the priority upon the three faculties of the soul. The understanding impresses biblical truths upon the affections. As a result, the affections are stirred, thereby freeing the will for greater conformity to God.

In writing *The Art of Divine Meditation*, Hall is motivated by his concern for what he calls 'the practice of true piety.'[63] He believes this practice is contingent upon meditation: 'the best improvement of Christianity.'[64] He goes

---

[60]   *Ibid.*, 168.

[61]   For a critique of Martz's theory that 'Calvinism' impeded the development of meditation among Protestants, see N. Gabo, 'The Art of Puritan Devotion,' *Seventeenth Century News* 26 (1968) 8.

[62]   Whilst it is true that Baxter leaned toward Amyraldism (i.e., hypothetical universalism), it is overstating the case to suggest that he was radically opposed to the Reformed theology of grace as understood by his contemporaries. See Packer, *Quest for Godliness*, 157-160; and Wallace, *Puritans and Predestination*, 132-140. For a critique of Amyraldism, see Benjamin Warfield, *The Plan of Salvation* (Grand Rapids: Eerdmans, 1984) 90-96.

[63]   Hall, 'The Epistle Dedicatory' in *Art of Divine Meditation*. In terms of sources, Hall acknowledges his indebtedness to 'one obscure nameless monk.' J. Booty argues that this is a reference to John Mauburnus' *Rosetum*. 'Joseph Hall, The Arte of Divine Meditation, and Anglican Spirituality' in *The Roots of the Modern Christian Tradition*, ed. E. R. Elder (Kalamazoo: Cistercian Publications, 1981) 203. Huntley rejects this suggestion, stating that whilst it is true that Hall quotes Mauburnus' scale, he also criticizes it for its 'darkness and coincidence.' Huntley believes that Hall's treatise is based on Thomas a Kempis' *The Imitation of Christ*. This is a collection of four treatises. The first three are exhortations to retreat from the world, to practice humility, obedience, purity, and poverty, to commune with God, Christ and the saints, and to reflect on Christ's life, passion, and the four last things. For the controversy surrounding authorship, see R. R. Post, 'Thomas a Kempis, the Author of the *Imitation*' in *The Modern Devotion: Confrontation with Reformation and Humanism* (Leiden: E. J. Brill, 1968) 521-550.

[64]   Hall, *Art of Divine Meditation*, I.

so far as to conclude that 'if there be any Christian duty whose omission is
notoriously shameful and prejudicial to the souls of professors, it is this of
meditation. This is the very end God hath given us our souls for; we misspend
them if we use them not thus.'[65] Hall defines meditation as 'a bending of the
mind upon some spiritual object, through divers forms of discourse, until our
thoughts come to an issue.'[66] This 'bending of the mind' takes two forms:
'extemporal' and 'deliberate.'[67] In his treatise, Hall elucidates deliberate
meditation, namely, that which is 'wrought out of the heart.'[68] He begins by
describing the necessary qualities of those who meditate. They must be pure in
heart, free from worldly distraction, and constant in their devotion.[69] Next, he
considers the circumstances necessary for meditation: place, time, and bodily
gesture.[70] Having done so, he touches on the appropriate matter for meditation,
namely, 'those matters in divinity which can most of all work compunction in
the heart and most stir us up to devotion.'[71] At this point, Hall arrives at his
main task: to describe the 'proceeding' of deliberate meditation. He writes, 'It
begins in the understanding, endeth in the affection; it begins in the brain,
descends to the heart; begins on earth, ascends to heaven, not suddenly but by
certain stairs and degrees till we come to the highest.'[72] These 'stairs and
degrees' are divided into two sections.

Meditation in the Mind

The first section concerns the practice of meditation in the mind.[73] Through a
series of questions, individuals seek to comprehend God's truth. These
questions are organized according to various 'heads,' including description,
division, causes, effects, subjects, qualities, contraries, comparisons, titles, and
testimonies.[74] Swinnock openly adopts Hall's approach, employing most of the
ten 'heads' mentioned above. He remarks:

---

[65]   *Ibid.*, XXXVII.

[66]   *Ibid.*, II.

[67]   For Hall's use of extemporal meditation, see *Occasional Meditations*. For a later
       Puritan example, see John Flavel, *Husbandry Spiritualized: The Heavenly Use of
       Earthly Things*, *Works*, V; and *Navigation Spiritualized: A New Compass for
       Seamen*, *Works*, V.

[68]   Hall, *Art of Divine Meditation*, II.

[69]   *Ibid.*, V-VIII.

[70]   *Ibid.*, IX-XI.

[71]   *Ibid.*, XII.

[72]   *Ibid.*, XVI.

[73]   *Ibid.*, XVI-XXVII.

[74]   Appealing to Thomas Wilson's *Rule of Reason* (1553), a best-selling textbook,
       Huntley observes that every schoolboy memorized these subject heads in Hall's
       time. *Bishop Joseph Hall and Protestant Meditation*, 22. By way of example, see
       Perkins, *Cases*, 130-135.

When thou hast fixed upon the subject, meditate, if it may be, on its causes, properties, effects, titles, comparisons, testimonies, contraries, all will help to illustrate the subject, and to quicken and advantage thee; they do all, as so many several windows, let in those beams which both enlighten the mind and warm the affections, but they must be considered in their places, and methodically. The parts of a watch jumbled together serve for no use, but each in their order make a rare and useful piece.[75]

Swinnock illustrates this 'methodical' approach by considering the 'sinfulness of sin' in its 'nature' (its opposition to God's 'being, law, and honour'), 'causes' (its 'father' is Satan and its 'mother' is humanity), 'properties' (it pollutes all humanity's 'natural, civil, spiritual actions'), and 'effects' (it results in 'temporal punishments, spiritual judgments, and eternal torments').[76] He also considers the 'excellency of holiness' in its 'nature' (its 'conformity to the pure nature'), its 'causes' (its principal cause is the Holy Spirit and its instrumental cause is the holy Scriptures), its 'names' (the image of God, the divine nature, the kingdom of heaven, etc.), and its 'effects' (pardon, peace, joy, adoption, growth, perseverance).[77] Like Hall, Swinnock firmly believes that such an approach will 'let in those beams which both enlighten the mind and warm the affections.' In terms of actual subjects for meditation,[78] Swinnock has in view 'the nature or attributes of God,' 'the states and offices of Christ,' 'the threefold state of man,' and 'the four last things'[79] – death, judgment, heaven, and hell.[80] All together then, Swinnock proposes seven 'divine weighty truths' as worthy for meditation.[81]

The Majesty of God

In terms of these 'weighty truths,' God's majesty is supreme. 'Above all,' writes Swinnock, 'meditate on the infinite majesty, purity, and mercy of that God against whom thou hast sinned.'[82] Charnock exhorts, 'Be often in the views of the excellencies of God.'[83] Gurnall encourages his readers to meditate

---

[75] *Christian Man's Calling*, II:426.

[76] *Ibid.*, II:427.

[77] *Ibid.*, II:428. By way of a third example, Swinnock considers God's Word in its causes, properties, names, and comparisons. *Ibid.*, II:429-450.

[78] For an extensive list of subject matter in Puritan meditation, see Beeke, *Puritan Reformed Spirituality*, 87-89.

[79] *Christian Man's Calling*, II:426.

[80] *Door of Salvation*, V:124. This expression 'four last things' is common among the Puritans. See Bolton, *Four Last Things*.

[81] *Door of Salvation*, V:124.

[82] *Christian Man's Calling*, I:113.

[83] Charnock, *Existence and Attributes of God*, I:172.

on the 'infinite holiness of God.'[84] Similarly, Baxter directs his audience to 'dwell on the meditations of the Almighty,' adding, 'One would think if I should set you no further task, and tell you of no other matters for meditation, this one should be enough; for this one is in a manner all.'[85]

Swinnock shares the fruit of his meditation upon the 'excellency of the boundless blessed God'[86] in his treatise, *The Incomparableness of God*. At the outset, he quotes the Psalmist, who asks, 'For who in the skies is comparable to the LORD?'[87] Swinnock answers this question in the negative, asserting that God is incomparable in his being, attributes, works, and words.[88] God's being is incomparable, because it 'alone is excellent.'[89] It is from himself, for himself, independent, perfect, universal, unchangeable, eternal, simple, infinite, and incomprehensible.[90] God's attributes are incomparable, because they are 'essential' to him,[91] the 'very essence' of him,[92] 'all one' in him,[93] and in the 'highest degree' in him.[94] God's works of creation, providence, and redemption are incomparable, because he acts irresistibly, arbitrarily, tirelessly, and independently.[95] Finally, God's words are incomparable, in that he speaks 'authoritatively,' 'condescendingly,' and 'effectually.'[96]

Meditation upon this incomparable God leads to the Psalmist's conclusion that no one 'in the skies is comparable to the LORD' and no one 'among the sons of the mighty is like the LORD.' This realization, in turn, leads to 'warmed and quickened' affections – 'incomparable awe and reverence,' 'incomparable humility and lowliness of spirit,' 'incomparable love,' 'incomparable trust,' and 'incomparable obedience in the course of our lives.'[97] Swinnock would agree wholeheartedly with Baxter's claim that the 'best

---

[84] Gurnall, *Christian in Complete Armour*, I:476-477.

[85] Baxter, *Directions and Persuasions*, *Practical Works*, 543. Also see *Christian Directory*, 72.

[86] *Incomparableness of God*, IV:376.

[87] Ps. 89:6-7.

[88] Shepard demonstrates that God is glorious in his essence, attributes, persons, and works. *Sincere Convert*, 14-17. Bayly writes of God's essence, persons, and attributes. *Practice of Piety*, 3-27. Baxter focuses on God's being and attributes. *Divine Life*, *Practical Works*, 125-187.

[89] *Incomparableness of God*, IV:386-387.

[90] *Ibid*., IV:388-400. For a treatment of the incomparableness of God's immutability, see Edward Pearse, *A Beam of the Divine Glory* (1674; Morgan: Soli Deo Gloria, 1998).

[91] *Incomparableness of God*, IV:422.

[92] *Ibid*., IV:423.

[93] *Ibid*.

[94] *Ibid*., IV:424.

[95] *Ibid*., IV:435-441.

[96] *Ibid*., IV:445-448.

[97] *Ibid*., IV:472-476.

Christian' is the one 'that hath the fullest impression made upon his soul, by the knowledge of God in all his attributes.'[98]

The Severity of Sin

This glimpse of God's majesty leads the individual to a greater appreciation of sin's severity.[99] According to Swinnock, 'Man never comes to a right knowledge of himself, what a pitiful, abominable wretch he is, till he comes to a right knowledge of God, what an excellent incomparable majesty he is.'[100] Charnock shares this view: 'In the consideration of God's holiness we are minded of our own impurity... so his immensity should make us, according to our own nature, appear little in our own eyes.'[101] In this, the Puritans echo Calvin, who states, 'Man is never sufficiently touched and affected by the awareness of his lowly estate until he has compared himself with God's majesty.'[102] Swinnock explains that the individual only comes to a 'right knowledge' of sin's severity in the light of God's majesty, because it is only then that sin is seen as an attack against the incomparable God.

> The worth and dignity of the object doth exceedingly heighten and aggravate the offence. How horrid then is sin, and of how heinous a nature, when it offendeth and opposeth not kings, the highest of men, not angels, the highest of creatures, but God, the highest of beings; the incomparable God, to whom kings and angels, yea, the whole creation is less than nothing... Sin is incomparably malignant, because the God principally injured by it is incomparably excellent.[103]

For Swinnock, sin is 'incomparably malignant,' because it is 'a breach of this incomparable God's law, a violation of his command, a contradiction of his will,' 'a contempt of this incomparable God's authority, a slighting his dominion, a denying his sovereignty,' 'a dishonouring this incomparable God,' and 'a fighting with, and to its power, a destroying this incomparable God.'[104] Swinnock states, 'Truly, sin is such a monster, such a devil, that were its power equal to its spite, and its strength to its malice, the living God should not live a moment... all sin is God-murder.'[105] Such a view of sin results in 'warmed and

---

[98] Baxter, *Divine Life, Practical Works*, 127.
[99] For Bayly's meditation upon 'the misery of a man not reconciled to God in Christ,' see *Practice of Piety*, 28-44. For Alleine, see *Sure Guide to Heaven*, 102-104. For Joseph Ussher, see *A Method for Meditation; or, A Manuall of Divine Duties, fit for every Christians Practice* (London, 1656) 93-125.
[100] *Incomparableness of God*, IV:474.
[101] Charnock, *Existence and Attributes of God*, I:395.
[102] Calvin, *Institutes*, I:II:3.
[103] *Incomparableness of God*, IV:456.
[104] *Ibid.*, IV:457-458.
[105] *Ibid.*, IV:458-459.

quickened' affections whereby individuals 'loathe' themselves 'for being so base, so vile, so unworthy.'[106]

The Beauty of Christ

In terms of Swinnock's 'sacred' subjects, God's majesty and sin's severity are followed by Christ's beauty (i.e., his 'states and offices').[107] This order is common among the Puritans. Bayly, for example, writes, 'And forasmuch as there can be no true piety without the knowledge of God; nor any good practice without the knowledge of a man's own self; we will therefore lay down the knowledge of God's majesty, and man's misery, as the first and chiefest grounds of the Practice of Piety.'[108] Alleine acknowledges that 'till men are weary and heavy laden, and pricked at heart, and quite sick of sin, they will not come to Christ for cure, nor sincerely enquire, "What shall we do?"'[109] In other words, Christ's beauty is only appreciated against the backdrop of God's majesty and sin's severity. Baxter exhorts, 'Never think of sin and hell alone; but as the way to the thoughts of Christ and grace.'[110]

With that foundation, Swinnock encourages his readers to meditate upon Christ's passion and affection. Concerning the former, Swinnock begins with Christ's incarnation, and proceeds to consider his virgin birth, public ministry, agony in the garden, and suffering upon the cross.[111] Regarding Christ's affection, Swinnock writes:

> His name is love, his nature is love, all his expressions were love, all his actions were love: he bought love, he preached love, his lips dropped love, he practiced love, he lived in love, he was sick of love; nay, he died for love; it was love that took upon him our nature; it was love that walked in our flesh; it was love that went up and down doing good; it was love that took our infirmities; it was love that gave sight to the blind, speech to the dumb, ears to the deaf, life to the dead; it was love that was hungry, and thirsty, and weary; it was love that was in a bloody agony; it was love that was sorrowful unto his own death, and my life; it was love that was betrayed, apprehended, derided, scourged, condemned, and crucified; it was love that had his head pierced with thorns, his back with cords, his hands and feet with nails, and his side with a spear; it was love that cried out, 'Weep not for me, weep for yourselves:' 'Father, forgive them, they know not what they do.'

---

[106] For more on this, see Bolton, *Helps to Humiliation* in *Four Last Things*, 123-144.

[107] For John Owen's meditation upon Christ, see *Meditations and Discourses on the Glory of Christ*, *Works*, I.

[108] Bayly, *Practice of Piety*, 2.

[109] Alleine, *Sure Guide to Heaven*, 101.

[110] Baxter, *Christian Directory*, 265.

[111] *Christian Man's Calling*, I:192-197.

Love left a glorious crown, and love climbed a shameful cross. O dearest Saviour, whither did thy love carry thee![112]

Swinnock declares that he could lose himself 'in this pleasant maze of Christ's love.'[113] He encourages his readers to do the same. Likewise, Gurnall exhorts, 'Bathe thy soul with the frequent meditation of Christ's love.'[114] Such meditation results in 'warmed and quickened' affections – a 'ravished' heart.[115] It causes the regenerate to 'love him dearly, love him entirely, love him above all, love him more than all.'[116]

The Certainty of Death

To these three subjects, Swinnock adds 'the four last things.'[117] The first is death's certainty: 'If thou wouldst exercise thyself to godliness, think often of thy dying day.'[118] Based upon Psalm 73:26,[119] he shows the folly of living for the flesh (i.e., the temporal) instead of the soul (i.e., the eternal).[120] To quicken his readers to this truth, he asks a series of questions:[121] (1) 'Dost thou not know that death will come certainly?' (2) 'Dost thou not know that death may come suddenly?' (3) 'Dost thou not know that, whensoever death come, it will be too late to prepare for it?' (4) 'Dost thou not know that thy dying hour will be a trying hour?' (5) 'Dost thou not know the misery of every carnal man at death?' (6) 'Dost thou know the felicity which upon thy death thou shouldst enter into if thou wert prepared for it?'[122] Swinnock is convinced that meditation upon these questions results in 'warmed and quickened' affections – it awakens people from their slumber, thereby causing them to mortify their affections for the temporal and kindle their affections for the eternal.

The Finality of Judgment

Inseparable from death is judgment. Swinnock writes, 'If thou wouldst exercise

---

[112] *Ibid.*, I:199. See I:209-210.

[113] *Ibid.*

[114] Gurnall, *Christian in Complete Armour*, I:120.

[115] *Christian Man's Calling*, I:200.

[116] *Ibid.*, I:210.

[117] Calvin's call for meditation on 'the future life' encompasses the same themes as the 'four last things' and certainly has the same end in view. *Institutes*, III:IX:1-6.

[118] *Christian Man's Calling*, III:119. Also see *Fading of the Flesh*, III:470. For Bolton, see *Four Last Things*, 67-74.

[119] 'My flesh and my heart may fail, But God is the strength of my heart and my portion forever.'

[120] *Fading of the Flesh*, III:430.

[121] *Ibid.*, III:437-453.

[122] *Ibid.*, III:458-469.

thyself to godliness, meditate much upon the day of judgment.'[123] He exhorts his readers to consider 'the holiness of the Judge,' 'the strictness of his proceedings,' 'the weight of the sentence,' 'the felicity of the godly at that day,' and 'the misery of sinners at that day.'[124] Likewise, Bolton instructs individuals to ponder what it will be like to face Christ,[125] to give an exact account of 'all things done in the flesh,'[126] to witness the disclosure of all 'secret sins' and 'closet villanies,'[127] and to 'hear that dreadful sentence of damnation to eternal torments and horror.'[128] Most people refuse to meditate upon this day, thereby accounting for their neglect of religion. With this in mind, Gurnall writes, 'Surely thou wilt not easily sleep while this trumpet, that shall call all mankind to judgment, shall sound in thy ear. The reason why men sleep so soundly in security is, because they either do not believe this, or at least do not think of it seriously so as to expect it.'[129] For Swinnock, thinking 'seriously' upon this day results in 'warmed and quickened' affections – 'thou wilt be stirred up to judge thyself, to repent of sin, to ensure an interest in Christ the Judge, to keep a good conscience, and so to think, speak, and act as one that must be judged by the law of liberty.'[130]

The Misery of Hell

Any discussion of judgment ultimately leads to the subject of hell. Swinnock describes hell as a 'privative' misery. This means sinners suffer because of what they lose, namely, 'earthly delights,' 'carnal contentments,' 'spiritual preferment,' 'the society of all the godly,' 'hope,' their 'precious soul,' and 'the infinitely blessed God.'[131] In brief, 'they lose the Lord Jesus Christ, the Prince of Life, the Lord of glory, the fairest of ten thousand, the only begotten of the Father, the heir of all things.'[132] Similarly, Bolton speaks of the 'privation of God's glorious presence, and eternal separation from those everlasting joys, felicities, and bliss above.'[133] He refers to this as 'the more horrible part of hell.'[134]

Swinnock also describes hell as a 'positive' misery. This means sinners suffer because of what they gain. He explains, 'the wicked shall in the other

[123] *Christian Man's Calling*, III:131.
[124] *Ibid.*, III:133-135.
[125] Bolton, *Four Last Things*, 76.
[126] *Ibid.*, 78.
[127] *Ibid.*, 79.
[128] *Ibid.*, 80.
[129] Gurnall, *Christian in Complete Armour*, II:507.
[130] *Christian Man's Calling*, III:140.
[131] *Heaven and Hell*, III:262.
[132] *Sinner's Last Sentence*, V:279-280.
[133] Bolton, *Four Last Things*, 82.
[134] *Ibid.*

world depart from Christ into fire... They shall not only be stripped of all good... but also be filled with all evil.'[135] At that time, they will gain 'a perfection of sin' – 'Here sin is thy sin and defilement, but there it will be thy hell, thy punishment. Here thou sportest with it, but there thou shalt smart for it. Now it is thy pleasure, but then it will be thine everlasting pain.'[136] In addition, they will gain 'a fullness of sorrow.' For Bolton, this is 'the pain of sense' – 'the extremity, exquisiteness, and eternity whereof, no tongue can possibly express, or heart conceive.'[137]

Finally, Swinnock describes hell as 'eternal,' stating, 'Because the authority of an infinite God is despised, the law of an infinite God disobeyed, the love of an infinite God undervalued, and the image of an infinite God defaced by sin, therefore there is an infinite demerit in sin: and because man cannot give satisfaction infinite in value, therefore he must give that satisfaction which is infinite in time, or rather in its eternity.'[138] Bolton adds that the 'conception of the everlastingness of the torments' and the 'hopelessness of ever coming out of hell' will be 'another hell.'[139]

The Glory of Heaven

The last of Swinnock's 'sacred' subjects is heaven's glory.[140] In *Heaven and Hell Epitomised*, he chooses Philippians 1:21 as his principal text: 'For me to live is Christ, and to die is gain.' From these words, he derives this doctrine: 'That such as have Christ for their life, gain by death.'[141] In terms of 'privative' gain, they obtain freedom from the evil of sin, that is, freedom from the commission of sin and the temptation to sin.[142] They also obtain freedom from the evil of suffering.[143] In terms of 'positive' gain, they obtain the company of perfect Christians, the nearest communion with Christ, and the full and immediate fruition of God.[144] For Swinnock, this consideration of heaven's glory produces heavenly mindedness. Wallace provides the following insight into the importance of this motif among the Puritans:

---

[135] *Sinner's Last Sentence*, V:297.

[136] *Heaven and Hell*, III:276.

[137] Bolton, *Four Last Things*, 86.

[138] *Sinner's Last Sentence*, V:305.

[139] *Ibid.*, 90-91.

[140] For Bayly on this, see *Practice of Piety*, 45-75. Swinnock never hints at his eschatological position. For an overview of Puritan eschatology, see Iain Murray, *The Puritan Hope: Revival and the Interpretation of Prophecy* (Edinburgh: Banner of Truth, 1998).

[141] *Heaven and Hell*, III:230.

[142] *Ibid.*, III:237.

[143] *Ibid.*, III:240.

[144] *Ibid.*, III:249.

Heavenly mindedness was the spiritual person's foretaste of the joys of heaven through meditation. This not only strengthened the soul for earthly trials but was one place in Puritan spirituality where the mystical element entered. The heavenly minded person was absorbed in divine things, weaned from earth, and advanced in communion with God because proleptically transported into that blessed state where the saints see God and enjoy his presence forever... To meditate on that state, binding one's heart so closely to God that all else paled into insignificance, was the aim of the heavenly minded.[145]

This 'aim' is confirmed in Baxter, who remarks, 'I would not have you cast off your other meditations; but surely as heaven hath the pre-eminence in perfection, it should have it also in our meditation. That which will make us most happy when we possess it, will make us most joyful when we meditate upon it.'[146] Concerning the joys of heaven, Bolton tells his readers to consider 'the place which God and all his blessed ones inhabit eternally,'[147] 'the inestimable glory of it,'[148] 'the beauty and blessedness of glorified bodies,'[149] and 'the unutterable happiness of the soul.'[150]

Meditation in the Affections

The second section of Hall's 'stairs and degrees' concerns the practice of meditation in the affections.[151] For him, this 'is the very soul of meditation, whereto all that is past serveth but as an instrument.'[152] It involves the pressing of divine truths upon the affections through seven steps: taste, complaint, hearty wish, confession, petition, enforcement, and confidence. Although Swinnock never mentions these seven steps, he certainly shares Hall's desire to press divine truths upon the affections. For Swinnock, this is done by 'serious consideration ... an act of the practical understanding, whereby it reflecteth

---

[145] Wallace, *The Spirituality of Later English Puritans*, xvii. For a study of the relationship between heavenly meditation and mysticism, see Chan, *The Puritan Meditative Tradition,* 117-143.

[146] Baxter, *Saints' Everlasting Rest, Practical Works*, 91.

[147] Bolton, *Four Last Things*, 96.

[148] *Ibid.*, 103.

[149] *Ibid.*, 105.

[150] *Ibid.*, 113.

[151] Hall, *Art of Divine Meditation*, XXVIII-XXXIV. Writing in 1656, Ussher articulates the same two-pronged approach, stating, 'The work consists of these two principall faculties of the soul; First, the Understanding, to which I referre the Memory; Secondly the Will, to which I referre the Affections.' In terms of the former, meditation involves a 'calling to mind' whereby a biblical subject is remembered and debated. In terms of the latter, meditation involves a 'laying to heart' these truths: 'First look backwards, and say, what have I done? Secondly look forewards, and say, what will I do?" *Method for Meditation*, 37-39.

[152] Hall, *Art of Divine Meditation*, XXVIII.

upon its actions and intentions, and comparing them with the rule of the word, proceedeth to lay its command upon the will and affections to put what is good in execution.'[153] For his part, Baxter remarks, 'The understanding having received truths, lays them up in the memory, and consideration conveys them from thence to the affections.'[154] Again, 'This heavenly work is promoted by the particular exercise of the affections... when the judgment hath determined, and faith hath apprehended the truth of our happiness, then may our meditation proceed to raise our affections.'[155]

In terms of methodology, Swinnock employs several techniques, including consideration, imagination, and soliloquy. Of these, soliloquy is by far the most prominent.[156] He directs his readers 'to conference' with themselves[157] or 'to commune' with their 'hearts.'[158]

> If thou wouldst walk closely with God, and keep even with him, reckon daily with him, call thyself to a strict scrutiny: What do I? How live I? Where am I? Is the work I do warrantable by the word or no? Is my life the life of faith, of holiness, or no? Am I in God's way, under his protection, or no? Have I truth of grace, the power of godliness, or do I please myself with the form of it? Do I thrive and increase in grace, or do I decay and decline? Suppose I were to die this night, what ground have I to hope for heaven? What assurance that I shall escape the power and rage of frightful devils? What evidences have I that I am a new creature, engrafted into Christ, and thereby entitled to life and bliss? Thus feel the pulse of thy soul, inquire into its state, visit it often, and see how it doth.[159]

From this, it is evident that soliloquies consist of a series of questions and answers, designed to make people 'feel the pulse of their soul' for the purpose of self-evaluation. Ussher puts it like this: 'The main business is to see how the matter stands between God, and my own soul.'[160] Baxter refers to soliloquies as 'awakening questions.'[161] Gurnall states, 'Reflect upon thyself, and bestow a few serious thoughts upon thy own behaviour – what it hath been towards God and man all along the day.'[162]

In his treatise, *The Fading of the Flesh*, Swinnock provides an example of soliloquy, writing, 'I must tell thee, the essence and heart of religion consisteth in the choice of thy portion; nay, thy happiness dependeth wholly upon thy taking of the blessed God for thine utmost end and chiefest good; therefore if

---

[153] *Door of Salvation*, V:123.

[154] Baxter, *Saints' Everlasting Rest, Practical Works*, 96.

[155] *Ibid.*, 97.

[156] For Baxter's use of soliloquy, see *Christian Directory*, 133,249-259.

[157] *Christian Man's Calling*, II:450-451.

[158] *Ibid.*, II:451.

[159] *Ibid.*, III:144.

[160] Ussher, *Method for Meditation*, 36.

[161] Baxter, *Directions and Persuasions, Practical Works*, 548.

[162] Gurnall, *Christian in Complete Armour*, I:240.

thou mistakest here, thou art lost for ever.'[163] He urges individuals to determine
if God is their 'utmost end and chiefest good.' He does so by asking three
questions. First, 'in what channel doth the stream of thy desires run?' 'Thou
mayest judge of the state of thy soul by thy desires; if thou desirest chiefly the
trash of the world, thy spiritual state is not right, thy heart is not right in the
sight of God.' Second, 'what is the feast at which thou sittest with most
delight?' 'If this Sun of righteousness only causeth day in thine heart when he
ariseth; and if he be set, notwithstanding all the candles of creatures, it is still
night with thee, then God is thy portion.' Third, 'what is the calling which thou
followest with greatest eagerness and earnestness?' 'The Christian, who hath
the blessed God for his portion, strives and labours, and watcheth and prayeth,
and weepeth, and thinks no time too much, no pains too great, no cost enough
for the enjoyment of his God.'[164]

Meditation in the Will

Returning to Swinnock's definition, the result of meditation is that the
affections are 'warmed and quickened' and the will's 'resolution heightened
and strengthened thereby, against what is evil, and for that which is good.' By
meditating upon God's glory, sin's severity, Christ's beauty, and the other
'sacred' subjects, the affections are 'warmed and quickened,' meaning love is
stirred toward the greatest good (i.e., God) and hatred is stirred toward the
greatest evil (i.e., sin). The remaining affections follow accordingly. This is the
fear of God.

As a result, the resolution of the will is 'heightened and strengthened'
against 'what is evil, and for that which is good.' Gurnall explains it like this:
'Affections are actuated when their object is before them. If we love a person,
love is excited by sight of him, or anything that minds us of him; if we hate
one, our blood riseth much more against him when before us.'[165] For Gurnall,
meditation produces this effect like 'bellows to fire.'[166] For Swinnock, this
means the regenerate love God and hate sin. This, in turn, leads them to
perform with zeal the other spiritual duties whereby the Holy Spirit effects his
work of renewal. The final result, according to Swinnock, is the mortification
of sin.[167] He remarks:

---

[163] *Fading of the Flesh*, IV:22.

[164] *Ibid.*, IV:24-25. An important discipline that facilitates meditation is the keeping of
a journal. Watkins comments, 'In such a book the practice of mortification could be
systematized and he could record the outcome of this meditation.' *The Puritan
Experience*, 18.

[165] Gurnall, *Christian in Complete Armour*, I:240.

[166] *Ibid.*

[167] Gleason considers the place of meditation in Calvin's doctrine of sanctification,
commenting, 'Calvin sees the fundamental problem to be within man, in his flesh,
rather than in his environment – the world. Hence, the object of mortification is not

I have in two or three authors read of five men that met together, and asked each other what means they used to abstain from sin? The first said, the thoughts of the certainty of death, and uncertainty of the time, moved him to live every day as if it were his last day. The second said, he meditated of the day of judgment, and the torments of hell, and they frighted him from meddling with his dangerous enemy, sin. The third considered of the deformity of sin, and beauty of holiness. The fourth, of the abundant happiness provided in heaven for holy ones. The last continually thought of the Lord Jesus Christ and his love, and this made him ashamed to sin against God.[168]

In short, for Swinnock, the way to 'abstain from sin' is by meditating upon 'the certainty of death,' 'the day of judgment,' 'the torments of hell,' 'the deformity of sin,' 'the beauty of holiness,' 'the abundant happiness provided in heaven,' and 'the Lord Jesus Christ.' These themes make the regenerate 'ashamed to sin against God.'

The key to this process is the 'practical knowledge,' produced by meditation. Swinnock writes, 'They who know the infiniteness and immensity of his being, cannot but... esteem all things as nothing to him,' 'they who know the power of God cannot but fear him, and stand in awe of his presence,' 'they who know the eternity of God, will choose him before temporal vanities,' 'they who know the wisdom of God will submit to his providences, and acquiesce in all his dispensations,' 'they who know the faithfulness of God will credit his word, and make him the object of their hope and faith,' 'they who know the mercy, and love, and goodness of God, will love, and admire, and trust, and praise him,' 'they who know the holiness of God will sanctify him in their approaches to him, and walk humbly and watchfully with him,' and 'they who know the anger of God will stand in awe, and not sin.'[169] He adds, 'O reader, be confident of this, the more thou knowest of the excellencies of God, the more thou wilt prize his Son, submit to his Spirit, crucify the flesh, condemn the world, fear to offend him, study to please him, the more holy thou wilt be in all manner of conversation.'[170]

The Puritan Meditative Tradition

Simon Chan classifies the above approach to meditation as 'ascetical piety.' He traces its development from the 1590s when initial Puritan theories of

---

the world, but our love for the world arising from the flesh.' *John Calvin and John Owen on Mortification*, 66-67. For Calvin, meditation upon the future life enables the individual to mortify fleshly (inordinate) longings for the present life. Swinnock's approach is similar.

[168] *Heaven and Hell*, III:344.

[169] *Christian Man's Calling*, III:154-155.

[170] *Ibid.*, III:156.

meditation were based on a 'mediate conception of grace.'[171]According to this concept, 'God does not work directly in the world but chooses to operate at the natural and human level.'[172] For Chan, this view began with Perkins and Greenham, who 'represent a stage in the development of meditation where its function was more clearly understood and its broader significance increasingly appreciated.'[173] From here, Richard Rogers – the first Puritan to produce an extensive manual of piety (*The Seven Treatises*) – made meditation a major focus in Puritan religious experience.[174] With Hall's *The Art of Divine Meditation*, the last ingredient was inserted into the mix, namely, 'a practical scheme for stirring up the affections.'[175] For this reason, Hall 'exerted the greatest influence on puritan thinking on the subject for the rest of the century.'[176] As already mentioned, Chan describes this meditative tradition as 'ascetical piety.' By this, he means that it affirms 'the use of certain religious exercises for the mortification of the flesh and the formation of virtues.'[177] Quite simply, through 'disciplined effort revolving around a *regula vitae*,' individuals accumulate 'graces'[178] – the most important component of the *regula vitae* being meditation.

Chan maintains that Puritan 'ascetical piety' neglects the role of the Holy Spirit in religious experience, commenting, 'The Holy Spirit is given scant attention in their exposition of the devotional life. If ever the Spirit is mentioned it is only incidental to their main focus, which is on duties as means of grace. Theoretically at least, they recognize that the "inner operation of the Holy Spirit" must accompany the use of the means... Yet in practice, the Spirit and the means are so inextricably joined that one needs only be concerned with the careful observance of duties.'[179] Chan notes that not all of the Puritans succumb to this tendency. He sees in Sibbes, for example, 'a more conscious reliance on the Spirit.'[180] As a result, for him, meditation becomes 'a duty stripped of much of its ascetical precision.'[181] Chan believes this emphasis reaches its zenith in Owen, who stresses 'the priority of the work of the Spirit *along with* the means rather than *in* and *through* the means.'[182] For Owen,

---

[171]   Chan, *Puritan Meditative Tradition*, 9.
[172]   *Ibid.*
[173]   *Ibid.*, 47.
[174]   *Ibid.*, 59.
[175]   *Ibid.*, 60.
[176]   *Ibid.*, 61.
[177]   *Ibid.*, 144.
[178]   *Ibid.*, 161-162. For Chan, 'such a view of godliness is not unlike the catholic concept of sainthood.' *Ibid.*, 146.
[179]   *Ibid.*, 188-189.
[180]   *Ibid.*, 196.
[181]   *Ibid.*, 200.
[182]   *Ibid.*, 205. His italics.

therefore, the Holy Spirit is 'utterly determinative.'[183] 'Simply put,' remarks Chan, 'Owen sees a basic disjunction in the two levels of the Spirit's working: his working *in* the means and *with* the means. The former at best produces only a "moral persuasion" which is nothing compared to the "physical immediate operation of the Spirit."'[184] Such a work of the Spirit does not rule out the use of means, however it does still require the immediate operation of the Spirit upon the soul's faculties. For Chan, this distinguishes Owen (and like-minded Puritans) from ascetical piety.

Without question, Chan sheds much light on the practice of Puritan meditation, however his definition of ascetical piety requires some clarification – particularly, his treatment of the relationship between the Holy Spirit and the means of grace. Chan lists Swinnock's *The Christian Man's Calling* among those Puritan devotional guides, which 'set out systematically to direct the individual through the various stages of his spiritual pilgrimage.'[185] In so doing, Chan includes Swinnock under the banner of 'ascetical spirituality.'[186] This is problematic. To suggest that Swinnock's emphasis upon the Holy Spirit's work through spiritual duties (the *regula vitae*) translates into a serious neglect of the Holy Spirit's immediate work upon the soul's faculties is difficult to defend.

Despite his devotion to the means of grace, Swinnock never loses sight of the fact that they are ineffectual apart from the sovereign work of the Holy Spirit. He comments, 'All our power for sacred performances is wholly from another... God must give us fresh supplies of his Spirit in every duty, or they cannot be rightly performed.'[187] Again, 'The Christian hath no natural power for these spiritual performances, but God gives them his Spirit for this purpose, that he might be enabled to do sacred duties, with suitable graces... The Christian... pulls and hales at his own heavy heart in a duty, to perform the duty aright, and yet makes nothing of it till the Spirit comes and helps him, and then he goes along comfortably through the duty.'[188] Therefore, the Holy Spirit works through means in the lives of the regenerate. However, he also works with means directly upon the soul's faculties in order to stir 'suitable graces,' the most important of which is faith. These 'graces' are absolutely necessary for the effectual use of means. For Swinnock, therefore, there is nothing inherently efficacious or particularly meritorious about spiritual duties (including meditation). They are simply means. In *The Christian Man's*

---

[183] *Ibid.*, 206.

[184] *Ibid.*, 206-207. His italics.

[185] *Ibid.*, 145. For Chan's use of *Christian Man's Calling*, see 10-11,68,94,95,98,106-108,112,113. He does not list any of Swinnock's other works in his bibliography. Some, such as *Door of Salvation*, may have served to set Swinnock's emphasis on spiritual duties in its larger context.

[186] Chan, *Puritan Meditative Tradition*, 146.

[187] *Pastor's Farewell*, IV:75.

[188] *Christian Man's Calling*, I:94.

Calling, he provides a detailed guide for their use. However, his attention to them must be understood in a much larger framework, in which he never loses sight of the immediate work of the Holy Spirit.

This clarification concerning Swinnock in no way discredits Chan's assertion that some Puritans viewed the disciplined use of spiritual duties as a means of accumulating 'graces.' There is no doubt whatsoever that some lost sight of the immediate work of the Holy Spirit, thereby placing their trust in the means themselves. However, Chan's misreading of Swinnock begs the question as to whether or not the teaching of a few necessarily translates into an entire 'Puritan meditative tradition' known as 'ascetical piety.' It also raises serious doubts concerning the alleged discrepancy between Bolton and Swinnock on the one hand and Sibbes and Owen on the other.

Conclusion

The intent of this chapter was to consider the place of meditation in Swinnock's spirituality. To sum up, Swinnock firmly believes that meditation is the starting-point for mortification in the regenerate. This is necessarily so given the fact that the mind is the leading faculty of the soul. He exhorts:

> Reader, be persuaded, therefore, to study this knowledge of God; think no labour too much for it; pray, and read, and hear, and confer, and mourn that thou mayest know God. Believe it, it is a jewel that will pay thee well for all thy pains. Incline thine ear unto wisdom, and apply thy heart unto understanding. Yea, if thou criest after knowledge, and liftest up thy voice for understanding; if thou seekest her as silver, and searchest for her as for hid treasures, then shalt thou understand the fear of the Lord, and find the knowledge of God... (Prov. 2:2-6).[189]

Swinnock is not alone in this conviction. Baxter is so convinced of the absolute necessity of meditation to spiritual renewal that he writes: 'If, by this means, thou dost not find an increase of all thy graces, and dost not grow beyond the stature of common Christians, and art not made more serviceable in thy place, and more precious in the eyes of all discerning persons; if thy soul enjoy not more communion with God, and thy life be not fuller of comfort, and hast it not readier by thee at a dying hour: then cast away these directions, and exclaim against me for ever as a deceiver.'[190]

For Puritans like Swinnock, it is true that 'man's highest faculty' is 'his reason.'[191] However, it is equally true that the mind is 'the means by which grace influences human beings.'[192] In other words, the head is the gateway to the heart. As Davies observes, this means that the Puritan 'devotional life was

---

[189]   *Ibid.*, III:158.

[190]   Baxter, *Saints' Everlasting Rest, Practical Works*, 90.

[191]   Watkins, The Puritan Experience, 230.

[192]   Sceats, 'The Experience of Grace,' 9.

not a cold, grey, cerebral piety, for it changed the affections and therefore transformed the wills of those who used it.'[193]

---

[193] Davies, *Worship and Theology in England*, 130.

Conclusion

As is evident from the preceding discussion, Swinnock believes 'there is an excellency in all knowledge. Knowledge is the eye of the soul, to direct it in its motions; it is the lamp, the light of the soul, set up by God himself to guide it in its actions.'[1] This is not a mere 'notional speculative knowledge,' but an 'experimental knowledge.' It is 'such a knowledge as affecteth the heart with love to him, and fear of him, and hatred of what is contrary to him; true knowledge takes the heart as well as takes the head… Right knowledge, though it begins at the head, doth not end there, but falls down upon the heart to affect that, and floweth out in the life to order and regulate that.'[2] For Swinnock, therefore, 'true knowledge' entails the proper ordering of the soul's faculties. And it is this concept of the fear of God that rests at the foundation of his spirituality.

This concept has been the primary focus of this thesis – a study set within the parameters of three objectives. It only remains to evaluate the extent to which these have been realized.

The first objective was to demonstrate that Swinnock's Puritanism is his spirituality as shaped by his understanding of sanctification. Without question, his political and ecclesiastical convictions would have earned him the label *Puritan*. He was a Presbyterian, Parliamentarian, and Dissenter – all known as *Puritanism* at some point during the seventeenth century. However, these convictions take second place to his spirituality. He writes, 'If the God upon whom thou livest, by whom thou movest, from whom thou hast thy being, may be heard, thou wilt wink on the world, crucify the flesh, loathe thyself for thy filth and folly, and devote thy heart and soul to his fear.'[3] Everything pales in comparison to Swinnock's devotion to holiness. And it is this 'severe discipline of a few whimsical puritans'[4] – more than anything else – that defines him.

This observation brings some needed balance to a field of study in which piety often takes a back seat to political, ecclesiastical, and social issues. These definitions of Puritanism are important; however, it is unfortunate when they obscure the spiritual meaning of the term. This thesis confirms, in the words of Packer, that 'Puritanism was at heart a spiritual movement, passionately concerned with God and godliness.'[5]

The second objective was to identify the foundation to Swinnock's doctrine

---

[1] *Incomparableness of God*, IV:481.
[2] *Ibid.*, IV:481-482.
[3] *Christian Man's Calling*, I:195.
[4] *Door of Salvation*, V:206.
[5] Packer, Quest for Godliness, 28.

of sanctification. In a word, it is his teleological understanding of the fear of God as the proper ordering of the soul's faculties after the image of God. This thesis does not deny the importance of other doctrines to Swinnock's belief system. There are many concepts and paradigms that intersect in his mind. However, it has shown that his teleological understanding of the fear of God shapes his convictions regarding sin, regeneration, faith, sanctification, assurance, and many other doctrines that are pivotal to the development of his spirituality. This teleological emphasis spans the divide among many Presbyterians and Episcopalians, Conformists and Nonconformists, Royalists and Parliamentarians. This fact has been made evident by comparing Swinnock's views with those of Charnock, Baxter, Flavel, Bunyan, Perkins, Owen, Gouge, and others. Whilst he may have disagreed with some of these men on issues such as the role of the civil magistrate, the form of church government, the mode of water baptism, or the extent of the atonement, he most certainly shared their conviction regarding the 'life of godliness.' As Baxter asserts, it is 'living unto God as God, as being absolutely addicted to him.'[6]

The relationship between this teleological understanding of the fear of God and Swinnock's experience has also been clearly established in this study.

(1) Believing that the fear of God involves the renewing of the soul's affections, Swinnock states, 'They which know experimentally what the sanctification of the Holy Ghost meaneth, are few indeed.'[7] By regeneration, the affections embrace God as the greatest good. The soul's love is set upon God. As a result, it desires God and delights in God. Conversely, the soul's hatred is set upon sin. As a result, it fears sin and sorrows for sin. This is at the heart of Swinnock's spirituality – the conviction that people must experience an affective appropriation of grace.

(2) Believing that the fear of God makes a divorce between sin and the soul, Swinnock seeks to cleanse himself 'from all filthiness of the flesh and spirit, perfecting holiness in the fear of God.'[8] When the soul embraces God as the greatest good, it hates sin because it is hostile to God. This conviction provides the necessary impetus for mortification. For Swinnock, therefore, the Christian's 'great care is every day to conquer his corruptions... his great end and endeavour, in every providence and every ordinance, is, not the repression, but the ruin of this evil of sin.'[9]

(3) Believing that the fear of God is manifested in obedience, Swinnock applies the Bible to all of life, writing, 'Whether a Christian be eating or drinking, or buying or selling, or ploughing or sowing, or riding or walking, whatever he be doing, or wherever he be going, he must be always in the fear

---

[6]   Baxter, *Christian Directory*, 63.
[7]   *Heaven and Hell*, III:205.
[8]   2 Cor. 7:1.
[9]   *Door of Salvation*, V:97.

of the Lord. Godliness must be his guide, his measure, and his end... Every moment must be devoted to God; and as all seasons, so all actions must be sacred.'[10] Simply put, the individual, who delights in God, delights in God's Law.

(4) Believing that the fear of God moderates 'ill-directed' affections, Swinnock seeks to exercise self-control in all of life. He fears idolatry – the substitution of self for God as the soul's satisfaction. This danger exists in relation to all actions, vocations, relations, and conditions. Related to this, Swinnock is aware that, in the regenerate, the affections are caught between the sensitive and rational appetites as the image of God is restored. In this condition, his goal is 'self-mastery' – the moderation of the sensitive appetite.

(5) Believing that the fear of God is cultivated through means, Swinnock exercises himself 'unto godliness,'[11] applying himself to 'secret, private, and public duties.' He views praying, reading and hearing God's Word, and receiving the Lord's Supper as 'conduit-pipes' whereby the Holy Spirit stirs the affections; particularly, on the Sabbath – 'the market-day for the soul.'[12] For Swinnock, the soul that delights in God will delight in the means that lead to God.

(6) Believing that the fear of God 'is seminally in the knowledge of God, and floweth from it,'[13] Swinnock devotes himself to a life of structured meditation. He believes it is the common denominator among the means of grace. As the mind meditates upon God's majesty, sin's severity, Christ's beauty, and the four last things, the Holy Spirit works upon the affections. Love is stirred toward the greatest good (i.e., God) and hatred is stirred toward the greatest evil (i.e., sin). The remaining affections follow accordingly. This stirring of the affections is manifested in a greater resolve against sin.

A misunderstanding of the above motifs often gives rise to the portrayal of Puritans as legalists, ascetics, or stoics. This study has confirmed that Swinnock is none of these. He writes, 'Zeal is the heat or intensity of the affections; it is a holy warmth, whereby our love and anger are drawn out to the utmost for God and his glory.'[14] Such zeal is implanted by the Holy Sprit and manifested in a desire to mortify sin, obey God, moderate affections, and pursue disciplines. This is not legalism, asceticism, or stoicism. For Swinnock, it is simply the life of godliness.

The third objective was to locate Swinnock in a tradition extending back to Augustine through Calvin. The intention was not to enter into every facet of this relationship. Nor was the intention to present Swinnock as an exact replica of these men. The purpose was simply to place his concept of the fear of God in

---

[10]   *Christian Man's Calling*, I:85.

[11]   1 Tim. 4:7.

[12]   *Christian Man's Calling*, I:226.

[13]   *Ibid.*, III:154.

[14]   *Ibid.*, II:296.

a historical setting. As far as the 'Calvin versus the Calvinists debate' is concerned, this study – at the very least – casts doubt upon the notion that there is a serious discrepancy between the theology of Calvin and the theology of Puritans like Swinnock. The Puritans are not an exact copy of Calvin. However, the suggestion that they are fundamentally incompatible with Calvin is difficult to defend. This is particularly true of their spirituality. In his *Catechism*, Calvin writes:

> True piety consists... in a sincere feeling which loves God as Father as much as it fears and reverences Him as Lord, embraces His righteousness, and dreads offending Him worse than death. And whoever have been endowed with this piety dare not fashion out of their own rashness any God for themselves. Rather, they seek from Him the knowledge of the true God, and conceive Him just as He shows and declares Himself to be.[15]

Clearly, for Calvin, true piety is affective piety.[16] He confirms this in his *Institutes*, stating, 'Here indeed is pure and real religion: faith so joined with an earnest fear of God that this fear also embraces willing reverence, and carries with it such legitimate worship as is prescribed in the law.'[17] As demonstrated in this thesis, 'earnest fear of God' is the essence of Swinnock's spirituality. It is the impression of God's greatness and goodness upon the soul. It is a sensible (or inclinational) knowledge of God that is summed up in Augustine's cry, 'How sweet was it to me on a sudden to be without these sweet vanities! thou, Lord, who art the true sweetness, didst take them from me and enter in thyself, who art more pleasant than all pleasure, and more clear than all light.'[18] When this 'true sweetness' is impressed upon the soul's faculties, the fear of God takes hold.

As mentioned in the introduction, Swinnock is essentially a forgotten Puritan. Almost four centuries after his death, he is virtually lost to history. This is unfortunate, because he provides a valuable glimpse into the 'practical religion' of seventeenth-century English Puritanism. Although most of the details of his life are hidden from view, his sermons and treatises offer

---

[15] Calvin, *First Catechism* (published in French in 1537 and Latin in 1538) as found in F. L. Battles, *The Piety of Calvin: An Anthology Illustrative of the Spirituality of the Reformer* (Grand Rapids: Baker Books, 1978) 13. For references to similar comments in Calvin's commentaries, see 14-15.

[16] In relation to this, Warfield remarks, 'In the form he has given this statement the element of reverence (*reverentia*) appears to be made the formative element: piety is reverence, although it is not reverence without love. But if it is not reverence in and of itself but only the reverence which is informed by love, love after all may be held to become the determining element of true piety.' *Calvin and Augustine* (Philadelphia: Presbyterian and Reformed, 1971) 173.

[17] Calvin, *Institutes*, I:II:2. Also see I:II:1.

[18] As quoted by Swinnock in *Christian Man's Calling*, III:185.

sufficient material from which to glean a good understanding of his spirituality. Whilst there remains much work to be done – there are many subjects in the last four chapters that could be dissertations in their own right – this present work has presented his understanding of the fear of God as foundational to his spirituality. Swinnock was a man, enthralled with the incomparable God, seeking to live 'in the fear of the LORD always.'[19]

---

[19]   Prov. 23:17.

Bibliography

Primary Sources

Alleine, J. *A Sure Guide to Heaven; or, An Alarm to the Unconverted* (1671; Edinburgh: Banner of Truth, 1989).

Ames, W. *Medulla Theologiae (The Marrow of Theology)*, translated from the third Latin edition by J. D. Eusden (1629; Grand Rapids: Baker Books, 1997).

Aristotle. *The Works of Aristotle: Vol. I-XIII*, ed. W. D. Ross (Oxford University Press, 1963).

    Categories.

    Nicomachean Ethics.

    The Soul.

Augustine. *A Select Library of the Nicene and Post-Nicene Fathers of the Christian Church: Vol. I-VIII*, ed. P. Schaff (New York: Random House, 1948).

    Confessions.

    Enchiridion.

    Our Lord's Sermon on the Mount, according to Matthew.

    The City of God.

    The Trinity.

—— *The Fathers of the Church: Vol. LIX*, ed. R. J. Deferrari (Washington: Catholic University Press of America, 1968).

    Grace and Free Will.

    The Free Choice of the Will.

Bagshawe, E. *The Life and Death of Mr. Robert Bolton* in R. Bolton, *The Four Last Things: Death, Judgement, Hell, and Heaven* (London, 1635).

Baxter, R. *A Christian Directory* (1673) in *The Practical Works of Richard Baxter, Vol. I* (London: George Virtue, 1846; rpt., Morgan: Soli Deo Gloria, 2000).

—— *The Practical Works of Richard Baxter: Select Treatises* (London: Blackie & Son, 1863; rpt., Grand Rapids: Baker Book House, 1981).

    A Call to the Unconverted to Turn and Live.

    A Treatise of Conversion Addressed to the Ignorant and Ungodly.

    Directions and Persuasions to a Sound Conversion.

    Directions to Weak Christians for their Establishment, Growth and Perseverance.

    Dying Thoughts upon Philippians 1:23.

    Now or Never: or, The Believer Justified and Directed.

    The Character of a Sound Confirmed Christian.

    The Divine Life.

    The Mischiefs of Self-Ignorance and the Benefits of Self-Acquaintance.

    The Saints' Everlasting Rest.

—— *The Reformed Pastor: Shewing the Nature of the Pastoral Work* (1656; London: J. Nisbet, 1860).

Bayly, L. *The Practice of Piety: Directing a Christian How to Walk, that He May Please God* (1613; London: Hamilton, Adams, and Co., 1842; rpt., Morgan: Soli Deo Gloria, 2003).

Bolton, R. *A Discourse about the State of True Happinesse: Delivered in Certaine Sermons in Oxford, and at Pauls Crosse* (London, 1611).

— *Helps to Humiliation* in *The Four Last Things: Death, Judgement, Hell, and Heaven* (1633; Religious Tract Society, 1830; rpt., Morgan: Soli Deo Gloria, 1994).

— *The Carnal Professor, Discovering the Woeful Slavery of a Man Guided by the Flesh* (1634; Hamilton, Adams, and Co., 1838; rpt., Ligoneir: Soli Deo Gloria, 1992).

— *The Four Last Things: Death, Judgement, Hell, and Heaven* (1633; Religious Tract Society, 1830; rpt., Morgan: Soli Deo Gloria, 1994).

Bolton, S. *The True Bounds of Christian Freedom* (1645; Edinburgh: Banner of Truth, 1964; rpt., 1978).

Brooks, T. *Heaven on Earth: A Treatise on Christian Assurance* (1654) in *The Works of Thomas Brooks: Vol. I-VI* (Edinburgh: Banner of Truth, 1980).

Bullinger, H. *The Christen State of Matrimonye*, trans. M. Coverdale (1541; rpt., Amsterdam: Theatrum Orbis Terrarum, 1974).

Bunyan, J. *The Miscellaneous Works of John Bunyan*, ed. R. L. Greaves (Oxford: Clarendon Press, 1981).

    A Holy Life: The Beauty of Christianity.

    A Treatise of the Fear of God.

    I Will Pray With the Spirit and I Will Pray With the Understanding Also; or, A Discourse Touching Prayer from 1 Corinthians 14:15.

    Questions about the Nature and Perpetuity of the Seventh-Day-Sabbath. And Proof, that the First Day of the Week is the True Christian-Sabbath.

    The Greatness of the Soul, And Unspeakableness of the Loss thereof, &c.

    The Holy War, Made by King Shaddai upon Diabolus, for the Regaining of the Metropolis of the World; or, The Losing and Taking again of the Town of Mansoul.

    The Pilgrim's Progress from this World to that which is to come.

Burroughs, J. *Gospel Fear* (London, 1674).

— *The Evil of Evils; or, The Exceeding Sinfulness of Sin* (London, 1654).

— *The Rare Jewel of Christian Contentment* (1648; Edinburgh: Banner of Truth, 1964; rpt., 1987).

Calamy, E. *Nonconformist's Memorial* (London, 1802).

Calvin, J. *Calvin's Commentaries Vol. I-XXII* (Grand Rapids: Baker Books, 2003).

    The Epistle of the Apostle Paul to the Romans.

    The First Book of Moses called Genesis.

    The First Epistle of the Apostle Paul to the Thessalonians.

— *Institutes of the Christian Religion* in *The Library of Christian Classics: Vol. XX-XXI*, ed. J. T. McNeill (Philadelphia: Westminster Press, 1960).

— *The Bondage and Liberation of the Will*, ed. A. N. S. Lane (Grand Rapids: Baker Books, 1996).

Charnock, S. *Discourses Upon the Existence and Attributes of God: Vol. I-II* (London: Robert Carter & Brothers, 1853; rpt., Grand Rapids: Baker Books, 1990).

— *The Works of Stephen Charnock: Vol. III*, ed. J. Nichol (London, 1865; rpt., Edinburgh: Banner of Truth, 1986).

    A Discourse of God's Being the Author of Reconciliation.

> *A Discourse of the Cleansing Virtue of Christ's Blood.*
> *A Discourse of the Efficient of Regeneration.*
> *A Discourse of the Nature of Regeneration.*
> *A Discourse of the Word, the Instrument of Regeneration.*
> *The Necessity of Regeneration.*

Cyprian. *Treatises Attributed to Cyprian* in *The Ante-Nicene Fathers* (Grand Rapids: Eerdmans, 1951) V:589.

Edwards, J. *Charity and Its Fruits: Christian Love as Manifested in the Heart and Life* (1852; Edinburgh: Banner of Truth, 1969; rpt., 2000).

— *The Works of Jonathan Edwards: Vol. I-II* (1834; rpt., Peabody: Hendrickson, 1998).
> *A Treatise Concerning Religious Affections.*
> *The Freedom of the Will.*

Flavel, J. *The Works of John Flavel: Vol. I-VI* (London: W. Baynes and Son, 1820; rpt., London: Banner of Truth, 1968).
> *A Practical Treatise on Fear: Its Varieties, Uses, Causes, Effects, and Remedies.*
> *Divine Conduct; or, The Mystery of Providence: A Treatise upon Psalm 57:2.*
> *Husbandry Spiritualized: The Heavenly Use of Earthly Things.*
> *Navigation Spiritualized: A New Compass for Seaman.*
> *Pneumatologia: A Treatise on the Soul of Man.*
> *Saint Indeed; or, The Great Work of a Christian, Opened and Pressed.*
> *The Fountain of Life; or, A Display of Christ in His Essential and Mediatorial Glory.*
> *The Method of Grace in the Gospel Redemption.*
> *The Reasonableness of Personal Reformation and the Necessity of Conversion.*

Gouge, W. *Of Domesticall Duties: Eight Treatises* (London, 1622).

Greenham, R. *A Treatise of the Sabbath* in *The Works of Richard Greenham* (London, 1612).

Gregory. *Four Homilies* in *The Ante-Nicene Fathers* (Grand Rapids: Eerdmans, 1951) VI:62-63.

Gurnall, W. *The Christian in Complete Armour: A Treatise of the Saints' War against the Devil* (1662-1665; London: Blackie & Son, 1864; rpt., Edinburgh: Banner of Truth, 1995).

Guthrie, W. *A Short Treatise of the Christian's Great Interest* (1658; rpt., Edinburgh: James Watson, 1720).

Hall, J. *Occasional Meditations* and *The Art of Divine Meditation* in F. L. Huntley, *Bishop Joseph Hall and Protestant Meditation in Seventeenth Century England: A Study with the Texts of the Art of Divine Meditation (1606) and Occasional Meditations (1633)* (Binghamton: Centre for Medieval and Early Renaissance Studies, 1981).

Hall, T. *The Beauty of Magistracy* (1659) in *The Works of George Swinnock: Vol. IV*, ed. J. Nichol (London, 1868; rpt., Edinburgh: Banner of Truth, 1992).

Ignatius. *The Spiritual Exercises of St. Ignatius of Loyola*, trans. E. Mullan (New York: P. J. Kenedy & Sons, 1914).

Irenaeus. *Irenaeus Against Heresies* in *The Ante-Nicene Fathers* (Grand Rapids: Eerdmans, 1951) I:547.

Kempis, Thomas. *The Imitation of Christ*, ed. H. C. Gardiner (New York: Doubleday &

Company, 1955).

Laud, W. *A Relation of the Conference Between William Laud and Mr. Fisher the Jesuit* in *The Works of William Laud*, ed. J. H. Parker (Oxford, 1857).

Luther, M. *Luther's Works*, ed. H. T. Lehmann (Philadelphia: Fortress Press, 1960).

> *An Admonition Concerning the Sacrament of the Body and Blood of our Lord.*
> *That these Words of Christ, 'This is My Body,' Etc., Still Stand Firm Against the Fanatics.*
> *The Babylonian Captivity of the Church.*
> *The Bondage of the Will.*
> *To the Christian Nobility of the German Nation Concerning the Reform of the Christian Estate.*

— *The Freedom of a Christian* in *Reformation Writings of Martin Luther* (London: Lutterworth Press, 1952).

Manton, T. *An Exposition on the Epistle of James* (1693; London: Banner of Truth, 1968).

— *The Complete Works of Thomas Manton* (Worthington: Maranatha Publication).

> *A Description of the True Circumcision.*
> *An Exposition, With Notes, Upon the Epistle of Jude.*
> *A Practical Exposition of the Lord's Prayer.*
> *Several Sermons Upon the CXIX Psalm.*

Marshall, W. *The Gospel Mystery of Sanctification* (1670; Grand Rapids: Reformation Heritage Books, 1999).

Owen, J. *The Works of John Owen: Vol. I-XVI*, ed. W. H. Gould (London: Johnstone & Hunter, 1850; rpt., Edinburgh: Banner of Truth, 1977).

> *Discourse on the Holy Spirit.*
> *Meditations and Discourses on the Glory of Christ.*
> *The Death of Death in the Death of Christ.*
> *The Doctrine of Justification by Faith.*
> *The Mortification of Sin.*

Pearse, E. *A Beam of the Divine Glory* (1674; Morgan: Soli Deo Gloria, 1998).

Perkins, W. *The Whole Treatise of the Cases of Conscience: Distinguished into Three Parts* (London: John Legate, 1632).

— *A Godly and Learned Exposition upon Christs Sermon in the Mount* in *The Works of William Perkins* (London, 1631).

— *The Works of William Perkins: Vol. I-III* (London: John Legate, 1608).

> *An Exposition of the Symbole or Creede of the Apostles, According to the Tenour of the Scriptures, and the Consent of Orthodoxe Fathers of the Church.*
> *A Reformed Catholike; or, A declaration shewing how neere we may come to the present Church of Rome in sundry points of Religion: and wherein we must for ever depart from them.*
> *Armilla Aurea (A Golden Chaine; or, The Description of Theologie Containing the Order and the Causes of Salvation and Damnation, According to Gods Word).*
> *A Treatise of Gods Free Grace, and Mans Free-Will.*
> *A Treatise of the Vocations; or, Callings of man, with the sorts and kinds of them, and the right use thereof.*
> *A Treatise Tending unto a Declaration, Whether a Man be in the Estate of*

  Damnation, or in the Estate of Grace.

  Of Gods free grace and mans free will.

  The Arte of Divine Prophesying; or, A treatise concerning the sacred and onely true manner and methode of preaching.

  Two Treatises: I. Of the Nature and Practice of Repentance. II. Of the Combate of the Flesh and Spirit.

Prynne, W. *Canterburies Doome; or, The First Part of a Compleat History of the Commitment, Charge, Tryall, Condemnation, Execution of William Laud* (London, 1646).

Reynolds, E. *A Treatise of the Passions and Faculties of the Soul* (London, 1640).

Shepard, T. *Autobiography* and *Journal* in *God's Plot: The Paradoxes of Puritan Piety*, ed. M. McGiffert (University of Massachusetts Press, 1972).

— *The Doctrine of the Sabbath* (London, 1650).

— *The Parable of the Ten Virgins* (1695) in *The Works of Thomas Shepard, Vol. II* (Ligoneir: Soli Deo Gloria, 1990).

— *The Sincere Convert and the Sound Believer* (Boston Doctrinal Tract and Book Society, 1853; rpt., Morgan: Soli Deo Gloria, 1999).

  The Sincere Convert: Discovering the Small Number of True Believers and the Great Difficulty of Saving Conversion.

  The Sound Believer: A Treatise of Evangelical Conversion in *The Sincere Convert and the Sound Believer.*

Sibbes, R. *Glorious Freedom; or, The Excellency of the Gospel above the Law* (1639; Edinburgh: Banner of Truth, 2000).

— *The Bruised Reed* (1630; Edinburgh: Banner of Truth, 1998).

Swinnock, G. *The Life and Death of Mr. Thomas Wilson, Minister of Maidstone, in the County of Kent, M.A.* (London, 1672).

— *The Works of George Swinnock: Vol. I-V*, ed. James Nichol (London, 1868; rpt., Edinburgh: Banner of Truth, 1992).

  Christian Man's Calling; or, A treatise of making religion ones business: Parts I, II, III (1661-1665).

  Door of Salvation Opened by the Key of Regeneration; or, A treatise containing the nature, necessity, marks and means of regeneration: as also the duty of the regenerate (1660).

  Fading of the Flesh and Flourishing of the Faith; or, One cast for eternity: with the only way to throw it well: as also the gracious persons incomparable portion (1662).

  Gods Are Men; or, Magistrates are mortal (1657).

  Men Are Gods; or, The dignity of magistracy, and the duty of the magistrate (1659).

  Ουρανος και ταρταρος; *or, Heaven and hell epitomized: the true Christian characterized, as also an exhortation with motives, means and directions to be speedy and serious about the work of conversion Heaven and Hell Epitomized* (1658).

  Pastor's Farewell and wish of welfare to his people; or, A valedictory sermon (1660).

  Sinner's last sentence to eternal punishment, for sins of omission: wherein is discovered the nature, causes and cure of those sins (1675).

  Treatise of the incomparableness of God in his being, attributes, works and word: opened and applied (1672).

Tertullian. *On Monogamy* in *The Ante-Nicene Fathers* (Grand Rapids: Eerdmans, 1951) III:59-72.

Ussher, J. *A Method for Meditation; or, A Manuall of Divine Duties, fit for every Christians Practice* (London, 1656).

Venning, R. *The Sinfulness of Sin; or, The Plague of Plagues* (1669; Edinburgh: Banner of Truth, 1965; rpt., 1993).

Watson, T. *A Body of Divinity Contained in Sermons Upon the Westminster Assembly's Catechism* (1692; 1890; rpt., London: Banner of Truth, 1958).

— *All Things for Good; or, The Divine Cordial* (1663; Edinburgh: Banner of Truth, 1986; rpt., 1994).

— *The Beatitudes* (1660; Edinburgh: Banner of Truth, 1994).

— *The Doctrine of Repentance* (1668; Edinburgh: Banner of Truth, 1994).

— *The Godly Man's Picture* (1666; Edinburgh: Banner of Truth, 1999).

— *The Lord's Prayer* (1692; 1890; rpt., Edinburgh: Banner of Truth, 1999).

— *The Mischief of Sin* (1671; Pittsburgh: Soli Deo Gloria, 1994).

Wilson, T. *David's Zeal for Zion, a sermon preached before the honourable House of Commons, April 4, 1641* (London, 1641).

— *Jerichoes Down-Fall, As it was Presented in a Sermon preached in St. Margarets Westminster, before the Honourable House of Commons, at the late Solemne Fast, September 28, 1642* (London, 1643).

Zwingli, U. *Commentary on True and False Religion*, eds. S. M. Jackson and C. N. Heller (Durham: Labyrinth Press, 1981).

Secondary Sources

Allison, C. F. *The Rise of Moralism: The Proclamation of the Gospel from Hooker to Baxter* (New York: Seabury Press, 1966).

Amussen, S. D. 'Gender, Family and the Social Order, 1560-1725' in *Order and Disorder in Early Modern England*, eds. A. Fletcher and J. Stevenson (Cambridge University Press, 1985) 196-217.

Arendt, H. *The Life of the Mind* (New York: Harcourt Brace Jovanovich, 1981).

Armstrong, B. *Calvinism and the Amyraut Heresy: Protestant Scholasticism and Humanism in Seventeenth-Century France* (University of Wisconsin Press, 1969).

— 'Puritan Spirituality: The Tension of Bible and Experience' in *The Roots of the Modern Christian Tradition*, ed. E. R. Elder (Kalamazoo: Cistercian Publications, 1984) 229-248.

Battles, F. L. *The Piety of Calvin: An Anthology Illustrative of the Spirituality of the Reformer* (Grand Rapids: Baker Books, 1978).

Bauckham, R. J. 'Sabbath and Sunday in the Protestant Tradition' in *From Sabbath to Lord's Day: A Biblical, Historical and Theological Investigation*, ed. D. A. Carson (Grand Rapids: Zondervan, 1982) 311-342.

— 'The Lord's Day' in *From Sabbath to Lord's Day: A Biblical, Historical and Theological Investigation*, ed. D. Carson (Grand Rapids: Zondervan, 1982) 221-250.

Beale, P. J. 'Sanctifying the Outer Life' in *Aspects of Sanctification* (London: Westminster Conference, 1981) 62-77.

Beeke, J. R. *Assurance of Faith: Calvin, English Puritanism, and the Dutch Second*

Reformation (New York: Peter Lang, 1991).

—— *Puritan Evangelism: A Biblical Approach* (Grand Rapids: Reformation Heritage Books, 1999).

—— *Puritan Reformed Spirituality* (Grand Rapids: Reformation Heritage Books, 2004).

Berkouwer, G. C. *Studies in Dogmatics – Man: The Image of God* (Grand Rapids: Eerdmans, 1978).

—— *Studies in Dogmatics – The Providence of God* (Grand Rapids: Eerdmans, 1974).

Booty, J. 'Joseph Hall, The Arte of Divine Meditation, and Anglican Spirituality' in *The Roots of the Modern Christian Tradition*, ed. E. R. Elder (Kalamazoo: Cistercian Publications, 1984) 200-228.

Bourke, V. J. *Will in Western Thought: An Historico-Critical Survey* (New York: Sheed and Ward, 1964).

Braund, E. 'Daily Life Among the Puritans' in *Puritan Papers: Vol. I*, ed. D. M. Lloyd-Jones (Phillipsburg: Presbyterian and Reformed, 2000) 155-166.

Brooke, C. and Highfield, R., eds., *Oxford & Cambridge* (Cambridge University Press, 1988).

Brooks, B. *The Lives of the Puritans: Vol. I-III* (1813; rpt., Morgan: Soli Deo Gloria, 1996).

Caiger, J. A. 'Preaching – Puritan and Reformed' in *Puritan Papers: Vol. II*, ed. J. I. Packer (Phillipsburg: Presbyterian and Reformed, 2001) 161-185.

Campbell, T. A. 'Affective Piety in Seventeenth-Century British Calvinism' in *The Religion of the Heart* (University of South Carolina Press, 1991) 42-69.

Carson, D. A. *Divine Sovereignty and Human Responsibility: Biblical Perspectives in Tension* (Atlanta: John Knox Press, 1981).

—— 'Introduction' in *From Sabbath to Lord's Day: A Biblical, Historical, and Theological Investigation*, ed. D. Carson (Grand Rapids: Zondervan, 1982).

—— *The Sermon on the Mount* (Grand Rapids: Baker Books, 1978).

Chadwick, H. 'The Ascetic Ideal in the History of the Church,' in *Monks, Hermits and the Ascetic Tradition: Studies in Church History, Vol. 22*, ed. W. J. Sheils (Basil Blackwell, 1985) 1-24.

Chamblin, K. 'The Law of Moses and the Law of Christ' in *Continuity and Discontinuity: Perspectives on the Relationship Between the Old and New Testaments*, ed. J. S. Feinberg (Wheaton: Crossway, 1988) 181-202.

Chantry, W. *Call the Sabbath a Delight* (Edinburgh: Banner of Truth, 1991).

Cohen, C. L. *God's Caress: The Psychology of Puritan Religious Experience* (Oxford University Press, 1986).

Collinson, P. *English Puritanism* (London: Historical Association, 1983).

—— *Godly People: Essays on English Protestantism and Puritanism* (London: Hambledon Press, 1983).

Cook, P. 'The Life and Work of a Minister According to the Puritans' in *Puritan Papers: Vol. I*, ed. D. M. Lloyd-Jones (Phillipsburg: Presbyterian and Reformed, 2000) 177-189.

Coolidge, J. S. *The Pauline Renaissance in England: Puritanism and the Bible* (Oxford: Clarendon Press, 1970).

Costello, W. T. *The Scholastic Curriculum at Early Seventeenth Century Cambridge* (Harvard University Press, 1958).

Cragg, G. R. *Puritanism in the Period of the Great Persecution, 1660-1688* (Cambridge University Press, 1957).

Dabney, R. 'The Christian Sabbath' in *Discussions: Evangelical and Theological* (London: Banner of Truth, 1967) I:496-550.

Davies, A. A. 'The Holy Spirit in Puritan Experience' in *Faith and Ferment* (London: Westminster Conference, 1982) 18-31.

Davies, H. *The Vigilant God: Providence in the Thought of Augustine, Aquinas, Calvin and Barth* (New York: Peter Lang, 1992).

— *The Worship of the English Puritans* (Morgan: Soli Deo Gloria, 1997).

— *Worship and Theology in England from Andrewes to Baxter and Fox, 1603-1690* (Princeton University Press, 1975).

Davies, J. *The Caroline Captivity of the Church: Charles I and the Remoulding of Anglicanism, 1625-1641* (Oxford: Clarendon Press, 1992).

De Lacey, D. R. 'The Sabbath/Sunday Question and the Law in the Pauline Corpus' in *From Sabbath to Lord's Day: A Biblical, Historical and Theological Investigation*, ed. D. A. Carson (Grand Rapids: Zondervan, 1982) 159-196.

Dennison, J. T. *The Market Day of the Soul: The Puritan Doctrine of the Sabbath in England* (Lanham: University Press of America, 1983).

— 'The Perpetuity and Change of the Sabbath' in *Soli Deo Gloria: Essays in Reformed Theology*, ed. R. C. Sproul (Nutley: Presbyterian and Reformed, 1976) 146-155.

Dever, M. E. *Richard Sibbes: Puritanism and Calvinism in Late Elizabethan and Early Stuart England* (Macon: Mercer University Press, 2000).

Dressler, H. H. P. 'The Sabbath in the Old Testament' in *From Sabbath to Lord's Day: A Biblical, Historical and Theological Investigation*, ed. D. A. Carson (Grand Rapids: Zondervan, 1982) 21-42.

Eales, J. 'Kent and the English Civil Wars, 1640-1660' in *Government and Politics in Kent, 1640-1914*, ed. F. Lansberry (Kent: Boydell Press, 2001) 1-32.

Eveson, P. H. 'Martin Luther and his Sacramental Teaching' in *Union and Communion, 1529-1979* (London: Westminster Conference, 1979) 7-21.

Feinberg, J. S. *The Many Faces of Evil: Theological Systems and the Problem of Evil* (Grand Rapids: Zondervan, 1994).

Ferguson, S. B. *John Owen on the Christian Life* (Edinburgh: Banner of Truth, 1987).

Fiering, N. *Moral Philosophy at Seventeenth-Century Harvard: A Discipline in Tradition* (University of North Carolina Press, 1981).

Fletcher, A. *Gender, Sex and Subordination in England 1500-1800* (Yale University Press, 1995).

— *Outbreak of the English Civil War* (New York University Press, 1981).

— 'The Protestant Idea of Marriage in Early Modern England' in *Religion, Culture, and Society in Early Modern Britain*, eds. A. Fletcher and P. Roberts (Cambridge University Press, 1994) 161-181.

Foh, S. T. *Women and the Word of God: A Response to Biblical Feminism* (Phillipsburg: Presbyterian and Reformed, 1979).

Foster, J., ed., *Alumni Oxonienses: The Members of the University of Oxford, 1500-1714* (Oxford: Parker, 1891).

Fraser, A. *Cromwell: Our Chief of Men* (London: Phoenix Press, 2001).

Gaffin, R. B. *Calvin and the Sabbath* (Ross-shire: Christian Focus, 1998).

Gerrish, B. A. *Grace and Gratitude: The Eucharist Theology of John Calvin* (Minneapolis: Fortress Press, 1993).

Godfrey, W. R. 'Law and Gospel' in *New Dictionary of Theology*, eds. S. B. Ferguson, D. F. Wright, and J. I. Packer (Downers Grove: InterVarsity Press, 1988) 379-380.

Gleason, R. C. *John Calvin and John Owen on Mortification* (New York: Peter Lang, 1995).

Greaves, R. L. 'The Nature of the Puritan Tradition,' *Reformation, Conformity and Dissent: Essays in Honour of Geoffrey Nuttall*, ed. R. B. Knox (London: Epworth Press, 1977) 255-273.

Gribben, C. *The Irish Puritans: James Ussher and the Reformation of the Church* (Auburn: Evangelical Press, 2003).

Griffiths, S. *Redeem the Time: Sin in the Writings of John Owen* (Ross-shire: Christian Focus, 2001).

Gwyn-Thomas, J. 'The Puritan Doctrine of Christian Joy' in *Puritan Papers: Vol. II*, ed. J. I. Packer (Phillipsburg: Presbyterian and Reformed, 2001) 119-140.

Hageman, H. G. 'Reformed Spirituality' in *Protestant Spiritual Traditions*, ed. F. C. Senn (New York: Paulist, 1986) 55-79.

Hall, B. 'Calvin Against the Calvinists' in *John Calvin: A Collection of Distinguishing Essays*, ed. G. E. Duffield (Grand Rapids: Eerdmans, 1966) 19-37.

— 'Puritanism: The Problem of Definition' in *Humanists and Protestants: 1500-1900* (Edinburgh: T & T Clark, 1990) 237-254.

Haller, W. *The Rise of Puritanism* (New York: Harper Torchbooks, 1957).

Hambrick-Stowe, C. J. 'Puritan Spirituality in America' in *Christian Spirituality III*, eds. L. Dupré and D. E. Saliers (New York: Crossroad Publishing, 1989) 338-353.

Hardman, S. 'Puritan Asceticism and the Type of Sacrifice,' in *Monks, Hermits and the Ascetic Tradition: Studies in Church History, Vol. 22*, ed. W. J. Sheils (Basil Blackwell, 1985) 285-297.

Hasker, W. *Providence, Evil and the Openness of God* (New York: Routledge, 2004).

Helm, P. *Calvin and the Calvinists* (Edinburgh: Banner of Truth, 1982).

Hendriksen, W. *A Commentary on I & II Timothy and Titus* (London: Banner of Truth, 1964).

— *Exposition of Colossians and Philemon: New Testament Commentary* (Grand Rapids: Baker Books, 1964).

Hesselink, I. J. *Calvin's Concept of the Law* (Allison Park: Pickwick Publications, 1992).

Hill, C. *Society and Puritanism in Pre-Revolutionary England* (London: Panther Books, 1969).

Hinson, E. G. 'Baptist and Quaker Spirituality' in *Christian Spirituality III*, eds. L. Dupré and D. E. Saliers (New York: Crossroad Publishing, 1989) 324-338.

— 'Puritan Spirituality' in *Protestant Spiritual Traditions*, ed. F. C. Senn (New York: Paulist Press, 1986) 165-181.

Hodge, C. *Systematic Theology: Vol. I-III* (Peabody: Hendrickson, 2001).

Hoitenga, D. *John Calvin and the Will: A Critique and Corrective* (Grand Rapids: Baker Books, 1997).

Holifield, E. B. *The Covenant Sealed: The Development of Puritan Sacramental Theology in Old and New England, 1570-1720* (Yale University Press, 1974).

Holmes, S. R. *God of Grace & God of Glory: An Account of the Theology of Jonathan Edwards* (Grand Rapids: Eerdmans, 2000).

Hulse, E. 'Sanctifying the Lord's Day: Reformed and Puritan Attitudes' in *Aspects of Sanctification* (London: Westminster Conference, 1982) 78-102.

— *Who are the Puritans?* (Darlington: Evangelical Press, 2000).

Hunter, A. M. *The Teaching of Calvin* (Westwood: Fleming H. Revell, 1950).

Huntley, F. L. *Bishop Joseph Hall and Protestant Meditation in Seventeenth Century England: A Study with the Texts of the Art of Divine Meditation (1606) and Occasional Meditations (1633)* (Binghamton: Centre for Medieval and Early Renaissance Studies, 1981).

Jewett, P. K. *The Lord's Day: A Theological Guide to the Christian Day of Worship* (Grand Rapids: Eerdmans, 1971).

Jones, J., ed., *Balliol College: A History 1263-1939* (Oxford University Press, 1988).

Kaufmann, U. M. *The Pilgrim's Progress and Traditions in Puritan Meditation* (Yale University Press, 1966).

Keeble, N. H. 'Puritan Spirituality' in *The Westminster Dictionary of Christian Spirituality*, ed. G. S. Wakefield (Philadelphia: Westminster Press, 1983) 323-326.

Kendall, R. T. *Calvin and English Calvinism to 1649* (Oxford University Press, 1979).

— 'The Puritan Modification of Calvin's Theology' in *John Calvin: His Influence in the Western World*, ed. W. S. Reid (Grand Rapids: Zondervan, 1982) 199-214.

Kevan, E. F. *The Grace of Law* (Ligonier: Soli Deo Gloria, 1993).

— 'The Law and the Covenants – A Study in John Ball' in *Puritan Papers: Vol. I*, ed. D. M. Lloyd-Jones (Phillipsburg: Presbyterian and Reformed, 2000) 45-58.

Knappen, M. M. *Tudor Puritanism: A Chapter in the History of Idealism* (University of Chicago Press, 1970).

Koehler, L. *A Search for Power* (University of Illinois Press, 1980).

Lake, P. *Anglicans and Puritans? Presbyterianism and English Conformist Thought from Whitgift to Hooker* (London: Unwin Hyman, 1988).

Lamont, W. M. *Godly Rule: Politics and Religion, 1603-1660* (New York: St. Martin's Press, 1969).

Lane, A. N. S. 'John Calvin: The Witness of the Holy Spirit' in *Faith and Ferment* (London: Westminster Conference, 1982) 1-17.

Leader, D. R. *A History of the University of Cambridge: Vol. I* (Cambridge University Press, 1994).

Leith, J. H. *John Calvin's Doctrine of the Christian Life* (Louisville: John Knox Press, 1989).

— 'The Doctrine of the Will in the *Institutes of the Christian Religion*' in *Reformatio Perennis: Essays on Calvin and the Reformation in Honour of Ford Lewis Battles*, ed. B. A. Gerrish and R. Bendetto (Pittsburgh: Pickwick Press, 1981) 49-66.

Letham, R. 'Faith and Assurance in Early Calvinism: A Model of Continuity and Diversity' in *Later Calvinism: International Perspectives*, ed. W. F. Graham (Kirksville: Sixteenth Century Journal, 1992) 355-384.

Lewis, P. *The Genius of Puritanism* (Morgan: Soli Deo Gloria, 1996).

Lillback, P. *The Binding of God: Calvin's Role in the Development of Covenant Theology* (Grand Rapids: Baker Books, 2001).

Lincoln, A. T. 'From Sabbath to Lord's Day: A Biblical and Theological Perspective' in *From Sabbath to Lord's Day: A Biblical, Historical and Theological Investigation*, ed. D. A. Carson (Grand Rapids: Zondervan, 1982) 343-412.

— 'Sabbath, Rest, and Eschatology in the New Testament' in *From Sabbath to Lord's Day: A Biblical, Historical and Theological Investigation*, ed. D. A. Carson (Grand Rapids: Zondervan, 1982) 197-220.

Lloyd-Jones, M. *Studies in the Sermon on the Mount: Vol. I-II* (Grand Rapids: Eerdmans, 1962).

— *The Puritans: Their Origins and Successors* (Edinburgh: Banner of Truth, 2002).

Lovelace, R. C. 'The Anatomy of Puritan Piety: English Puritan Devotional Literature, 1600-1640' in *Christian Spirituality III*, eds. L. Dupré and D. E. Saliers (New York: Crossroad Publishing, 1989) 294-323.

MacLeod, D. 'Luther and Calvin on the Place of the Law' in *Living the Christian Life* (London: Westminster Conference, 1974) 5-13.

Mallett, C. E. *A History of the University of Oxford: Vol. I-II* (New York: Barnes & Noble, 1968).

Marlowe, J. *The Puritan Tradition in English Life* (London: Cresset Press, 1956).

Marsden, G. M. 'Perry Miller's Rehabilitation of the Puritans: A Critique' in *Reckoning With the Past: Historical Essays on American Evangelicalism from the Institute for the Study of American Evangelicals*, ed. D. G. Hart (Grand Rapids: Baker Books, 1995) 23-38.

Martz, L. *The Poetry of Meditation* (Yale University Press, 1962).

McGee, J. S. *The Godly Man in Stuart England: Anglicans, Puritans, and the Two Tables, 1620-1670* (Yale University Press, 1976).

McGrath, A. *Christian Spirituality* (Oxford: Blackwell Publishers, 1999).

McGuckin, J. A. 'Christian Asceticism and the Early School of Alexandria,' in *Monks, Hermits and the Ascetic Tradition: Studies in Church History, Vol. 22*, ed. W. J. Sheils (Basil Blackwell, 1985) 25-39.

McSorley, H. J. *Luther: Right or Wrong? An Ecumenical-Theological Study of Luther's Major Work, The Bondage of the Will* (New York: Newman Press, 1969).

Miller, P. *The New England Mind: The Seventeenth Century* (Harvard University Press, 1963).

Moo, D. 'The Law of Moses or the Law of Christ' in *Continuity and Discontinuity: Perspectives on the Relationship Between the Old and New Testaments*, ed. J. S. Feinberg (Wheaton: Crossway Books, 1988) 203-220.

Moore-Crispin, D. R. '"The Real Absence:" Ulrich Zwingli's View of the Lord's Supper?' in *Union and Communion* (London: Westminster Conference, 1979) 22-33.

Morgan, E. S. *The Puritan Dilemma: The Story of John Winthrop* (Boston: Little, Brown & Co., 1958).

— *The Puritan Family: Religion and Domestic Relations in Seventeenth-Century New England* (New York: Harper & Row, 1956).

Morgan, I. *Puritan Spirituality* (London: Epworth Press, 1973).

Morgan, J. *Godly Learning: Puritan Attitudes Towards Reason, Learning, and Education, 1560-1640* (Cambridge University Press, 1986).

Muller, R. *Christ and the Decree: Christology and Predestination in Reformed Theology from Calvin to Perkins* (Grand Rapids: Baker Books, 1986).

Murray, I. H. *The Puritan Hope: Revival and the Interpretation of Prophecy* (Edinburgh: Banner of Truth, 1998).

— 'The Puritans and the Doctrine of Election' in *Puritan Papers: Vol. I*, ed. M. Lloyd-Jones (Phillipsburg: Presbyterian and Reformed, 2000) 3-16.

Murray, J. *Principles of Conduct* (Grand Rapids: Eerdmans, 1957).

— 'The Moral Law and the Fourth Commandment' in *Collected Writings* (Edinburgh: Banner of Truth, 1982) I:193-228.

Neal, D. *The History of the Puritans; or, Protestant Nonconformists; from the Reformation in 1517 to the Revolution in 1688: Vol. I-III* (London: Thomas Tegg and Son, 1837; rpt., Minneapolis, Klock & Klock, 1979).

New, J. F. H. *Anglican and Puritan: The Basis of Their Opposition, 1588-1640* (Stanford, 1964).

Nicholls, J. D. '"Union with Christ:" John Calvin on the Lord's Supper' in *Union and Communion* (London: Westminster Conference, 1979) 35-53.

Nuttall, G. F. *The Holy Spirit in Puritan Faith and Experience* (University of Chicago Press, 1992).

Packer, J. I. *A Quest for Godliness: The Puritan Vision of the Christian Life* (Wheaton: Crossway Books, 1990).

— *Knowing God* (London: Hodder and Stoughton, 1975).

— *The Redemption and Restoration of Man in the Thought of Richard Baxter* (Vancouver: Regent College Publishing and Carlisle: Paternoster Press, 2003).

Parker, K. L. *The English Sabbath: A Study of Doctrine and Discipline from the Reformation to the Civil War* (Cambridge University Press, 1988).

Peterson, R. 'Continuity and Discontinuity: The Debate Throughout Church History' in *Continuity and Discontinuity: Perspectives on the Relationship Between the Old and New Testaments*, ed. J. S. Feinberg (Wheaton: Crossway Books, 1988) 17-36.

Pettit, N. *The Heart Prepared: Grace and Conversion in Puritan Spiritual Life* (Middletown: Wesleyan University Press, 1989).

Piper, J. *Desiring God: Meditations of a Christian Hedonist* (Sisters: Multonomah Press, 1996).

Porter, H. C. *Reformation and Reaction in Tudor Cambridge* (Cambridge University Press, 1958).

Post, R. R. 'Thomas a Kempis, the Author of the *Imitation*' in *The Modern Devotion: Confrontation with Reformation and Humanism: Vol. III* in *Studies in Medieval and Reformation Thought*, ed. H. O. Oberman (Leiden: E. J. Brill, 1968) 521-550.

Primus, J. H. 'Calvin and the Puritan Sabbath: A Comparative Study' in *Exploring the Heritage of John Calvin*, ed. David E. Holwerda (Grand Rapids: Baker Books, 1976) 40-75.

— *Holy Time: Moderate Puritanism and the Sabbath* (Macon: Mercer University Press, 1989).

Richard, L. *The Spirituality of John Calvin* (Atlanta: John Knox Press, 1974).

Roberts, H. W. '"The Cup of Blessing:" Puritan and Separatist Sacramental Discourses' in *Union and Communion* (London: Westminster Conference, 1979) 55-71.

Rolston, H. *John Calvin Versus the Westminster Confession* (Richmond: John Knox Press, 1972).

Rowen, H. H., ed. *From Absolutism to Revolution, 1648-1848* (New York: Macmillan Publishing, 1963).

Rupp, G. 'A Devotion of Rapture in English Puritanism,' *Reformation, Conformity and Dissent: Essays in Honour of Geoffrey Nuttall*, ed. R. B. Knox (London: Epworth Press, 1977) 115-131.

Russell, C. *The Causes of the English Civil War* (Oxford University Press, 1990).

Ryken, L. *Worldly Saints: The Puritans as They Really Were* (Grand Rapids: Zondervan, 1986).

Ryle, J. C. 'A Biographical Account of the Author' in W. Gurnall, *The Christian in Complete Armour: A Treatise of the Saints' War against the Devil* (London: Blackie & Sons, 1864; rpt., Edinburgh: Banner of Truth, 1995).

Ryrie, C. *Dispensationalism Today* (Chicago: Moody Press, 1965).

Sasse, H. *This is My Body: Luther's Contention for the Real Presence in the Sacrament of the Altar* (Lutheran Publishing House, 1977).

Schaff, P. *The Creeds of Christendom: Vol. I-III* (Grand Rapids: Baker Books, 1998).

Schlatter, R. B. *The Social Ideas of Religious Leaders, 1660-1688* (New York: Octagon Books, 1971).

Schucking, L. L. *The Puritan Family* (London: Routledge & Kegan Paul, 1969).

Seaver, P. *Puritan Lectureships: The Politics of Religious Dissent 1560-1662* (Stanford University Press, 1977).

— *Wallington's World: A Puritan Artisan in Seventeenth-Century London* (Stanford University Press, 1985).

Solberg, W. U. *Redeem the Time: The Puritan Sabbath in Early America* (Harvard University Press, 1977).

Sommerville, C. J. *Popular Religion in Restoration England* (University Press of Florida, 1977).

Song, Y. *Theology and Piety in the Reformed Federal Thought of William Perkins and John Preston* (Lewiston: Edwin Mellen, 1998).

Spufford, M. 'Puritanism and Social Control?' in *Order and Disorder in Early Modern England*, eds. A. Fletcher and J. Stevenson (Cambridge University Press, 1985) 41-57.

— 'The Importance of the Lord's Supper to Dissenters' in *The World of Rural Dissenters, 1520-1575* (Cambridge University Press, 1995) 86-102.

Stachniewski, J. *The Persecutory Imagination: English Puritanism and the Literature of Religious Despair* (Oxford University Press, 1991).

Stone, L. *The Family, Sex and Marriage in England, 1500-1800* (New York: Harper & Row, 1977).

Stott, J. *The Message of Ephesians: God's New Society* in *The Bible Speaks Today*, eds. J. A. Motyer and J. Stott (Downers Grove: InterVarsity Press, 1986).

— *The Message of the Sermon on the Mount* in *The Bible Speaks Today*, eds. J. A. Motyer and J. Stott (Downers Grove: InterVarsity Press, 1978).

Stout, H. S. *The New England Soul: Preaching and the Religious Culture in Colonial New England* (Oxford University Press, 1988).

Tanner, J. R., ed., *The Historical Register of the University of Cambridge to the Year 1910* (Cambridge University Press, 1917).

Thomas, D. *Proclaiming the Incomprehensible God: Calvin's Teaching on Job* (Ross-shire: Christian Focus, 2004).

Thomas, M. *The Extent of the Atonement: A Dilemma for Reformed Theology from Calvin to the Consensus (1536 to 1675)* (Bletchley: Paternoster, 1997).

Toon, P. *From Mind to Heart: Christian Meditation Today* (Grand Rapids: Baker Books, 1987).

— *Puritans and Calvinism* (Swengel: Reiner Publications, 1973).

Torrance, T. F. *Calvin's Doctrine of Man* (Grand Rapids: Eerdmans, 1957).

Trevor-Roper, H. R. *Archbishop Laud* (London: Phoenix Press, 2000).

Turner, M. M. B. 'The Sabbath, Sunday, and the Law in Luke/Acts' in *From Sabbath to Lord's Day: A Biblical, Historical and Theological Investigation*, ed. D. A. Carson (Grand Rapids: Zondervan, 1982) 99-158.

Tyacke, N. *Anti-Calvinists: The Rise of English Arminianism, c. 1590-1640* (Oxford University Press, 1987).

Venn, J., ed., *Alumni Cantabrigienses: A biographical list of all known students at the University of Cambridge from the earliest times to 1900* (Cambridge University

Press, 1922).

Von Rohr, J. *The Covenant of Grace in Puritan Thought* (Atlanta: Scholars Press, 1986).

Vos, G. *Biblical Theology: Old and New Testaments* (Edinburgh: Banner of Truth, 1992).

Wallace, D. D. *Puritans and Predestination: Grace in English Protestant Theology, 1525-1695* (University of North Carolina Press, 1982).

— *The Spirituality of the Later English Puritans* (Macon: Mercer University Press, 1987).

Warfield, B. B. *Calvin and Augustine* (Philadelphia: Presbyterian and Reformed, 1971).

— *The Plan of Salvation* (Grand Rapids: Eerdmans, 1984).

— *The Westminster Assembly and Its Work* in *The Works of Benjamin Warfield: Vol. I-X* (Grand Rapids: Baker Books, 2003).

Watkins, O. C. *The Puritan Experience* (London: Routledge & Kegan Paul, 1972).

Watts, M. R. *The Dissenters* (Oxford: Clarendon Press, 1978).

Webber, D. 'Sanctifying the Inner Life' in *Aspects of Sanctification* (London: Westminster Conference, 1981) 41-61.

Webb, W. J. *Slaves, Women and Homosexuals: Exploring the Hermeneutics of Cultural Analysis* (Downers Grove: InterVarsity Press, 2001).

Weber, M. *The Protestant Ethic and the Spirit of Capitalism* (New York: Scribner, 1976).

Weir, D. *The Origins of the Federal Theology in Sixteenth-Century Reformation Thought* (Oxford University Press, 1990).

Wendel, F. *Calvin: Origins and Development of His Religious Thought* (New York: Harper and Row, 1963).

Whitaker, W. *Sunday in Tudor and Stuart Times* (London, 1933).

White, H. C. *English Devotional Literature [Prose] 1600-1640* (New York: Haskell House, 1966).

Whitney, D. S. *Spiritual Disciplines for the Christian Life* (Colorado Springs: NavPress, 1991).

Wilson, J. F. *Pulpit in Parliament: Puritanism during the English Civil Wars 1640-1648* (Princeton University Press, 1969).

Yule, G. 'Luther and the Ascetic Life,' in *Monks, Hermits and the Ascetic Tradition: Studies in Church History, Vol. 22*, ed. W. J. Sheils (Basil Blackwell, 1985) 229-239.

Articles

Atkins, J. M. 'Calvinist Bishops, Church Unity, and the Rise of Arminianism,' *Albion* 18 (1986) 411-427.

Bangs, C. '"All the Best Bishoprics and Deaneries:" The Enigma of Arminian Politics,' *Church History* 42 (1973) 5-16.

— 'Arminius and the Reformation,' *Church History* 30 (1961) 155-170.

Bauckham, R. 'Marian Exiles and Cambridge Puritanism: James Pilkington's 'Halfe a Score,'" *Journal of Ecclesiastical History* 26 (1975) 137-148.

Beeke, J. R. 'Personal Assurance of Faith: The Puritans and Chapter 18.2 of the Westminster Confession,' *Westminster Theological Journal* 55 (1993) 1-30.

Bell, C. 'Calvin and the Extent of the Atonement,' *Evangelical Quarterly* 55 (1983)

115-123.

Bierma, L. 'Federal Theology in the Sixteenth Century: Two Traditions?' *Westminster Theological Journal* 45 (1983) 304-321.

— 'The Role of Covenant Theology in Early Reformed Orthodoxy,' *Sixteenth Century Journal* 21 (1990) 453-462.

Black, J. W. 'Richard Baxter's Bucerian Reformation,' *Westminster Theological Journal* 63 (2001) 327-349.

Boersma, H. 'Calvin and the Extent of the Atonement,' *Evangelical Quarterly* 64 (1992) 333-355.

Bondos-Greene, S. A. 'The End of an Era: Cambridge Puritanism and the Christ's College Election of 1609,' *Historical Journal* 25 (1982) 197-208.

Boughton, L. C. 'Choice and Action: William Ames's Concept of the Mind's Operation in Moral Decisions,' *Church History* 56 (1987) 188-203.

Bozeman, T. D. 'Federal Theology and the National Covenant: An Elizabethan Case Study,' *Church History* 61 (1992) 394-407.

Brauer, J. C. 'Puritan Mysticism and the Development of Liberalism,' *Church History* 19 (1950) 151-170.

— 'The Nature of English Puritanism: Three Interpretations,' *Church History* 23 (1954) 99-108.

— 'Types of Puritan Piety,' *Church History* 56 (1987) 39-58.

Breen, T. H. 'The Non-Existent Controversy: Puritan and Anglican Attitudes on Work and Wealth, 1600-1640,' *Church History* 25 (1966) 273-287.

Breward, I. 'The Abolition of Puritanism,' *Journal of Religious History* 7 (1972) 20-34.

— 'The Significance of William Perkins,' *Journal of Religious History* 4 (1966) 113-128.

Calder, I. M. 'A Seventeenth Century Attempt to Purify the Anglican Church,' *American Historical Review* 53 (1948) 760-775.

Christianson, P. 'Reformers and the Church of England under Elizabeth I and the Early Stuarts,' *Journal of Ecclesiastical History* 31 (1980) 463-482.

Clark, P. 'Josias Nicholls and Religious Radicalism,' *Journal of Ecclesiastical History* 28 (1977) 133-150.

Cohen, C. L. 'Two Biblical Models of Conversion: An Example of Puritan Hermeneutics,' *Church History* 58 (1989) 182-196.

Collinson, P. 'A Comment: Concerning the Name Puritan,' *Journal of Ecclesiastical History* 31 (1980) 483-488.

Daly, J. W. 'John Bramhall and the Theoretical Problems of Royalist Moderation,' *The Journal of British Studies* 11 (1971) 26-44.

Davies, K. 'The sacred condition of equality – how original were Puritan doctrines of marriage?' *Social History* 2 (1977) 563-580.

Davis, J. L. 'Mystical Versus Enthusiastic Sensibility,' *Journal of the History of Ideas* 4 (1943) 301-319.

Doriani, D. 'The Puritans, Sex, and Pleasure,' *Westminster Theological Journal* 53 (1991) 125-143.

Dowey, E. A. 'Law in Luther and Calvin,' *Theology Today* 41 (1984) 146-153.

Emerson, E. 'Calvin and Covenant Theology,' *Church History* 25 (1956) 136-144.

Fincham, K. 'Prelacy and Politics: Archbishop Abbot's Defence of Protestant Orthodoxy,' *Historical Research* 61 (1988) 36-64.

Fincham, K. and Lake, P. 'The Ecclesiastical Policy of King James I,' *Journal of British*

Studies 24 (1985) 169-207.

Finlayson, M. G. 'Puritanism and Puritans: Labels or Libels?' *Canadian Journal of History* 8 (1973) 203-223.

Fisher, R. M. 'The Origins of Divinity Lectureships at the Inns of Court, 1569-1585,' *Journal of Ecclesiastical History* 29 (1978) 145-162.

Frye, R. 'The Teachings of Classical Puritanism on Conjugal Love,' *Studies in the Renaissance* 2 (1955) 148-159.

Fulcher, J. R. 'Puritans and the Passions: The Faculty Psychology in American Puritanism,' *Journal of the History of the Behavioural Sciences* 9 (1973) 123-139.

George, C. H. 'A Social Interpretation of English Puritanism,' *The Journal of Modern History* 25 (1953) 327-342.

Gerrish, B. A. 'The Lord's Supper in the Reformed Confessions,' *Theology Today* 23 (1966) 224-243.

Gessert, R. A. 'The Integrity of Faith: An Inquiry into the Meaning of the Law in the Thought of John Calvin,' *Scottish Journal of Theology* 13 (1960) 247-261.

Godrey, W. R. 'Reformed Thought on the Extent of the Atonement to 1618,' *Westminster Theological Journal* 37 (1975) 133-171.

Gorman, G. E. 'A Laudian Attempt to "Tune the Pulpit:" Peter Heylyn and His Sermon Against the Feoffees for the Purchase of Impropriations,' *Journal of Religious History* 8 (1975) 333-349.

Greaves, R. L. 'The Origins of English Sabbatarian Thought,' *Sixteenth Century Journal* 12 (1981) 19-34.

— 'The Puritan-Nonconformist Tradition in England, 1560-1700: Historiographical Reflections,' *Albion* 17 (1985) 449-486.

Hawkes, R. M. 'The Logic of Assurance in English Puritan Theology,' *Westminster Theological Journal* 52 (1990) 247-261.

Helm, P. 'Calvin (and Zwingli) on Divine Providence,' *Calvin Theological Journal* 29 (1994) 388-405.

— 'Calvin, English Calvinism and the Logic of Doctrinal Development,' *Scottish Journal of Theology* 34 (1981) 179-185.

Herbert, J. C. 'William Perkins's A Reformed Catholic: A Psycho-Cultural Interpretation,' *Church History* 51 (1982) 7-23.

Hoekema, A. 'The Covenant of Grace in Calvin's Teaching,' *Calvin Theological Journal* 2 (1967) 133-161.

Hoyle, D. 'A Commons Investigation of Arminianism and Popery in Cambridge on the Eve of the Civil War,' *Historical Journal* 29 (1986) 419-425.

Jewett, P. K. 'Concerning the Allegorical Interpretation of Scripture,' *Westminster Theological Journal* 17 (1954) 1-20.

Jones, R. T. 'Union With Christ: The Existential Nerve of Puritan Piety,' *Tyndale Bulletin* 41 (1990) 186-208.

Kalu, O. U. 'Bishops and Puritans in Early Jacobean England: A Perspective on Methodology,' *Church History* 45 (1976) 469-489.

— 'Continuity in Change: Bishops of London and Religious Dissent in Early Stuart England,' *Journal of British Studies* 18 (1978) 28-45.

Karlberg, M. W. 'The Original State of Adam: Tensions Within Reformed Theology,' *Evangelical Quarterly* 87 (1987) 291-309.

Keddie, G. J. 'Unfallible Certenty of the Pardon of Sinne and Life Everlasting: The Doctrine of Assurance in the Theology of William Perkins (1558-1602),'

Evangelical Quarterly 48 (1976) 230-244.

Kinlaw, C. J. 'Determinism and the Hiddenness of God in Calvin's Theology,' *Religious Studies* 24 (1988) 497-510.

Kline, M. G. 'Of Works and Grace,' *Presbyterion* 12 (1983) 85-92.

Lake, P. 'Calvinism and the English Church, 1570-1635,' *Past and Present* 114 (1987) 32-76.

— 'Constitutional Consensus and Puritan Opposition in the 1620s: Thomas Scott and the Spanish Match,' *Historical Journal* 25 (1982) 805-825.

— 'The Dilemma of the Establishment Puritan: The Cambridge Heads and the Case of Francis Johnson and Cuthbert Bainbrigg,' *Journal of Ecclesiastical History* 29 (1978) 23-35.

Lamont, W. 'The Rise of Arminianism Reconsidered,' *Past and Present* 107 (1985) 227-231.

Lane, A. N. S. 'Did Calvin Believe in Free Will?' *Vox Evangelica* 12 (1981) 72-90.

— Review of R. T. Kendall's 'Calvin and English Calvinism to 1649,' *Themelios* 6 (1980) 29-31.

— 'The Quest for the Historical Calvin,' *Evangelical Quarterly* 55 (1983) 95-113.

Lea, T. D. 'The Hermeneutics of the Puritans,' *Journal of the Evangelical Theological Society* 39 (1996) 271-284.

Leites, E. 'The Duty to Desire: Love, Friendship, and Sexuality in Some Puritan Theories of Marriage,' *Journal of Social History* 15 (1982) 383-403.

Leithart, P. J. 'Stoic Elements in Calvin's Doctrine of the Christian Life. Part I: Original Corruption, Natural Law, and the Order of the Soul,' *Westminster Theological Journal* 55 (1993) 31-54.

— 'Stoic Elements in Calvin's Doctrine of the Christian Life. Part II: Mortification,' *Westminster Theological Journal* 55 (1993) 191-208.

— 'Stoic Elements in Calvin's Doctrine of the Christian Life. Part III: Christian Moderation,' *Westminster Theological Journal* 56 (1994) 59-85.

Letham, R. 'The *Foedus Operum*: Some Factors Accounting for its Development,' *The Sixteenth Century Journal* 14 (1983) 457-467.

Looney, J. 'Undergraduate Education at Early Stuart Cambridge,' *History of Education* 10 (1981) 9-19.

Maclear, J. F. 'The Influence of the Puritan Clergy on the House of Commons: 1625-1629,' *Church History* 14 (1945) 272-289.

McGiffert, M. 'Grace and Works: The Rise and Division of Covenant Identity in Elizabethan Puritanism,' *Harvard Theological Review* 75 (1982) 463-505.

— 'The Perkinsian Moment of Federal Theology,' *Calvin Theological Journal* 29 (1994) 117-148.

McGrath, G. J. 'Grace and Duty in Puritan Spirituality,' *Grove Spirituality Series* 37 (1991).

McWilliams, D. B. 'The Covenant Theology of the *Westminster Confession of Faith* and Recent Criticism,' *Westminster Theological Journal* 53 (1991) 109-124.

Michaelsen, R. S. 'Changes in the Puritan Concept of Calling or Vocation,' *The New England Quarterly* 26 (1953) 315-336.

Middlekauff, R. 'Piety and Intellect in Puritanism,' *William and Mary Quarterly* 22 (1965) 457-470.

Milton, A. Review of Nicholas Tyacke's 'Anti-Calvinists: The Rise of English Arminianism,' *Journal of Ecclesiastical History* 39 (1988) 613-616.

Moller, J. 'The Beginnings of Puritan Covenant Theology,' *Journal of Ecclesiastical History* 14 (1963) 46-67.

Mosse, G. L. 'Puritan Political Thought and the "Cases of Conscience,"' *Church History* 23 (1954) 109-117.

Muller, R. A. 'Covenant and Conscience in English Reformed Theology: Three Variations on a 17th Century Theme,' *Westminster Theological Journal* 42 (1980) 308-334.

— '*Fides* and *Cognitio* in Relation to the Problem of Intellect and Will in the Theology of John Calvin,' *Calvin Theological Journal* 25 (1990) 207-224.

— 'Perkins' *A Golden Chain*: Predestinarian System or Schematized Ordo Salutis,' *Sixteenth Century Journal* 9 (1978) 69-81.

— 'The Priority of the Intellect in the Soteriology of Jacob Arminius,' *Westminster Theological Journal* 55 (1993) 55-72.

Nicole, R. 'John Calvin's View of the Extent of the Atonement,' *Westminster Theological Journal* 47 (1985) 197-225.

Partee, C. 'Calvin's Central Dogma Again,' *Sixteenth Century Journal* 18 (1987) 191-199.

Peyer, E. de 'Calvin's Doctrine of Divine Providence,' *Evangelical Quarterly* 10 (1938) 30-44.

Reid, W. S. Review of R. T. Kendall's 'Calvin and English Calvinism to 1649 in Westminster' in *Theological Journal* 43 (1980) 155-164.

Rolston, H. 'Responsible Man in Reformed Theology: Calvin versus the Westminster Confession,' *Scottish Journal of Theology* 23 (1970) 129-155.

Sceats, D. 'The Experience of Grace: Aspects of the Faith and Spirituality of the Puritans,' *Grove Spirituality Series* 62 (1997).

Schwarz, M. L. 'Lay Anglicanism and the Crisis of the English Church in the Early Seventeenth Century,' *Albion* 14 (1982) 1-19.

Seaver, P. 'The Puritan Work Ethic Revisited,' *Journal of British Studies* 19 (1980) 35-53.

Shaw, M. R. 'Drama in the Meeting House: The Concept of Conversion in the Theology of William Perkins,' *Westminster Theological Journal* 45 (1983) 41-72.

— 'William Perkins and the New Pelagians: Another Look at the Cambridge Predestination Controversy of the 1590s,' *Westminster Theological Journal* 58 (1996) 267-301.

Shriver, F. 'Hampton Court Re-Visited: James I and the Puritans,' *Journal of Ecclesiastical History* 33 (1982) 48-71.

— 'Orthodoxy and Diplomacy: James I and the Vorstius Affair,' *The English Historical Review* 336 (1970) 449-474.

Simpson, A. 'Saints in Arms: English Puritanism as Political Utopianism,' *Church History* 23 (1954) 119-125.

Sommerville, C. J. 'Interpreting Seventeenth-Century English Religion as Movements,' *Church History* 69 (2000) 749-769.

— 'The Anti-Puritan Work Ethic,' *Journal of British Studies* 20 (1981) 70-81.

Sommerville, J. P. 'The Royal Supremacy and Episcopacy "Jure Divino," 1603-1640,' *Journal of Ecclesiastical History* 34 (1983) 548-558.

Sprunger, K. L. 'English and Dutch Sabbatarianism and the Development of Puritan Social Theology,' *Church History* 51 (1982) 24-38.

Stearns, R. P. 'Assessing the New England Mind,' *Church History* 10 (1941) 246-262.

Stoever, W. K. B. 'Nature, Grace and John Cotton: The Theological Dimension in the New England Antinomian Controversy,' *Church History* 44 (1975) 22-33.

Strehle, S. 'The Extent of the Atonement and the Synod of Dort,' *Westminster Theological Journal* 51 (1989) 1-23.

Tipson, B. 'Invisible Saints: The "Judgment of Charity" in the Early New England Churches,' *Church History* 44 (1975) 460-471.

Todd, M. '"An Act of Discretion:" Evangelical Conformity and the Puritan Dons,' *Albion* 18 (1986) 581-599.

— 'Humanists, Puritans and the Spiritualized Household,' *Church History* 49 (1980) 18-34.

Torrance, J. B. 'Covenant or Contract? A Study of the Theological Background of Worship in Seventeenth-Century Scotland,' *Scottish Journal of Theology* 23 (1970) 51-76.

Tylenda, J. N. 'Calvin and Christ's Presence in the Supper – True or Real,' *Scottish Journal of Theology* 27 (1974) 65-75.

Trinterud, L. 'The Origins of Puritanism,' *Church History* 20 (1951) 37-57.

VanderMolen, R. J. 'Providence as Mystery, Providence as Revelation: Puritan and Anglican Modifications of John Calvin's Doctrine of Providence,' *Church History* 47 (1978) 27-47.

Von Rohr, J. 'Covenant and Assurance in Early English Puritanism,' *Church History* 34 (1965) 195-203.

White, P. 'The Rise of Arminianism Reconsidered,' *Past and Present* 101 (1983) 34-54.

Wiener, C. Z. 'The Beleaguered Isle: A Study of Elizabethan and Early Jacobean Anti-Catholicism,' *Past and Present* 51 (1971) 27-62.

Winship, M. P. 'Weak Christians, Backsliders, and Carnal Gospelers: Assurance of Salvation and the Pastoral Origins of Puritan Practical Divinity in the 1580s,' *Church History* 70 (2001) 462-481.

Wright, L. B. 'William Perkins: Elizabethan Apostle of "Practical Divinity,"' *Huntington Library Quarterly* 3 (1940) 171-196.

Yule, G. 'Theological Developments in Elizabethan Puritanism,' *Journal of Religious History* I (1960) 16-25.

Zakai, A. 'The Gospel of Reformation: The Origins of the Great Puritan Migration,' *Journal of Ecclesiastical History* 37 (1986) 584-602.

General Works of Reference

Dictionary of National Biography, ed. S. Lee (London: Smith, Elder & Co., 1909).

Documents of the Christian Church, ed. H. Bettenson (Oxford University Press, 1963).

Encyclopaedia of Religion and Ethics, ed. J. Hastings (Edinburgh: T & T Clark, 1913).

Historical Register of the University of Oxford to the End of the Trinity Term 1888 (Oxford: Clarendon Press, 1888).

Oxford Dictionary of the Christian Church, ed. F. L. Cross (Oxford University Press, 1966).

Unpublished Thesis

Chan, S. *The Puritan Meditative Tradition, 1599-1691: A Study of Ascetical Piety* (PhD
   Dissertation, Cambridge University, 1986).

Index

Studies in Christian History and Thought
(All titles uniform with this volume)
Dates in bold are of projected publication

David Bebbington
Holiness in Nineteenth-Century England
David Bebbington stresses the relationship of movements of spirituality to changes in their cultural setting, especially the legacies of the Enlightenment and Romanticism. He shows that these broad shifts in ideological mood had a profound effect on the ways in which piety was conceptualized and practised. Holiness was intimately bound up with the spirit of the age.
2000 / 0-85364-981-2 / viii + 98pp

J. William Black
Reformation Pastors
Richard Baxter and the Ideal of the Reformed Pastor
This work examines Richard Baxter's *Gildas Salvianus, The Reformed Pastor* (1656) and explores each aspect of his pastoral strategy in light of his own concern for 'reformation' and in the broader context of Edwardian, Elizabethan and early Stuart pastoral ideals and practice.
2003 / 1-84227-190-3 / xxii + 308pp

James Bruce
Prophecy, Miracles, Angels, *and* Heavenly Light?
The Eschatology, Pneumatology and Missiology of Adomnán's Life of Columba
This book surveys approaches to the marvellous in hagiography, providing the first critique of Plummer's hypothesis of Irish saga origin. It then analyses the uniquely systematized phenomena in the *Life of Columba* from Adomnán's seventh-century theological perspective, identifying the coming of the eschatological Kingdom as the key to understanding.
2004 / 1-84227-227-6 / xviii + 286pp

Colin J. Bulley
The Priesthood of Some Believers
Developments from the General to the Special Priesthood in the Christian Literature of the First Three Centuries
The first in-depth treatment of early Christian texts on the priesthood of all believers shows that the developing priesthood of the ordained related closely to the division between laity and clergy and had deleterious effects on the practice of the general priesthood.
2000 / 1-84227-034-6 / xii + 336pp

Anthony R. Cross (ed.)
Ecumenism and History
Studies in Honour of John H.Y. Briggs
This collection of essays examines the inter-relationships between the two fields in which Professor Briggs has contributed so much: history—particularly Baptist and Nonconformist—and the ecumenical movement. With contributions from colleagues and former research students from Britain, Europe and North America, *Ecumenism and History* provides wide-ranging studies in important aspects of Christian history, theology and ecumenical studies.
2002 / 1-84227-135-0 / xx + 362pp

Maggi Dawn
Confessions of an Inquiring Spirit
Form as Constitutive of Meaning in S.T. Coleridge's Theological Writing
This study of Coleridge's *Confessions* focuses on its confessional, epistolary and fragmentary form, suggesting that attention to these features significantly affects its interpretation. Bringing a close study of these three literary forms, the author suggests ways in which they nuance the text with particular understandings of the Trinity, and of a kenotic christology. Some parallels are drawn between Romantic and postmodern dilemmas concerning the authority of the biblical text.
2006 / 1-84227-255-1 / approx. 224 pp

Ruth Gouldbourne
The Flesh and the Feminine
Gender and Theology in the Writings of Caspar Schwenckfeld
Caspar Schwenckfeld and his movement exemplify one of the radical communities of the sixteenth century. Challenging theological and liturgical norms, they also found themselves challenging social and particularly gender assumptions. In this book, the issues of the relationship between radical theology and the understanding of gender are considered.
2005 / 1-84227-048-6 / approx. 304pp

Crawford Gribben
Puritan Millennialism
Literature and Theology, 1550–1682
Puritan Millennialism surveys the growth, impact and eventual decline of puritan millennialism throughout England, Scotland and Ireland, arguing that it was much more diverse than has frequently been suggested. This Paternoster edition is revised and extended from the original 2000 text.
2007 / 1-84227-372-8 / approx. 320pp

Galen K. Johnson
Prisoner of Conscience
John Bunyan on Self, Community and Christian Faith
This is an interdisciplinary study of John Bunyan's understanding of conscience across his autobiographical, theological and fictional writings, investigating whether conscience always deserves fidelity, and how Bunyan's view of conscience affects his relationship both to modern Western individualism and historic Christianity.

2003 / 1-84227-223-3 / xvi + 236pp

R.T. Kendall
Calvin and English Calvinism to 1649
The author's thesis is that those who formed the Westminster Confession of Faith, which is regarded as Calvinism, in fact departed from John Calvin on two points: (1) the extent of the atonement and (2) the ground of assurance of salvation.

1997 / 0-85364-827-1 / xii + 264pp

Timothy Larsen
Friends of Religious Equality
Nonconformist Politics in Mid-Victorian England
During the middle decades of the nineteenth century the English Nonconformist community developed a coherent political philosophy of its own, of which a central tenet was the principle of religious equality (in contrast to the stereotype of Evangelical Dissenters). The Dissenting community fought for the civil rights of Roman Catholics, non-Christians and even atheists on an issue of principle which had its flowering in the enthusiastic and undivided support which Nonconformity gave to the campaign for Jewish emancipation. This reissued study examines the political efforts and ideas of English Nonconformists during the period, covering the whole range of national issues raised, from state education to the Crimean War. It offers a case study of a theologically conservative group defending religious pluralism in the civic sphere, showing that the concept of religious equality was a grand vision at the centre of the political philosophy of the Dissenters.

2007 / 1-84227-402-3 / x + 300pp

Byung-Ho Moon
Christ the Mediator of the Law
Calvin's Christological Understanding of the Law as the Rule of Living and Life-Giving
This book explores the coherence between Christology and soteriology in Calvin's theology of the law, examining its intellectual origins and his position on the concept and extent of Christ's mediation of the law. A comparative study between Calvin and contemporary Reformers—Luther, Bucer, Melancthon and Bullinger—and his opponent Michael Servetus is made for the purpose of pointing out the unique feature of Calvin's Christological understanding of the law.

2005 / 1-84227-318-3 / approx. 370pp

John Eifion Morgan-Wynne
Holy Spirit and Religious Experience in Christian Writings, c.AD 90–200
This study examines how far Christians in the third to fifth generations (c.AD 90–200) attributed their sense of encounter with the divine presence, their sense of illumination in the truth or guidance in decision-making, and their sense of ethical empowerment to the activity of the Holy Spirit in their lives.

2005 / 1-84227-319-1 / approx. 350pp

James I. Packer
The Redemption and Restoration of Man in the Thought of Richard Baxter
James I. Packer provides a full and sympathetic exposition of Richard Baxter's doctrine of humanity, created and fallen; its redemption by Christ Jesus; and its restoration in the image of God through the obedience of faith by the power of the Holy Spirit.

2002 / 1-84227-147-4 / 432pp

Andrew Partington,
Church and State
The Contribution of the Church of England Bishops to the House of Lords
during the Thatcher Years

In *Church and State*, Andrew Partington argues that the contribution of the Church of England bishops to the House of Lords during the Thatcher years was overwhelmingly critical of the government; failed to have a significant influence in the public realm; was inefficient, being undertaken by a minority of those eligible to sit on the Bench of Bishops; and was insufficiently moral and spiritual in its content to be distinctive. On the basis of this, and the likely reduction of the number of places available for Church of England bishops in a fully reformed Second Chamber, the author argues for an evolution in the Church of England's approach to the service of its bishops in the House of Lords. He proposes the Church of England works to overcome the genuine obstacles which hinder busy diocesan bishops from contributing to the debates of the House of Lords and to its life more informally.

2005 / 1-84227-334-5 / approx. 324pp

Michael Pasquarello III
God's Ploughman
Hugh Latimer: A 'Preaching Life' (1490–1555)

This construction of a 'preaching life' situates Hugh Latimer within the larger religious, political and intellectual world of late medieval England. Neither biography, intellectual history, nor analysis of discrete sermon texts, this book is a work of homiletic history which draws from the details of Latimer's milieu to construct an interpretive framework for the preaching performances that formed the core of his identity as a religious reformer. Its goal is to illumine the practical wisdom embodied in the content, form and style of Latimer's preaching, and to recapture a sense of its overarching purpose, movement, and transforming force during the reform of sixteenth-century England.

2006 / 1-84227-336-1 / approx. 250pp

Alan P.F. Sell
Enlightenment, Ecumenism, Evangel
Theological Themes and Thinkers 1550–2000

This book consists of papers in which such interlocking topics as the Enlightenment, the problem of authority, the development of doctrine, spirituality, ecumenism, theological method and the heart of the gospel are discussed. Issues of significance to the church at large are explored with special reference to writers from the Reformed and Dissenting traditions.

2005 / 1-84227-330-2 / xviii + 422pp

Alan P.F. Sell
Hinterland Theology
Some Reformed and Dissenting Adjustments

Many books have been written on theology's 'giants' and significant trends, but what of those lesser-known writers who adjusted to them? In this book some hinterland theologians of the British Reformed and Dissenting traditions, who followed in the wake of toleration, the Evangelical Revival, the rise of modern biblical criticism and Karl Barth, are allowed to have their say. They include Thomas Ridgley, Ralph Wardlaw, T.V. Tymms and N.H.G. Robinson.

2006 / 1-84227-331-0 / approx. 350pp

Alan P.F. Sell and Anthony R. Cross (eds)
Protestant Nonconformity in the Twentieth Century

In this collection of essays scholars representative of a number of Nonconformist traditions reflect thematically on Nonconformists' life and witness during the twentieth century. Among the subjects reviewed are biblical studies, theology, worship, evangelism and spirituality, and ecumenism. Over and above its immediate interest, this collection provides a marker to future scholars and others wishing to know how some of their forebears assessed Nonconformity's contribution to a variety of fields during the century leading up to Christianity's third millennium.

2003 / 1-84227-221-7 / x + 398pp

Mark Smith
Religion in Industrial Society
Oldham and Saddleworth 1740–1865

This book analyses the way British churches sought to meet the challenge of industrialization and urbanization during the period 1740–1865. Working from a case-study of Oldham and Saddleworth, Mark Smith challenges the received view that the Anglican Church in the eighteenth century was characterized by complacency and inertia, and reveals Anglicanism's vigorous and creative response to the new conditions. He reassesses the significance of the centrally directed church reforms of the mid-nineteenth century, and emphasizes the importance of local energy and enthusiasm. Charting the growth of denominational pluralism in Oldham and Saddleworth, Dr Smith compares the strengths and weaknesses of the various Anglican and Nonconformist approaches to promoting church growth. He also demonstrates the extent to which all the churches participated in a common culture shaped by the influence of evangelicalism, and shows that active co-operation between the churches rather than denominational conflict dominated. This revised and updated edition of Dr Smith's challenging and original study makes an important contribution both to the social history of religion and to urban studies.

2006 / 1-84227-335-3 / approx. 300pp

Martin Sutherland
Peace, Toleration and Decay
The Ecclesiology of Later Stuart Dissent
This fresh analysis brings to light the complexity and fragility of the later Stuart Nonconformist consensus. Recent findings on wider seventeenth-century thought are incorporated into a new picture of the dynamics of Dissent and the roots of evangelicalism.
2003 / 1-84227-152-0 / xxii + 216pp

G. Michael Thomas
The Extent of the Atonement
A Dilemma for Reformed Theology from Calvin to the Consensus
A study of the way Reformed theology addressed the question, 'Did Christ die for all, or for the elect only?', commencing with John Calvin, and including debates with Lutheranism, the Synod of Dort and the teaching of Moïse Amyraut.
1997 / 0-85364-828-X / x + 278pp

David M. Thompson
Baptism, Church and Society in Britain from the Evangelical Revival to
Baptism, Eucharist and Ministry
The theology and practice of baptism have not received the attention they deserve. How important is faith? What does baptismal regeneration mean? Is baptism a bond of unity between Christians? This book discusses the theology of baptism and popular belief and practice in England and Wales from the Evangelical Revival to the publication of the World Council of Churches' consensus statement on *Baptism, Eucharist and Ministry* (1982).
2005 / 1-84227-393-0 / approx. 224pp

Mark D. Thompson
A Sure Ground on Which to Stand
The Relation of Authority and Interpretive Method of Luther's Approach to Scripture
The best interpreter of Luther is Luther himself. Unfortunately many modern studies have superimposed contemporary agendas upon this sixteenth-century Reformer's writings. This fresh study examines Luther's own words to find an explanation for his robust confidence in the Scriptures, a confidence that generated the famous 'stand' at Worms in 1521.
2004 / 1-84227-145-8 / xvi + 322pp

Carl R. Trueman and R.S. Clark (eds)
Protestant Scholasticism
Essays in Reassessment

Traditionally Protestant theology, between Luther's early reforming career and the dawn of the Enlightenment, has been seen in terms of decline and fall into the wastelands of rationalism and scholastic speculation. In this volume a number of scholars question such an interpretation. The editors argue that the development of post-Reformation Protestantism can only be understood when a proper historical model of doctrinal change is adopted. This historical concern underlies the subsequent studies of theologians such as Calvin, Beza, Olevian, Baxter, and the two Turrentini. The result is a significantly different reading of the development of Protestant Orthodoxy, one which both challenges the older scholarly interpretations and clichés about the relationship of Protestantism to, among other things, scholasticism and rationalism, and which demonstrates the fruitfulness of the new, historical approach.

1999 / 0-85364-853-0 / xx + 344pp

Shawn D. Wright
Our Sovereign Refuge
The Pastoral Theology of Theodore Beza

Our Sovereign Refuge is a study of the pastoral theology of the Protestant reformer who inherited the mantle of leadership in the Reformed church from John Calvin. Countering a common view of Beza as supremely a 'scholastic' theologian who deviated from Calvin's biblical focus, Wright uncovers a new portrait. He was not a cold and rigid academic theologian obsessed with probing the eternal decrees of God. Rather, by placing him in his pastoral context and by noting his concerns in his pastoral and biblical treatises, Wright shows that Beza was fundamentally a committed Christian who was troubled by the vicissitudes of life in the second half of the sixteenth century. He believed that the biblical truth of the supreme sovereignty of God alone could support Christians on their earthly pilgrimage to heaven. This pastoral and personal portrait forms the heart of Wright's argument.

2004 / 1-84227-252-7 / xviii + 308pp

Paternoster
9 Holdom Avenue,
Bletchley,
Milton Keynes MK1 1QR,
United Kingdom
Web: www.authenticmedia.co.uk/paternoster